OXFORD LEGAL HISTORY SERIES

General Editors

PAUL BRAND

JOSHUA GETZLER

DANIEL HULSEBOSCH

AND

AMALIA KESSLER

Federal Ground

OXFORD LEGAL HISTORY SERIES

General Editors

Paul Brand, Joshua Getzler, Daniel Hulsebosch, and Amalia Kessler

This series presents original work in legal history from all periods. Contributions to the series analyze diverse legal traditions, including common law; ius commune, civilian, and canon law; colonial, imperial, and international law; and customary, religious, and non-Western cultures of law. The series embraces methods ranging from doctrinal and juristic analysis through to every variety of historical, social-scientific, and philosophical enquiry. A leading purpose of the series is to investigate how legal ideas and practices operated in larger historical contexts. Our authors trace changes in legal thought and practice and the interactions of law with political and constitutional institutions and wider movements in social, economic, cultural, and intellectual life.

OTHER TITLES IN THIS SERIES

Priests of the Law
Roman Law and the Making of the Common Law's First Professionals
Thomas J. McSweeney

Capitalism Before Corporations
The Morality of Business Associations and the Roots of Commercial Equity and Law
Andreas Televantos

Federal Ground

Governing Property and Violence in the First U.S. Territories

GREGORY ABLAVSKY

OXFORD
UNIVERSITY PRESS

OXFORD
UNIVERSITY PRESS

Oxford University Press is a department of the University of Oxford. It furthers the University's objective of excellence in research, scholarship, and education by publishing worldwide. Oxford is a registered trade mark of Oxford University Press in the UK and certain other countries.

Published in the United States of America by Oxford University Press
198 Madison Avenue, New York, NY 10016, United States of America.

Library of Congress Cataloging-in-Publication Data

Names: Ablavsky, Gregory, author.
Title: Federal ground : governing property and violence in
the first U.S. territories / Gregory Ablavsky.
Description: New York : Oxford University Press, [2021] |
Series: Oxford legal history series | Includes index.
Identifiers: LCCN 2020029865 | ISBN 9780190905699 (hardback) |
ISBN 9780190905729 (digital-online) | ISBN 9780190905712 (epub) |
ISBN 9780190905705 (updf)
Subjects: LCSH: Public lands—United States—History. |
Land tenure—Law and legislation—United States—History. |
Land titles—United States—States—History.
Classification: LCC KF5605 .A73 2019 | DDC 346.7304/4—dc23
LC record available at https://lccn.loc.gov/2020029865

DOI: 10.1093/oso/9780190905699.001.0001

5 7 9 8 6 4

Printed by Integrated Books International, United States of America

Note to Readers

This publication is designed to provide accurate and authoritative information in regard to the subject matter covered. It is based upon sources believed to be accurate and reliable and is intended to be current as of the time it was written. It is sold with the understanding that the publisher is not engaged in rendering legal, accounting, or other professional services. If legal advice or other expert assistance is required, the services of a competent professional person should be sought. Also, to confirm that the information has not been affected or changed by recent developments, traditional legal research techniques should be used, including checking primary sources where appropriate.

(Based on the Declaration of Principles jointly adopted by a Committee of the American Bar Association and a Committee of Publishers and Associations.)

In loving memory of Trudi Luthi.

Contents

Note on Terminology

In 1796, a Cincinnati newspaper article complained that Arthur St. Clair, the governor of the Northwest Territory, "appears to look down upon the citizens of the North-Western Territory": in "speaking of them," he "seems cautiously to avoid the common and respectful appellations of inhabitants, or citizens, and with great art, and in a dimunitive way, makes use of the term Settlers."[1]

As this anonymous author reminds us, terms in the early United States were fraught with questions of power, and choosing them necessarily involves taking sides. I frequently use "Anglo-American" to describe citizens of the United States who arrived in the federal territories in the late eighteenth century. This term is overinclusive—many, but hardly all, of these recent immigrants originally hailed from the British Isles—but it distinguishes them from the territories' preexisting French residents, who were also legally U.S. citizens. I also describe U.S. citizens of European descent as "white," a racial category well known and understood at the time to distinguish Euro-Americans from Indigenous peoples.

I follow both Governor St. Clair and his anonymous critic in different contexts. I often refer to "U.S. citizens" more broadly and "territorial citizens" more specifically in contradistinction to Indigenous peoples, even though the meaning of U.S. citizenship, especially in the territories, was still hazy at this time. I also speak of territorial "inhabitants" or "residents"—although, unlike the newspaper author, I use the term to mean *all* people living in the territories, not just whites. Like St. Clair, I use the term "settler," although I usually mean it literally, to describe people who settled and claimed a particular parcel of land. At the time, Anglo-Americans almost exclusively referred to whites as settlers, but I have tried to be specific to avoid the pernicious suggestion that Indigenous peoples and others did not also settle land.

In general, I favor the term Native to describe the descendants of the Indigenous peoples of North America, and I capitalize it to signify its status as a marker of national status—as a member of a Native nation—as well as of ethnicity. At times, particularly when I speak of the views of federal officials and others, I use the term "Indian," the more common parlance of the time. Similarly, federal officials used the terms "tribes" and "nations" interchangeably to describe Native polities. I have generally favored "nation": scholars have debated how accurate this label was for Native polities, but, by the late eighteenth century, Native peoples insisted on it despite internal divisions: "It is very Certain that we are a nation known by the name of the Cherokees, but we are Divided," Cherokee leaders told federal officials in 1797. I use Natives' national affiliations when speaking of a single nation or its members.[2]

Introduction

In November 1791, Secretary of State Thomas Jefferson wrote a report for Congress: a dense, four-thousand-word catalog tracing a welter of land claims in two newly established jurisdictions in the so-called western country. One jurisdiction, the Northwest Territory, was former Virginian land that extended west of Pennsylvania across much of the current Midwest; the other, the Southwest Territory, was a recently ceded portion of North Carolina congruent with present-day Tennessee.[1]

Under the new constitution, these two territories were under sole federal jurisdiction following a decade of debate about the regions' future. Eight years earlier, at the end of the Revolution, Great Britain had surrendered its claim to sovereignty and ownership over much of eastern North America, including these future territories, to the new United States. Existing states had claimed the lands beyond the Appalachians under their colonial charters, but, after heated arguments, nearly all had ceded their purported rights to both jurisdiction and title to the nascent federal government. The Continental Congress had then enacted a series of foundational laws—the Land Ordinance of 1785, the Northwest Ordinance of 1787—to administer the new federal sovereignty over the region. These statutes cast this vast expanse as blank canvas on which to plot the future: they envisioned that the federal government would draw new boundaries, transforming western lands into rectangular parcels of property and into new states admitted into the union on "equal footing" with existing states.[2]

Jefferson's 1791 report revealed a sharply different portrait of the two territories from these earlier statutes. Eager to open a land office, Congress had charged the Washington administration with determining how much federal land actually existed within these new territories. After months of research, Jefferson revealed that the supposedly federal territories were not vacant lands waiting to be subdivided and sold. On the contrary, both teemed with people asserting ownership—many Native peoples, whose rights Jefferson set to one side, but also land companies, French villagers, Revolutionary War veterans, and roughly forty thousand Anglo-American migrants, many alleging title under prior state laws. All told, Jefferson reported, non-Natives claimed over twenty-one million acres of territorial land. Apparently overwhelmed, Congress did not return to the land office question for another four years. It would ultimately take federal officials over a century to unspool this tangle of ownership.[3]

Federal Ground. Gregory Ablavsky, Oxford University Press (2021). © Gregory Ablavsky.
DOI: 10.1093/oso/9780190905699.003.0001

This little-known report reveals a larger history concealed by the more-famous foundational documents that preceded it: a story of how, in attempting to transform the early American West, the federal government was itself remade. *Federal Ground* recounts that process. Like Jefferson's report, it focuses on the first two federal territories, the Southwest Territory (Figure 1) and the Northwest Territory (Figure 2). Also like the report, it begins with an indisputable reality, albeit one that Congress had earlier attempted to deny: the lands it carved up on paper were not empty. This simple fact had important consequences. Because the territories' existing residents refused to be ignored, federal officials would, however reluctantly, have to grapple with them and their claims. Yet this tedious labor of administration, rather than faraway imaginings traced on a map, proved the foundation for the new government's authority in the territories.

This focus on practical governance helps explain the paradox of federal power in the territories: it was at once everywhere and nowhere. Nearly everyone in the territories routinely engaged with federal authority, yet federal representatives remained vanishingly few, often a handful of men bewailing their limited power to control territorial residents. This apparent contradiction stemmed from the nature of governance in the territories. For territorial residents, the new federal government was less an institution than a resource, a font of law and money. Federal officials sought to direct this resource toward their desired goals, but they faced competition from many others—Native peoples, territorial citizens, eastern land speculators, French *habitants*—who often proved more adept at conscripting federal authority.

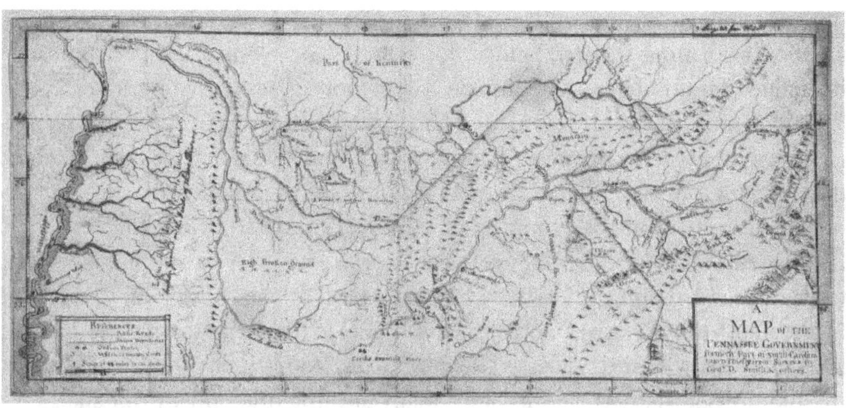

Figure 1: "A Map of the Tennasee Government, Formerly Part of North Carolina, Taken Chiefly by General D. Smith and Others" [1795]. Courtesy of American Philosophical Society. Based on surveys by Territorial Secretary Daniel Smith, this map portrays the Southwest Territory, which later became the state of Tennessee.

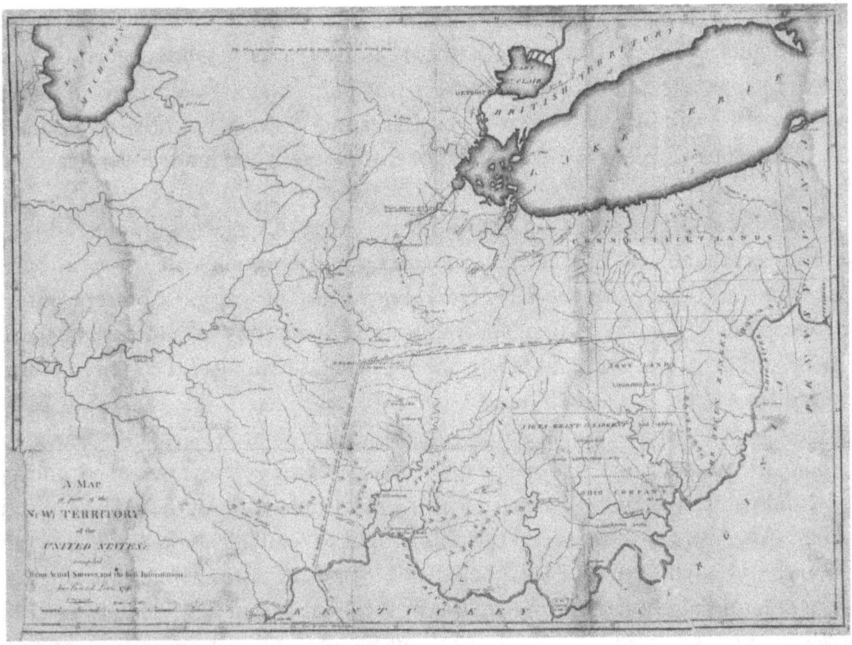

Figure 2: *Map of Part of the N. W. Territory of the United States* (1796), from *Carey's General Atlas* (Philadelphia: M. Carey, 1800). Courtesy of the New York Public Library. This map depicts the original boundaries of the Northwest Territory, which encompassed the present-day states of Ohio, Illinois, Indiana, Michigan, Wisconsin, and part of Minnesota.

The result of this contest was that government got things done, but not always the things that officials set out to do. Administrators' carefully laid plans frequently crumbled. Instead, prodded by residents, officials stumbled toward makeshift solutions. Yet this continual resolution of demands insinuated federal authority ever deeper into the lives of territorial residents. Over time, these ad hoc precedents were cobbled together and labeled "systems." As a result, a government distrusted by the people exploiting it, and rarely able to control events or dictate outcomes, slowly transformed a continent.

THE NEWLY ADOPTED U.S. CONSTITUTION charged the national government with important responsibilities: overseeing foreign diplomacy, managing a national economy, supporting an army, arbitrating interstate disputes, regulating public lands, and governing "Indian affairs," a term broadly encompassing relations between the United States and Native nations. Many of these powers were not new. They echoed authority ostensibly enjoyed by the British Crown during imperial rule as well as by the Continental Congress under the Articles of Confederation. But throughout the 1780s, even as it crafted grand plans for the expansive new nation, Congress was often unable to employ its paper powers, thwarted by recalcitrant states. In response, the new Constitution gave the federal government greater powers of enforcement and made federal law the "supreme law of the land."[4]

Opponents of the new Constitution feared that this newly empowered federal government would overwhelm formerly autonomous states. Yet, in both personnel and authority, the early federal government was most present not in state capitals but in the liminal spaces around the nation's ragged edges, where states' authority was thin and where the supposed territory of the United States butted up against the jurisdictions of other sovereigns. In this sense, the early federal government was what scholars have labeled an imperial state, seeking to project the new nation's tenuous power into the places where it was most uncertain and contested. One such space was the maritime world of the high seas and urban waterfront, where federal officials sought to regulate and tax free-flowing goods and people. Another was the lands beyond the Appalachian Mountains, a vast region barely settled by Anglo-Americans that had long defied imperial assertions of "sovereignty"—an amorphous yet ubiquitous term indicating recognized right of rule and ultimate authority.[5]

The vision of the new nation's political elite for what they called the West resembled the aspirations of their British predecessors. Like nearly all Anglo-Americans of the era, they regarded the region's colonization by white settlers as the inevitable consequence of a westward torrent of people driven by a seemingly insatiable land hunger. The federal government could not stop this flow, federal leaders believed, but it could manage it. In place of what they regarded as violence and anarchy, they sought to establish a colonial process that was peaceful, orderly, and systematic, while strongly attaching the region to federal authority. The key was the creation of firm and evenhanded rules: fairly negotiated treaties with Native nations would ensure "peace and friendship"; unambiguous property laws would facilitate federal land sales, repaying the national debt. Rooted in pragmatism as well as concern for the "national character," this approach to colonization was broadly shared across the era's nascent partisan divisions. Proto-Federalists and Republicans alike agreed that regulated, nonviolent settlement would prove both "more just and less expensive," in the words of Thomas Jefferson.[6]

Despite this seeming consensus in Philadelphia, in much of the West the new federal government encountered the same resistance that had thwarted prior sovereigns' attempts at peace and order. In particular, notwithstanding state cessions, large portions of the West still ostensibly remained within New York, Georgia, and Kentucky (part of Virginia until it became a state in 1792). These states embraced a different vision of settlement—one that aggressively asserted state ownership and jurisdiction over these contested regions. For the next forty years, federal and state leaders squabbled over the scope of their respective powers and the pace of colonization.[7]

The creation of the federal territories from the western lands ceded to the United States was a constitutional innovation intended to avoid such conflicts. The territories were unique sites of federal authority in a double sense. For one, many of the new federal government's nationwide responsibilities concentrated there. At the time of their creation, the two federal territories were home to the entire federal public domain, to most of the "Indian country" within the United States, to most of the nation's international borders, and to the whole U.S. Army (admittedly, initially a meager eight hundred or so soldiers).[8]

But the territories were also federal ground in a formal constitutional sense. Territories were states-in-waiting, to be admitted to the union once they reached sixty thousand free inhabitants. Until then, the Constitution and the Northwest Ordinance placed the territories and their non-Native residents under sole federal control. The president would appoint a territorial governor, secretary, three judges, and senior militia officers; the governor would in turn appoint all other officials, including local magistrates. In the first stage of territorial governance, the governor and judges would together enact laws. Once the territory had five thousand free adult male inhabitants, it entered the second stage, with an elected legislature and the right to a nonvoting delegate to Congress (ultimately, neither territory reached this stage until shortly before statehood). Both before and after statehood, the federal government would control "the primary disposal of the soil," the right to own and sell the territories' unclaimed land.[9]

As the only part of the United States outside state borders, the territories offered the federal government the opportunity to enact a national vision unimpeded by state sovereignty or even much formal local control. The territories' principal value, one U.S. senator argued, was that "the clashing claims and encroachments of the St[ates] on [federal] Constitutional powers are thereby silenced." This unified rule, denounced as "oppressive and tyrannical" by many territorial citizens, made the territories an exclusively federal space in a nation of divided authority. As one historian has put it, "The territories, not the capital, were the repository of national authority."[10]

Much rested on federal rule's success in the first two territories. As the grandiose, quasi-constitutional language of the Northwest Ordinance suggested, the Anglo-American political elite did not regard the Northwest and Southwest Territories solely as remote corners of the nation to be shepherded toward statehood. These first territories were also proving grounds for a "new mod[e]led" governance intended to administer U.S. imperialism going forward. Anglo-Americans anticipated—correctly, in hindsight—that nearly the entire trans-Appalachian West, and perhaps still more of the continent, would eventually pass through territorial rule. In this sense, in governing the Northwest and Southwest Territories, the federal government was plotting its, and the nation's, future.[11]

FIXATED RELENTLESSLY FORWARD, THE territorial model ignored the complicated past and present of the regions it deemed territories. Proclaiming new jurisdictions did not alter these preexisting realities. Both territories remained what they had been since time immemorial: Native homelands. "Indians is all we see, know or hear of," one army officer there reported. What the United States called the Southwest Territory was the northern edge of the Native South, where new Native confederacies had coalesced out of the collapse of prior Mississippian societies. Long affiliated collections of villages and regions, the emergent Choctaws, Chickasaws, Muskogee Creeks, and Cherokees increasingly envisioned themselves, and were regarded by Euro-Americans, as cohesive nations; they owned and governed most of the lands in and around the Southwest Territory. The Northwest Territory encompassed a still more enormous swath of Native land. In the Territory's west, known as the Illinois Country, lived the Miami and Wabash Confederacies, while to the east, in the Ohio Country, were more recent migrants, the Delawares, Shawnees, and Wyandots. Trade and diplomacy tied these regions' multiethnic towns to the Haudenosaunee to the east, the Anishinaabeg to the west and north, as well as to the Native confederacies to the south.[12]

For still others, particularly the small pockets of Europeans who had long lived alongside Native peoples, the territories were borderlands where multiple sovereigns had contested for decades. So-called Indian country men worked within Native communities as traders and diplomats, while in the early eighteenth century French villagers formed small settlements along the Mississippi and Wabash Rivers. During and after the Revolution, they had been joined by increasing numbers of Anglo-Americans, who exploited the regions' uncertain status to make new settlements. While most of these settlers headed to Kentucky—a part of the state of Virginia sandwiched between the two territories—some spilled north, crossing the Ohio River into the Northwest Territory. Others, heading south, formed two detached outposts in what would become the Southwest Territory: the Cumberland District, clustered around what would become Nashville, and Watauga, later renamed the Washington and Hamilton Districts, in the western foothills of the Smoky Mountains. These settlements established their own governments with little involvement from North Carolina, which purported to govern them.[13]

Meanwhile, nearly encircling the new federal territories were European empires eager to cabin, and perhaps even stifle, the new United States. North of the Northwest Territory was British Canada; flouting the Treaty of Paris, the British also retained posts, most notably Detroit, *within* the Territory. To the Territory's west, across the Mississippi River, lay Spanish jurisdiction; the Spanish loomed even larger over the Southwest Territory, surrounded to the south and west by Spanish Louisiana and Florida. The boundaries between these British, Spanish, and U.S. territories remained hazy and contested, ambiguity that the Europeans seized on to court the regions' Native peoples.[14]

Viewed from the perspective of their existing residents and in light of their history, then, the new territories arguably represented the United States at its weakest, not strongest. Long the graveyard of empires, the Native South and the Illinois and Ohio Countries had seen would-be sovereigns—France, Britain, Spain, Virginia, North Carolina—come and go, constantly redrawing boundaries of jurisdiction and property. Little had stuck; sovereignty and effective control remained with Native nations. There seemed little prospect that the federal government would succeed where others had failed. Few territorial inhabitants identified as citizens of the United States, and even those who plausibly bore that label showed little affection for the distant new government that claimed to rule them.[15]

THE CONTRADICTION BETWEEN THESE TWO REALITIES—between nearly unchecked formal federal sovereignty and the preexisting jumble of claims to property, authority, and jurisdiction wrought by centuries of Native power and imperial struggle—lay at the core of territorial governance. Before it could enact any grand plans for the West, the federal government would have to resolve this tangle. This collision proved the cause for a tremendous amount of work, as well as a significant, if ironic, source for federal power in the regions.[16]

Describing and capturing federal power in the first territories presents two key challenges. The first is defining what, and who, counts as "federal"; the second is establishing and measuring what we mean by "power."

WHEN TERRITORIAL RESIDENTS SPOKE of the "national," "general," or "federal" government, they were describing a loose hierarchy with an at-times ambiguous relationship to federal authority. At one end, in distant Philadelphia, were cabinet members charged with key responsibilities: the secretary of state supervised territorial governance, the secretary of war oversaw the military and Indian affairs, and the secretary of the treasury managed federal lands. Henry Knox, Timothy

Pickering, James McHenry, and others who held these offices had strong views on both federal power and how the territories should be run. Yet they were not only hampered by distance and imperfect control, they also had to share authority with a fractious Congress.[17]

At the other end of the hierarchy were the local officials who governed daily life in the territories—militia officers, justices of the peace, sheriffs. Formally, these officials, selected by the territorial governor, were federal officers. "[A]ll persons in authority" in the territories, one U.S. attorney general opined, "derive their authority from the present constitution of the United States." But in practice, local governance in the territories was nearly identical in both structure and personnel to what had existed under state rule; often, the sole acknowledgment of the advent of federal sovereignty was a new caption in the county record book. Similar to town and county officials elsewhere, the local notables rechristened as territorial officers enjoyed authority based on their claim to represent the community, not the United States.[18]

Mediating between these two groups was the presidentially appointed territorial administration, especially the territorial governor and secretary. Territorial citizens and cabinet officials alike regarded these officers as the clearest federal representatives in the territories. Citizens appealed to them for federal aid or blamed them for unpopular federal policies; cabinet officials requested information or relayed commands. The governor in particular served as an administrative jack-of-all-trades: Congress anointed him not only head of the territorial government but also superintendent of Indian affairs, adjudicator of land claims, overseer of land auctions, and occasional military commander.[19]

The men who filled these posts in the two territories differed in how they approached their roles. In the Northwest Territory, Governor Arthur St. Clair (Figure 3), a Pennsylvanian, and Secretary Winthrop Sargent, from Massachusetts, were both Continental Army veterans who uncompromisingly defended federal power—which they often conflated with their own authority. The arrogant St. Clair reportedly "could not beare dictation by inferiors or those of Under rank to him," while the "very obnoxious" Sargent "wishe[d] to make every Person submit to his will." Both men spent their tenures roiled in disputes, creating an administrative record that one observer described as a "history of bickerings and discontents."[20]

In the Southwest Territory, by contrast, prominent locals with fewer federal ties filled both offices. Governor William Blount (Figure 4) was a North Carolinian land speculator deemed the "properest man" by the state's congressional delegation, while Secretary Daniel Smith was a well-regarded resident of the Cumberland District. But, while both men navigated local politics more skillfully than St. Clair or Sargent did, they proved unreliable enforcers of their higher-ups' aims. The especially calculating Blount used his office to advance his

Figure 3: William Blount (1749–1800) by Washington B. Cooper. Courtesy of Tennessee State Museum—Tennessee Historical Society.

Figure 4: Arthur St. Clair (1736–1818) by Charles Wilson Peale, from life, 1782–1784. Courtesy of Independence National Historical Park.

own career and his enormous land dealings, earning him the Muskogee Creek appellation "Fushe Micco"—the "Dirt King."[21]

As superintendents of Indian affairs, Blount and St. Clair also nominally oversaw the War Office's Indian Department in the territories—a separate, loose network of agents, clerks, and translators who extended federal authority into Native lands. Federal officials wanted two things from these officers: influence among Native nations and loyalty to the federal government. Yet these attributes often ran in opposite directions. From necessity, Blount and St. Clair relied on "back-country m[e]n" who knew Native communities intimately from years living among them, yet neither fully trusted nor controlled these peripatetic, self-promoting schemers of dubious allegiances. Urged "to send among the Indians Men more steady and reserv[e]d," the War Department began to appoint recent graduates of Princeton and Dartmouth. These well-bred young men were obedient but reportedly "wholly ignorant and unacquainted with the practices and customs of indians." Regardless of origin, Indian agents faced suspicion from Natives and territorial citizens alike. Frontier whites were especially hostile, alleging that "the very officers of the United States are treacherously leagued with the savage tribes"; one group even attempted to hang the federal agent to the Cherokees.[22]

THE INTERACTION BETWEEN THESE multiple sites of authority, spread thinly across vast distances and mediated through a constant flow of paper, collectively constituted the federal government in the territories. Reconstructing federal authority there thus requires reading records of high law and policy—congressional debates, reports like Jefferson's, federal statutes—alongside the documents of workaday territorial governance now scattered throughout personal papers and local repositories: court minutes, surveys, deeds, and everyday correspondence.[23]

Though crafted largely by officials, this archive demonstrates that the primary architects of federal authority in the territories were not autonomous bureaucrats. Instead, federal representatives thought themselves besieged and powerless before the demands of the borderlands' residents: Anglo-American territorial citizens, French *habitants*, empire-building land speculators, Revolutionary War veterans, and, most influential of all, the regions' diverse Native peoples. All pressed claims on the federal government, sometimes using long-standing formal channels—petitions, court cases, diplomatic negotiations—and other times practicing raucous politics "out of doors," in newspapers, pamphlets, mobs, and even violence. Though each method of claims-making had its own norms, territorial inhabitants deployed them in tandem toward the same end: to push the federal government to do what they wanted, often successfully.[24]

But this archive also poses a challenge: it portrays territorial inhabitants not on their own terms but through federal officials' flawed perceptions. Blinkered by ignorance, disdain, and self-interest, these officials often poorly grasped Anglo-American citizens, let alone French *habitants* or the Native peoples they homogenized into Indians. All men, they envisioned power as a masculine preserve, blinding them to women's authority, especially in Native societies. As a rich borderlands literature demonstrates, interpreting such sources against the grain can help reconstruct claimants' perspective. But reading them through their authors' eyes illuminates the encounter between territorial inhabitants and federal authority in a different way. However inaccurate, officials' (mis) understandings mattered because they undergird federal action and law.

Paradoxically, officials' arrogant efforts to comprehend territorial inhabitants demonstrated those residents' power. Federal officials could not simply wish existing inhabitants away, nor were they strong enough to project naked stereotypes into policy. Rather, with varying degrees of good faith and sincerity, they became amateur ethnographers of the people whose claims they encountered, and fashioned the federal government based on what they grasped. They focused on law, especially Indigenous law, which played an important, if unheralded, role in early federal governance. Though federal officials were ill-equipped and biased interpreters of what they saw, comprehending unfamiliar cultures was difficult work; present-day scholars are still modest about how certainly they can reconstruct these borderland societies. For their part, territorial residents similarly failed to understand federal officials, or so those officials thought, complaining that residents' "imperfect perceptions" of federal intentions sowed discord and confusion. Territorial governance was built on these many layers of misapprehension.[25]

MEASURING FEDERAL POWER PRESENTS another challenge. Scholars have posited many models for assessing state authority, expressed in terms of autonomy and capacity, or contrasting infrastructural and despotic power. Historians of the early federal government have been at pains to move beyond long-standing debates about strength and weakness, insisting that this early state governed not less but differently than its later incarnations, and in ways not always captured in existing accounts. Yet stressing what the federal government was *not* leaves open the question of what exactly the federal government *was*.[26]

Citizens of the early United States understood governmental power through comparison. They contrasted themselves with Native nations, whom they caricatured as "without government"—a "free people, knowing neither law and restraint." They also looked to Europe, particularly the fiscal-military state ascendant in eighteenth-century Britain and France, which Anglo-Americans regarded with mix of envy and anxiety: this was, perhaps, too much government. As the leading edge of U.S. colonialism, the territories more closely resembled a garrison state than anywhere else in the early United States. But even there, where early national military power was at its height, the federal government could only rarely impose its will directly through violence, and only at tremendous cost in both money and legitimacy. For most places in the territories, most of the time, federal power was more amorphous than large numbers of regular soldiers.[27]

Though they occasionally embraced militaristic models, advocates like Alexander Hamilton and especially James Madison also spoke of another aspiration for the new federal government: that it would provide a "neutral forum" or "impartial and unbiassed" tribunal to arbitrate among competing interests. Far from a call for a minimal state, this understanding harkened to another European model of state formation, one we might dub the adjudicatory state. In prior centuries, European monarchs had consolidated authority by creating institutions that attracted litigants and displaced local sources of justice. This process played out even more sharply in global spaces of European empires, as borderlands contests over jurisdictional politics built imperial states. Some in the early territories explicitly connected this adjudicatory role with federal authority: "There is perhaps nothing that contributes more to induce an affectionate Submission to any power," Arthur St. Clair argued of territorial governance, "than the habit of looking up to that power as the depositary and dispenser of Justice in the last resort."[28]

Federal law and adjudication did come to play an outsized role in the early territories, albeit more through federal officials' ersatz resolution schemes than in courts. Yet this outcome yielded little "affectionate Submission," partly because St. Clair misunderstood law's role in the early republic. Similarly to a mid-twentieth-century historiography devoted to federal "policy," St. Clair believed law was crafted in the capital and then imposed on the territories through federal statutes and officials. This perspective not only claims too much coherence for a fractitious federal government's ad hoc pursuit of much-debated aims, but it also overlooks how law in the early United States functioned: it was less an adjunct of state power than a "zone of contestation." Federal law became ubiquitous in the territories not despite but often *because* of the resistance of territorial inhabitants, who offered their own interpretations of federal law at odds with the readings of officials like St. Clair.[29]

Territorial residents had long-standing laws of their own, yet they turned to federal law because it offered them two valuable goods. One was legitimacy. Residents did not have to believe in the federal government or its authority to conscript federal law as a useful weapon to defend their claims amidst the post-revolutionary churn—often against officials spouting that same law, but also against each other, especially in the scramble to validate ownership and sovereignty. The other good that federal law promised was more literal: material goods. Sometimes this came in the form of federally sanctioned land title; other times, it came as federally supplied arms, food, clothing, and cash.

In a broader sense, what federal law offered territorial residents was rights. Like the rest of the early United States, the territories were alive with assertions of "right of soil," "right of jurisdiction," and "rights of sovereignty"; even Native leaders couched their claims in such rights-talk. Rights sometimes carry a libertarian smack as limitations on governments, but in the early territories they were an appeal *to* government, a craving for official validation to help ward off challenges to ownership and autonomy. Federal officials mattered, then, because they controlled the alchemy by which territorial residents' *claims* became *rights* under federal law.[30]

This authority did not translate straightforwardly into conventional measures of state power. Rarely could the federal government dictate outcomes in the territories; often it could not even stop its resources from supporting goals officials abhorred. Neither, though, did the federal government operate out of sight. On the contrary, territorial residents, keenly aware that their would-be rights hinged on federal recognition, had to grapple with federal authority constantly, even after the territories became supposedly autonomous states. The consequence in the early territories was something the early republic supposedly lacked—a sense of the state. The ubiquity of federal law meant that the federal government set the terms and language of debate, even when it could not prescribe the result. When, later on, the federal government built more explicit instantiations of its power—more familiar bureaucracies like the General Land Office or Bureau of Indian Affairs—it did so on the foundation of this abstract but meaningful authority.

THIS CONTEST OVER FEDERAL AUTHORITY occurred in *both* the Southwest and Northwest Territories. The first two federal territories were linked by their shared jurisdictional status, as Jefferson's report suggests, as well as by a steady flow of people and information between them. Yet historians have generally not considered the two territories in tandem: they have seen them as divided by both the legality of chattel slavery and the role of the federal government.[31]

The Northwest Ordinance governed *both* the Northwest and Southwest Territories, with a single exception: Congress specifically excised the provision banning slavery and involuntary servitude when it extended the Ordinance over the Southwest Territory. But this purported legal divide between slave and free proved yet another line on a map. As recent scholarship has underscored, the enslavement of Indigenous and African peoples, already long present in what became the Northwest Territory, persisted notwithstanding the Ordinance. As for the Southwest Territory, in the 1790s the region's anticipated future as a plantation society remained mostly yet to come, especially while Native violence thwarted Anglo-American settlement. Under federal rule, both territories were borderlands where centuries of Indigenous captivity intersected with the more recent advent of chattel slavery inflicted on African-Americans; in both, ownership of humans was entangled with wider uncertainties of title and with the fraught ties of bondage linking Natives and whites.[32]

Historians have also juxtaposed the federal government's purported success in the Northwest Territory—a topic on which they have lavished attention—against its seeming failure in the Southwest Territory, which a sparse historiography has depicted as the victim of federal neglect. *Federal Ground* reverses this focus and emphasizes the lesser-known Southwest Territory to challenge this narrative, which too readily credits territorial citizens' strategic and self-serving complaints. Read critically, such cries—readily heard north of the Ohio, too—suggest not federal authority's absence but the opposite: territorial citizens' dependence on the federal government and their frustration when it failed to support their aims. Not for the last time in U.S. history, some of the loudest critics of federal power were among its greatest beneficiaries.[33]

THIS RISE OF FEDERAL AUTHORITY played out in two closely intertwined areas that dominated governance in both territories: property, the focus of Part I, and violence between Natives and territorial citizens, the subject of Part II.

The United States was born land-obsessed, as recent scholarship has stressed. To many Anglo-Americans, the Revolution had vindicated their claim to own the vast spaces beyond the Appalachians. These western lands became the new nation's arguably most valuable asset: cheap now, they promised to rise inexorably in value as Anglo-Americans migrated west. In the territories, as Chapter One explores, this rabid land market intersected with a plethora of sources of title—deeds from Native nations, grants from state governments, occupancy rights. This property pluralism created a quagmire that made ownership highly uncertain. Chapter Two examines the federal government's initial attempt to resolve this tangle: the creation of federally sanctioned land companies. Yet as these companies, too, succumbed to the speculative lure of uncertain ownership, their ensuing failure exacerbated confusion. The result, as Chapter Three recounts, was that federal officials spent the next decade and a half reluctantly sifting through these preexisting property claims. However unplanned, this effort slowly worked to translate the territories' crazy quilt of ownership into title derived from federal authority.[34]

Violence between Natives and their white neighbors in the territories presented its own morass. Blaming endemic conflict on a shared borderlands culture of racial hatred and warfare, federal administrators sought to establish the federal government as the ultimate arbiter of legitimate violence. As Chapter Four explores, they sought to enshrine federal sovereignty through criminal law, securing impartial justice to Natives and U.S. citizens alike, while, as Chapter Five demonstrates, federal officials also attempted to ensure that Congress alone authorized legitimate armed conflict. Yet criminal punishment and command proved ineffective, and so, as Chapter Six considers, federal officials hit on another source of authority—money. Throughout the 1790s, federal funds flowed into the territories to both Natives and whites as compensation for unpunished crimes and an attempt to secure tenuous loyalties. A crude, expensive, and often ineffective tool at achieving federal goals, this money nonetheless reoriented the territories, as both Natives and non-Natives looked to the federal treasury for redress of wrongs committed by the other.

Part III considers the end of territorial rule as both territories sought statehood. In 1796, the Southwest Territory became the first territory to become a state. As Chapter Seven examines, this new state of Tennessee then challenged continued federal authority over property and Indian affairs within its borders. This only partially successful effort helped ensure that, when part of the Northwest Territory became Ohio in 1802, Congress safeguarded the authority accumulated under territorial rule. As a result, claims-making on the federal government—and the federal role in resolving those claims—persisted even after territorial rule ended. Whether welcomed or despised, federal law and authority had become consequential.

WE CURRENTLY HAVE TWO seemingly contradictory stories about the early American West. One depicts a space of robust, nearly unchallenged federal authority. The other describes a borderland marked by flux, contestation, and uncertain sovereignty, where the success of the United States in securing its tenuous hold was, in the words of one historian, the "most unlikely scenario of all."[35]

This book argues that these two accounts are not only complementary but mutually explanatory. It was the people of the borderlands themselves, as much as distant officials, who built the federal state in the early territories as a response to uncertainty. Even as they deflected grand schemes crafted in Philadelphia, they dragooned the federal government, with its promise of law and money, to bolster their claims amidst the free-for-all in the territories. But once invited in, federal power proved persistent.

In hindsight, this gamble on the federal government might seem a mistake, as federal authority rarely proved a boon for most borderlands residents, whether Natives, French, or marginal white settlers. But territorial inhabitants did not know this outcome when they took these risks. Many confronted possibly profound loss with few options; others chanced enormous gain. Although residents sensed the broad stakes, territorial struggles over ownership and jurisdiction played out one parcel of land, one violent dispute at a time. For those caught in these lengthy, local conflicts, federal law promised not only resolution but possibly even protection for deeply felt rights. For many in the territories, this offer was too tempting to resist.

PART I
PROPERTY

1
Sources of Title in the Territories

Jefferson's 1791 report depicted a property morass. Under federal law, nearly the entire Southwest Territory still belonged to the Cherokee and Chickasaw Nations, while Delawares, Shawnees, Miamis, and other Native nations owned most of the Northwest Territory. But even in the small corners where Native title had been "cleared," in Jefferson's parlance, the secretary recounted endless "claims of citizens"—to thirteen million acres in the Northwest Territory and over eight million in the smaller Southwest Territory. These claims came from multiple sources, but Jefferson focused on two. The first were prior state land grants under Virginian and North Carolinian law that the federal government was now obliged to honor. The second set of claims came from white settlers throughout the territories who asserted ownership "without Right or License," in Jefferson's view, but who were actually claiming under well-established principles of occupancy codified in earlier state land laws.[1]

The ownership tangle in both territories resulted from what might be termed property pluralism—the proliferation of multiple sources of ownership with disputed legitimacy. Such pluralism was neither new nor limited to the territories, of course. Ownership of land in North America had long been a complicated patchwork, as diverse Indigenous property laws collided with the title schemes European colonizers had cobbled together to dispossess Native owners and distribute land to individual colonists, usually through grant or sale by colonial governments.[2]

Yet property pluralism was both particularly acute and significant in the Northwest and Southwest Territories, for two reasons. The first was timing. The American Revolution—described by one historian as a "watershed era in the history of American landed property"—unsettled prior practice. After the war, Anglo-Americans debated anew the political economy of landed property and its relationship to power. Remaking land law in light of ascendant republican principles, states stripped common-law property of its feudal vestiges and enthroned the unrestricted, freely alienable title known as fee simple absolute. This streamlining helped further transform land into an easily salable commodity that might reward investment by rising in value—a conception of ownership that fueled a speculative "mania" or "fever" building since the Seven Years' War. Land companies dreaming of enormous settlements mushroomed, and the prospect of huge

Federal Ground. Gregory Ablavsky, Oxford University Press (2021). © Gregory Ablavsky.
DOI: 10.1093/oso/9780190905699.003.0002

returns lured elite and middling Anglo-Americans alike to hazard capital on what was pejoratively called "land jobbing."[3]

The second factor that exacerbated the territories' property pluralism was jurisdictional chaos. As Anglo-Americans interpreted it, British defeat had reopened sovereignty and ownership beyond the Appalachians. With U.S. law on these questions hazy and contested, land companies, states, the federal government, and individual U.S. citizens scrambled to claim millions of now supposedly available acres, often with little regard for existing Native owners. This free-for-all posed a substantial legal question: In a region with so many conflicting claims, which sources of ownership would Anglo-American law recognize and deem legitimate?

The contest over this issue unfolded throughout the early American West, in regions under ostensible state control, as well as in the federal territories. In Iroquoia, the Haudenosaunee, New Yorkers, and federal officials fought over the nature of Native title; in Maine, large-scale speculators battled claimants asserting possession based on occupancy; and in Kentucky, Virginia's land laws rendered "the Titles to the landed Estates . . . so very uncertain, that the Chance is at least three to One, that a Man who purchases there must defend his Title by a Lawsuit, the Expense of which will ruine a new Settler."[4]

Yet federal jurisdiction made the question of ownership in the territories both distinctive and particularly significant. Some states were temporarily land rich in the Revolution's wake, but their control over "waste and unappropriated lands"—the public domain—would, Anglo-Americans anticipated, soon cease. By 1790, every state except Georgia had ceded any claim to western lands to the federal government, and states that still retained substantial public land within their remaining borders, like New York or Virginia, were rapidly selling these lands off. In 1789, for instance, one congressman declared Kentucky "already full."[5]

With limited state public lands dwindling, the future public domain, Anglo-Americans believed, would be federally owned and distributed. This expectation gave what happened in the Northwest and Southwest Territories broader import. Both Congress and federal officials regarded their decisions there as precedents that would govern property when, as they anticipated, the United States expanded across the continent. This frame made the federal determination of which territorial property rights to honor, and which to repudiate, strikingly consequential.

But property pluralism also ensured that any federal recrafting of ownership in the territories would be neither quick nor easy. Past property regimes, it turned out, were sticky and hard to displace. The challenge was not simply, as many scholars have suggested, a gap between formal and informal property law—officials wielding new statutes confronting "squatters" citing customary law. Rather, long-standing property concepts and positive law were entwined in the territories: most claimants, even Native nations invoking immemorial title or would-be settlers citing improvement or occupancy, could point to some piece of government-sanctioned paper—a grant, deed, warrant, or treaty— that purported to give them ownership. The durability of chains of title gave such property rights, even when dubious, a kind of immortality—especially in the territories, where state cessions mandated that the federal government honor prior land schemes. The result, as Jefferson's report underscored, was that the past still weighed heavily on regions imagined as the proving ground for new ideas of ownership.[6]

Free Consent

"The most good faith shall always be observed toward the Indians," the Northwest Ordinance proclaimed. "[T]heir lands and property shall never be taken from them without their consent."[7]

This assertion glossed over much complex law. The intricate land tenures of English common law dissolved "property" into multiple overlapping individual and communal claims to specific uses and resources, readily separating title from possession and current from future rights. Property law in the late eighteenth-century United States, especially in the territories, shed some of these intricacies—Anglo-American law increasingly labeled most land "allodial," meaning free of feudal incidents—but created others: as we shall see, state property law provided uncertain future rights contingent on governmental action that one attorney general would later label "a kind of inchoate title to the fee simple of lands." Such a flexible system could readily recognize Native title: as scholars have traced, the key question was not whether Native peoples "owned" land in some abstract sense, but which rights of ownership Anglo-American law would recognize. The Northwest Ordinance said little on this fraught issue. Its language merely codified what had become common understanding: Native peoples held some kind of ill-defined but legally protected interest in their land.[8]

More distinctive was the Ordinance's focus on Native "consent." This language exemplified post-revolutionary Anglo-American political thought, which envisioned consent as the principal basis for legitimate power, recasting relationships like citizenship or family. Consent also had strong foundations within Indigenous legal culture: Native leaders routinely invoked the concept to explain what they demanded in their land transactions with the United States. Yet this shared vocabulary of consent did not resolve disagreements; it focused them. In the territories, three legal understandings of Native consent to land sales vied for supremacy—that of speculators, the federal government, and Native leaders themselves. These diverging views produced triplicate land claims that crisscrossed the Northwest and Southwest Territories, spawning confusion and violence.[9]

When Europeans began to settle in what became the Northwest and Southwest Territories in the eighteenth century, they followed long-standing practice and individually purchased lands from those they believed to be its Native owners. Though largely indistinguishable from Euro-American land practice, the resulting deeds sometimes showed greater solicitude for Native consent. One Piankeshaw (Peeyankihšiaki) deed from Vincennes, for instance, recorded that the interpreter had translated the contract to the Native sellers, "th[e]y understanding him and consenting."[10]

Such written performances of Native consent, made for the benefit of Anglo-American law, often misrepresented the realities they supposedly recorded. Indian deeds from the 1770s and 1780s proliferated in the territories, describing large payments; "in reality," Miami leader Little Turtle reported, "none of these titles have cost more than a Gallon of Rum." Anglo-Americans notoriously sought out any Natives willing to sign, even when, Little Turtle further complained, the purported sellers "were never trusted by Indians with any part of their affairs." Such shortcomings led Anglo-Americans to describe such purchases "barefaced pocket picking."[11]

As we shall see, uncertain, even fraudulent land documents were rife in early America, yet the problem of Native consent was particularly acute: Anglo-Americans could not easily assess its legitimacy, and Native power made violating norms of consent costly. By the late eighteenth century, most colonies had banned individual purchases of Native lands for over a century, and, in 1763, the British Crown proclaimed that, to prevent Native "Dissatisfaction" and "Discontent," only the Crown could legally purchase Native lands—a legal principle known as preemption.[12]

Yet imperial laws codifying preemption were freely flouted amidst the borderlands' lucrative land traffic. If purported Native consent could secure ownership of a few acres of land, such consent could, under the same logic, pass title to millions more. In 1775, North Carolinian Richard Henderson, head of the Transylvania Company, bought "several millions of Acres" of Cherokee land, including much of present-day central Tennessee. The same year, the Illinois and Wabash Companies made the second of two purchases of a similarly enormous tract in the Illinois Country from the Illinois and Piankeshaw Nations.[13]

The companies knew these purchases violated British law. Yet the Revolution had empowered new sovereigns over the region—the states—to whom the companies now pressed the validity of Native consent. Henderson Company partners told North Carolina's legislature that their purchase had occurred in "the most fair and open manner" and "with the consent of the head men and warriors as [well as] of the said [Cherokee] Nation at large." (The Cherokees disagreed;

they argued that Henderson had failed to secure the support of the requisite chiefs.) For its part, the Illinois and Wabash Company (the two companies merged in 1779) argued that consideration for the purchases was valid, the negotiation "of the most public notoriety," and the "meaning and interpretation of the parties were interpreted and explained by persons duly qualified." Yet these arguments failed: after heated debate, both Virginia and North Carolina adopted constitutions reiterating the right of preemption.[14]

Yet, when both states ceded their western lands, the companies hoped that the regions' newest sovereign, Congress, might recognize Native consent. They nearly succeeded: in its waning days, the Continental Congress stated that "however improper it may be in general to countenance private purchases from the Indians," the Illinois and Wabash Company's transaction appeared to be "fairly conducted." But in the end, the new federal government followed its imperial predecessor and embraced preemption. One of the new nation's first statutes, the Trade and Intercourse Act of 1790, drafted by Secretary of War Henry Knox, barred private purchases of Indian lands; subsequent versions established criminal penalties for such purchases. The point of the law, James Madison later stressed, was to ensure that "this whole business should be under the absolute and sole direction of the public authority."[15]

The Trade and Intercourse Act's success in achieving this goal was mixed. After its enactment, Congress turned decisively against the Illinois and Wabash Company, and would-be speculators lamented that the law "entirely deranged [their] Plans." Yet many in the territories now simply kept their schemes to purchase Native land "a profound Secret." Those who engaged in this "Wildest of all Wild Speculations" hoped they could persuade or dupe some authority into honoring their bargains. Even territorial officials made purchases of "immense extent," anticipating using their connections to secure confirmation—albeit in letters that they urged be burned after reading.[16]

Others defied federal law more openly. Some leased Native land, a ploy criminalized in 1796 that nonetheless persisted: one Tennessee country traveler stayed with a man who rented his land from the Cherokee Nation. Other would-be purchasers rejected federal authority altogether: one group leasing from Kaskaskias in the Illinois Country said that "Congress has nothing to do with the lands but that they belong to the Indians who may dispose of them as they please."[17]

By the 1790s, then, the federal government had repudiated, and even criminalized, the speculators' vision of Native consent. Yet the promise that Native signatures on a deed might yield valid title proved a vision that refused to die. Despite a centuries-long cloud of illegality, the lure of private purchases from Native nations floated through the territories' property practice long after the federal government had condemned it.

Like the speculators, the federal government used the unsettled aftermath of the Revolution to redefine Native consent—or, more accurately, abolish it from Anglo-American law altogether. Imperious in victory, federal representatives now asserted conquest. "[T]he British King . . . has cast you off, and given us your country," a congressional commissioner told Shawnees, Delawares, and Wyandots in the Ohio Country in 1785. "We plainly tell you that this country belongs to the United States." This arrogance's predictable result was Native resistance. "[I]f your people had not told the Indians that their lands belonged to you," an unnamed Native leader of the Wabash Confederacy told a federal emissary, "you would have had no war."[18]

Confronted with Native power, the United States quickly retreated. As "the main spring of the distressing War on our frontiers," federal officials concluded, conquest theory "cannot be too explicitly renounced." Instead, Secretary of War Knox emphasized, the United States would only claim lands "ceded by treaties made with the full understanding and free consent of the Chiefs."[19]

Knox and other officials articulated what such "free consent" involved. Although the resulting treaties, like the speculators' deeds, recorded Native consent through signatures on legal documents, federal officers believed that Native consent required more than written formalities. In 1790, Knox gave Governor William Blount of the Southwest Territory explicit instructions for upcoming negotiations with the Cherokee Nation. "However desireable" a cession, lands could be purchased only "by the free and unconstrained consent of a full and fair representation of the Cherokees, who are the proper proprietors of the lands to be relinquished, and with their full understanding of the act they are performing, and the consideration they are to receive as an equivalent." Knox's successor Timothy Pickering told Anthony Wayne, in advance of 1795 negotiations with the Ohio Country nations, that Native leaders should "feel that they are at perfect liberty to speak their opinions and to sign or refuse to sign." Above all, Pickering insisted, "[o]ne great principle ought to govern all the negociations, *a rigid adherence to truth*."[20]

Notably, this conception of consent required federal officials to understand and honor at least some Native law. Federal officials, for instance, worked to grasp how Native communities allocated authority. This was not always a simple task: power in both the Native South and Ohio Country was decentralized, often resting with individual villages or clans in what one observer called a "foederal union." Yet federal officials still attempted to obey Native norms when possible. When Miami leader Kaweahatta refused to negotiate with Major John Hamtramck as "no more then a war Capttain"—invoking the divide between war and peace leaders within Miami society—Brigadier General Rufus Putnam donned civilian attire and took the title of Indian agent to meet with him.[21]

Such a distinction might be considered "trivial" or "Laughable," Putnam observed, but he disagreed. When negotiating with Native nations, he argued, "we ought to accommodate our selves to their ideas of propriety especially those which they consider binding on them." Henry Knox shared this view. "The United States may conform to the modes and customs of the [I]ndians in the disposal of their lands," he informed Congress, "without the least injury to the national dignity."[22]

Federal officials sold their efforts to suppress private land purchases and adhere to Native law governing consent as a kind of humanitarianism: federal law would now "protect the Indian Lands [a]gainst . . . Bad men" who "wish[ed to] cheat not only the Indians but their own nation," Timothy Pickering asserted. Rightly skeptical of such self-serving rhetoric, scholars have critiqued preemption as a "partisan fiction asserted to dispossess native people."[23]

Yet federal officials' efforts to enshrine Native consent reflected neither benevolence nor duplicity as much as the federal government's institutional interest in ensuring clarity and certainty of title, a goal embraced by nearly every federal official. Native consent was simply too dangerous and powerful a legal tool to permit outside federal control: a land market that sanctioned private purchases from Native peoples could never offer solid and predictable ownership. As for adhering to what they perceived as Native law governing consent, federal officials emphasized that this approach avoided "misconstructions on either side" that had led to "depredations and war." In short, safeguarding Native consent, at least as federal officials grasped it, was less an act of altruism than a legal principle that would help realize federal aspirations for stability, especially for property in the territories.[24]

A Free and Lawful Treaty

In principle, then, federal officials embraced Native norms about what consent required—the full understanding of Native leaders, the absence of duress, and the appropriate authority of Native leaders. Yet Native leaders still often contested with federal officials over whether a particular treaty embodied Native consent. At the roots of these contentions was a deeper divergence between Native and federal understandings of consent, especially around finality, as one particularly well-documented treaty, the Treaty of Holston between the United States and the Cherokee Nation, suggests.

In late June 1791, Governor William Blount and other territorial officials met an estimated twelve hundred Cherokees on the Holston River, at the site of what would soon become Knoxville. It was a grand ceremonial occasion, as representatives from the two nations assembled under a purpose-built arbor. After several weeks of negotiations, Blount and forty-one Cherokee leaders signed the first treaty between the Cherokee Nation and the reconstituted United States. The treaty ceded Cherokee land in the upper Tennessee River Valley, as well as a diamond-shaped tract forty miles around Nashville (Figure 1.1), for an annuity of $1,000.[25]

Formally, the treaty adhered to Knox's rigorous instructions about consent. The forty-one Cherokee signatories—recorded in transliterated Cherokee alongside English sobriquets—included the Nation's key leaders, many of whom, like Blount, had risen to prominence amidst postwar violence and jurisdictional uncertainty. As Blount well knew, the Cherokee Nation had long been divided into regions centered around influential towns, with its prewar political hub in the Overhill towns, located twenty-five miles south of the treaty ground in the Smokies' western foothills. The treaty's first two Cherokee signatories came from that region. After North Carolinians murdered Old Tassel, the Overhill Towns' leader, in 1788, Scolocutta (Hanging Maw) assumed leadership of the region. "I am the Head man of my Nation as Governor Blount is of the white people," Scolocutta subsequently pronounced. But, just as Blount answered to President George Washington, the Cherokee Nation later selected Keanetoah (Little Turkey), also from the Overhill Towns, as what Blount called "its great and principle Chief." Though Keanetoah did not attend the Holston negotiations, his vocal representative, Culcoah (known as the Creek Linguister or the Boots), enjoyed pride of place as the first Cherokee signatory.[26]

Yet Blount achieved an even greater diplomatic coup by securing the agreement of the leaders of the increasingly influential five Lower Towns, known to Anglo-Americans as the Chickamaugas. This region had coalesced along the Tennessee River during the Revolution, as Anglo-American violence displaced many Cherokees westward. Further from Anglo-American settlements and closer to Spanish Florida, the region, centered in Will's Town, produced a cadre of younger leaders more openly skeptical of the United States than their Overhill counterparts. These towns' most important leaders nonetheless signed: Kunokeski, or John Watts, Old Tassel's nephew, whom Blount considered the Lower Towns' "principal Chief"; Chuquilatague, or Doublehead; and Nenetooyah, whom Anglo-Americans called Bloody Fellow, the most outspoken Lower Town leader at the negotiations.[27]

Blount's apparent success pleased both Knox and Congress. Opining that Blount had followed the president's instructions, Congress readily ratified the treaty, and on November 11, 1791, President Washington proclaimed it the law of the land. Knox congratulated Blount: "in pursuance of so good a work," he wrote, "you will never want the firm support of the Supreme executive of the United States."[28]

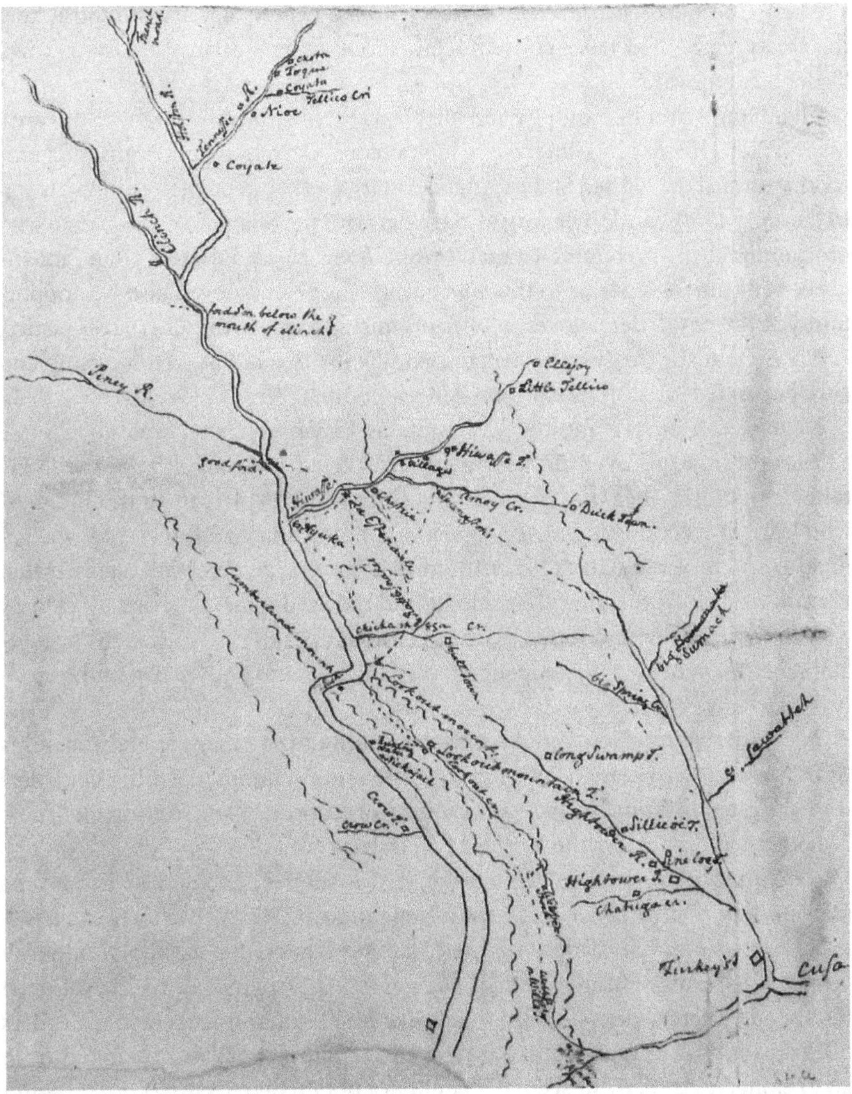

Figure 1.1: "Bounds of the Cherokee Treaty" (July 2, 1791), Folder 5, Harry Innes Papers, Manuscript Division, Library of Congress. This map, enclosed in a letter from William Blount to Harry Innes, marks the boundaries of the Treaty of Holston.

Many Cherokees, however, disagreed with the United States' assumption that the treaty embodied their consent—few more actively than the Lower Town leader Nenetooyah.

Like Blount and his complicated allegiances, Nenetooyah sought to advance his own and his nation's interests simultaneously. He had good cause for animosity toward the United States; Anglo-Americans had reportedly killed his son in the early 1780s, and so he forged close ties with the Spanish in Louisiana, who proclaimed him "preferable to many white men" and possessed of an "intelligence very much Superior to that of a Savage." Yet Nenetooyah also saw opportunity in the new federal government's promises to secure the Cherokees justice, and arrived at the treaty expecting to rekindle the two nations' relationship and curb endemic violence. He came away disappointed.[29]

Nenetooyah offered multiple accounts as to why Holston was not a "free and lawful treat[y]" even if the United States tried to "make it appear so." He told his Spanish allies that the treaty had not been "explained to the Indians," who learned its contents only upon arriving home, nor had it received "the general consent of the nation." In still other accounts, Nenetooyah claimed that Blount had bribed the interpreters to lie and changed material terms by secretly altering boundaries and reducing the promised annuities. Using such "fraudulent means," Nenetooyah complained, the United States had "usurped the lands of the Indians."[30]

But Nenetooyah also offered another account of the Treaty of Holston—this time directly to Secretary of War Knox, when he and a number of other Cherokee leaders visited in January 1792. "I am come to ask of you," Nenetooyah told Knox, "whether he [Blount] was authorized to purchase our lands."[31]

Nenetooyah's account to Knox suggested a subtler violation of the norms surrounding Native consent. Despite Nenetooyah's hopes, Blount was relentlessly fixated on land, badgering the Cherokee leaders on the topic for seven days straight. Attempting to outlast the governor, Nenetooyah had questioned Blount's disinterestedness—Carolinians like him "would not observe the orders of Congress or any body else." He attempted to circumvent Blount, demanding to go to Congress directly to see if he "could not obtain better satisfaction." Blount said there was no point, as he represented federal authority, and noted that Nenetooyah could not afford the journey without federal support.[32]

Nenetooyah read in Blount's statement an implicit threat of violence. Realizing that he and the other Cherokees were "in [Blount's] power," Nenetooyah agreed to part with a small parcel of land in return for safe passage. This concession immediately prompted intense bargaining. Blount made extravagant demands, which Nenetooyah repeatedly rejected; after "a good deal of dispute," Blount persuaded the Cherokees to craft a line along a mountain ridge in present-day eastern Tennessee. Negotiation then shifted to price. Blount offered Nenetooyah the annuity authorized by Knox—$1,000 annually. Insulted, Nenetooyah told Blount that the annuity was too small: the sum "would not buy a breech clout [cloth] for each of my nation." But, when Blount promised to write to Congress to authorize more funds, Nenetooyah and the other Cherokees agreed to sign the treaty.[33]

Nenetooyah's account may have been tailored for his audience, but it closely corresponded with the United States' own record of the treaty proceedings; it also demonstrated that Blount's voracious demands for land had violated Knox's instructions, at least in spirit. Yet Knox proved surprisingly unsympathetic, offering only a small increase in the annuity, to $1,500 per year. The secretary pointed out that the president, the Cabinet, and the Senate had all concluded that the treaty was "a good satisfactory treaty, as well for the red as the white people," and so "confirmed it, printed it as you here see, and it has become the law of the land."[34]

Consent, in short, might require a process, but one that had a clear and defined end. Once a treaty had gone through the constitutional machinery, it was no longer open for renegotiation—a law of nations principle that the United States also articulated in negotiations with the British. Law, as Knox deployed the term, connoted finality.[35]

Nenetooyah and the other Cherokee leaders did not share Knox's understanding of law. Their contrasting view appeared in a letter they wrote to the Spanish after Holston: "[T]hey never questioned the legality of their former treaties," the leaders stated, "because under the British government they were treated with justice and humanity." This understanding of legality appears in other Native statements of the time. "[H]ow can a treaty of this kind be binding," Delawares in the Ohio Country reportedly complained, "where all the stipulations are one side, where all is concession on the one part and no friend ship appears on the other?" For Cherokees, consent was not a single moment entombed in a document; it was an ongoing commitment to justice and fair dealing.[36]

The consequence of this understanding of consent was the Cherokees regarded the Treaty of Holston as the beginning, not the end, of discussions. In June 1792, Cherokee leaders, including Keanetoah and Scolocutta, gathered in council at the town of Ustanali to hear about the Philadelphia trip, "to know if the President had altered the lines." Disappointed at the news that he had not—"every thing is not to our satisfaction," the council complained—Keanetoah once again appealed to the president for a different boundary: "if this can be done, it will be a great happiness, and establish a permanent peace."[37]

The Ustanali council suggests that, on questions of consent, Cherokee leaders like Keanetoah and federal officials like Blount were talking past each other: scholars have long juxtaposed Native peoples' relational understandings of treaties with Anglo-Americans' more transactional views. But this account is doubly misleading. First, it ignores the actual content of federal law. Some officials, like Blount, sought to reduce treaties to mere deeds—formulaic language with the only operative terms names, prices, and boundaries—but other officials, like Knox, rejected that view, and the treaties' text supported them. The Treaty of Holston did not address cession until Article IV; like most eighteenth-century treaties with both European and Indigenous sovereigns, the rest of the text spoke of "permanent peace and friendship." Secondly, Blount and others, well aware of Cherokee norms around consent, insisted that Cherokees also understood federal law. Keanetoah "kn[e]w the President could not grant him the line he asked," Blount's informants told him, but the Cherokee leader was constrained, by the "nature of Indian Government," to placate younger, more aggressive leadership. "[S]uch is the fear of the Headmen of loosing their consequence," Blount reported, "that it is very rare that one of them on such occasions will declare they did sell lands, and if they do admit they did, to save their consequence will say they were wrong advised by some bad man, or deceived by the purchasor, and in either case Indians do not consider the bargain binding." Blount also attributed the newfound Cherokee critique of the Holston line to European interference. The Holston boundary "is nothing," the Cherokee leader Young Frog reportedly murmured during Keanetoah's speech; "then we had nobody to back us; now we have, and can get to that line"—meaning, according to the federal translator present, "the Spaniards."[38]

In short, Blount and others understood the Cherokees' legal arguments, but discounted them based on a theory of law. If expediency or realpolitik undergird Keanetoah's complaints, then his critiques did not reflect sincere legal norms; they were, as James Madison wrote in a similar context, mere "pretext." This was an odd position for a thinker like Madison, who built a constitutional philosophy around self-interest; it was jarring, too, in an era when legal writers increasingly accepted reasons of state as the foundation for the law of nations. Unwilling to go so far, Henry Knox, for one, credited Keanetoah's complaints: "I have had some doubts whether that part of the line was agreeable to the opinion of the Cherokees generally," he responded upon learning of them, "and it really appears to me that something will yet be to be arranged on that subject." But Knox's ultimate arrangement—tripling the Cherokee annuity, to $5,000—demonstrated the limits to even his recognition of Native law. An important win for Cherokee conceptions of consent, this compensation still did not grant the Nation the altered boundary it sought. Some Native norms, it seemed, could not be accommodated.[39]

Violating Cherokee understandings of consent had consequences. In the aftermath of his visit to Philadelphia, Nenetooyah proclaimed himself satisfied: "[W]e rejoice in the prospect of our future welfare, under the protection of

Congress." But the federal government failed to meet these expectations; reports stated that the Cherokees waited six months for their grievances to be redressed, but received no relief. "The bloody Fellow [Nenetooyah] then said," this informant related, "Congress are Liars general washington is a Liar & governour Blount is a Liar." Months later, Nenetooyah was reportedly urging the Lower Towns to war against the United States.[40]

As Knox's action demonstrated, the divide between the Cherokee Nation and the United States over consent was ultimately less about finality than about a different norm: equality. The United States was, in fact, willing to reopen treaty boundaries and past guarantees—but only in one direction, only when, at the next treaty, it asked for more Cherokee land. No matter how much Knox and other federal officials sought to outwardly conform to Native norms, such purchases would always lack the ongoing commitment to fair dealing and equality that Cherokee leaders demanded, since, as both parties well knew, these bargains were predicated on inequality. Cherokee leaders understood and assented to these treaties, but they did not freely enter them. "We objected to giving up so much land," Nenetooyah reported to Knox of Holston, "but, for the sake of peace and quietness, we did it." For their part, federal officials increasingly regarded their commitment to Native consent not as a recognition of equality but a gratuitous reflection of magnanimity: "[W]e are strong enough to take land," William Blount had informed Nenetooyah at Holston, "but will not do it because we will not be guilty of injustice." Blount's bluster was misleading—as the retreat from conquest theory shows, federal officials, too, had to accept others' law for the sake of "peace"—but his words pointed toward the future. Justice, particularly as construed by people as self-dealing as Blount, proved a thin reed for Native peoples. Even as Native consent remained a surprisingly durable, if often flouted, feature of federal law, that law defined the concept in ways that diverged ever further from Native understandings.[41]

In the early territories, the three divergent standards for Native consent had another immediate consequence: they yielded overlapping claims of ownership to the same land. Federal officials had anticipated that their embrace and enforcement of consensual Native land sales would create unambiguous chains of title unmarred by fraud, abuse, or Native discontent. Instead, land contentions persisted so long as dubious Indian deeds and contested treaties remained the foundation for ownership.

Indiscriminate Location

For all the federal attention it consumed, Native title occupied little space in Jefferson's report. Jefferson spent much more time on long lists of claims tracing to state land laws. He calculated North Carolina had already granted 5.4 million acres of the Southwest Territory—20 percent of its entire landmass—while, in the Northwest Territory, the Virginia Military District, pledged to the state to satisfy its promises to veterans, filled 15 percent of present-day Ohio.[42]

The paradoxical existence of state title schemes within the only parts of the United States *outside* state borders reflected Virginia and North Carolina's brief moments of post-revolutionary control. When these two states ceded their lands to the federal government, they formally stipulated that their land grants would retain the "same force and effect" as they had enjoyed under state sovereignty.[43]

The nature of these state land systems significantly undercut certainty of title in the territories. Both North Carolina and Virginia adopted a loosely regulated system of land distribution known as "indiscriminate location" that spawned inchoate land rights and conflicting claims. The resulting confusion benefited large-scale speculators, while undermining stable ownership. Even smallholders who sought only self-sufficiency became unwilling gamblers on the validity of title.

As codified by Virginia and North Carolina during the Revolution, the system of indiscriminate location required four steps to obtain title to the states' western lands. First, would-be owners had to appear at a state-run land office with a written description of the land they wished to purchase and pay the per-acre fees, usually quite low. The state entry taker then recorded the claim and assigned it a number. A pause of a few months followed to allow challengers to dispute the claim, a process known as filing a *caveat*. Second, barring a caveat, the entry taker issued a document called a *warrant* that instructed the county surveyor to survey the claim. Third, the surveyor returned a map and description of the property's borders, known as a *plat*, to the state secretary. Fourth and finally, if the plat was unchallenged, the secretary issued a *grant*—a document that officially passed title from the state to the new owner. The new owner recorded the grant in the local county court.[44]

These laws regulated indiscriminate location unevenly. The statutes precisely instructed entry takers on how to record claims, even specifying margins and paper size, yet left claimants to locate lands and avoid conflicting claims on their own. This lax oversight frustrated critics—one congressman of the era complained that the system "create[d] law-suits" costing more than the disputed lands—but others argued this loosely controlled process served administrators and claimants alike. It avoided elaborate, expensive bureaucracies: states could distribute lands from a single land office staffed by an entry taker and a couple of clerks, paid entirely by fees. As for claimants, indiscriminate location promised to reward first occupants, translating their knowledge of the land into the best entries, and to serve smallholders, who could obtain property cheaply.[45]

As for the problem of conflicting claims, proponents argued it was less significant than it seemed. Maps and records might be spotty, Jefferson observed in his report, but surveyors, land agents, and others "on the Spot" would "possess local Informations . . . so as to be able to keep clear of each others Rights." And if a "Conflict of Claims should arise," the caveat system dispatched such disputes to be tried in the county courts, where, Jefferson anticipated, "a local Judge will doubtless be provided to decide them without Delay." In short, in its reliance on localism and close scrutiny of state officials, indiscriminate location reflected widespread post-revolutionary models for governance.[46]

Yet what followed the enactment of North Carolina and Virginia's land laws was not the orderly unfolding of Jeffersonian communitarianism; it was a chaotic land rush. Within three years of North Carolina opening its land office, nearly 4.4 million acres had already been entered, most in the name of a few powerful individuals. "[S]cheming and capable men executed their plans," North Carolina's governor would later lament, "and swallowed up the property of the state."[47]

In explaining this outcome, commentators past and present stressed venality and corruption—what the state governor bemoaned as the "[m]ost atrocious frauds and scandals." Record books contained mysterious erasures, forgeries, and unauthorized duplicate warrants. Speculators deployed straw purchasers to avoid statutory limits. In a Nashville tavern, a young Andrew Jackson witnessed a drunk Continental Army major duped into signing forged military certificates.[48]

But much of the scramble for lands under indiscriminate location reflected, not outright fraud, but the multiple ways that the powerful and well-connected could tilt the poorly supervised land system in their favor. Rather than pay in specie, which, even at nominal prices, would have made the vast tracts prohibitively expensive, speculators paid in heavily discounted state debt certificates or military warrants. In the Virginia Military District—"a Country where there is more Sharpers than any I have been in," one correspondent recorded—surveyors demanded extortionate payment in kind for their services, up to half of the land they surveyed. Such rates quickly made them the region's wealthiest and most influential men.[49]

The creation of the territories further facilitated the land grab. Among the most prominent of North Carolina's land speculators were the Blount family, who collectively made 2,760 entries in North Carolina's land office. The Blounts then helped secure North Carolina's cession of its western lands to the federal government, with William Blount exploiting his connections to become governor of the new Southwest Territory. Blount was thrilled to learn of his new post. "[M]y Western Lands have become so great an object to me that it had become absolutely necessary that I should go to the Western Country to secure them," he wrote a confidant. He was sure that "my present Appointment" would "enhance[] their Value."[50]

The jurisdictional shift helped insulate the Blounts' land speculations from *both* state and federal interference. By the time North Carolina eventually turned against the Blounts—William's brother John Gray Blount was the subject of a 1794 grand jury presentment against "land Jobbers" whose "unsufferable monopoly" had "accumulated to themselves the vacant Lands of this State"—most Blount land lay outside the state in the new federal jurisdiction. Yet even there, federal authority was nominal: not only was Blount the Territory's governor, but North Carolina's cession bound the federal government to adhere to state land law as it existed at the time of cession.[51]

In this sense, the creation of the federal territories was testament less to a national commitment to federal ownership than to the power of people like the Blounts. Rather than physically moving between jurisdictions, they forum-shopped simply by swapping the sovereigns that controlled their lands. In the process, they converted an ostensibly national patrimony to their own interest.

A Traffic in Parchment

Among the Blounts' greatest allies in their speculative efforts were confusion and uncertainty—which the state land systems offered in abundance. It turned out that, in the vast domains opened for settlement, Anglo-Americans lacked the local knowledge would supposedly prevent indiscriminate location from devolving into a chaotic jumble.

This uncertainty unfolded first in what would become the Southwest Territory. North Carolinians knew virtually nothing of the vast territory they claimed to own, and the entries they made in the state land office reflected this ignorance. One representative warrant described two thousand acres of land over five hundred miles away from the land office lying "between the river Tennisee & Missippi [a roughly hundred-mile distance] & upon a small river or Creek, lying on both sides inclosing a tree Mark M.B. standg among a parcel chopd & Deaded trees."[52]

Inevitably, such hazy claims overlapped. Yet their vagueness also ensured that claimants could not possibly know about these conflicts when they filed, when the statutes imagined expeditious resolution through caveat suits. Instead, conflicting claims only became apparent years later, usually well after initial claimants had sold their inchoate rights to new settlers migrating into the Tennessee and Cumberland Valleys in the late 1780s. These settlers told similar stories: after years of peaceful occupancy, a neighbor might mention a conflicting claim, or there might be a knock on the door from a stranger, who produced a document granting title to the same land. The result was often litigation, as land disputes tracing to the 1780s clogged court dockets in the Southwest Territory and, later, Tennessee.[53]

Most of these suits were tried under the writ of ejectment. Compared to other common-law writs involving real estate, ejectment was more flexible and less technical, and so had long been the favored method to resolve ownership disputes. The writ did have one quirk: originally available only to tenants, ejectment required litigants testing fee simple ownership to invent fictitious leaseholders like "Richard Fenn" or "John Doe." But once an ejectment suit got to court, its resolution was relatively straightforward: plaintiff and defendant argued for the merits of their respective titles, and a local jury decided whose claim was stronger.[54]

Yet North Carolinian law ensured that such comparatively straightforward resolutions rarely ended the litigation. Land was valuable, and so litigants routinely appealed to the three regional appellate courts known as superior courts. Further complicating matters was North Carolina's distinctive equity practice, which persisted in the Southwest Territory.[55]

In England, equity offered an alternative legal system, rooted in a separate system of chancery courts, intended to do justice when the common-law writ system foreclosed relief. Equity suits differed from suits at law: they were traditionally decided by judges, not juries, and usually required lengthy, and elaborately written, prayers for relief.[56]

North Carolina adopted some of these aspects of English equity, especially the long briefs, but changed others. Rather than having separate chancery courts, the state vested both equity and law jurisdiction in superior court judges. Even odder, unlike in England, nearly any dispute could be reheard in equity. In essence, this gave litigants yet another appeal without any deference to prior judgments, sometimes before the same judges who had heard the original case at law—who could, and did, sometimes overturn their own decisions.[57]

Multiple appeals with increasing formality made land litigation in the Southwest Territory long, expensive, and unpredictable. Faced with the prospect of a lawsuit, some landowners simply bought out contrary claims, even seemingly frivolous ones. James Miller purchased a rival claim from one Hutchings, not because he thought Hutchings had the stronger claim but because "it was the easiest mode of quieting the title and saving any difficulty either in law or equity respecting the title." Unsurprisingly, this practice only encouraged more claims: Miller later confronted additional claimants to portions of his land.[58]

In other instances, multiple opportunities to relitigate had the opposite effect, encouraging claimants to fight instead of settle. In one instance, a litigant refused his opponent's offer to give up ownership, having concluding that "bringing Suit," and winning monetary damages, "would be the best way to Sell his land." Another litigant refused to bargain with his adversary even after losing in court: he would seek "a pull or twist in Equity" instead.[59]

But it was not the courts alone that caused uncertainty; the land system itself yielded unpredictable results. Perhaps the most common land dispute occurred when there were two entries for the same tract: that is, two claimants had entered the same land in the state entry book. The law dealing with such controversies was well established: the older ("elder") entry prevailed, leaving later claimants without title. Yet avoiding such conflicts proved more difficult than this clear rule might suggest. In the 1799 case of *King v. Daniel*, for instance, James Daniel purchased a parcel for which Thomas King had obtained a warrant (the document instructing the county surveyor to survey the parcel preliminary to a state grant). According to Daniel, King had told him that the warrant was based on entry number twenty-one in the entry book: because entries were made sequentially, the low number was valuable because it was almost certainly elder to other claims. But King asserted that twenty-one was merely the informal number he had used in subdividing the lands. It turned out there was, in fact, an "earlier and better" claim to Daniel's land, as a court determined when it evicted him from his parcel. After litigation in both law and equity, Daniel ultimately prevailed against King, but reportedly received far less in damages than the land was worth—never mind the attorneys' fees for the interminable proceedings.[60]

In other instances, purchasers attempted to mitigate risk by requiring sellers to promise that their claim to the land was the first and best entry by including a so-called warranty of the title in the deed. Yet such guarantees often just converted title disputes into debt litigation, where the legal question was whether contractual nonperformance excused the refusal or failure to pay a promissory note. These cases frequently arose when settling an estate after an individual's death, requiring rehashing title issues from years or even decades earlier.[61]

North Carolina law foreclosed another possible solution to land disputes. The common-law doctrine of adverse possession resolved ancient property conflicts by honoring the title of someone who *acted* as if they owned the land for a certain amount of time—in North Carolina, a relatively short seven years—even if they were not, initially, the property's recorded owner. But state courts ruled that this seven-year period began only once there was a *grant*: that is, once formal title had passed from the state. Given the many lengthy steps that indiscriminate location required before a grant issued, this statutory period usually did not start running, if ever, until long after a claimant entered a tract. Moreover, state courts increasingly limited adverse possession to claimants who could show what was called "color of title," usually interpreted to require a defective grant—which, of course, provided little help to those holding warrants, entries, and the plethora of other inchoate titles under indiscriminate location. Controversies over adverse possession would later dominate antebellum Tennessee, but under territorial rule the doctrine offered claimants little relief.[62]

The problem of conflicting land rights produced escalating frustration in the Southwest Territory. In 1796, residents, including Andrew Jackson, appealed to North Carolina's legislature to argue that those holding "junior" entries were "in justice" just as entitled to land as "elder" entrants, as they, too, had paid the state for their claims. In fact, North Carolina's land law already purported to offered them a solution. Under the terms of the state's cession, those denied land rights by an earlier entry could obtain a so-called "supernumerary" warrant, a sort of rain check that allowed frustrated claimants to make a new claim on unclaimed lands.[63]

In practice, supernumerary warrants became yet another floating potential source of ownership, exacerbating confusion. In the 1800 case of *Criswell v. Donalson*, Criswell bought a parcel of land but lacked the physical warrant from the state. So he hired a man named Tyrell to go to the state land office to secure his warrant. Tyrell instead defrauded his employer. Knowing that Criswell lacked any documents showing title, Tyrell used a supernumerary warrant to claim Criswell's lands, which Tyrell then sold to a third man, Evans. Evans sued to evict Criswell, who, lacking "any grant or title which could be admitted to read as evidence in a court of common law," lost. Such cases underscore how smallholders tried to scrupulously adhere to the law, and yet time, distance, unreliable intermediaries, and the state's lackluster efforts undermined their ownership.[64]

In the Northwest Territory's Virginia Military District, Virginians proved just as land-mad as North Carolinians. Surveyors were already on the ground when the state began to grant the region's lands in August 1787; in just over a year, claimants had filed for 1.4 million acres of land. But unlike in the Southwest Territory, Congress asserted some control over the District's distribution. In 1788, the Continental Congress voided all of Virginia's prior grants for failing to comply with the Act of Cession. Two years later, Congress mandated that the War Department determine Virginia veterans' eligibility and the U.S. Secretary of State maintain records of all entries. Virginia would still handle land recordation and surveying, but the ultimate patent would issue from the United States. These precautions would ensure, one congressman stated, that "the public never could be defrauded of an acre of land."[65]

Virginians did not appreciate federal efforts to regulate the District's lands. Congress's "vague" and "uncertain" procedures, both veterans and the state's legislature bemoaned, would "totally derange the business," causing "great delays" and "tedious and expensive [law]suits." These complaints argued, in what became a common refrain, that federal efforts violated the terms of cession: the federal intervention constituted "judging ex parte of private property, which we think ourselves secured in by the laws of this State," the veterans alleged. Congress maintained its system, but it indulged claimants by continually extending the filing deadlines. Hybrid state-federal authority over the District's lands also caused delays and bureaucratic conflicts, prompting two U.S. Supreme Court decisions.[66]

Yet the most fundamental question—how the District's lands would be distributed—lay outside federal control. Bound by cession, Congress legislated that all locations must occur "agreeably to the laws of Virginia," using the state's system of indiscriminate location nearly identical to North Carolina's, creating complicated and ill-defined plots (Figure 1.2). Just as in the Southwest Territory, the consequence was seemingly endless litigation (although, especially because patents did not issue until 1796, much it came only after the region had been admitted as the new state of Ohio). Disputes over the validity of entries and patents were over thirty-three times higher in the Virginia Military District than elsewhere in Ohio, one recent survey of Ohio Supreme Court decisions concluded. That court was well aware of the problem: "[T]he uncertainty of title,

Figure 1.2: "Land Survey for Nathaniel Massie," Oct. 10, 1796, Virginia Military District Surveys, Library of Virginia, Richmond, Va. This survey shows the convoluted borders of tracts typical of property in the District.

in the Virginia military district, is proverbial," it observed in one 1825 case. "[I]n many cases it is impossible to ascertain the existence of conflicting claims, till they are set up by the claimants." These entanglements engulfed the U.S. Supreme Court, too, which waded into what one justice labeled the "peculiar system of the Virginia land law" in the District dozens of times. The Court heard its last case involving title in the District in 1887; Congress, for its part, finally stopped honoring claims based on Virginia's bounty warrants in 1906.[67]

Indiscriminate location's dominance in the territories produced two ironies. The first was how this loosely regulated system undercut the purposes it supposedly served. Indiscriminate location was not designed to secure clarity but to make landownership cheap, decentralized, and democratic. But in the territories, indiscriminate location secured neither certainty nor autonomy. Rather, it swept smallholders like James Daniel and James Criswell into the maw of the hungry land market, even as it allowed well-connected men like William Blount to exploit the disarray it sowed.

The problem was that indiscriminate location was built for a communitarian world, already fading in the East, that never existed among Anglo-Americans in the early American West. From the beginning, would-be claimants had viewed western lands principally as *title*—the promise of governmental recognition through law. Endless litigation only heightened this conception: as litigants chased conflicting verdicts, the property concept that ownership exists only as far as the state acknowledged an individual's right against all comers was no mere theory but the lived experience of many territorial citizens.[68]

Title, moreover, was a commodity, vendible and exchangeable in networks of credit and debt. Virginia's system of indiscriminate location created a mere "traffic in parchment," that state's most eminent jurist St. George Tucker complained: "[P]atents for lands . . . land-warrants, military rights to lands, certificates of survey, nay, even bonds to procure, survey, and patent lands" had, the staunch republican and Jeffersonian recorded, "become a species of mercantile paper passing from hand to hand." This system, Tucker lamented, spawned "endless lawsuits"; it served principally "those who wish only to deceive and defraud others, who buy, merely to sell; who regard not in what miseries or perplexities they may involve ignorant persons."[69]

Tucker captured indiscriminate location's second irony when he urged that a buyer who sought "peaceable possession of his lands" should forgo Virginia and instead "turn his eyes to the northwest of the Ohio"—that is, to the federal lands of the Northwest Territory. But it was arguably there, and to an even greater extent in the Southwest Territory, where state land systems reached their full fluorescence. There, outside the states and within the ostensibly federal jurisdiction, federal territorial courts and their state successors adjudicated the disputes produced by North Carolina's and Virginia's decisions to run their land offices on the cheap. This outcome frustrated many federal officials, for whom such uncertainty was antithetical to the clear chains of ownership they wished to construct. But the acts of cession kept large swaths of these ostensibly federal domains under state jurisdiction and authority. Moreover, the federal government had to accommodate, and even hire, local notables like William Blount—men whose inescapable prominence and power stemmed precisely from their success in exploiting state law to gain landed wealth.[70]

First Occupancy

Alongside indiscriminate location, with its often-illusory benefits to smallholders, both Virginia and North Carolina also recognized a property law doctrine explicitly designed to serve smallholders' interests: so-called "preemption rights." Preemption in this context had a meaning different from its application in Indian affairs: it granted the first settlers who improved a parcel of land the first right to purchase it from the state, notwithstanding competing claims.[71]

The struggle over preemption rights in the early republic centered on two regions in the territories. In the Northwest Territory, officials and settlers contested for the north bank of the Ohio River, across from present-day Kentucky and West Virginia, then both part of Virginia. And in what became the Southwest Territory, North Carolinians poured into the French Broad region in the western foothills of the Smoky Mountains. In both regions, white settlement was illegal under federal and state law—and yet widespread. A federal army officer estimated that there were twenty-one hundred families settled on the north shore of the Ohio River in 1785, while North Carolina's governor placed the number of white families south of the French Broad River in 1788 at fifteen hundred. In both regions, a tangled battle over the legality of these settlers' claims to ownership occurred, one that underscored that the federal government was merely one of multiple overlapping sources of law in the early territories.[72]

Preemption rights were rooted in a widespread and deep-rooted Anglo-American discourse of improvement—the principle that occupancy, coupled with clearing, planting, or building on land, could yield title—that served as a vernacular property law in the borderlands. Though few on the late eighteenth-century frontier had read John Locke, they unwittingly echoed him when they described the West as "almost a State of Nature," with land free for the taking. In such a world, as one attorney argued in a 1794 Southwest Territory case, "first occupancy agreeable to the Laws of nature gave . . . an Equitable title to the land." But these ideas of improvement were not universally accepted, having long clashed with more positivist models of land distribution based on government grant. In colonial Pennsylvania and New York, government officials had battled those they deemed "intruders" and fruitlessly sought to extract payment.[73]

The creation of the federal domain in the 1780s and 1790s opened a new arena for contestation in this long-running contest over ownership. But this was not much of a competition. Though advocates of preemption rights had some champions in Congress, most federal administrators shared their predecessors' implacable opposition to occupancy claims.[74]

At core, this hostility was about money. Whatever their political allegiance, nearly everyone connected to the cash-strapped national government envisioned the new national domain as an asset whose sale could repay the enormous sums the United States had borrowed to finance the war. "The only adequate fund I can conceive for the payment of our debts," a congressman wrote to John Adams, echoing the sentiments of many, "are our western Lands." Yet preemption rights threatened to undermine any effort to secure revenue. What are "commonly called improvements" in the Northwest Territory, Governor Arthur St. Clair reported, consisted of "marking or deadening a few trees, or throwing a few logs together in the form of a cabin." Claimants could satisfy this loose standard far too easily. "[N]o Man would give 400 Dollars for a Farm which One Days work would serve," one U.S. Army officer observed. If preemption rights were recognized, he noted, the "whole Federal Territory will not raise One thousand Pounds."[75]

Preemption rights challenged the public fisc in another way, too. Western lands were not in a state of nature; they were owned by Native nations. Preemption rights encouraged Anglo-Americans to invade Indian country on the belief that, when the lands were purchased from Natives (an event the settlers regarded as inevitable), they would have the first claim. "All our acts of No. Carolina seem to favour intruders," Senator Benjamin Hawkins noted, by granting them title "under the appellation of occupants." Thus it was, Hawkins lamented, "that by violating a solemn treaty these people could acquire this *right of occupancy*."[76]

Such casual disregard of Native land rights would, George Washington feared, "inevitably produce a war," the costs of which would be borne by the government. "[G]ratify[ing] a few intruders," Thomas Jefferson bemoaned of the Southwest Territory, would "cost the other inhabitants of the U.S. a thousand times" the land's value. It was cheaper and "more just," Jefferson concluded, to "make war" against the intruders than Native nations.[77]

Early on, then, Congress issued a proclamation banning settlement north of the Ohio River on lands not purchased directly from the federal government. North Carolina followed suit: although it allowed its citizens to claim land in every other part of its western territory, the state forbade settlement in the French Broad region, site of the most important Upper Cherokee towns (Figure 1.3). When white settlers defied these orders and claimed occupancy rights anyway, governmental officials disdained the intruders as "banditti" and "adventurers." Above all, they were "lawless," the adjective routinely used to describe Anglo-American settlers who openly defied government edicts. They were, one official insisted, people who "wish to live under no government."[78]

Those asserting rights based on occupation, of course, did not regard themselves as lawless. Rather, as historians have traced in other contexts in the early United States, claims of lawlessness masked the conflict between multiple legal discourses. The "intruders" crafted legal narratives that cast them as "faithful subjects of the common wealth of America" by appealing alternately to state property law and principles of self-governance.[79]

Preemption rights might have been rooted in natural law, but during the Revolution, states began to codify improvement in their land laws. In 1777, North Carolina granted claimants who "possessed and actually improved" vacant lands the right to obtain 640 acres "in preference to all others"—a right reinforced and expanded in subsequent land statutes. In 1779, the Virginia legislature granted first settlers who had "built any house or hut, or made other improvements" the first right to purchase one thousand acres of land at the nominal state price of roughly two cents per acre. As a result, claimants could, and did, assert preemption rights under state law in Kentucky and all of the Southwest Territory—except the French Broad region. Like other property rights, preemption rights were recorded before local courts and freely bought and sold, and offered a powerful tool for asserting title.[80]

Claimants north of the Ohio and south of the French Broad hoped to similarly codify preemption rights in their regions. The intruders sought to "derive a Title to themselves by prior Occupancy according to the Mode which has heretofore prevaild in Virginia & Pensylvania," one observer in the Northwest Territory wrote. Their principal tool was a seemingly endless stream of petitions and appeals submitted to government officials. Sometimes, pleading ignorance, they argued that they were just following well-established custom. "Thos prohibatory Laws [banning their settlement] are Nevar sufficiently promulgated and have never hitherto been put in Execution," one group of French Broad settlers complained to North Carolina's legislature. "[W]e did not transgress your laws from a refractory disposition, but only followed the practice of the different states who had unapropriated lands to settled, who from time immemorial confirmed the actual settlers in their settlements upon their paying the price settled by Law." Other times they used moral suasion, claiming title based on suffering at Native hands and rhetorically parading widowed mothers and fatherless children before legislators. They were desperate, one group of petitioners argued: if expelled, we "must take up with hunger for [a] companion and familiarly shake hands with the cold hand of poverty."[81]

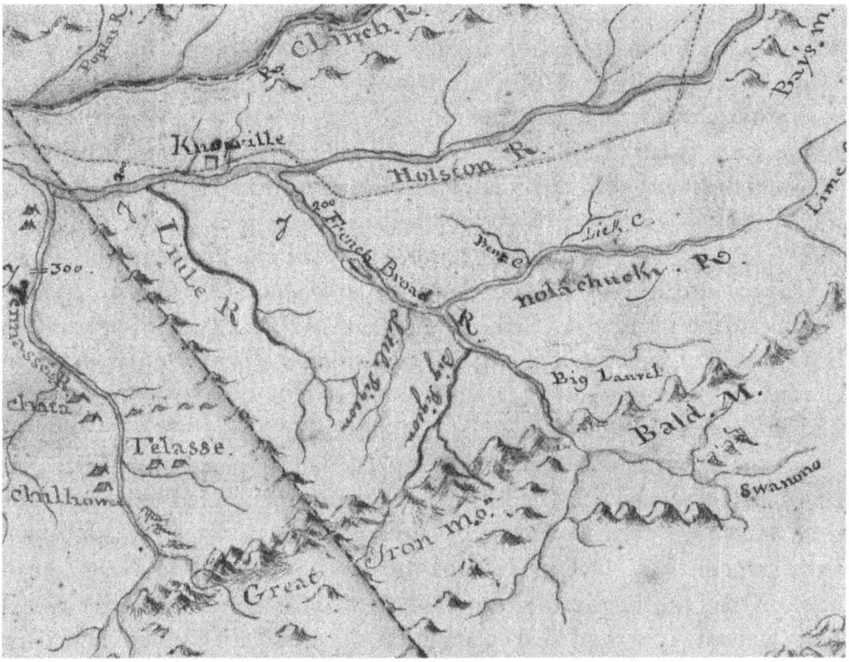

Figure 1.3: Selection from "A Map of the Tennassee Government" showing the French Broad region. North Carolina land law barred settlement *south* of the French Broad River. The dotted line along the ridge of mountains shows the boundary of the 1791 Treaty of Holston, where the federal government purchased land *east* of the line.

Such proclamations of legal and moral entitlement invariably prefaced pleas for indulgence. Every petition appealed for a land office and the opportunity to buy occupied lands "at a moderate price." Barring that, petitioners asked, always, for more time—to bring in their crops, to appeal to yet another official. The settlers "generally promise compliance" with orders for removal, one federal officer along the Ohio wrote, "but I observe it is with a degree of reluctance, and that they are fond of construing every indulgence, in the most favorable and extensive manner for themselves." Unless forced off, he reported, "there will be no end to their craveing for future indulgence."[82]

But the petitions reveal only a partial perspective of the intruders' legal understanding. Unsurprisingly, in their appeals to government, the occupiers strategically reiterated their lawfulness. "We do not pretend Claim Right or title to Land till we obtain it in a Constitutional Manner," one group along the Ohio reassured a federal official, while French Broad inhabitants loyally committed "to support [North Carolina's] laws and Constitution." Yet the petitions were vague about what precisely constitutionalism meant. To the officials who read them, constitutionalism implied obedience to proper authority. Yet outside the bounds of the petitions, the intruders invoked a more capacious understanding of constitutionalism, one that vindicated the people's right to form their own governments—what historians have dubbed self-sovereignty. If their petitions failed and the state would not honor their claims, the occupiers concluded, they would constitute a new state.[83]

Though it echoed revolutionary natural-law rhetoric, this language of self-governance also relied on formal law. One anonymous Northwest Territory pamphlet denied that the federal government had the power to interfere in the Ohio Valley settlements, promiscuously citing the pursuit of happiness in the Declaration of Independence, the guarantees of possessing property in the Massachusetts and Pennsylvania Declarations of Rights, and the right to form a new state in the Pennsylvania Bill of Rights. The pamphlet's author was perhaps John Amberson, who published an advertisement posted throughout the white settlements north of the Ohio. "I do certify that all mankind," Amberson wrote, paraphrasing the Pennsylvania provision, "agreeable to every constitution formed in America, have an undoubted right to pass into every vacant country, and there to form their constitution." Amberson thus proposed that the region's settlers form their own state. This effort fizzled, but the intruders nonetheless elected their own justices of the peace who issued writs and decided cases without sanction from any state or federal government.[84]

Settlers in the French Broad region went further: they did try to create their own state, dubbed "Franklin," crafting a constitution that established a separate legislature, executive, and court system. Franklin's perhaps core purpose was to legalize the intruders' titles, and the would-be state's leaders immediately concluded a land agreement with the Cherokee Nation. Under any law but that of Franklin, this purported Treaty of Dumplin Creek was invalid, little more than a gussied-up speculator's Indian deed. The Cherokees immediately disavowed it: the nation had refused to negotiate with the Franklinites, influential Upper Cherokee leader Old Tassel assured an Indian agent, because they did not represent the United States. Instead, "some of our young men went to See what they wanted," only to tell the Anglo-Americans "that they no Authority to Treat about Lands."[85]

Yet this purported treaty was pretext enough for the Franklinites to proclaim the disputed territory "their Ground." They proceeded to open a land office that sold off the Upper Cherokees' "Belov'd Town Chota & several of their cornfields," leading panicked Cherokee leaders to appeal to federal officials for help. "[W]e look upon the white people that Lives in the new State very deceitfull," Keanetoah told a federal representative. "[W]e have Experienced them, and are much affraid of them." North Carolina and the federal government ordered the Franklinites off

Cherokee land, but the Franklinites—promising to "Hold [the land] in Defiance of Every power"—refused to acknowledge the authority of either sovereign. "[T] hey Had Knowledge Enough to Judge for themselves," one group of Franklinites informed a North Carolinian official trying to expel them, "that they should not ask North Carolina Nor no other person how they ware to B. Governd."[86]

In 1788, after intense factionalism and a brief battle, Franklin imploded, and North Carolina resumed control over the region. But, still excluded from civil government because of their illegal settlement, some of the French Broad settlers formed a new "convention of the people" and drafted a new "social compact." The resulting articles of association adopted the laws and constitution of North Carolina but maintained the civil and military officers appointed by Franklin. Above all, they insisted on the validity of the Treaty of Dumplin Creek—and therefore their land titles.[87]

Aggressive assertions of autonomy like Amberson's and the state of Franklin led government officials to regard those who violated state and federal law by settling north of the Ohio and south of the French Broad as fundamental threats to constituted order. But the settlers' vision of creating new jurisdictions amidst the swirl of contesting authorities in the 1780s was not bizarre; after all, the creation of new states was the fundamental purpose of the territories. Nor did these intruders wish to live under "no government." On the contrary, they dearly wanted government, but of a particular kind—above all, one that would honor their claims to the land. When they failed to achieve this goal through petitions that cast them as lawful actors, they sought to build their own states to vindicate their ownership.

Federal Law

Rather than no government, claimants got the federal government, which, after North Carolina 1790's cession, governed both the French Broad and Ohio Valleys. Federal officials now sought to establish the primacy of the federal law of property over the occupiers' law but quickly discovered they had limited options.

In theory, the federal government, like other landowners, could expel the intruders through eviction proceedings. But officials were skeptical. If federal officials opted for court proceedings, the United States might as well "throw open this country to every person who pleases to take possession of it," wrote Governor St. Clair, "for not one of [the intruders], I am certain, will ever be removed of civil process."[88]

Instead, north of the Ohio, federal officials resorted to force to enforce Congress's ban on unauthorized settlements. The removal of "all intruders" from federal lands was "the first object" for the few hundred federal soldiers stationed along the Ohio, Secretary of War Knox instructed their commander, Colonel Josiah Harmar: "[T]he payment of the public debt" required that he immediately "expel from the public lands, those lawless men who have acted in defiance of the orders and interest of the United States." Harmar was only too pleased to "give . . . *federal Law*" at gunpoint. Throughout 1785 and 1786, detachments of federal soldiers ranged the Ohio, ordering settlers to leave their cabins and burning the homes and crops they left behind.[89]

This contest over ownership threatened violence, as Major John Armstrong discovered as he fulfilled Harmar's orders. Settlers frequently defied Armstrong: some simply "laugh[ed]" when he read his orders, while one man named Ross, after "cast[ing] many reflections on the Honorable the Congress," insisted that he "was determined to hold his possession." Armstrong had Ross arrested and hauled off in chains. Others armed themselves, backing down only when Armstrong promised to fire on any armed party. When Armstrong entered the intruders' homes, he discovered loopholes and barricades.[90]

Yet even this raw exercise of federal power was often unavailing. Despite repeated expulsions, settlers returned, sometimes two or three times: Ross vowed that, if his house were destroyed, he would "build six more in the course of a week." The failure of unvarnished federal force to stop such intrusions demonstrated to many that the federal government was powerless to halt the inexorable tide of westward expansion. "A few may be dislodged," one observer noted of the efforts to expel intruders, "but they will soon become too numerous for this to be easily effected." One congressman argued that "it was not in the power of any force on earth" to halt Anglo-Americans' westward movement.[91]

Yet the cat-and-mouse game along the Ohio was misleading. The federal government could not prevent crude huts, but most of the occupiers wanted to do more than just hold the land; as their repeated petitions demonstrated, they wanted title. Federal actions long denied them this resource.

This dynamic was particularly clear in the Southwest Territory's French Broad region, where the legal situation was especially tangled. North Carolina repeatedly refused to recognize the intruders' land rights on Cherokee territory, deeming it "impolitic." But the state did offer the intruders one key concession. In its cession to the federal government, North Carolina stipulated that the transfer "shall not prevent the people now residing south of French Broad . . . from entering their pre-emptions in that tract, should an office be opened for that purpose, under an act of the present General Assembly."[92]

The creation of this tentative land right, contingent on future legislative decisions, sowed more confusion. It encouraged the region's settlers to remain, anticipating that the state would fulfill its implicit promise. Yet the assembly consistently declined to do so, perhaps reasoning that the region was now the federal government's problem.

In 1791, the French Broad region's ownership switched. After the Cherokee cession at the Treaty of Holston, federal law now deemed the region *federal* land, with the roughly three hundred thousand newly purchased acres "the only Lands open to [federal] Disposal" in the entire Southwest Territory. Yet, as Jefferson noted, any such "Disposal" ignored the thousands of white families already there claiming ownership.[93]

As in the Ohio Valley, then, the French Broad region presented a conflict between federal title and occupancy rights. But federal officials responded differently. In place of the harsh course the government pursued in the Northwest Territory, Secretary of State Jefferson urged Governor William Blount only to require a vague acknowledgment of federal title from the occupiers. That way, Jefferson suggested, "you will secure the right of the U.S. with as little trouble and injury to the intruders and grantees as you can."[94]

This contrasting approach likely reflected that, unlike military men like Knox and Harmar and their demands for obedience, Jefferson had some sympathy for the intruders' arguments, even acknowledging that "equitable circumstances" might justify their claims. And there were only a handful of federal soldiers in the Southwest Territory to evict them anyway. But the reluctance to use federal force also likely reflected a *third* set of claimants asserting title to the region alongside the federal government and the occupiers.[95]

This third set of claims stemmed, yet again, from North Carolina's complex land law. As discussed previously, when claimants could not obtain their original land rights because of a prior conflicting entry, North Carolina issued supernumerary warrants, which allowed claimants relocate their land rights elsewhere. When William Blount arrived in the Southwest Territory in autumn 1790, he discovered that residents were using these supernumerary warrants to obtain North Carolinian grants on the French Broad lands. This, Blount was convinced, was illegal—"directly against both the Words and Spirit . . . of the laws of No. Carolina"—because state law had explicitly declared the region Cherokee land. (This illegality did not personally trouble Blount, however: he had earlier instructed his associates to buy up warrants to invest in this "scheme," cautioning, "my name never to appear.")[96]

Yet these claimants had their own legal theory: because supernumerary warrants were part of North Carolina's land law, the federal government had to honor them under the act of cession. Despite this argument's obvious opportunism—the claimants were, after all, flagrantly defying North Carolina law in attempting to settle the region—North Carolina Governor Alexander Martin backed this interpretation. At Jefferson's behest, Martin grudgingly issued a proclamation against the supernumerary warrant scheme, but observed that any past and future grants were still legally valid and enforceable under the act of cession.[97]

White French Broad settlers asserting occupancy rights regarded these supernumerary warrants as an ever graver challenge to their claim to ownership than federal title. In 1794, they sent a remarkable petition to Congress, in which they appealed, yet again, for recognition of their "right of pre-emption to their hard-earned improvements and possessions" when a land office opened. But they also requested something more surprising. Many of them, they stated, had purchased the supernumerary warrants and "laid them on their lands," as a way to bolster their title claim. They now asked that Congress honor their warrants—but theirs alone: "stranger[s]" who engaged in the same scheme using the same kind of warrants, they argued, should be prevented from seizing title "from the holder and improver of the land."[98]

As the intruders' unanswered petition underscores, the region's confusing array of sources of title offered claimants little certainty as to which law would ultimately yield ownership. So they hedged, obtaining multiple sources to minimize the risk of dispossession. For instance, right around the time of the petition, land speculator Robert King offered Robert Wilson, one of the French Broad intruders, a state supernumerary warrant to bolster his preemption right title. Wilson refused: he "did not wish to risque his money for a Grant," he stated, "because he conceived the grants Obtained in that tract of Country would be illegal and void." But King "insisted that [such] grants . . . would be good and valid in law," and so Wilson agreed, with an important limitation: King had to provide a bond promising to obtain the tract "in fee simple . . . derived from the United States whenever the federal Office for the sale of said land should opened (provided the title and conveyance from North Carolina . . . should be found insufficient)."[99]

In the end, Wilson got cold feet and backed out; a decade later, King and Wilson filed conflicting law and equity suits over Wilson's promissory note. But even as these cases wound their way through court, the question that had first prompted the now contested transaction—who owned the French Broad lands—was still not settled.[100]

The wranglings in the French Broad region differed from the ideological, and at times literal, standoffs over preemption rights elsewhere—between claimants invoking natural law and officials who evicted "lawless" intruders at gunpoint—that captured the imagination of commentators past and present. Yet the French Broad occupants were not distinctive; they exemplified long-neglected aspects of the legal struggle over preemption rights. The discourses of improvement they invoked were largely grounded in state statutes, and reflected expediency as much as deeply held concepts of ownership: claimants could, and did, readily grasp for any source of title that might bolster their land claims. Moreover, although claimants slipped into anti-state rhetoric when it suited their purposes, they ultimately relied on governments to validate their ownership, especially against competing claimants. As both their petitions and actions demonstrate, what these "lawless" settlers craved above all was law—law, from whatever source, that would protect their lands in the midst of the territorial ownership scramble.

But in the early territories, law could not provide the security of title that claimants sought. Instead, preemption rights served as yet another legal trump in the myriad contests to secure lands in the territories. Like the state land systems more generally, these rights often failed to serve the smallholders they supposedly benefited, even as they further exacerbated the territories' property confusion. Alongside Native title, inchoate rights under state land law, and federal assertions of ownership, preemption rights proved yet another way that multiple people could claim to own the same piece of ground.

Confusion was the hallmark of the territories' property pluralism. This uncertainty created significant, if risky, opportunities to obtain land cheaply, but it also imposed enormous costs on anyone who sought defensible title. Such unsettled and contingent ownership became, as St. George Tucker's comments suggested, an important foil for thinking about property in the early republic—an example of how *not* to regulate title. As a result, federal land law, however shifting and tentative, was defined in opposition to the existing chaos. Whatever system replaced the current free-for-all in the territories, officials' strong preference was for clarity, finality, and the absence of conflict—the administrative virtues. Federal lands, one booster of the Northwest Territory optimistically if inaccurately wrote, would have a "great advantage" over lands elsewhere: "*the Title is indisputable.*"[101]

Yet consensus about the diagnosis did not extend to the cure. Territorial residents argued sharply about what kind of property system would yield unambiguous title—a disagreement echoed in Congress, too. During the two years leading up to Jefferson's report, representatives had fiercely contended over how best to achieve clarity. Survey prior to sale, the rectangular grid, the location of federal land offices, the price per acre—all were hotly contested, with congressmen drawing disparate conclusions about the lessons of prior land practices. When one congressman praised New York's system, another wanted it well described "in order that the United States may avoid it." When one congressman lauded indiscriminate location, others attacked it, with one North Carolinian noting that his state's system had allowed "persons rich in securities and cash" to seize the best lands. Despite substantial opposition, advocates in the House successfully passed a bill honoring preemption rights—which promptly died in the Senate.[102]

Nonetheless, Congress did coalesce around some legal principles: it quickly codified the sole federal right to purchase land from Native nations, and its early refusal to recognize preemption rights became part of a stubborn pattern to resist any general statutory acknowledgment of occupancy. Yet these laws only partially and haltingly recast ownership in the territories. It would take forty years, and the intervention of the Supreme Court, in a case involving the Illinois and Wabash Company, before the persistent dream of private purchases from Natives finally died. Similarly, Anglo-American settlers waged, ultimately successfully, a forty-year campaign to overturn the federal government's hostility to preemption rights.[103]

As these examples suggest, the property mess in the territories proved too tangled, and there were too many other legitimate sources of land law, for new concepts of ownership dictated from Philadelphia to displace past practices. Rather than a resolution, state cessions of the territorial property morass to the federal government marked the beginning of a decades-long struggle over the source and nature of title in early America.

Congress seemingly recognized this reality when, confronted with Jefferson's report, it abandoned its initial haste and did not return to the land office project for over four years. The growing conflict between Native nations and the federal government in the Northwest Territory had largely rendered the question moot anyway: there was little demand for land in a war zone.[104]

But one of the land office bill's strongest proponents attributed its demise to another cause: well-placed opposition from existing federally backed land companies, who sought to block competition. These companies, many thought, might solve the territories' property muddle. Events played out differently.[105]

2

The Land Company Experiment

At core, the intense fights over land distribution in the post-revolutionary United States were contests about democracy and political economy. During and immediately after the Revolution, republicanism—which celebrated extensive smallholdings as the foundation of civic virtue—dominated. As we have seen, North Carolina and Virginia's wartime land systems sought to make western land widely and cheaply available to individual white men, even if in practice speculators adeptly exploited these laws. The federal government initially followed a similar approach: the Land Ordinance of 1785 created government-run land auctions for small parcels of 640 acres. But by the late 1780s, as the fiscal reality of the enormous war debt set in, governments began to opt for a simpler, if less egalitarian, approach: they directly alienated millions of acres of public land to wealthy investors, pejoratively labeled "land jobbers," who sought to profit through resale. Loosely organized into land companies, these efforts differed from prerevolutionary endeavors like the Illinois and Wabash or Henderson Companies in that they obtained both title and blessing from Anglo-American governments.[1]

The federal government led the way. In summer 1787—after two years of federal land auctions had sold a meager 150,000 acres—a cash-strapped Continental Congress agreed to sell 7.5 million acres of federal land in the Northwest Territory to the Ohio, Scioto, and Miami Companies for current and future payments that would extinguish nearly $5 million in federal debt. The deals, one proponent bragged, "far exceeded any private contract ever made before in the United States"—but not for long, as states quickly followed the federal example. In just a few years' span, legislatures in Massachusetts (1788, 1792), Connecticut (1794, 1795), and New York (1791) had also sold title to millions of acres of public domain to land companies. The largest sale occurred in Georgia, where, in 1789, the legislature transferred nearly the state's entire purported western territory—fifteen million acres directly south of the Southwest Territory—to the Tennessee, South Carolina, and Mississippi Companies.[2]

In the late 1780s and 1790s, then, both the federal and state governments embarked on a vast experiment to use land companies to distribute public land. But this experiment's implications differed for the two sets of sovereigns. States like Connecticut and Georgia were offloading their entire public domains,

Federal Ground. Gregory Ablavsky, Oxford University Press (2021). © Gregory Ablavsky.
DOI: 10.1093/oso/9780190905699.003.0003

leaving little remaining to sell. By contrast, even after its 1787 contracts, the federal government retained over twenty-one million acres still to be distributed, an amount that the United States anticipated would only grow as it purchased still more Native land. For the federal government, then, the land company project, adopted in a moment of financial desperation, was something closer to an actual experiment: a test to see whether such large-scale land sales furthered federal aims. Hotly debated in Congress from the moment it first took up federal lands in 1789—no issue attracted more attention or controversy there than whether to continue to sell federal land "by the million acres"—much of this experiment unfolded in the territories, where land companies undertook the work of settlement.[3]

Events there underscored why land companies were such an appealing, yet controversial, approach to distribute public lands. Anglo-American governments had long passed the risks and responsibilities of colonialism onto government-backed companies, and had routinely relied on towns and municipal corporations to allocate title. Anglo-Americans were also familiar with imperial corporate behemoths like the British East India Company, which echoed many states' own origins as English joint-stock companies. Yet, though the post-revolutionary land companies reflected long-standing practices of governance and empire, many Anglo-Americans viewed them as a threat to the public good. A republican critique bemoaned how land companies exploited public assets for personal enrichment. Another line of attack came from the Washington administration. Even as they speculated heavily in lands themselves, men like Henry Knox feared that the new, state-created land companies would echo their prerevolutionary predecessors and challenge their project of orderly, regulated settlement under federal supremacy, especially in Indian affairs.[4]

Georgia's Tennessee Company exemplified this threat. The Company did not clearly own what it was attempting to settle, since the federal government, Spain, South Carolina, and above all the Cherokee, Creek, and Chickasaw Nations all asserted title contrary to Georgia's claim. Moreover, the Company's creator, Zachariah Cox, basing himself in the Southwest Territory, openly defied territorial officials and plotted to violate federal law by settling Native land. Such shortsighted pursuit of profit, federal officials feared, would exacerbate uncertain ownership, alienate Native confederacies, and undermine the federal claim to sovereignty.

In the Northwest Territory, the Ohio, Scioto, and Miami Companies purported to offer a different approach. Historians have noted how these companies sold themselves as extensions of federal authority, but they have missed their broader confluence with federal aims, as the companies promised to replace the territories' haphazard property schemes and curb land speculation's seeming anarchic impulses. The companies would do so through what they called "System," a resonant term that implied particular commitments. For one, system embraced the Washington administration's pursuit of friendship with Native nations—an economic as well as humanitarian goal tied to land value. For another, literal system would create clear ownership by distributing lands methodically. This approach, proponents insisted, would offer "a wise model for the future settlement of all the federal lands."[5]

That, at least, was the ideology. In practice, "system" proved self-serving rhetoric. When the promise of remade Indian affairs collapsed into open violence, the backers of both the Ohio and Miami Companies alleged that the federal government had opportunistically taken advantage of their financial and personal risk without providing the support they believed implicit in the partnership. From the perspective of federal officials, the federally created land companies proved little different from the Tennessee Company, as they, too, succumbed to the lure of inchoate and uncertain ownership. When their speculative gambles failed dramatically, these land companies left property messes that fell to Congress to resolve, exacerbating rather than clarifying the tangle of title in the territories.

A Wild Speculator

Like many who gambled on title in the early United States, Zachariah Cox began his career as a surveyor. Cox, a Georgian, first became interested in western lands in 1785, when he sought to lead a group of other Georgians to Muscle Shoals, also known as the "Bent" of the Tennessee.[6]

Located in present-day Alabama, the Bent was one of the most strategically significant locations in the Southeast (Figures 2.1 and 2.2). The southernmost point of the vital Tennessee River, it linked the region to the Gulf of Mexico via a short portage. At the junction of Cherokee, Creek, and Chickasaw territories, the Bent had long served as a center of trade and diplomacy among the three nations. These prospects for Indian and riverine commerce attracted would-be speculators, including Cox, over the 1780s.[7]

These plans fizzled, but Cox's hopes revived in 1789. That year, Georgia—pressed for cash and with little desire to actually govern the vast western borderland it claimed to own—simply sold its supposed western territory, most of present-day Mississippi and Alabama, to three land companies. One of them, the Cox-created Tennessee Company, purchased 3.5 million acres centered at the Bent, at a heavily discounted price of 1.3 cents per acre, to be paid within

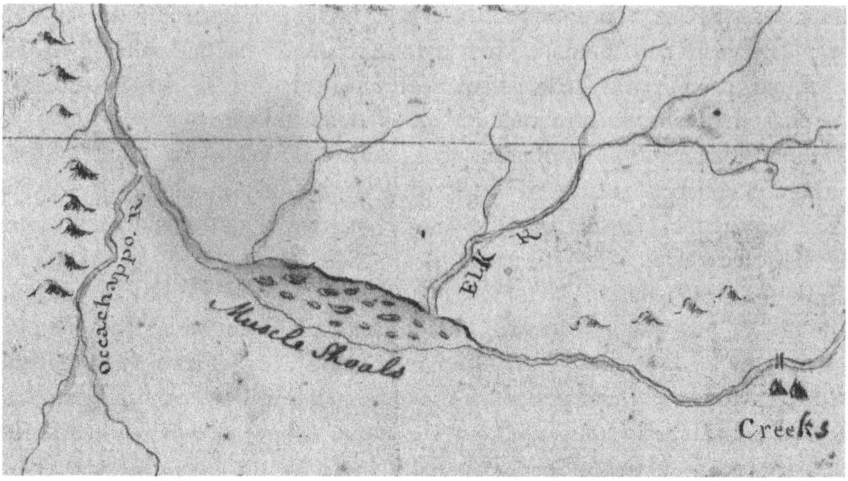

Figure 2.1: Selection from "A Map of the Tennassee Government" showing Muscle Shoals.

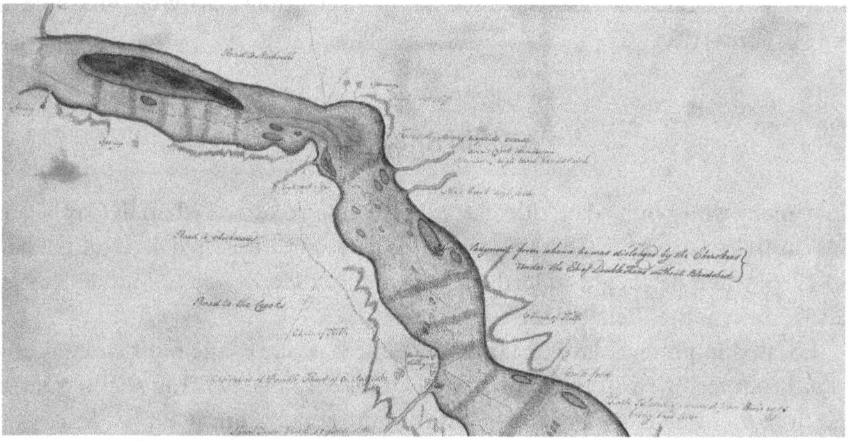

Figure 2.2: "A Sketch of the Muscle Shoals of the Tennessee River," c.1802. Courtesy of the American Philosophical Society. This later map of Shoals contains a notation describing Cox's eviction in 1791: It records the location of "Coxe's lodgment from whence he was dislodged by the Cherokees under the Chief Double Head without Bloodshed."

two years. The other two companies received millions more acres at similar prices. The bargain price reflected significant doubts over whether Georgia owned the land it was selling. In particular, federal treaty guaranteed the property rights of the resident Creek, Chickasaw, and Cherokee Nations to the region. Georgia resolved this dilemma by requiring the land companies to extinguish Native claims and keep the state "free from all charge and expences" from Indian affairs.[8]

These sales of dubiously owned land represented the first of the Yazoo sales—later decried as the "Yazoo fraud"—that convulsed early American politics, finance, and law for decades. Yet, in focusing on later financial and courtroom maneuverings, historians have neglected the literal ground-level fight for control of the southern borderlands precipitated by Cox's immediate goal—settling his newly purchased land.[9]

Cox headquartered his efforts in the Southwest Territory, which lay just north of the Tennessee's Company's tract. Advertising free land to any who would raise a crop at the Bent, Cox and thirty-one armed men traveled to the Shoals in spring 1791. In a widely reprinted letter, Cox reported meeting with Chickasaw and Cherokee representatives, who supposedly assured Cox of their friendship. (Reports suggested that Cox had told Native leaders only of plans to trade, keeping mum about his planned settlement.)[10]

For federal officials, Georgia's sale of the contested borderlands directly challenged federal authority over Indian affairs. Both Secretary of War Henry Knox and Secretary of State Thomas Jefferson concluded the contracts were illegal, since, Knox reasoned, the federal government possessed the "only constitutional right" of negotiating with Native nations. President Washington himself denounced the consequences that Cox's plans would have on relations with Native nations. "Notwithstanding the existing laws [and] solemn Treaties," he angrily wrote, "agents for the Tennessee company are at this moment by public advertisements under the signature of a *Zachariah Cox* encouraging by offers of land, & other inducements, a settlement at the Mussle-Shoals."[11]

Washington's fears proved well founded. When word of Cox's proposal reached Cherokee leaders gathered to negotiate what became the Treaty of Holston, they became "exasperated" and "Indigna[n]t" at this "open violation" of past agreements, complaining that Governor William Blount was simply "amus[ing] them with friendly Talk." During his subsequent visit to Philadelphia, Cherokee leader Nenetooyah specifically demanded that the federal government halt the Tennessee Company's planned settlement.[12]

Cox's assault on Native title similarly angered the Creeks. "The Tennesee Companies Grant," Creek leader Alexander McGillivray observed, "includes every foot of our, the Cherokees & Chickasaw Hunting Grounds."[13] Recognizing McGillivray's importance, Cox sent an agent to meet him: a "Talkative Chap," McGillivray recounted, who sought to "Cajole me into measures by the most profuse and wild promises he could invent." Yet McGillivray spurned the overture. "[T]hese wild Speculators," he recounted, "must think me as mercenary, base & unprincipled as themselves by presuming to address me on such a Subject."[14]

To placate Native demands, Henry Knox commanded Governor Blount to prevent the settlement "at all events." Yet Blount failed to stop Cox in the Southwest Territory. Instead, he turned to Native jurisdiction to enforce federal law, reportedly informing the Cherokees that, because Cox "was acting without any Permission or Authority of the Supreme Government," the Nation had "leave to intercept" his party. McGillivray reached a similar legal conclusion. "This Measure of Messr. Cox I conceivd to be a flagrant Violation of the treaty [between the United States and Creek Nation], because Congress had pledgd themselves not to Countenance the Georgia Grants to the Yasou & Tennessee Companys," McGillivray wrote, which "left me at liberty to act hostilely against them if they should presume to Settle the Countrys in question." McGillivray sent a force to destroy Cox's settlement, but they found the Shoals abandoned: Cox's party had stayed only briefly to trade with some Chickasaws before heading back upriver, reportedly after being expelled by neighboring Cherokees. McGillivray posted guards in case the Georgian returned.[15]

Cox's retreat to the Southwest Territory roiled the territorial government. Blount had Cox and his men hauled before the Washington District Superior Court for violating the federal Trade and Intercourse Act's prohibition on purchasing Native land, but the result was not what the governor hoped. "The Grand Jury would [not] find the bill against Cox and others," he complained, lamenting that the decision "has given the Company a sort of triumph in the Eyes of ignorant People over Government"; Territorial Secretary Daniel Smith bemoaned that Cox's acquittal led many "to believe the laws cannot punish them for settling at the shoals."[16]

Defiant, Cox announced plans to return to the Shoals the following year. Blount responded by barring Cox from the Southwest Territory; any "injudicious" citizens who joined him, he warned, would be hauled "before the federal court." Federal Territorial Judge David Campbell reminded a grand jury that Indian treaties were the "supreme Law of the Land"—a widely circulated charge that reportedly "operated much to the disgrace of those Adventurers."[17]

Yet it was Native power and financial worries, not federal law, that ultimately doomed Cox's plans. Cox and his men would be "mad . . . to attempt another Settlement," one newspaper observed, without "a force sufficient to act in opposition to all the Southern Indian Tribes." Meanwhile, Cox found himself unable to scrounge together the money needed to pay Georgia, which insisted on hard currency rather than near-worthless state currency. "Your good friends the Muscle shoal Compy. have faild to make pay[men]t," a sarcastic correspondent informed Governor Blount.[18]

Cox's early abortive efforts at settlement have long been cast as a minor footnote in the larger drama surrounding the Yazoo sales that came to dominate American finance and law. But at the time, Cox's plan was seen, not as a borderland picaresque, but as a serious threat "inimical to the United States." Without settling a foot of land, Cox had convulsed the Creek, Cherokee, and Chickasaw Nations, the Southwest Territory, and the Washington administration.[19]

Cox seemed so dangerous because such unregulated land speculations fundamentally challenged federal officials' vision of orderly settlement under national authority. For one, Cox had little patience for the federal project to remake Indian affairs. Like an earlier generation of speculators, Cox, heedless of Native power, sought only to bribe or cajole Native leaders into providing a fig leaf of legality to Native dispossession. For another, Cox's opportunistic machinations rested on the same dubious assertions of uncertain title that federal officials wanted to quash. In asserting ownership based on Georgia's contested claim, Cox created the sort of intricate, decades-long property struggle across multiple legal fora (including, as we shall see, the federal government) that already plagued the borderlands. Finally, Cox's plan underscored how quickly claims of ownership bled into assertions of law, power, and jurisdiction—in short, of sovereignty. Cox's efforts terrified federal officials who feared that such self-created governments would thwart their efforts to firmly establish national authority in the West.

Yet neither federal law, nor the Native power that had actually thwarted the scheme, deterred Cox or Georgia. In 1795, after Cox and like-minded associates liberally plied the state legislature with bribes, Georgia once again sold its western lands to several companies—including nearly three million acres around Muscle Shoals to a renewed Tennessee Company for $60,000. Unlike the 1789 purchases, this land grab caused outrage in Georgia; a newly elected legislature not only repealed the sales but literally burned the earlier statute. An undaunted Cox pushed on with his plans for settlement.[20]

The Advantages of System

While Cox struggled to establish his claim to the Muscle Shoals, in the Northwest Territory another land company began to settle a similar governmental grant for millions of acres. The Ohio Company resembled the Tennessee Company in more than its riverine name. It employed the same business model of trading government debt for government land. And like Cox, the Company's main organizer, Rufus Putnam, from a middling central Massachusetts family, had earlier worked as a surveyor. Yet there was a key difference between the two companies: in contrast to the Tennessee Company's antagonistic relationship to national authority, Putnam's endeavor enjoyed the federal government's active encouragement and support.[21]

From the beginning, the Ohio Company's backers cast their land speculation as a nationalist project of "lasting consequence to the *American Empire*." In

1786, Putnam—a former brigadier general in the Continental Army—gathered similarly civic-minded veterans in Boston to draft the Company's articles of association. "[M]uch opposed to the monopoly of lands" which concentrated "much power in the hands of the few," as Putnam told George Washington, the Company embraced a democratic political economy of settlement. Instead of solely enriching the Company's directors, the articles established a shareholding structure that allowed any investor to transform federal debt into western land. Each of the one thousand Company shares cost $1,000 in certificates, the heavily discounted debt that the federal government had issued to fund the Revolution; no individual could purchase more than five. The Company would then use the accumulated capital to purchase federal land in the Ohio Country, which would then, akin to New England towns, be divided among the shareholders "by lot."[22]

In summer 1787, with share selling well underway, the Company dispatched Manasseh Cutler, a minister and political neophyte, to negotiate with the Continental Congress to purchase federal land. In New York, Cutler dined with Congress's then-president—Arthur St. Clair—and with his fellow Bay Stater Secretary at War Henry Knox; he later joined both men in visiting foreign ministers. Cutler's timing was propitious. One day after his arrival, he recorded, he "was furnished with the Ordinance establishing a Government in Western federal Territory. It is in a degree new modled—the amendments I proposed have all been made, except one."[23]

Cutler's undefined role in shaping the Northwest Ordinance underscores how closely that document's template for the territories dovetailed with the Ohio Company's aims. The Ordinance established the model of orderly territorial governance under firm federal authority that St. Clair, Knox, and other Washington administration officials later sought to enact. Cutler recognized the congruence between this vision and the Ohio Company's own goals, and so strategically emphasized what he sincerely believed: that unlike other land companies, the Company would *further* the Ordinance's goals rather than impede them. The Company, he stressed, promised "regular," "judicious," and above all "Systematic" settlement. Cutler knew his audience. Cutler's negotiating counterpart, Board of Treasury President Samuel Osgood—yet another Bay Stater—lamented that, notwithstanding "the advantages of *System* in a new Settlement," "System had never before been attempted" in colonizing western lands. The confluence between Ohio Company's proposal and federal aims led Osgood to proclaim the "plan . . . the best ever formed in Amer[ic]a."[24]

System, as used by Cutler and Osgood, involved several components, all defined in opposition to the past practices that had made territorial property chaotic. The first was the process of land distribution itself. The Company would adhere to prior rectangular survey, remaking western property along the neat lines that Congress had ineffectually sought to create in the Land Ordinance of

1785. This approach "exempt[ed] the United States from the greatest part of the expense" of actual surveying, even as it would "instantly enhance the value of [remaining] federal lands." The second was a rejection of occupation and intruders, whom Cutler, echoing Knox and others, referred to as "lawless banditti" who "seized" federal lands while disdaining national authority. Company settlers, Cutler emphasized, would be "strongly attached to the federal Government."[25]

System also encompassed relations with the Company's Delaware, Shawnee, and Wyandot neighbors. Leaders of the Ohio Company readily took up the Northwest Ordinance's aim of "peace and friendship" with Native nations. "*I want* to embrace them in the arms of Friendship," Rufus Putnam wrote John Heckewelder, a Moravian missionary working among the Delawares on the Ohio, to reassure him of the Company's intentions. "*I want* to be made acquainted with them, *I want* to have them Introduced to our Settlement in a friendly manner *I want* them to live by us and with us if they please I want (if I may be permited to speak it) I want that we should do them good and not evil."[26]

The key to securing cross-cultural peace, Putnam and others believed, was the Company's land practices. Unlike other land companies, they had no desire to settle land that Native nations still owned: the Company's lands, Cutler boasted, had been "confirmed to the United States by sundry Tribes of Indians" in federal treaties. Similarly, Native consent to cessions was as important to Putnam as it was to Knox: "I wish the land may be purchased from them [the Indians] on the principle of Bargain and Sale," he wrote, echoing Knox's rhetoric, "and not wrested from them as a condition of giveing them Peace." Company leaders were equally confident that the "New England Mode of Settlement" would facilitate cross-cultural cooperation. Because the Ohio Company settlers would be "Farmers or Mecannicks and not Hunters," they, unlike the "Big Knives"—a derogatory Native label for the refractory existing settlers readily adopted by antagonistic Company officials—had no need to invade Native lands and kill their game.[27]

Cutler's commitment to system and federal authority was genuine, but he was not above playing on congressional fears of unregulated land speculation to bolster his case. When negotiations flagged, he threatened to turn instead to the states, or even to follow earlier land speculators and enter "contracts with the natives." Coupled with the parlous state of national finance, such threats to undercut federal authority and aims had their effect. After some political horse-trading and haggling over price, Congress finally agreed to sell the Company 1.5 million acres of land along the Ohio River in return for the Company's $1 million in federal certificates—half due up front, the other half due in seven years. The nominal price of sixty-six cents per acre in certificates worked out, in specie, to eight cents per acre.[28]

On October 27, the Ohio Company and Congress formalized their agreement—the first of two congressional contracts that Manasseh Cutler signed that day. Confronted with a $143,000 shortfall in the Ohio Company's down payment, Cutler struck a side bargain with New York financier William Duer. In exchange for the needed money, Duer proposed establishing a second company known as the Scioto Company. This company, to be "kept a profound secret," would purchase five million acres along the Ohio River west of the Ohio Company's purchase. Unlike the Ohio Company, there would be no down payment—just six future installments at sixty-six cents per acre. A skeptical Rufus Putnam insisted on keeping the two endeavors apart. Yet the two companies remained entangled, with both contracts signed on the same day by the same people: Cutler and Ohio Company Secretary Winthrop Sargent. The contracts codified some aspects of Cutler's promises of system—they stipulated, for instance, that the companies undertake surveying based on the 1785 Ordinance, and required reserving lands for education—but otherwise Congress trusted the civic-minded New Englanders.[29]

The Scioto Company's model, offering access to federal land with no down payment at all, allured would-be purchasers, and Congress quickly confronted multiple copycat proposals. Ultimately, only one such scheme came to fruition: the purchase of one million acres in the Northwest Territory by an entity known as the Miami Company.[30]

Unlike the Ohio Company and its elaborate governance structure, the Miami Company was largely the project of one man, John Cleves Symmes, a New Jersey representative in the Continental Congress. Symmes had reconnoitered the Northwest Territory in early 1787, and, days after the Ohio and Scioto deals had been agreed on, he asked Congress to buy one million acres under the same terms as the Scioto agreement. The land in question lay along the Ohio between the Great Miami and Little Miami Rivers, downriver from the Ohio and Scioto purchases and just west of the Virginia Military District.[31]

From the outset, Symmes never claimed the same public-mindedness constantly invoked by the Ohio Company's promoters. He focused unabashedly on the land's promise for his settlers—and for himself. Yet Symmes also believed that his business interests and the federal government's desire for regulated settlement aligned, since he hoped to lure settlers fatigued with chaotic ownership with the promise of clear title. In Kentucky, across the Ohio River from the Miami Company's land, "titles of land are not easily ascertained [and] frequently very doubtful," he reminded prospective purchasers. By contrast, because he adhered to the rectangular grid survey, "title to the Miami lands will be clear and certain, and no possible doubt thereto can arise."[32]

Similarly, although Symmes never saw himself as a promoter of a new federal Indian policy the way that Ohio Company boosters did, he, too, embraced the Washington administration's tropes of friendship. For him, this approach offered yet another way to further differentiate his company's properties from Kentucky lands. "[P]erhaps," he slyly suggested, if the Kentuckians "would act as moderately towards [Natives], they might live in as much safety as the people of this purchase."[33]

Symmes's commitment to self-interest, in short, did not make him equivalent to the reckless speculators like Cox who supposedly blithely ignored the public good; like the Ohio Company, the Miami Company would serve federal aims of clear title and peaceful settlement. In its own way, Symmes's endeavor was an even bolder experiment than the New Englanders' project: rather than claiming the mantle of the national interest, Symmes unabashedly sought to profit from his bargain. Yet even such a businessman, Symmes argued, might, for reasons of enlightened self-interest, pursue policies that would channel land speculation away from chaos and toward system.

Company Towns

On April 7, 1788, Rufus Putnam and forty-eight selected men reached the confluence of the Ohio and Muskingum Rivers, the center of the Ohio Company's settlement (Figure 2.3), and immediately began the process of surveying a new town that the Company dubbed Marietta. While Putnam toiled, "Ohio fever" struck New England. "No property commands money like the Ohio Lands," Cutler gleefully reported. Some subscribers were wealthy and influential; others, relatively humble, put down what they could. By May 1788, all shares had been subscribed, and traded at double their initial cost. There were skeptics, but Cutler dismissed them as afflicted by a "new disorder" of "Ohio-Phobia." The disease's small-minded sufferers were quite unlike the Company's patriotic proponents, who worked to "extend the American Empire—increase our internal wealth—& render us more respectable abroad."[34]

Cutler's vision of harmony between the Ohio Company and national authority seemed to be playing out in Marietta. Nearly all the territorial officials appointed under the new Northwest Ordinance were also Company officers: Company directors James Varnum and Samuel Parsons constituted two of the Northwest Territory's three congressionally appointed federal judges (after Parsons's early death, Rufus Putnam replaced him as judge), while Winthrop Sargent, the Company's secretary, was also Secretary of the Northwest Territory, its second executive.

For the few federal officials without such a position, the Ohio Company quickly set about using the asset it had—land—to secure their support, donating parcels to the commander, officers, and soldiers stationed at Fort Harmar in Marietta, and even offering Secretary of War Knox a share. The Company was especially eager to attach Governor Arthur St. Clair, making him a shareholder

Figure 2.3: "Plan of the Ohio Companys Purchase." Courtesy of the Ohio History Connection, Image AL07517. This map illustrates how the Company used the rectangular grid to distribute its land holdings.

while gifting him a number of additional lots. Such gestures were "a little selfish," one Company proprietor admitted, since they "wish[ed] [St. Clair] to make the Muskingum [i.e., Marietta] the seat of government, and place of his residence." This proximity to power would, they anticipated, make the Company's lands more valuable. In July 1788, St. Clair satisfied these hopes, as the governor arrived in Marietta and gave a brief speech praising the Ohio Company for its commitment to "order." "This is the birth-day of this Western World," one proprietor rhapsodized, expressing the view that the Territory's origins lay in the union of the Company's settlement with constituted federal authority.[35]

Matters progressed less well in the Miami Company settlement, where Symmes created the town of "North Bend" on a curve along the Ohio River. Unlike the orderly settlement at the Ohio Company's center, North Bend initially consisted only of "one family . . . and a few stragling hunters." And while Marietta had a federal fort, North Bend had to content itself with a handful of soldiers. Yet there was still similar overlap between the Miami Company and federal governance: after Territorial Judge James Varnum also died, Symmes assumed Varnum's judicial office.[36]

Despite their differences, both Marietta and North Bend were pockets of Anglo-American settlement in the midst of a multiethnic Native world. As a result, though sole responsibility for managing Indian affairs ostensibly lay with the federal government, both towns became centers for diplomacy and trade with surrounding Native communities.

Cross-cultural curiosity, exchange, and even seeming friendship quickly marked early Marietta. Rufus Putnam's first meal in the town was a banquet attended by "Captain Pipe"—the Delaware leader Konieschquanoheel, the region's most significant Native leader—and twenty other Delawares. When Putnam told Pipe of the Ohio Company's "business," Pipe reportedly proclaimed that his nation "should be happy to live by us." Samuel Parsons similarly reported that the Delawares "profess a great Friendship for the *Yankees* who they distinguish from the Settlers on the Virginia Shore."[37]

Soon, neighboring Wyandots and Delawares—"our Indian friends," as Putnam dubbed them—were reportedly coming to Marietta "almost every day." A particularly strong bond formed around Marietta's public celebrations. When General Varnum died in January 1789, local Native leaders marched in his funeral cortege. Local Delawares also attended Marietta's first July Fourth celebration, where toasts were raised to Captain Pipe as well as Governor St. Clair and the new U.S. Constitution. Company proprietor John May, heading one of the tables, was bemused when one of the Delaware leaders greeted him: "How do you do, brother Yankee." He seated the Delaware man next to him and watched as he ate freely and tried to join in the toasts. "He labored with all his might to speak them," May recorded, "but made very poor work of it." May noted that he had shaken hands with most local Delawares since his arrival.[38]

North Bend offered similar stories. Symmes's settlers first met their Native neighbors in spring 1789, when three surveyors, encountering a Shawnee group, tried to flee and then prepared to fight. As a surveyor trained his rifle on a Shawnee, he was startled to see the man lift his hat, raise his hand in greeting, and call out, in English, that they were friends. Led to a nearby blockhouse, the Shawnees and their "unexpected . . . visit" reassured North Bend's residents of their neighbors' friendly intentions. Soon, Symmes reported, "the white and red people began to form a sociable neighborhood," with "our hunters frequently taking shelter for the night at the Indians camps; and the Indians with their squaws spending whole days and nights at the blockhouse." A Moravian missionary passing through North Bend reported that Symmes, "by his treatment of the Indians," had "gained their love and friendship, which is a better protection for this place than a regiment of soldiers would be."[39]

These invocations of tropes of friendly Indians—often relayed in letters sent back east, and sometimes published—served both companies' purposes, as perceived amity with Natives was key to their success in attracting settlers and investors. "The greatest present discouragement is the fear of Indians," Cutler informed Putnam, instructing him to censor letters back to ensure that "first impressions" of Indians were positive. "Terreble Stories" of phantasmagorical attacks spread anyway. Such vague reports of Indians, "magnified . . . a thousand fold," constituted "our Principal Obstruction to Settlement." Symmes confronted the same challenge: he even alleged that neighboring Kentuckians, their "jealousy & ill will" provoked by "the friendly manner we have with the Indians," deliberately spread false stories that all settlers in the Miami Purchase had been tomahawked. "I fear I shall be nearly stripped of settlers and left with one dozen soldiers only," Symmes lamented as the rumors dissuaded prospective purchasers.[40]

This tidy alignment between business interests and reports of Native friendship suggests some ventriloquism by the companies. Yet neighboring Delawares, Wyandots, and Shawnees had their own reasons to pursue close relationships with the new arrivals. In particular, recognizing the blurred lines between the companies and federal authority, Natives understood that ties with the new settlers might bolster their connections to the United States and secure access to trade goods. The Delaware Captain Pipe, for instance, seemed to see the newly arrived New Englanders as an extension of the federal soldiers stationed at Fort Harmar, with whom he had already cultivated a closer relationship. The Shawnees near North Bend were even more explicit in their aims. They had, they later informed Symmes, held a council and resolved to send George, an Anglo-American taken prisoner a decade earlier, to meet their "new white brother's": it was George who had greeted the surveyors in English. Soon afterward, a Shawnee leader Symmes called "Capt. Blackbeard" met Symmes in person and expressed his interest in a "free intercourse with us" to "exchange their peltry for the articles which they much wanted." Blackbeard proceeded to suss out the relationship between Symmes and federal authority, pressing Symmes "how far I was supported by the United States, and whether the thirteen fires had sent me hither." In response, Symmes unfurled an American flag, pointed to his federal military escort, and offered up his seal of commission, which Blackbeard examined closely. These symbols, paired with Symmes's proclamations, evidently persuaded Blackbeard of Symmes's authority and intentions; the leader "appeared entirely sattisfied of the friendship of Congelis (for so they pronounce Congress) towards the red people." The Shawnees then took advantage of the trade goods promised by their new alliance: for the next four weeks, Blackbeard and his companions availed themselves of Symmes's hospitality, before departing "in a most friendly manner."[41]

As narrated by Putnam and Symmes, events in Marietta and North Bend suggested close harmony between the interests of Native leaders, federal officials, and the land companies: all sought to create a new foundation for their relations based on the promise of friendship. As implicit outposts of federal authority, the companies' towns seemed to fulfill the aspiration that they could displace unregulated models of settlement and the violence they produced.

No Weight with Government

Tensions nonetheless existed below the seeming harmony between federal and company interests. Symmes complained of inadequate federal aid, bewailing that visiting Shawnees "lived chiefly at my expense (nor was it a very small one, as they had whisky at their pleasure gratis.)." Not only did the federal government failed to reimburse him for these expenses, it could not even support the pittance of federal soldiers stationed at North Bend, whom Symmes fed from his own pocket—only for them to trade his food for liquor. "I have indeed lost sight of any succor from the United States," Symmes complained.[42]

An undercurrent of suspicion also lay beneath the supposed friendship between Natives and the new arrivals. Their perceptions shaped by long-standing narratives of Native duplicity, Anglo-American settlers did not credit their neighbors' apparent goodwill: John May thought them "a set of creatures not to be trusted." "[N]ot withstanding [the Indians'] professed friendship," one Marietta settler wrote, "there is a guard placed every night." Symmes shared this distrust. "They are a subtil enemy," he wrote of the Shawnees, "& all their boasted friendship may be only to learn our numbers, and what state of defence we are in." There are hints, too, that local Native leaders were not as pleased with the companies' presence as they professed. When Captain Pipe first met Rufus Putnam, for instance, he told the Ohio Company leader that he "did not expect any people would come on to settle before the treaty [of Fort Harmar]," suggesting discontent about the federal government's presumptuous appropriation of Delaware lands.[43]

Recasting Indian affairs, then, proved harder than the companies anticipated. Both Natives and non-Natives were well aware of the violence and bloodshed occurring elsewhere in the Ohio Country. Many Ohio Native communities, sharing Pipe's frustration with federal land grabs, had begun to form a diffuse but wide-reaching confederacy with the shared goal of repudiating federal treaties and confirming the Ohio River as the border between Native lands and the United States. Small groups of angered Natives raided boats traveling down the Ohio; Henry Knox responded by authorizing an expedition against the presumed source of the attacks, the towns of the Wabash Confederacy along the Maumee River, several hundred miles from the Ohio Company's settlement. The campaign, in autumn 1790, proved a disorderly disaster for the United States and merely encouraged further attacks.[44]

Yet the New Englanders displayed little anxiety about living in what was rapidly becoming a war zone, believing that their systematic land policies mitigated any Native threat. "[T]he Indians themselves remark in their Towns, that we settle compactly & not in the scatterd manner in which the Frontiers have been generally Settled," Samuel Parsons observed, "& no Attempt [to attack] can be made without meeting the whole force in the Settlement."[45]

Events soon tested Parsons's proposition. At sunset on Sunday, January 2, 1791, a group of Wyandots and Delawares stopped in at Big Bottom, a collection of a little over twenty Ohio Company settlers located up Muskingum Creek from Marietta. Friendly with the Company settlers, the Natives conversed and dined with two of them, Francis and Isaac Choate. In the midst of talking, the Choates heard gunfire. The Natives told the alarmed Choates they were now their prisoners. Three other men from the settlement were also taken prisoner; two escaped to seek help. A relief party arrived from Marietta the next day to discover a grisly scene. The settlement's other twelve settlers, confined in the blockhouse, had all been killed and the building burnt. Only charred, unidentifiable bodies remained.[46]

"Our prospects are much changed," wrote an alarmed Rufus Putnam on learning of the attack, which became known as the Big Bottom Massacre. "[I]n stead of peace and friendship with our Indian neighbours a horid Savage war Stairs us in the face." As Big Bottom demonstrated, familiarity bred a particularly vicious and personal form of warfare. When a Native killed a "mulatto boy" in the middle of the Ohio River, in plain view of Marietta, one Ohio Company settler thought he "recognize[d] the Indian, as one whom he had known aforetime." Later in 1791, a scouting party—led by a man whose father had been killed in an Indian raid—shot a Native man. The party decapitated the Native and mounted his head on a pole, which was displayed in front of the garrison, while the body was brought to the river, "where it was literalley Cutt up, & Boiled." News of this brutality spread through Indian country; one Native remarked, "*Oh white Man boil Indian.—No. Good.*"[47]

Such actions have led one historian to identify the Big Bottom Massacre as the moment when the idealistic New Englanders abandoned their humanitarian impulses and "bec[a]me Kentuckians." But it would be more accurate to describe it as the instant when the Ohio Company became disillusioned with federal authority. Re-examining the federal treaties with the Delawares and Wyandots, Rufus Putnam discovered that many of the Company's lands "were rather wrested then fairly purchased": even at treaties where compensation was paid, Putnam noted representation was "very partial" and many nations "never consented to what was don." In Putnam's view, the Ohio Company settlers were victims of the government's failure to follow its own land policy of "fair dealing" and secure true Native consent.[48]

The federal government's half-hearted efforts at protection further tested the Ohio Company settlers' trust. Putnam had been confident that, in the event of war, Marietta would become the headquarters for the federal army. But, even as rumors abounded that two or three thousand Ohio Country Natives would soon attack Marietta, nearly all the federal soldiers moved downriver to the newly constructed Fort Washington, the staging ground for another, and even larger, expedition. With Marietta "defenceless," Putnam appealed to Secretary of War Knox and even President Washington for aid. Invoking the implicit partnership between the Ohio Company and the federal government, Putnam insisted the interests of the "united States in general" were at stake. If the federal government effectively protected settlements established "under [its] authority," then the public lands would "rapid[ly]" sell, "Sink[ing] many millions of . . . National Debt." But if such protection was not forthcoming, "the consequence" was clear: the lands would be "Seized on by privit adventurers who will pay little or no reguard to the laws of the United States or the rights of the natives."[49]

In response to Putnam's appeals, federal officers dispatched a single cannon. The message was clear: the Ohio Company had to rely on its own resources to survive. Days after the attack at Big Bottom, the Company agreed to call out the militia under its authority and at its own expense, with the "highest confidence" that Congress would later "reimburse the necessary expense we shall be at in defending ourselves against the Common Enemy." Meanwhile, Ohio Company settlers retreated to defensible stockades, while Native war parties destroyed the houses and cattle they left behind. White settlers began abandoning the settlement in droves: nearly half of the initial forty-eight who had traveled with Putnam fled. "Our Settlement does not encrease," one Marietta resident complained, "we are circumscribed within narrow Limits & are heartily tired of the Indian War, & with its present Management see no End to it."[50]

Marietta's loss was, ostensibly, Judge Symmes's gain. His colony, too, had suffered Native hands: days after the Big Bottom attack, there had been a similar assault on a blockhouse protecting the Miami Purchase. But Symmes proved the beneficiary of the new federal military policy: Fort Washington, the new center of military operations, lay within the Miami Company's tract. "Judge Sims's Settlement it is apprehend by many is building up at our expense," complained one Marietta resident. "[W]e have discovered that some of our Great Men are going to move down"—including Governor St. Clair, who relocated to the nascent town of Losantiville, soon renamed Cincinnati, surrounding Fort Washington.[51]

Yet Cincinnati's newfound prosperity caused its own tensions between federal interests and Symmes's investments. Symmes had happily sold Cincinnati land to eager purchasers: his original application to Congress, after all, had included all the land between the Great and Little Miami Rivers. But the contract he had actually *signed* differed from his proposal: it set a boundary twenty miles *west* of the Little Miami—which excluded Cincinnati. All of Symmes's purported sales in the town rested on invalid title.[52]

Governor St. Clair was shocked to discover that Symmes had, in essence, created an entire town of intruders. "I could not conceive," the incredulous St. Clair wrote, that "considerable Settlements . . . had been made, not only without authority, but directly in the face of it, and by a Person invested with high Office of a Judge of the Territory." Settlement, St. Clair lectured the judge, could only occur based on "a regular and proper authority . . . founded on an actual purchase or previous contract," and not on bare expectation. To protect future "unwary" purchasers and guard federal title, St. Clair issued an official proclamation barring further settlement and subjecting settlers around Fort Washington to martial law. Symmes took deep umbrage at St. Clair's "harsh sentences," alleging that the governor's actions "border[ed] hard" on "acts of tyranny." St. Clair's proclamations, Symmes told a colleague, "have convulsed these settlements beyond your conception." Ultimately, Congress, to clean up Symmes's mess, retroactively granted him the land under Cincinnati.[53]

Despite this seeming act of indulgence, as well as divergent fortunes of the Ohio and Miami Companies during the war, both Putnam and Symmes ended up similarly embittered against a federal government that they had envisioned as a partner and source of prosperity. Both felt that the government had taken advantage of them, offloading the risks of settlement onto them while failing to fulfill its implicit promise of support. Putnam never forgave the federal government's abandonment of Marietta at its moment of crisis, concluding that the Ohio Company had paid for federal failure to follow its own Indian policy of land purchase: he bitterly recalled how, although the Company expended nearly $15,000 on the Indian war, Congress only repaid about $2600. Symmes, too, was angry about money. He later recalled how he had created a "respectable settlement" at his own expense, spending $4,000 supporting "starving emigrants" and paying "presents" to the Indians. Yet all these services to the nation, Symmes lamented, had "no weight with Government."[54]

The advent of the Northwest Indian War had tested the promise of the harmony between the companies and federal interests—and found it lacking. For

Putnam, the federal government had failed to fulfill its implicit obligations to defend settlements made under its own authority; for Symmes, tyrannical federal officers attacked his claims to ownership.

But, if the leaders of the Ohio and Miami Companies had reason for frustration with the federal government, federal officials soon had cause for anger with them, too. Symmes's Cincinnati speculation merely foreshadowed the complexities of ownership that both companies would create and force Congress to resolve.

Naked Preemption

The Ohio Company's promise to support federal authority and remake relationships with Native nations was inseparable from its core purpose—to recraft how land was distributed. Under the Company's elaborate scheme, each shareholder would receive a house lot in Marietta and then receive individual plots of increasing size that would then radiate outward from the town. Parcels would be assigned by lottery. "By this mode of Division," one investor wrote, "the Proprietors will be enabled to make Settlement by preveously forming a Sistem by which they will bind themselves to adhere to fixed Principals for that purpose."[55]

This "Sistem," proponents believed, would tamp down on the excesses of land speculation. All shareholders would receive the same acreage and kinds of parcels, and, because parcels would be assigned randomly, no one could cherry-pick the most valuable lots. Theirs was a structured and egalitarian vision of land distribution, in opposition to the frantic grab for riches that generally characterized the era's land speculation.

That, at least, was the plan. "The Division of the land into Cities Towns . . . was a well digested System to read within the Town of Boston," one army officer reported, "but . . . on putting the System into execution there were innumerable embarrassments." System, it turned out, neither provided flexibility nor suppressed opportunities to gamble on land value. As one investor complained, "Speculation was ushered in to their System at an early period."[56]

Fights about lands around Marietta "very much disturbed the peace of the Society" from the beginning. Company settlers were upset with their locations, or complained about the "scandalous errors" in surveying. But the most contentious issue proved the "donation lands," an innovation intended to protect against Native attack. The Company withdrew one hundred acres from each share to offer to new arrivals who would bear arms and construct proper defenses. Yet this policy "opened such doors for . . . speculation on speculation." Few claimants actually settled; most, "more anxious to fill their purses than increase the Settlement," quickly resold the lands to "real settlers" for $50 to $100. These settlers often arrived entirely destitute, lacking animals, farm tools, furniture; half reportedly did not even own a pot. Meanwhile, settlers denounced the donation committees created to enforce the system as arbitrary and self-dealing, with one settlement nicknaming theirs the "Damnation Committee."[57]

These repeated controversies caused widespread grumbling. "[M]ost of the transactions of the Ohio Company," one investor complained, "ha[ve] generally been conducted in a mode that reflects little Credit on the abilities or intentions of the various Managers." But the contentions over small-scale speculations paled in comparison to the fights over the Scioto Company, the existence of which was quickly revealed. The "very great impropriety" of Cutler and Sargent's gamble, regarded as a "dirty speculation," caused "*general* . . . dissatisfaction" among the shareholders.[58]

This criticism was well taken, since the Scioto Company turned out to be precisely the sort of risky land speculation that the Ohio Company had sought to displace—one that relied on boosterism, questionable title, and paper promises to create overnight wealth from hoodwinked investors. The Scioto Company owned nothing; it held only a contract to purchase lands from the federal government in the future at a fixed price—"the naked preemption." To secure the money for these future payments, the Company's investors had to sell their contingent promise of title for immediate cash.[59]

The Company's proprietors opted to market the lands in Europe, hoping to profit from the disorder of the French Revolution. Although enthusiastic, Cutler and Sargent contributed little to the venture, which quickly escaped their control even as it entangled them in a complicated financial web created by William Duer and his agents. On his own accord, the Scioto Company's agent in France decided that the mere promise of future title was "too light and dangerous a ground to attempt retailing upon." He instead created a shell company to contract with the Scioto Company for land that he could then dubiously market as fee simple property.[60]

As with the Ohio Company in New England, the promise of western lands caused something of a cultural sensation in France. In late 1790, four hundred French settlers arrived at a settlement, grandly named Gallipolis in their honor, along the Ohio downriver from Marietta. The "town" in fact consisted of a few crude huts hastily constructed by Rufus Putnam. But the French settlers' greatest shock was the discovery that "all the apparently legal Documents" shewn to "Seduc[e]" them with the "Solidity of the Titles" were frauds. The Scioto Company did not actually own any land it could sell, and, even if it had, Gallipolis was located within the Ohio Company's tract. Governor St. Clair bemoaned how little this endeavor corresponded with the repeated invocation of national interests by Cutler, Putnam, and Sargent. The "interested speculation of a few men, pursued with too great avidity," he feared, "would destroy American character abroad."[61]

The Gallipolis fiasco occurred just as the Ohio Company confronted its own financial difficulties. The second installment of $500,000 for its lands loomed, but the Company entirely lacked the funds to comply. Under the contract terms, if the Company failed to pay, it would forfeit the entire tract. The problem was an irony at the heart of the Company's finances: although the Company was both reliant on, and an investment in, federal state-building, its ability to raise capital depended on the low price of federal certificates. The ratification of the U.S. Constitution—an event the Ohio Company settlers celebrated—undermined the company's financial stability. As public confidence in the government's financial health rose, federal certificates' value also rose, and with this shift, "people . . . began to look upon securities better than western Land."[62]

Once again, the Scioto Company offered a potential solution. In February 1791, William Duer, Manasseh Cutler, and Winthrop Sargent met in New York to resolve the Gallipolis mess. With it clear to all that the Scioto Company would fail, the proprietors now vied to shed themselves of responsibility for the French settlers. They decided that Duer would pay for 148 forfeited Ohio Company shares, which would then entitle the French to those shares' lands.[63]

A year later, Cutler and Putnam traveled to Philadelphia to petition Congress. Their goal was to secure title to whatever lands they could, based only on their earlier down payment and some military bounty warrants they had cobbled together. To advance their claim, they harped on the services they had performed for the nation by funding their own expenses during the Northwest Indian War. Surely Congress's goal could not have been "to raise the value of [Congress'] Land at the expence exertions and risk of others but to make an actual Settlement." They concluded with a threat: unless Congress relieved settlers "from that state of suspence and uncertainty respecting their title," they would no longer defend their lands but "immediately retreat to some place of greater security."[64]

The Ohio Company's request passed through Congress nearly unopposed, likely reflecting the federal government's desperate need for settlers in the midst of the Northwest Indian War. Ultimately, Congress granted the Company nearly one million acres for payments already made, with an additional one hundred thousand acres to compensate for the donation lands.[65]

Yet news of disaster came at the same moment as the Company's triumph. For over a year, the Ohio Company had fruitlessly sought to get Duer and the Scioto Company to live up to their agreement to purchase the 148 shares, finally moving toward litigation. But now, without payment, Duer's finances collapsed in spectacular fashion, destroying private fortunes "from Georgia to New Hampshire." Duer was imprisoned, where he mostly remained until his death seven years later. His collapse suddenly constricted the ties of debt that bound together the

Ohio and Scioto Companies. In Philadelphia, Putnam was arrested and had to pay off over $2,000 in Scioto debts to obtain release.[66]

With the Scioto Company defunct, the Gallipolis settlers turned to territorial authorities for relief. Yet, unsurprisingly, federal officials—many of whom were also Scioto Company officers—proved unsympathetic: Secretary Winthrop Sargent, a Scioto Company director, hotly denied being "in any degree accessary to your misfortunes." Refusing to "allow these companies to lead them by the nose any longer," the French resolved to "appeal directly to Congress." Congress referred the matter to the attorney general, who was pessimistic about recovery through a lawsuit against the Ohio Company. An angry Senate instead demanded that the Ohio Company directors appear before it, threatening to rescind portions of the Company's grant. Demonstrating the deterioration of relations between the Company and the federal government, the directors refused to appear.[67]

In 1795, Congress finally resolved the mess on its own, compensating the Gallipolis settlers with 24,000 acres of federal land elsewhere in the Northwest Territory. As for Gallipolis itself, the town's settlers were forced to (re)purchase the townsite from the Ohio Company for $1.25 per acre—nearly twice what the Ohio Company had paid Congress for the same land.[68]

With its title secured by Congress, the business affairs of the Ohio Company wound to a slow conclusion. After four years of surveying, the final division was made in 1796: each settler finally received 1,173 acres, dispersed in six lots. Shareholders even received a modest dividend from funds the Company managed to scrounge together. With that, the Ohio Company largely dissolved.[69]

Measured against other land speculations, and compared with earlier abortive federal efforts to distribute land, the Ohio Company was arguably a success. Though Marietta never became the booming center Putnam and Cutler had envisioned, the company had conveyed clear title, secured a small return for investors, and created a stable settlement in a landscape littered with failed land schemes.

Yet for many at the time, the Ohio Company felt like a failure. The endeavor had always been more than another land company; it had promised to channel the era's rampant land speculation to further nationalist ends of stability and secure title. Assessed against this goal, the Company came up short. Its entanglement with the Scioto Company involved it in the same chancy, uncertain claims to ownership that "system" was intended to avoid. Resentful federal officials found themselves giving land away for free as they had to resolve, at public expense, the tangled knot created by the Company's avarice. "[P]rejudices . . . against the Ohio Company" were felt "very strongly," one visitor to Congress reported, because the Company was so "deeply implicated" in the Gallipolis mess. Many in Congress likely shared one embittered investor's disappointment. "I should be glad to have done with the business," he wrote. "And if wishing was not vanity; I should wish I had not never heard of the Ohio Company."[70]

Endless Disputes

Like the Ohio Company, Symmes found that his embrace of system also struggled to tame more speculative approaches to land. When he first arrived, Symmes had been thronged by Kentuckians eager to settle. Yet, not only were these would-be settlers "very ungovernable and seditious," they lacked both means and intent to pay. They "had no other views than speculation," Symmes complained, and most quickly returned to Kentucky to resell their (still unpurchased) land rights to their neighbors. When they inevitably defaulted, the Kentuckians "vented their spleen in abuses & calumnies" of Symmes. Other prospective buyers similarly contracted with Symmes for hundreds of thousands of acres, and yet seldom paid. Large or small, few buyers viewed land as a long-term investment; the possibility of reselling bare promises of future title excited far more interest.[71]

Of course, Symmes was engaged in the same endeavor, just on a grander scale: he had promised to pay Congress for the lands he contracted for, but, with so many purchasers defaulting, it was unlikely he could satisfy his contract. Months after the Ohio Company's renewed agreement with Congress, Symmes appeared to ask for a similar grant of the land he had already paid for. With little opposition, Symmes secured a statute affirming his purchase, and in 1794, President Washington patented him over three hundred thousand acres of land based on the funds he had scrounged together.[72]

Yet unlike the Ohio Company, Symmes was not content with this resolution. Rather, his success with Congress encouraged him to undertake still riskier speculation on bare promises of federal land. He insisted, dubiously, that his original contract entitled him to a full one million acres and so set out to amass $82,000 for another installment. Everything hinged on making payment. "Money will be the best argument that can be r[a]ised," Symmes stated, "though I had the logic and oratory of a Cicero, and the right of Adam to the soil." Yet the same rise in securities that had doomed the Ohio Company hamstrung Symmes, and, as 1796 stretched into 1797, there was no prospect of payment. But Symmes remained convinced that if he could just gather the money, he could force Congress's acquiescence. "I have read so many cases in point," Symmes stated, that "if we tender the Money, it is not in the power of Congress, constitutionally to take [the land] from us." Desperate for capital and confident of ultimate success, Symmes continued selling land outside of his bounds of his patent—lands, in other words, he did not own—based only on the expectation that he would eventually receive title from Congress once he had actually made payment.[73]

Symmes's freewheeling gamble with the public domain slowly attracted congressional attention. Albert Gallatin, a representative from western Pennsylvania with growing expertise on the public lands, took on the responsibility of explaining Symmes's contract to Congress. In 1796 and again 1797, he headed committees that investigated Symmes's contract and concluded that he had no right to the lands he claimed. In 1798, Symmes watched in horror as Gallatin proposed declaring the lands outside Symmes's patent forfeit; the bill became law the next year.[74]

As his house of cards collapsed around him, Symmes turned to whatever sources of power he had. He helped secure the election of his son-in-law, William Henry Harrison, as the Northwest Territory's nonvoting delegate to Congress. He also turned to another source of authority—his position as a judge on the General Court, the Northwest Territory's highest court.[75]

The overlap between company and federal authority in the Territory had long made some uneasy. Territorial citizens publicly complained that Symmes, "the first judge of the supreme court, is perhaps the greatest land jobber on the face of earth." Governor St. Clair had similarly pointed out that the land companies caused "endless disputes," and yet two of the three judges of the territorial General Court—Symmes and Rufus Putnam—headed these companies. "Every land dispute will be traced to some transaction of one or other of those Gentlemen in those capacities," St. Clair observed, "and they are to sit in Judgement upon them." St. Clair feared "Biass."[76]

Now, St. Clair's fears were seemingly being realized, as Symmes used his judicial authority to try to staunch lawsuits based on his dubious land sales. In one case, Symmes supposedly told some of purchasers of his lands that they should litigate their titles: if they lost below, they could appeal "into his Court, where they might be sure, he would not give Judgment against himself." In another suit before the General Court, the plaintiff argued that Symmes should recuse himself because he was "directly interested" in the outcome: because the defendant had purchased the disputed land from Symmes, the judge would himself be legally liable if title proved defective. Symmes refused, insisting he had "no interest" in the outcome. But then, after presiding over much of the trial, Symmes suddenly reversed himself. Now, he reportedly stepped down from the bench, "openly acknowledged that he was the person most interested in the event of the suit," and walked across the courtroom to the bar. There, he proceeded to "advocate[] [the case] for the defendant" to his (presumably astonished) fellow judges.[77]

Symmes allegedly also instructed purchasers to employ extrajudicial means to protect their title. When one disgruntled purchaser demanded back money he had paid for his land, Symmes refused. He urged the man instead to go home and "shoot or drown any person who might molest him"—an approach, Symmes claimed, that had worked for intruders elsewhere.[78]

Despite such extreme efforts, the Miami Company crumbled around Symmes. Besieged by lawsuits stripping him of tens of thousands of acres of land—he was arrested three times for debt in 1802 alone—Symmes slid toward penury. In a final appeal to Congress, Symmes stated that its statutes returning the disputed lands to the public domain were causing him "very great hardships, tending to the utter destruction . . . of his whole property." But the attorney general presented a lengthy report that determined that Symmes had no legal rights based on the contract—concluding, in fact, that Symmes owed the United States over $15,000 in compensation for his own breaches. Symmes never paid this debt. He died penniless in North Bend, Ohio—the town he had created—in 1814.[79]

He left behind a mess. As with the Scioto Company, Symmes had used implicit congressional backing to spin an elaborate scheme of debt and dubious title. Also as with Scioto, the costs of these reckless speculations ultimately fell on innocent purchasers—and the federal government. The nearly two thousand settlers who had purchased Symmes's dubious title bombarded Congress with petitions asserting that they would lose "their only support & means of subsistence." Congress felt constrained to offer them the right of preemption—the first right of refusal to purchase their lands—despite, as we have seen, stubbornly denying this privilege to other settlers. But Symmes's purchasers did not regard the opportunity to repurchase, at $2 per acre, lands that they had purchased for half that amount as munificence; Congress's action instead produced "very great alarm." Many could not exercise their preemptive rights because they had only verbal contracts with Symmes; others lacked money to make the purchase. Of the roughly one hundred thousand acres purchased under the preemption statute, thirty thousand were ultimately forfeit because the claimants lacked the down payment necessary; most of the rest went to speculators rather than the original purchasers.[80]

In 1789, when Congress first began debating federal lands, many advocated continued sales to large companies: one congressman noted that the 1787 sale had, in one swoop, promised to extinguish $5 million, an estimated one-fifth, of the nation's domestic debt. "Everybody is in favor of selling large tracts, rough & smooth, if we can," another congressman wrote to the Scioto Company's agent in France in April 1790. "I have no doubt all reasonable proposals will be accepted."[81]

These advocates received a boost three months later when Secretary of the Treasury Alexander Hamilton presented, at Congress's request, a "Plan for Disposing of the Public Lands." Compared to his successors in office, Hamilton spent little time on the public lands, and his short land plan paled compared to his voluminous reports on federal finance. Moreover, unlike many of his colleagues, Hamilton only dabbled in land speculation, although he did own five Ohio Company shares, yielding him lands he valued at $6,000. Nonetheless, Hamilton's report unequivocally embraced large-scale sales. "[A] plan for the sale of western lands," it concluded, should focus on "contracts for large purchases," especially to "monied individuals and companies, who will buy to sell again."[82]

Hamilton's report became the basis of a bill that passed the House but failed in the Senate. Events then overtook Congress, as Jefferson's 1791 report, coupled with the Northwest Indian War, derailed any immediate plans to open a land office. Congress did not return to the question of federal land distribution until December 1795, after the United States had defeated the Northwest Native Confederacy and, at the Treaty of Greenville, compelled the Native nations of the Ohio Country to sell millions more acres in the Northwest Territory.[83]

December 1795 was also the month that Congress first employed its contempt power for the first time. This confluence was not a coincidence. A man named Robert Randall approached several congressmen on behalf of a nebulous Detroit land company seeking twenty million acres of Native land in present-day Michigan, then part of the Northwest Territory. Confident that his associates' "great influence over the Indians" would secure the "extinction of the Indian title," Randall sought a congressional grant for the "fee simple of the land." His company would then divide the land into forty shares—twenty-four of which would be given to members of Congress.[84]

Randall had good reason to think his scheme might succeed. His appeal to the congressmen's self-interest was perhaps more brazen but not so different from past influence peddling employed by speculators as diverse as Cox and the Ohio Company. Yet Randall had misjudged: Congress proclaimed itself shocked and outraged, and ordered Randall's arrest and imprisonment.[85]

Randall's arrest evinced a growing suspicion of land companies on ample display when Congress turned again to a land office bill, which was the House's "principal business" for over two weeks in early 1796. The debates rehashed a decade's worth of unsettled issues over rectangular survey, minimum price, and preemption rights, but the key issue of contention remained the same as a half-decade earlier. "Much has been said about speculators and settlers," one congressman summarized.[86]

Yet the debate had shifted against large-scale sales in the intervening years. Although the land companies still had their advocates, most in Congress were hostile to any proposal that they deemed an "act of favoritism" toward wealthy buyers. "Persons of property," one congressman argued, "can generally accommodate themselves; we ought to accommodate the lower classes." In particular, many in Congress were now dubious of claims of public-spiritedness or national benefits from such investments. "[P]ersons whom we have supposed worthy of our confidence and esteem," one opined, had been "publicly practicing the meanest and most disgraceful arts and tricks of swindling"; the nation, he insisted, could not "suffer the execution of our land law to depend on the disinterestedness of an individual." Selling public land, one congressman concluded, "is a sort of transaction which should always be kept in the hands of Government, and not in those of speculators."[87]

Such comments firmly rejected the supposed symbiosis that had undergird the earlier sales to the Ohio, Scioto, and Miami Companies. Speculators would gain legitimate title, these projects' backers had argued, even as the federal government would, with minimal expenditure, establish a "system" to bolster aims of peace, clarity, and order in the territories. But just as many in Congress now argued, such harmony proved illusory. The companies discovered that their success depended on federal willingness to protect them and save their finances from their own worst excesses. For their part, Putnam and Symmes no less than Cox sought to secure quick returns by selling property that they did not yet own. Such gambles on contingent title, endemic to the era's land practice, produced uncertainty and imposed costs that someone had to bear—almost always innocent purchasers, but also often the federal government, which felt obligated to tidy up the messes the companies left behind. Better, many now concluded, for the federal government simply to undertake land distribution itself.

Although it is difficult to say how much events in the territories fueled these critiques, some in Congress specifically cited the companies' failures against such future sales. Some representatives, for instance, questioned the merits of Symmes's purchase. But the most explicit mention came from Albert Gallatin, quickly gaining a reputation as an expert on public lands, who described the company sales as bad policy. "In the year 1792 all the land west of the Ohio was disposed of to speculators at 1s. 6d per acre, and in a week afterwards sold for a dollar and a half," Gallatin observed, "so that the money which ought to have gone into the funds, went into the pocket of the moneyed men who purchased." To Gallatin, this experiment had demonstrated that the government should simply sell public lands directly. "Government would be, in effect, its own speculator."[88]

The Land Act of 1796 that Congress finally passed largely vindicated Gallatin. Half the land sold under its provisions would be small parcels of one square mile (640 acres), while the other half would be entire townships of six square miles (23,000 acres) intended for larger purchasers; all would be offered at public auction. Even these larger parcels were a far cry from transfers of millions of acres that had augured to become the dominant model earlier in the decade.[89]

Ultimately, 1796 statute's greatest achievement was administrative. The returns of the first public auction under the law, held in Pittsburg in October

1796, were so disappointingly small that it was never repeated. But, seeking to resolve nearly a decade of contentions over federal lands, the law helped establish an enduring federal bureaucracy to survey and distribute the public domain. Purchasers would buy from federal officers rather than Congress, and, unlike in most state systems, the federal government undertook the initial survey and distribution itself.[90]

This new bureaucracy's most active office was the new post of Surveyor General, charged with imposing the statute's rectangular grid on the landscape. Throughout the late 1790s, this office frenetically surveyed much of the public domain in present-day Ohio—three million acres in 1798 alone—leading the surveyor to argue that he and his men worked longer hours than "any Public Office within my Knowledge." As some in Congress had feared, this system of prior survey proved expensive—costing over $25,000 in 1799 alone, nearly three times what the government annually paid the Native nations of the Ohio Country for the same land.[91]

Yet this new federally administered scheme also demonstrated how the land companies had, literally, prepared the ground for the federal government. Nearly all these busy new federal surveyors had previously worked for the Ohio and Miami Companies—including the new surveyor general, Rufus Putnam, appointed to his new office just as he concluded his duties overseeing the Ohio Company.

3
The Rise of Federal Title

Less than two weeks after it enacted the seminal 1796 law governing the sale of federal lands in the Northwest Territory, Congress passed another statute that removed millions of acres of those same lands from sale. These so-called bounty lands would instead be awarded to former Continental Army soldiers to satisfy promises of title that the United States had made two decades earlier, during the Revolution. The statute was brief, with four short sections that sketched where these lands were to be located and how they were to be distributed.[1]

Even before the statute passed, veterans began sending dozens of letters to the Treasury Department, which the law charged with overseeing the bounty lands' distribution. The letters, many signed only with a mark, all alleged that fraudsters had swindled the veterans of their land rights; they asked the Secretary of the Treasury to enter caveats against these crooked claims. This request had no grounding in the sparse statute's provisions; it instead echoed state practices, recounted earlier, that allowed challengers to formally object to a land grant and transfer their dispute to a local court. But the veterans' appeals went still further by asking the Treasury Department itself, rather than courts, to resolve their complaints.[2]

The veterans' unbidden letters exemplified the ubiquity of federal adjudication of land rights in the early territories. As we have seen, the federal government sought to displace some earlier sources of title there even as it resolved the tangles created when the land companies collapsed. But, through the 1790s, the government also spent considerable effort giving away land to satisfy preexisting claims—much more land, in the end, than it sold. Over the course of the decade, Congress enacted fifteen laws conferring title on worthy claimants: converted Moravian Delawares, road developers, a federal Indian interpreter. During the same time, it passed a single statute, the 1796 land law, to govern the lands' *sale*.[3]

This work involved more than the straightforward confirmation of existing land rights. Rather, the federal government was engaged in a kind of alchemy, taking sources of title that it recognized as valid but inchoate and transforming them into official federal documents, like treaties and land grants, that purported to offer definitive federal title. This process required discretion, as federal officials determined which land rights they were legally and morally obligated to honor, and translation, as they struggled to interpret other peoples' property laws.

Federal Ground. Gregory Ablavsky, Oxford University Press (2021). © Gregory Ablavsky.
DOI: 10.1093/oso/9780190905699.003.0004

As the letters flooding the Treasury Department suggest, the federal role arbitrating property rights was often unsought; it arose from the demands of would-be owners themselves. Besides the veterans, there were two other especially significant sets of territorial claimants that pressed their claims: Native nations and the French residents of the Illinois Country known as *habitants*.

In one sense, these groups' decision to turn to the federal government to confirm their property was surprising. Though federal officials conflated title with official government documents, this definition had little purchase in much of the territories, where the federal government lacked effective local control. Natives and *habitants* alike had long managed without formal title as federal officials conceived it; both associated ownership less with the market than with community, and so their property law reflected long-standing customary practices and acknowledged overlapping claims. Federal officials found this form of ownership maddeningly informal, even though it resembled long-standing Anglo-American land practices.

Yet Native peoples and *habitants* also recognized that the federal government was offering them an additional, increasingly important form of ownership—property rights that would be legible to outsiders. As Natives and French settlers knew from long experience, papers ostensibly bestowing ownership could impress officialdom and so help ward off federal claims. They also knew—as the veterans did even more keenly—that documents purporting ownership were increasingly a commodity, as distant speculative networks reached into the territories' remotest corners, threatening to dispossess those who lacked such paper proofs. As a result, the federal government's ability to produce titles that those *outside* the borderlands would consider valid became ever more significant for those *in* the borderlands, too.

Beyond a vague commitment to establishing clear title, the federal government was unsure how to resolve the property claims pressed upon it. Congress felt constrained to take them seriously both out of a sense of obligation and to bolster tenuous federal authority in the region. Many in the new government would have gladly let local courts adjudicate such property claims, as they did in most of the United States. But individual litigation could not create an entire property scheme from hundreds of existing rights, as French rights in the Illinois Country required, nor did Anglo-American courts assert authority over Native property in Indian country. The result was a jurisdictional and competence gap that Congress and the Washington administration turned to territorial officials to fill, largely because they were already there. These ad hoc, extrajudicial arbiters then decided claims' validity based on a loose knowledge of Native or French property law, often measuring claimants' rights against the strength of competing claims—what property scholars call relativity of title.[4]

Despite being arguably unwelcome and unplanned, such administrative adjudications did important work for the federal government, and so quickly became precedent. For one, they accomplished the essential but unsung task of resolving preexisting claims before any distribution of "vacant" federal lands could occur. For another, these officials were furthering the federal goal of crafting a more legible, more easily administered body of property rights. By producing a piece of paper from the federal government conferring title, these disputes made ownership appear to derive from the United States rather than from the plural sources that had previously undergirded property rights. This transformation toward a more positivist conception of ownership, centered in the national state, laid the literal groundwork for federal land offices and the century of federally overseen expansion that followed.

Tedious and Inconvenient

The United States was born, historians have traced, with a seemingly insatiable hunger for Native land. Although the dream of erasing Native ownership was as old as European colonization, only with the Revolution did the Anglo-American vision of seizing Native property and "extirpat[ing] their whole Savage race," in the words of one petition from Nashville, become both dominant and seemingly attainable. Even federal officials who despised such exterminatory rhetoric believed, albeit with pathos alongside anticipation, that Native nations' ownership was temporary. They may have sought to make the process of dispossession as orderly and consensual as possible, but few harbored doubts about the ultimate result: Native land would eventually be transformed into Anglo-American property.[5]

But what scholars have called the "logic of elimination" ran up against another logic: the fundamental principle of Anglo-American property law captured in the Latin maxim "nemo dat quod non habet"—no one could give what he did not have. In the context of Native land, this concept required the federal government to purchase land from sellers who actually owned the lands they purported to sell, if only to establish clear, valid chains of title. As congressional commissioner Samuel Parsons stated, "the security of the Title to those [western] lands is much concerned in procuring the confirmation . . . of the Indian Title." "Extinguishing" Native title on an unprecedented scale thus required first understanding the nature and scope of that title.[6]

Here, federal officials faced a challenge. However resolved, the long-running Anglo-American debates over how to define Native title with respect to fee simple ownership could not settle the question that confronted federal purchasers of Native land: *which* Native peoples owned *which* land. When Anglo-Americans fought over title, they looked to state and federal law to resolve their claims, but neither purported to define conflicting Native ownership rights *within* Indian country. Only one body of law had any claim to define ownership among Native communities: Indigenous property law.

Ironically and even perversely, then, the effort to eliminate Native ownership also mandated that federal officials attempt to understand, and even incorporate, Native law at the very moment they sought to displace it. This requirement thrust reluctant federal officials into the unlikely role of interpreters and even arbiters of Native concepts of ownership, as they dimly understood them. They undertook this responsibility with varying degrees of good faith and self-dealing, but all felt constrained to attempt the endeavor.[7]

There was another reason that federal officials found themselves adjudicating Native concepts of ownership: Native leaders demanded it of them. Federal officials might have had to determine which nation owned the lands they were purchasing, but they had little interest in going further to decide property *among* Native nations. Such "altercations among them about their boundaries," Secretary of War Timothy Pickering opined, were "tedious and . . . Inconvenient."[8]

Yet Native leaders repeatedly dragged federal officials into these disputes as they "insisted" that commissioners codify their nations' property rights in federal treaties. At the 1786 Treaty of Hopewell, for instance, federal commissioners sought to avoid the issue of boundaries between the Cherokee, Chickasaw, Creek, and Choctaw Nations by leaving it to "the respective tribes." Yet one Chickasaw leader demanded that the commissioners mark his nation's borders on the map. "[H]e wished," the commissioners reported, that "Congress would point out his lands to him, he wanted to know his own."[9]

This demanding Chickasaw leader was almost certainly Piomingo, whom Anglo-Americans sometimes called the Mountain Leader, a war leader who had risen to prominence in the Revolution's aftermath by pursuing a close alliance with the United States. Piomingo's statement at Hopewell was less a declaration of ignorance of his own nation's borders than an attempt to force *federal officials* to acknowledge Chickasaw territory—a gambit that Piomingo repeatedly, and forcefully, deployed as he sought to protect his nation's territory.[10]

Piomingo's aims were especially apparent at a 1792 meeting in Nashville between Chickasaw, Choctaw, Cherokee, and U.S. representatives. Governor William Blount had convened the meeting to introduce himself as Indian superintendent to Native leaders, but Piomingo quickly set the agenda: he wanted, he insisted, "to have boundaries settled." Piomingo drew out the map from

Hopewell and presented it to Blount. "This map is old, I want to have a new one," he proclaimed as he proceeded to describe his nation's borders.[11]

Piomingo's anxiety stemmed from reports that, at the Treaty of Holston, the Cherokees had sold land south and west of Nashville—land that the Chickasaws also claimed. The Cherokee leader Nontuaka, who had signed the Treaty of Holston and traveled to Philadelphia with Nenetooyah to negotiate with Knox, confirmed that it was true. But he argued that these lands had always been considered as a common hunting ground shared among the Chickasaws, Cherokees, Creeks, and Choctaws, and insisted that the only relevant boundary was between Native nations and the United States. "I never knew, before the present, that our people divided lines and made lines like white people," Nontuaka concluded. Piomingo offered a revealing response:

> By marking my boundary I did not mean to exclude other nations from the benefit of hunting on my lands. I knew the Cherokees had often pretended to take the whites by the hand, but instead of doing it in good faith, they are always sharpening their knives against them. I feared the whites, in retaliation, would fall on the Cherokees, and that they might take my land, supposing it belonged to the Cherokees: for this reason I have marked it.

Thus, as Piomingo made clear, neither Chickasaws nor Cherokees were the principal audience for these demarcated borders; they were targeted squarely at Blount and other federal officials. He was unambiguous about his motive to thwart Anglo-American dispossession: "To save my own land," he stated, "I made it plain."[12]

In the end, Piomingo's demands repeatedly forced the United States, despite its best efforts, to adjudicate ownership disputes *among* Native nations. Both the Cherokees and Chickasaws left the Nashville meeting with a copy of the newly marked map. Later on, when Piomingo proposed establishing a trading post along the Tennessee River, Secretary Pickering authorized it only "if the Chickasaws indisputably own the land, and the Cherokees do not claim it or also consent to the measure." Pickering even implicitly conceded the role of the United States in resolving intertribal property disputes in yet another controversy about Chickasaw territory, this time over the proper interpretation of a presidential proclamation protecting the Chickasaw Nation. President Washington, Pickering insisted, had clearly not intended "to decide the boundaries between the lands of different Indian nations"—"at least on the mere representation of only one of the parties," Pickering continued. Pickering's proviso suggested that, in some instances, the federal government would—and did—intervene to arbitrate property disputes among tribes.[13]

A Sort of Common Property

If federal officials were to decide which Native nations owned which land, they would have to attempt some understanding of the property law of the diverse Native nations they confronted. Federal officials were not the first Euro-Americans to undertake this project: they followed a long line of would-be ethnographers and Indian country travelers who sought to grasp Indigenous ideas of ownership. Transmitted back to Europe, these narratives often depicted Indigenous communities as peoples lacking private property. Fixated on ownership's origins, early modern European political theorists then translated these accounts into imagined histories in which Native nations' present stood in for property's purported past. Even a text as practical and staid as William Blackstone's ubiquitous *Commentaries on the Laws of England* recounted the creation of private property by tracing "the manners of many American nations."[14]

But the federal officials in charge of Indian affairs were politicians and military men, not philosophers. Although they at times relied on ethnographies—Henry Knox, for instance, copied William Bartram's travels in Indian country, and enlisted Moravian missionary John Heckewelder into federal service—most officials deployed more direct sources to learn about Native peoples. In the territories, Governor St. Clair and especially Governor Blount gathered information from a network of official and quasi-official Indian agents, many of whom were intermarried with Native women, knew Native languages, and had long lived in Indian country. Blount praised agent John McKee, previously a trader among the Cherokees, as possessing a deep "knowledge of Indians, their habits & dispositions"; he similarly commended interpreter James Carey for his "long and intimate" relationship with the Cherokees and "understanding [of] their language and connexion with them."[15]

Most often, though, federal officials turned to Natives themselves to try to understand Indigenous ownership. Knox had long conversations with Native leaders about their nations' histories and customs, and told others to do the same: he informed a federal negotiator in the Ohio Country that among the mission's "first objects" was "to ascertain *from the Indians* what tribes are the allowed proprietors" of the lands under discussion. Echoing this view, President Washington instructed the attorney general to determine which Native nations were the "acknowledged proprietors" of disputed land in the Ohio country based on which nations' claims were "conceded generally by other Indians bordering" those lands.[16]

Yet Washington's instructions contained an important qualification: at least "as far as the information shall be attainable." This qualification reflected the fact that federal officials found the Native property law related to them highly confusing. Secretary of War Pickering, for one, found Native descriptions of their boundaries "extremely vague."[17]

Some Native law translated clearly. Federal officials found it relatively easy to comprehend Native ownership of their villages and surrounding cornfields, forms of occupancy and improvement readily legible to Anglo-Americans. They could readily grasp, too, the temporal basis for these claims. The Miamis' lands had been "enjoyed by my forefathers time immemorial," the Miami chief Little Turtle told federal commissioners at the Treaty of Greenville. "[T]he print of my ancestors' houses are every where to be seen." Little Turtle's basis for property—its emphasis on occupancy, timelessness, and even its wording—could have been cribbed directly from Blackstone.[18]

Anglo-Americans could also usually understand Native practices of recordation. Some Native methods of marking territory—oral testimony, marks on the landscape—were opaque to federal officials, although they knew of their existence. Others they knew well but could not interpret directly: federal emissaries were well schooled in the significance of wampum, which they bought by the thousand to present at treaty sessions, yet they could not read wampum belts as Natives were reputedly able to do.[19]

Increasingly, though, Native leaders maintained written evidence of prior land transactions in what one Indian country visitor called "the archives, where all messages and reports are kept." At one federal treaty negotiation, an observer recorded, "the Indians produced a bundle of papers as records & ratifications of former treaties." Increasingly distrustful of Anglo-Americans' manipulations, many Native leaders began to demand written records of discussions and land transactions from their federal counterparts to forestall future disputes. At times, Native access to written texts caused federal officials alarm, since they were *too* legible in Anglo-American law. General James Wilkinson was highly "embarrass[ed]," for instance, when, in 1797, some Natives of an unspecified Ohio country nation presented him with a document that "asserted to be the original counterpart of the Treaty of Greenville left with the Indians." This copy, which Wilkinson believed a forgery, outlined borders different from those in the version ratified by the president and the Senate.[20]

But, when Native property law ventured away from such clear analogs to Anglo-American property, federal officials found Native title increasingly difficult to comprehend. They particularly struggled to grasp rights in the broad Native territories that Anglo-Americans denominated as "hunting grounds." Belying European theorists' assertions that Indigenous peoples had no ideas of property other than simple possession, these lands were the subject of a welter of overlapping national, village, clan, and individual-based entitlements, some exclusive and some communal. Traveler William Bartram complained that the terms "common" and "private property" were "too vague and general" to capture Native property rights to these regions. The Creek Nation's "Whole territory," he observed, was "divided by lines & boundaries amongst the different Tribes. . . .

yet every individual citizen of the Confederacy have the same equal right to hunt and range where he pleases," and owned what he secured. Even more befuddling to federal officials was the idea of communal land rights shared *among different* nations. Federal efforts to obtain Cherokee lands at Muscle Shoals—the center of much eager speculative attention, as recounted earlier—ran aground when the Cherokees declined to sell on the grounds that "they were not clearly our property" alone. They were, the Cherokees instructed the federal negotiators, "a sort of common property" among all the southeastern nations, and so could only be sold with the consent of all.[21]

Migration, particularly in response to Anglo-American colonialism, further complicated Native property rights. A particularly rich mixture of peoples lived in the Ohio and Illinois Countries, in what Richard White labeled the refugee zone. While some communities—the Miamis, Weas, and others of what Anglo-Americans dubbed the Wabash Confederacy—had long lived along the Ohio's tributaries, others, most notably the Delawares and Shawnees, were more recent arrivals pushed west and northward by Anglo-American settlement. Colonization had shaped the settlements of the southern Native confederacies, too. The chaos of the Revolution and its aftermath had particularly impacted the Cherokees, who shifted away from their historic upper settlements in the eastern part of the Southwest Territory, around their beloved town of Chota, and led many to push down the Tennessee River, forming the lower or Chickamauga towns.[22]

All this movement made it harder for Anglo-Americans to understand ownership patterns in Indian country. When a U.S. emissary arrived at a Kickapoo village north of Vincennes to invite them to a treaty, the Kickapoos replied, to the official's bafflement, that they could not act without consulting the "Ouiatonons [Weas], being the owners of their [the Kickapoos'] lands."[23]

Federal officials also struggled to grasp the relationship between ownership and gender in the matrilineal Native nations they encountered. These officials recognized, at least implicitly, the power that Native women enjoyed within their communities, stressing the "influence" that came from agents' marriage to Native women. St. Clair's predecessor as superintendent of Indian affairs, Richard Butler, was more explicit: he condemned negotiators who disregarded Native women from "want of Knowledge of Indian customs, as councils among the Indian women are by no means uncommon." But, because most of the Native nations in the territories relied on men to negotiate external relations, particularly on war matters, William Blount, Arthur St. Clair, and Henry Knox perceived the diplomatic world they operated in as largely masculine. Full of accounts of male Native leaders like Nenetooyah or Captain Pipe, their correspondence featured Native women only as generic "squaws" who were the subjects, not the agents, of diplomacy.[24]

Officials' blinkered view encompassed Native women's land ownership. As the farmers of the expansive cornfields that surrounded Native towns, Native women among the nations of both the Ohio Country and Native South enjoyed a particular entitlement to land, one they sometimes made explicit to federal officials. "We are *the owners of this land*—and it is ours," Haudenosaunee female elders lectured federal negotiators in 1791, "for it is we that plant it." These women made a plea recorded in St. Clair's papers as they sought to guard their title against U.S. encroachment: "Hear us therefore for we speak of things that Concern us and our Children." Like these Haudenosaunee women, Native women in the Ohio Country and Native South often sought to use their ownership to forestall land cessions to the United States. Yet neither St. Clair nor Blount seemed to hear or recognize Native women's claims. Although some individual Indian agents recognized the gendered division of ownership and sought to exploit it, none of the treaties of cession Blount or St. Clair negotiated had any female signatories, nor is there any indication that they grasped the significance of Native women's property rights.[25]

Little of what federal officials found confusing and supposedly alien about Native property law—its communal, informal nature; its subdivision of land based on use rights; its recognition of women's ownership—was actually so different from Anglo-American practices, as historians have demonstrated. Native peoples were not the only territorial residents who claimed overlapping rights to ownership based on occupancy and uncertain texts, whose lives were marked by mobility and migration, or who allowed women greater property rights than the formalities of coverture suggested. And in presenting worn copies of treaties to assert ownership to federal officials, Native leaders differed little from Anglo-American claimants in the territories, with their tangles of warrants, deeds, and grants.[26]

But this similarity between Native and Anglo-American laws of property did not make federal officials' task simpler. The likeness, rather, reflected those aspects of Anglo-American property law in the territories—flexibility, informality, and custom—that federal officials were most anxious to displace. In this sense, the parallels between the property understandings of Natives and their white neighbors presented federal officials yet another challenge as they struggled to grasp and formalize unfamiliar law.

The Proper Owners

Federal officials differed in how they met this challenge—how they reconstructed Native property law. Some waded deeply into the contradictory statements on ownership made by multiple Native nations; others favored a bright-line approach based on occupancy. Two sets of property controversies—one over the Cumberland District in the Southwest Territory, the other over ownership of the Ohio Country—underscored these divergent approaches and brought them into conflict.

The Cumberland District consisted of a forty-mile triangle of Anglo-American settlement, centered around Nashville, separated from the rest of the Southwest Territory by Indian country. Anglo-Americans had first settled the region during the Revolution, claiming ownership based on Henderson's questionable 1775 purchase recounted earlier. In the 1785 Treaties of Hopewell with the Cherokees and Chickasaws as well as the 1791 Treaty of Holston with the Cherokees, federal negotiators had leveraged Henderson's claim into paper recognition of U.S. ownership and sovereignty over Cumberland. Nonetheless, Native leaders repeatedly objected to the Cumberland settlements, informing federal negotiators that the region remained a communally held hunting ground shared among the Creek, Cherokee, Chickasaw, and Choctaw Nations. In the early 1790s, the region became perhaps the most violent and blood-soaked part of the United States, as Anglo-Americans, Creeks, and Cherokees contested for ownership and control.[27]

Cherokee and Creek leaders alike insisted that Cumberland was illegally located on their shared land, but Governor Blount waded into what he understood as Native law to dismiss such claims as mere pretense. Based on "the greatest contiguity to hunting grounds, and the prior use of them"—which, he argued, provided "the best claim Indians can establish" for ownership—the lands properly belonged to the Chickasaws. In fact, Blount alleged, the Cherokees had supposedly "admitted the Chickasaw claim was just." And the Cherokees had no basis to assert ownership, he argued, since their homelands lay considerably further east. "[B]y the best information I can collect," Blount told the secretary of war, "the Claim of the Cherokees to the lands lying on Cumberland is a recent thing."[28]

Blount found the Creek claim even more unfathomable. Blount's Cherokee and Chickasaw informants told him that the Creek hunting grounds had stopped well below the Tennessee River, nearly one hundred miles south of Cumberland, and that the Creeks had hunted along the coast until the Georgians forced them inland. The nearest Creek village, he noted, was two hundred miles away from Nashville. At Tellico in 1794, Blount grilled Cherokee leaders to confirm his beliefs. "[I]s it not a fact," Blount leadingly asked Lower Cherokee leader Kunokeski (John Watts), "that in the division of the Lands among them red people . . . . [the] Tennessee bounds them [the Creeks] on the North?" "What you say about the Boundary of the Creek Land is right," Kunokeski reportedly replied. "[F]rom anything I have ever heard," Blount concluded, the Creeks had not even the "colour of claim" to "a foot of land" north of the Tennessee River.[29]

But some in the Washington administration disagreed with Blount's approach as well as his assessment of the Creeks' Cumberland claim. Secretary of War Pickering—who had a fraught relationship with Blount—was much more willing to credit the Creeks' own statements and actions in assessing their property rights. "The inveteracy with which the Creeks committed depredations on Cumberland," Pickering wrote, "satisfied me that they had some latent claim to the lands." Consulting with the federal agent to the Creeks, Pickering found "his answer justifies my suspicion. The Creeks said their claims on those lands had never been extinguished." As further proof of Creeks' legitimate claim to Cumberland, Pickering pointed out that, after the Creeks finally relinquished their claim at a recent conference, Creek violence against the Southwest Territory had ceased. For Pickering, these actions, rather than the testimony of neighboring tribes or purported immemorial usage, constituted the strongest evidence of Native property rights.[30]

A similar conflict played out in the Ohio Country, where federal officials confronted an equally complicated set of overlapping claims produced by an even more tangled history of Native mobility. The Wyandots, Shawnees, Delawares, and Mingoes, for instance, all claimed ownership of lands between Ohio River and Lake Erie in present-day eastern Ohio, despite their varying histories of migration. Further complicating matters was the assertion by the Haudenosaunee Confederacy that, even though its homeland was far away in Iroquoia (current upstate New York), it had conquered several of these nations, and so rightfully controlled their lands. Like the British before them, the United States relied on the Haudenosaunees' purported right of conquest to assert ownership. In 1784, the Haudenosaunee ceded lands *north* of the Ohio claimed "by virtue of former conquests" to the United States; the 1789 Treaty of Fort Harmar reconfirmed this cession.[31]

Given all this movement, some federal officials, following Blount's emphasis on immemorial usage, concluded that nations recently arrived in the Ohio Country lacked any ownership rights under Native law. The Continental Congress opined, for instance, that the Shawnees "are not considered *by the Indians* as a Nation having any Claim of Territory." Or, as treaty commissioner Samuel Parsons put it more bluntly, the Shawnees "do not own a Foot of Land in the World," a principle one trader believed applied to the Wyandots and Delawares as well.[32]

Other officials followed the course charted by Pickering and credited nations' ownership claims based on occupancy. Secretary of War Knox instructed negotiators to acknowledge nations "who were the actual occupants of the lands as the proper Owners thereof." This argument rested in part on analogy to Anglo-American legal concepts. In the eyes of one army officer, the Delawares were the "actual proprietors" of the lands in the eastern Ohio Country. But because other nations "now reside and hunt on those Grounds," they "by possession have attended a kind of claim." As these statements suggest, some Anglo-Americans concluded that under Native as well as Anglo-American law, occupancy itself could yield title.[33]

Occupancy proved a particularly salient legal concept in evaluating Haudenosaunee claims to the Ohio Country, which federal officials had begun to question. Initially, the leaders of the Six Nations had declared "their title to the lands . . . was acknowledged by *all* the Western Indians," but, when pressed, they "confessed that the four most hostile tribes denied their right to it." Timothy Pickering concluded that, "whatever claim the Six Nations might formerly have to the lands Westward of the Allegany, they long relinquished the same to the Delawares and others of the present Western Indians." The Six Nations' earlier cessions "I consider as affording us but the Shadow of a title" to the Ohio Country; the federal government would have to negotiate with the lands' actual inhabitants to extinguish their claims.[34]

In the end, in determining which property rights the federal government would honor, Pickering and Knox's broader approach, favoring occupancy and tribes' own statements of ownership, largely prevailed over Blount's crabbed and static vision, in which tribes' property rights derived only from his version of immemorial usage. This outcome likely did not reflect a repudiation of Blount's chauvinism and contradictions—ironic as it was for a man whose career and fortune rested on migration to reject Native mobility. Rather, the federal decision not to strongly contest Native nations' own assertions of their rights to ownership largely stemmed from expediency and simplicity. Federal officials found it easier to compensate tribes than to haggle over property rights or risk conflict. It was also more straightforward. Blount's stingy approach ironically required wading into Native history to uncover the "true" owners. Occupancy, by contrast, afforded officials a familiar and bright-line rule for adjudicating Native disputes.

Despite their differences, what both approaches to Native property shared was a keenly felt need to justify federal definitions of Native rights based on Native law, as legitimated by Native peoples themselves. Even Blount's imperialist interpretations ultimately relied on Chickasaw and Cherokee statements for authority. This history reflects, in part, the persistence of Native power. Most federal officials disliked trying to understand Indigenous property law, but Native leaders repeatedly forced them into this role. Similarly, Native nations' continued dominance meant that federal officials had to construct chains of ownership that Native peoples would themselves respect. For all that westward expansion involved the erasure of Native governance and property, the concern over valid title mandated federal officials' attempt, however half-hearted and self-serving, to understand Indigenous law.

But another consequence of this often-unwilling federal role was the aggrandizement of federal authority. Native peoples confronted constrained choices, and, as Piomingo's statements demonstrate, federal acknowledgment of Native title presented one of the only viable means to preserve Native lands against Anglo-American encroachments. But the effect was that property disputes under Native law came to be adjudicated within a federal forum, relying on incomplete federal understandings of Indigenous legal orders. This pattern, which held throughout the nineteenth and twentieth centuries, had pernicious consequences for Native peoples. It made Native title appear as if it existed merely at the sufferance of federal officials, and transformed Native property rights into "claims" whose validity hinged on legibility within formalized Anglo-American law. In this sense, even though federal officials embraced a vision of Native property law more sympathetic than most Anglo-Americans of the time, the rise of federal title increasingly came at the expense of Native ownership.[35]

French Usage

Throughout the late 1780s, as federal officials struggled to comprehend and apply Native property law, some of these same officials were working to interpret and codify another body of foreign law within the U.S. territories: that of the French residents of the Illinois Country in the Northwest Territory. These *habitants* had repeatedly petitioned the Continental Congress to confirm their property rights. So, soon after it enacted the Northwest Ordinance and appointed Arthur St. Clair as territorial governor, Congress instructed him to adjudicate and confirm these settlers' titles to their lands "according to the laws & Usages of the Governments under which they have respectively settled." In October 1789, President Washington urged St. Clair to go to the Illinois Country "as soon as possible." It was a "circumstance of some importance," Washington instructed, that the inhabitants be guaranteed their lands "by some known and fixed principles."[36]

The *habitants* were the descendants of settlers who had arrived in what Anglo-Americans labeled the Illinois Country in the late seventeenth and early eighteenth centuries, when the region was part of New France. They built villages along the rivers linking French Canada and Louisiana: Vincennes, along the Wabash River in present-day southern Indiana; Kaskaskia, Cahokia, and Prairie du Rocher, along the Mississippi River in present-day downstate Illinois. Remote outposts whose residents were closely tied to surrounding Native nations through kinship and intermarriage, these towns capitalized on their proximity to Natives to serve as entrepôts in the trade between the continent's vast Native interior and the Euroamerican commercial centers of Montreal and Detroit.[37]

These villages' strategic location along the Mississippi and Wabash subjected them to the vagaries of the long contest over the continent. By the late 1780s, formal sovereignty over the territory had switched three times. First, at the end of the Seven Years' War, the British had supplanted French rule. Then, during the American Revolution, the Virginians had invaded, displacing the British and ravaging the towns' economy, as the state's militia pillaged from the people they had supposedly liberated. Finally, sovereignty passed yet again in 1784, when Virginia ceded both ownership and jurisdiction to the federal government.[38]

When federal officials finally arrived at the villages beginning in the late 1780s, they were unimpressed, filtering their impressions through a haze of class and cultural contempt. Vincennes, the largest of the settlements, held only 330 families. Its economy wrecked by war, the town and its buildings were "low, Old, and ugly," many in "decay'd & even ruinous condition." (The situation in the other towns was similar: Kaskaskia was reportedly "nothing more then a heap of ruin.") Anglo-Americans had little respect for the inhabitants, whom they found "very Ignorant," even though, not knowing French, most officials could not speak with them. Their disdain also had a racial element. As a result of the inhabitants' "vicinity, trade, and intermarriages" with neighboring tribes, Vincennes residents were "a good deal on the savage establishment" and "barely . . . removed from the Indians"; many wore Native attire and had "brown complextions." Federal officials thought the residents ill-suited for American governance. "The people will not relish a free government," Territorial Judge John Cleves Symmes reported after a visit to Vincennes. "[T]hey say our laws are too complex, not to be understood, and tedious in operation—the command or order of the Military commandant is better law and spedier justice for them & what they prefer to all the legal systems found in Littleton and Blackstone."[39]

Contrary to Symmes's sneers, the French settlers possessed a legal system that depended on more than military whim. Their property law, based on a French legal code of codified customs known as *Coutumes de Paris*, was grounded in notarial practice, with formal, written deeds in standardized language sworn before public notaries. The settlers employed community schemes of marital property, which granted title to wives and husbands jointly, and measured lands in arpents, a French unit slightly smaller than the Anglo-American acre. They had developed a tripartite division for their lands—individually held town lots, river lots divided into long strips, and commons. Though the river lots were held individually, they were worked communally through an open-field system.[40]

Yet, just as Littleton and Blackstone were poor guides to the property law on the Anglo-American frontier, the French villagers' property practices reflected borderland exigencies as much as they did the *Coutumes*. In particular, land ownership did not have the salience for the *habitants* that it held for land-crazed Anglo-Americans. The mid-eighteenth-century Illinois Country had been the center of a booming flour industry, but thirty years of war and competition from Anglo-American farmers on the Ohio led the remaining *habitants* to turn to commerce, describing themselves as "chiefly addicted to the Indian trade." Anglo-Americans, unaware of this past, disdained the French they encountered as "indifferent Farmers." Communal farming and the settlements' remote location also meant that there was little to gain from engrossing enormous tracts: land held little commodity value without the prospect of ever-increasing prices driven by constant immigration.[41]

Land practice in the French villages thus reflected the informality of life in close-knit communities where residents knew each other's holdings. Boundaries were haphazard and imprecise; Vincennes was remarkable, an Anglo-American surveyor observed, for its "extreme irregularity." Written deeds spoke vaguely of lots extending "of the depth of one street to the next"; one land contract contained only a promise to sell along with the assurance that, "as soon as we see each other again I will straighten all things out."[42]

The Illinois Country's transfer to the federal government made the *habitants* anxious that their new sovereign would not recognize their informal property rights, especially after Congress forbade unauthorized settlements on public lands. "Placed at an immense distance from the seat of the federal government of America, your Petitioners have always lived in a dangerous security concerning the lands which they were wont to consider as their own," read one of several petitions addressed to the Continental Congress from the Illinois Country in 1787 appealing for confirmation of title, "and it is but of late that they have been awakened to fear & anxiety."[43]

The *habitants* were only one of many groups in the territories that importuned the federal government to honor property rights predating federal authority, yet the federal government proved more sympathetic to their claims than to rights founded on Indian purchases or preemption rights. The United States was not only anxious to secure the loyalty of these new citizens, but it also considered itself legally bound to recognize their ownership. The era's law of nations stipulated that a new sovereign was bound to honor rights of private property within a transferred territory. Moreover, like state land law, the *habitants*' rights were written into federal statute: Virginia's cession that stipulated that the French settlers "shall have their possessions and titles confirmed to them," while the Northwest Ordinance had promised that the French settlers' "laws and customs" concerning "the descent & conveyance of property" would remain binding.[44]

The Continental Congress responded to the *habitants*' appeals by establishing a generous standard. "[A]ncient settlers" who had lived in the villages in 1783 would not only have their claims confirmed, but would also each receive four hundred acres of land in the surrounding region. Congress also recognized that, given their informal property practices, the *habitants* might hold "equitable Titles to lands under some peculiar Customs established and recognized in the ancient French Colonies where no actual grants have passed." Rather than dispossess the villagers, Congress instructed St. Clair to honor these "equitable or Customary rights to Lands."[45]

St. Clair finally reached the Illinois and Wabash Countries in summer 1790, accompanied by Territorial Secretary Winthrop Sargent. The men instructed the towns' residents to appear before them with the papers and witnesses necessary to establish their claims to land, on which St. Clair and Sargent would pass judgment.[46]

This task proved more daunting than either Congress or President Washington likely anticipated. Part of the problem was volume: St. Clair received over four thousand land claims to adjudicate. An even more substantial problem was evidence. St. Clair and Sargent were accustomed to Anglo-American land recordation schemes, in which counties tracked parcels in official ledgers. The villages lacked anything comparable. "[N]o records are preserved," one official lamented. Grants from French and British officials had been scribbled on "small scrap[s] of paper" and passed to notaries who recorded them on "loose sheets." These notarial papers rarely survived: one notary had reportedly run off with all the public records, while other papers were simply scattered upon a notary's death. Notaries also passed deeds onto owners, but these records were either later "fraudulently destroyed" or entrusted to people Sargent thought "unacquainted with their consequence" who lost them: "for, by the French usage, [these deeds] are considered as family inheritance, and often descend to women and children."[47]

This informality extended beyond recordkeeping to encompass the sources of ownership. "The confusion of title here is a labyrinth of perplexity," Judge Symmes reported from Vincennes, "which requires the utmost care nay tenderness to set right." Symmes noted the "variety" of titles: "prescription, bar[e] possession—fraudulent deeds from those who had no right to sell." Title to much of the land around Vincennes rested on a purchase from the Piankeshaw Nation that had been made, the town's inhabitants insisted, in "utter[]" ignorance of the "laws of America, respecting land-affairs." Other portions of land were commons, which some settlers now sought to have distributed as individual lots.[48]

Anglo-Americans like Sargent and Symmes saw all these difficulties as evidence of French law's inferiority. Yet what they saw as deficiencies in legal norms mostly stemmed from the flexibility of property law in a society where the absence of a land market among strangers created little need to establish clear chains of title. The diverging gender norms that Sargent lambasted, for instance, reflected women's commercial power in towns where men were routinely away trading for months on end as much as it did French community property; many Anglo-American frontier communities discarded the formal strictures of common-law coverture, too.[49]

The fundamental challenge that confronted St. Clair and Sargent, then, was translating this customary land system suited for local needs into a formalized framework legible in Philadelphia and elsewhere, one in which ownership rested on legitimate sources of title established by written, impersonal evidence. Overseeing this act of translation gave St. Clair and Sargent tremendous discretion. The paucity of written evidence presented to them—"there is scarcely one case in twenty where the [written] title is complete," Sargent lamented—meant that they had to rely on "oral Testimony" about land ownership (though, in a rare fit of optimism, Sargent conceded that much of this testimony was "very good").[50]

This task thrust the Pennsylvanian St. Clair and the New Englander Sargent into the unlikely role of experts on French colonial land law, adjudicating questions for which, as for Native title, there was no law other than validity under prior local practice. St. Clair rejected one claim in Kaskaskia on the ground that it was former Jesuit land, which, he believed, French law provided "could not be alienated." He similarly rejected the land claims of *habitants* who had crossed the Mississippi to Spanish territory. Because their grants were not in fee simple but reverted to the king's domain when vacated—or so St. Clair interpreted French law—these tracts "strictly" belonged to the United States as the king's successor.[51]

The thorniest legal question, though, involved very recent rather than "ancient" claims. Shortly after the Virginians arrived in the Illinois Country, their militia commander, Lieutenant Todd, had authorized the local courts to make land grants—which they did right up through 1787, to the amount of 48,000 acres. Todd claimed this authority based on precedent: as local court officials explained to Sargent, "since the Establishment of this Country, the Commondants have always appeared to be vested with the powers to give Lands." Local courts then issued land grants citing both Todd—inflated to the "Chief Justice for the United States"—and "utmost necessity" for vindication.[52]

St. Clair recognized none of these authorities. He viewed Todd's grants as triply invalid: under Virginia law, Todd held no authority to grant land; even if he had, he could not delegate this power to the courts; and, even then, since most of the grants had occurred after Virginia's cession to the United States, they were "absolutely void." St. Clair accordingly "uniformly rejected" these grants as "altogether unauthorized" and "usurpation[s]" by "self created" officials.[53]

The irony in such assessments was how little they resembled the operation of a "free government" as envisioned by Judge Symmes. St. Clair and Sargent were not judges determining title in adversarial cases turning on the fineries of Blackstone. They were unelected federal administrators, appointed by a distant executive, passing judgment based on their own impoverished understandings of French law and practice. They became, in short, the latest in the line of "commandants" to rule over the *habitants* and their property.

Where St. Clair and Sargent differed from their French and British predecessors was in their insistence on formalizing local land practices. By the end of 1790, St. Clair, with Sargent's assistance, had ruled on the myriad claims presented him. Now, in place of the plural sources of ownership that had previously governed village life, St. Clair aspired to substitute a single valid title—a patent, issued by the sovereign's authorized representative, with the promise of an authoritative point of origin that St. Clair and Sargent had found so lacking.[54]

A Loose Manner

The French settlers, however, did not passively accept St. Clair's judgments. If the United States was more autocratic than Symmes believed, the *habitants* proved better equipped to navigate "free" institutions than he anticipated, as they again importuned Congress to recognize their disallowed claims. This foray into the early American culture of petitioning proved successful. Perhaps anxious to secure the allegiance of the French villagers in a volatile borderland, Congress in 1791 granted relief to many of the claimants St. Clair had denied without much debate. The statute provided that title based on purchases from local Indians as well as Todd's grants would be recognized so long as the lands had been "actually improved."[55]

Yet the French settlers confronted another, less appealing facet of Anglo-American governance as they faced interminable delays in securing their title. It proved hard to find a surveyor—St. Clair complained that the region contained only one man "who could run a single line"—and residents also got caught up in legal niceties, as Congress's statute had failed to specifically authorize the issuing of grants.[56]

The delay turned the forthcoming federal grants into yet another paper title promise in the early republic's parchment traffic. French residents—many of whom had already moved across the Mississippi into Spanish territory—began to cash out, transferring the promise of their grants to a "few speculators." When Territorial Judge George Turner came to Vincennes in 1794, he reported that "[b]y far the greater part [of the French settlers], having neither patience nor, as they say, much confidence left in the promise of Government, have sold their rights for little or nothing." Supposedly the *habitants*' land rights could be purchased for a rifle or a mediocre horse. When Governor St. Clair at last returned to the Illinois Country in 1795 to rule on expanded land rights authorized by the 1791 statute, he found the claims had proliferated: both the "old rights and [Todd's] Court Grants had become subjects of traffic, and scattered in different parts of the United States," he observed.[57]

St. Clair's return visit was largely a repeat of his first. Once again, he faced the challenge of adjudicating claims based on a vague standard, although in this case the confusion came from Congress: the requirement that settlers have constructed an "actual improvement" was, the governor complained, "not a very definite term." St. Clair delegated the task to Sargent to complete who, in 1797 and 1798, parceled out tracts of four hundred, two hundred, or twenty-five acres, based on his assessment of "improvement." After Sargent left for a new position, St. Clair struggled to make sense of the notes he had left behind. "[I]t is not easy to discover by what rule [Sargent's grants] were governed," he lamented. "[T]he people are extremely dissatisfied."[58]

Patents to the lands finally began to be issued in 1799. But, as with many territorial land sagas, confusion over title in the Illinois Country dragged on—past the region's inclusion in a new and separate Indiana Territory with Vincennes as its capital; even past the admission of Indiana and Illinois as states. Congress ultimately created a board of commissioners in 1804 to weigh unexamined claims anew, and in 1812, established a third board to reassess the validity of the grants made by St. Clair and his successors. These boards demonstrated that St. Clair's promise of definitive ownership was illusory. On the contrary, the new commissioners spoke of St. Clair just as the governor had dismissed the land practices of Todd and others, accusing him of managing the "business" in a "loose manner" and relying on ill-defined "bundles of papers" to determine claims. They uncovered copious evidence of fraud and self-dealing, in the form of perjured affidavits, faked transfers, and illegal interpolations in the entry books. And they hinted that St. Clair himself had profited from the haphazard process, confirming tens of thousands of acres to his son and associates. They did not wish to "impeach the character of any man," the commissioners observed, but if the facts made it "appear that something has indeed been 'rotten in Denmark,' we cannot help it." Yet, although the stream of petitions and congressional interventions involving the *habitant* lands did not end until the 1830s, Congress ultimately allowed most of St. Clair's seemingly questionable grants to stand.[59]

In hindsight, these opportunities for fraud and deceit, including by officials like St. Clair, tarnished these adjudications with the "very mire and filth of corruption," in the commissioners' words—a charge that later commentators have readily echoed. Yet the ubiquity of such "corruption" in all territorial land dealings, whether by states, land companies, or federal officials, suggests that this moralizing label distorts the structures of early American governance, as historians have repeatedly noted. For one, the parade of land-dealing territorial officials underscores that the ability to tilt property confusion to personal advantage was the primary route to influence, and public office, in the territories. For another, "corruption" was the consequence of discretion. Congress had empowered a single official, with little guidance, instruction, or oversight, to process thousands of ill-defined claims, for which there was no neutral or objective standard. More broadly still, as the federal government repeatedly discovered, there was no easy, cheap, or clean way to manage the chaotic collision between informal land systems with multiple poorly documented sources of ownership and the rapacious early American land market.[60]

The struggles to address the title of the French settlers were a harbinger of things to come. Even before Sargent had finished in the Illinois Country, he had begun to replicate the process in Detroit, an even larger former French settlement that had passed to U.S. sovereignty in 1796. Sargent was once again shocked by how "extreme loose[ly]" the inhabitants had dealt with land, with "scarcely a single Deed made where a Boundary was expressed"; he once again set about attempting to create order from perceived chaos. As the United States expanded into more former French and Spanish territory, federal officials encountered still more Vincennes and Detroits. Even as the federal land system envisioned tidily surveyed rectangular tracts marching across vacant land, the territory that the United States sought to incorporate was seldom empty or unclaimed by Europeans, let alone Native peoples. Resolving these claims consumed enormous amounts of federal time and resources over the nineteenth century.[61]

The challenges presented by prior Native and European ownership were more similar than sharp dichotomies between oral and written cultures, or between customary and formal law, would suggest. In both instances, often reluctant federal officials found themselves mired in alien property regimes, as they sought to use incomplete and contradictory oral and written evidence to translate informal ownership practices into a system where official documents granting well-defined and unambiguous title circulated as commodities. The difference lay in the purpose, not the nature, of the assessment. Federal officials interpreted Native title to extinguish it; they sought to understand the French villagers' title to confirm it. Undoubtedly racial, this distinction was also jurisdictional: it reflected the contrast between the quasi-foreign status of Native nations and French settlers' position as newly minted "citizens" of the United States.

Another parallel between Native and Euroamerican claims was the role of the federal government. As with Native title, arbitrating property rights within the French villages simultaneously burdened federal officials and expanded federal authority. In pressing their claims, the *habitants* merely pursued their self-interest; as their long history demonstrated, they had little interest in which sovereign assured their title. But, because these local decisions over property had, however accidentally, become a federal responsibility, the settlers' demands quickly gained an improbably outsized presence on the national agenda. Not just territorial officials but the president, his cabinet, and Congress all repeatedly intervened in these intensely local disputes.

The largely unintended outcome was the creation of a precedent bolstering federal power: that federal administrators would resolve, extrajudicially, preexisting Euroamerican ownership claims. Now, federally appointed commissioners would evaluate claims based on earlier property systems and laws and translate these preexisting, often inchoate rights into definitive, federally recognized land title. As a result, Congress ensured that petitions and appeals from remote borderlands villages, burdened with the minutiae of local property controversies, continued to flow eastward throughout the coming century.

Strictness and Caution

In 1796, Congress created another set of claimants to territorial lands when it established the U.S. Military District in the Northwest Territory. These lands would satisfy long-delayed federal promises of title—from one hundred acres (privates and noncommissioned officers) up to eleven hundred acres (major general)—made to entice Continental Army recruits during the Revolution.[62]

These bounty lands differed from the preexisting titles asserted by Native and French claimants in important ways. For one, as federally created rights, the bounty land promises did not require federal officials to interpret unfamiliar bodies of law; confirming these rights, officials believed, merely required following what Congress had directed. For another, as eager as the United States was to secure Native and French allegiance, veterans enjoyed special solicitude in the early republic. As scholars have traced, the new national government regarded claims based on military service as especially deserving of federal attention and protection, and veterans and their dependents were among the earliest beneficiaries of federal largesse. A deeply felt rhetoric of national obligation accordingly framed federal efforts to make good on its wartime promises to former soldiers.[63]

For both reasons, the framework for distributing veterans' titles under the 1796 statute was clearer than the ad hoc systems for resolving Native and French ownership. The Military District, the statute stipulated, would be surveyed on the same rectangular grid as the rest of the federal lands. Warrant holders would submit their claims to the secretary of the treasury, who would register them. The secretaries of the treasury, war, and state would then gather and hold a lottery that would priority rank all the confirmed warrant holders, who would then, in order, select tracts for the requisite acreage anywhere in the district. Any unclaimed land would be returned to the public domain for sale.[64]

But, despite these attempts at regulation, there was an important similarity between the veterans' land rights and other property claims: they, too, required federal action to translate inchoate entitlement into formal title. The careful precautions of prior survey and lottery did not obviate the fundamental challenge that had also plagued the French property rights: acknowledging contingent but perfectible land rights commodified them. Suddenly valuable, papers and certificates asserting these rights proliferated, their pedigree difficult to trace.

Thus, like other federal land promises early made and long delayed—with repeated extensions, the lottery for the bounty lands did not occur until four years after the statute passed, and even then claims persisted until the 1830s—federal bounty land warrants quickly became a speculative investment. One congressman said that he did not know a "single soldier" who still held one; another observed that they could be purchased for a "mere trifle." Speculation in the warrants was particularly intense in the Northwest Territory, as the experience of U.S. Army Captain John Armstrong illustrates. Armstrong schemed to acquire nearly fifty thousand acres in bounty lands, convincing eastern correspondents to buy up hundreds of military warrants until, as one reported, "the soldiers have quit calling on me." But Armstrong also had an advantage: as an army captain, he had ready access to soldiers and quickly set about buying up their bounty rights for a little over one pound a piece.[65]

This freewheeling market in bounty land certificates posed a challenge for the War Department and speculators alike. Congress was torn: it wanted to honor veterans' right to sell their entitlements but also guard against abuse. Recognizing that many soldiers had sold their rights "without any formal Conveyance," Congress instructed the secretary of war to honor either actual written conveyances *or* the presentation of a discharge from the army, even if not held by its original owner—unless, Congress continued, "fraud in Obtaining such discharge shall be proved."[66]

Such seemingly nominal requirements nonetheless often foiled bounty warrant purchasers, who in their zeal ignored even basic formalities. War Department clerks denied claims for many reasons: they lacked discharges, or the warrant had already been claimed, or the soldiers were ineligible, or the conveyances lacked a date or had not been sworn before a magistrate. One speculator found that fourteen hundred acres of his twenty-six-hundred-acre claim were rejected, while John Cleves Symmes's associate Jonathan Dayton complained that the military rights Symmes had purchased caused him "an inconceivable amount of trouble": despite over twenty visits to the War Office, he had still not received his warrants.[67]

Yet these minimal bureaucratic precautions also failed to halt fraud and abuse, complaints of which overwhelmed the War and Treasury Departments. The letters that poured in from veterans relayed numerous stories displaying what Secretary of War James McHenry called "[e]very devise of dishonest cunning." Henry Hill noted that the conveyance of his claim was supposedly executed in New York, where he had never been. John Redman said that a man who shared his name had claimed his patent. Judah Alden alleged that "two swindlers" in

Boston had taken his warrants. Others simply claimed that they had lost or misplaced their warrants.[68]

The question that federal administrators confronted was how much authority and responsibility they had to redress veterans' grievances. Unwilling to allow veterans to be deprived of their "hard earned dues," Secretary of War McHenry attempted to forestall the proliferation of forgeries by printing a broadside imposing stricter requirements on magistrates to swear to the conveyances' validity. Lacking any "other guard for individual rights to military lands," McHenry enjoined "strictness and caution . . . at the War Office," requiring that his clerks closely scrutinize all the warrants presented. Nonetheless, McHenry lamented, such careful examination "must often be ineffectual," due to "the great diversity of the Arts practiced to deceive."[69]

McHenry sought greater authority to delve into and adjudicate the substance of such allegations. He urged Congress to establish an administrative procedure in which federal officials would hear evidence on land warrants and rule on their validity. McHenry's proposal echoed earlier calls for a federal administrative tribunal for disputed land rights. Alexander Hamilton's 1790 land report had sought to empower land offices to "determine[]" the "controversies concerning rights to patents or grants of land" that arose in their district. A year later, Thomas Jefferson had similarly argued for "the establishment of a proper judicature for deciding speedily all land controversies between the public and individuals," but Congress had not acted.[70]

There was even precedent within the War Office. The customary practice before McHenry's arrival, he noted, was to permit claimants to file caveats without any statutory authorization. Moreover, in 1797, the U.S. attorney general had determined that the secretary of war must conduct a "proper inquiry" into a caveat filed for lands in the *Virginia* Military District that the War Office administered: the secretary must "investigate and decide" whether Virginian law had been violated, the attorney general concluded, including by obtaining sworn affidavits from witnesses.[71]

McHenry now urged that this approach be extended to the *federal* bounty lands. He proposed an administrative tribunal modeled on Pennsylvania's Board of Property, which had adjudicated disputed rights to land. This approach, McHenry believed, could benefit defrauded claimants compared to actions at law by shifting the burden of proof. Because the "rights appears [*sic*] to strongly to center" in the original holders, they should "stand upon the footing of Defendants," with the burden "on the other party to make out his own rights (as is understood to be legal principle) compleat."[72]

McHenry's proposed system of administrative adjudication contrasted with the approach advocated by Secretary of Treasury Oliver Wolcott, who was responsible for the actual distribution of lands (as opposed to the registering of bounty rights). Wolcott concluded that the 1796 statute granted him "no power to investigate or decide on the titles of the holder of military land Warrants." Exhausted by the constant caveats, he directed the recorder of deeds to inform claimants that "the merits of their claims can only be determined at Law"—that is, through the courts. Wolcott's approach reflected both statutory textualism as well as a grounding in state practice, where disputes were referred to courts rather than being adjudicated by the executive. Wolcott urged a similar solution for disputes that arose through the Land Office.[73]

On paper, Congress sided with Wolcott. Although it briefly flirted with McHenry's proposal, Congress never enacted such an administrative scheme, and later spurned petitioners who claimed their lands had been fraudulently taken, referring them to a "court of competent jurisdiction" to obtain "full and complete relief." Yet in practice, the War Department still found itself assessing land warrants' validity: in the decades following 1800, it rejected nearly four claims for every warrant that it issued. And in some respects, Congress itself fulfilled the role McHenry urged, albeit in ad hoc fashion. It constantly extended deadlines for filing, and, even while paying lip service to opposing legislative resolution of individual claims, it repeatedly passed statutes authorizing relief for individuals who had lost their bounty rights. After the War of 1812, Congress attempted to preemptively forestall the recurrence of earlier confusions by barring the transfer or sale of bounty rights; only soldiers themselves could claim them, though they could then sell the land warrants. This prohibition failed, and the land office found itself once again confronting caveats filed by disgruntled claimants; the new secretary of war ended up banning filings from attorneys altogether. In short, however much Congress and the executive wished to avoid getting dragged into determinations on individual claims, it proved difficult for federal officials to avoid making quasi-judicial decisions to afford meritorious claimants relief.[74]

The federal government's experience with the U.S. Military Reserve demonstrated that it was not vague boundaries or multiple sources of ownership alone that thrust the federal government into the territories' morass of conflicting property rights. Even when the federal government created the terms of ownership, disputes arose that required federal intervention—in part because the U.S. Constitution made the federal government responsible for the territories, and in part because the paper promises freely floating through the early republic made exploiting land systems too tempting to forgo. The result, whether in the context of Native, French, or veterans' claims, was federal administrators' ceaseless despair over fraud and confusion even as claimants demanded resolution from them.

For their part, bounty rights holders were no more advocates of federal bureaucratic power than Native leaders or French *habitants* were; they, too, merely followed the chain of authority in their efforts to secure relief. This process nonetheless oriented claimants toward Philadelphia, and later, Washington. The most significant speculators, like Captain Armstrong, often enjoyed privileged access to federal power; others from the territories served as intermediaries, gathering claims and journeying to the capital to press their cases. Those who could not travel wrote letters and petitioned Congress instead. Through this process, many citizens' prospects of landed wealth came to rest on the determinations of the federal government.

In spring 1800, the Northwest Territory's first nonvoting representative, William Henry Harrison, arrived in Congress. It was, Harrison reported to his constituents, a busy time. Congress was in the midst of addressing a half-dozen ongoing questions concerning the public lands: the recent bounty lands lottery; the title of settlers on Symmes's tract (an awkward issue for Harrison, Symmes's son-in-law); McHenry's caveat proposal; negotiations with Georgia over the cession of its western lands (complicated by the Yazoo purchases); and the status of public lands in the former Southwest Territory, now the state of Tennessee. It was as if Congress had determined to tidy, in five months, a decade's worth of confusions and uncertainties about ownership in the West.[75]

These many issues exemplified the land issues that had dominated the prior decade, as claimants had pressed federal officials to adjudicate their land rights. As Congress's legislative agenda underscored, this process had worked to distill the complicated and plural sources of ownership in the territories into a single document, a federal title that issued—eventually—under federal authority.

This rise of federal title was not a boon for most claimants. Native leaders rediscovered, as they likely already suspected, that the federal government was not a disinterested arbiter of their property rights. Meanwhile, federal land promises swept both French settlers and military bounty holders into the voracious maw of the early American land market. The result was often dramatically unequal distributions of land tilted in favor of those best equipped to navigate both the market and federal bureaucracy. In the U.S. Military District, for instance, 70 percent of the land ended up in the hands of a little over one hundred men, mostly nonveterans. By far the largest holder, claiming one-sixteenth of the region's 1.4 million acres, was Senator Jonathan Dayton, close associate of John Cleves Symmes (who himself located 36,000 acres in the District).[76]

This outcome—in which claimants elevated to authority a federal government that helped dispossess them—was ironic, perhaps even perverse. But it did not result from claimants' naiveté. Owners, particularly smallholders, constantly risked dispossession in the early territories. For many, their best hope was that some sovereign would recognize their title and make it legally binding. Many looked to state governments, but, as recounted earlier, they often confronted disappointment. Facing constrained choices, others turned instead to federal officials, who spouted promises of justice and equity that many likely believed. But dispossession nonetheless often followed, as even well-intentioned officials like Knox and McHenry often could not control the processes they purportedly oversaw. This apparent federal failure paradoxically became a source of federal power, as the federal government—inadvertently, and without any conscious plan—was perhaps the chief beneficiary of these claimants' efforts to obtain the elusive security of title.

Yet these issues were not Harrison's principal concern. "[A]mongst the variety of objects" concerning western lands, he reported, "none appeared to me of so much importance as the adoption of a system for the sale of public lands." Nearly as soon as he had arrived in Congress, Harrison had pushed for a committee to update the 1796 land statute, which he ultimately headed. Unlike its predecessor, this new land bill occasioned little debate, other than a brief and abortive effort by a Tennessean representative to codify preemption rights. On May 10, the bill became a law known, in honor of its chief promoter and drafter, as the Harrison Land Act.[77]

In the history of federal lands, the Harrison Land Act usually marks a beginning. The law maintained the rectangular grid and land auctions of its 1796 predecessor, but it also contained new provisions intended, in Harrison's words, "to give more favourable terms to that class of purchasers who are likely to become actual settlers." The law set 640 acres—known as one section—as the largest parcel size. Most significantly, it created regional land offices, the first four of which were in the Northwest Territory. Each office, staffed by a federally appointed register, would be the exclusive sale location for newly surveyed lands in its region. These lands would first be available in three-week-long auctions, and then, if unsold, at what the statute called "private sale," at a new minimum price of $2 per acre, although the law also extended purchasers yearlong terms of credit. The first land auction under the new law, at Chillicothe in spring 1801, brought in nearly as much revenue as all sales under the 1785 Land Ordinance and the 1796 Act combined.[78]

The Chillicothe land office remained open until 1877, a testament to the Harrison Act's long-lasting legacy. Although apparent only in hindsight, the law established the fundamental structures that governed sales of the public domain at least through the Civil War. By definitively resolving some issues—prior survey and rectangular sections—the statute channeled debate toward the terms within the law's framework that remained unsettled and that Congress could readily tweak. Fights over federal lands in the antebellum United States not only persisted but grew arguably even more heated and significant, given the important questions of political economy that they implicated. Yet, especially compared to the wide-ranging arguments of the 1790s, antebellum debates were surprisingly cramped. Congress increasingly jammed all the sweeping issues raised by the public lands into seemingly narrow policy decisions: minimum price, availability and length of credit, sale of full, half, or quarter sections—all the subject of endless contention in Congress. The Harrison Act had created a structure that proved unexpectedly durable.[79]

Yet, as the flurry of surrounding congressional activity seeking to tie up loose ends suggested, the Harrison Act also represented an end. Two decades of disagreement, controversy, and experiment had at last coalesced into something like the "system" that Harrison so desired. But this outcome was only possible because it built on years of hard, if largely unremarked, legal and administrative work: deciding, and legislating on, which sources of ownership would be recognized; attempting to use, and then abandoning, land companies to distribute the public domain; adjudicating, and often "extinguishing" through coercion, the titles of those whose property rights predated the United States. None of this work ended because Congress passed a single statute. On the contrary, the practices forged in these early decades persisted. Both sets of precedents replicated as the United States pushed its institutions westward across the continent into new federal territories, onto more already owned lands that the federal government sought to redistribute.

PART II
VIOLENCE

4
Federal Sovereignty

In the early 1790s, as Secretary of State Jefferson drafted his voluminous report on territorial lands, his colleague Secretary of War Henry Knox crafted his own set of influential reports. A former Boston bookseller risen to prominence during the Revolution, Knox was a staunch defender of federal and military authority. Prior to his cabinet appointment, he had had almost no experience with Native peoples. But, after Congress charged his War Department with governing Indian affairs, Knox became the new government's most distinctive and influential thinker about the relationship between the United States and Native nations.[1]

Knox's reports on Indian affairs identified an even more acute version of the same challenge Jefferson had traced: the weight of the past. "For some years past," Knox observed, Natives and whites in what became the territories had "exercis[ed] indiscriminate hostilities on each other" as they fought for sovereignty and land. The Revolution had intensified this brutal bloodshed outside the effective control of any government, an escalation that, in the territories, endured past the war's ostensible end.[2]

Knox viewed this violence between Natives and territorial citizens as a threat to federal interests. The territories were violent places generally—Anglo-Americans routinely assaulted and killed one another in territorial towns, as Native peoples did within their villages—but violence *between* Natives and whites was different: it was inherently political. As a large literature has traced, such cross-cultural bloodshed was a form of diplomacy that, while often intensely personal, also affected relations among sovereigns. Knox feared that such unregulated violence would undercut federal diplomatic efforts or, worse yet, drag the government into expensive open warfare. He accordingly instructed William Blount, Arthur St. Clair, and other officials to use their authority to end the ceaseless conflict.[3]

For Knox, the core problem was the lack of any neutral arbiter for the inevitable disagreements. "There can neither Justice or observance of treaties," he argued, "where every man claims to be the sole Judge in his own cause." The solution was for the federal government to assume this role, crafting and applying strict rules. "The administration of indian affairs," Knox argued, must be "conducted by fixed principles established by [federal] Law, and which being published should be rigidly enforced." Rather than subordinating Native peoples alone to federal will—a later leitmotif of federal Indian policy—Knox's effort aspired to subject Natives

Federal Ground. Gregory Ablavsky, Oxford University Press (2021). © Gregory Ablavsky.
DOI: 10.1093/oso/9780190905699.003.0005

and U.S. citizens *alike* to federal supremacy. "Government must keep both in awe by a strong hand," Knox wrote, "and compel them to be moderate and just."[4]

Knox's reports epitomized the Washington administration's plan to remake Indian affairs, one that we might call federal sovereignty. As in other areas of federal governance, this approach embraced an impartial and supreme federal law that would transcend local bias—a vision codified in the Trade and Intercourse Acts, a series of federal statutes expanded several times over the 1790s. These laws defined two distinct legal spaces: "ordinary jurisdiction," where local Anglo-American law and courts governed, and "Indian country," quasi-foreign territory owned and governed by Native nations. (Although the Acts applied nationwide, most Indian country—and most Indians—lay within the federal territories.) Between the two, the federal government would create, and police, a firm boundary. It would also vigorously punish both Native and white malefactors by exercising jurisdiction over cross-cultural crime. Killing or wounding an Indian in Indian country became, alongside piracy and treason, one of the small handful of federal crimes in the early United States.[5]

Yet as an effort to prevent violence, the Acts, and federal sovereignty more generally, failed. Cross-cultural boundaries remained permeable, and federal efforts to hold Natives and whites legally accountable for their crimes rarely succeeded. In explaining this failure, officials wrung their hands at their apparent powerlessness in the face of the "prejudice against Indians on the frontiers." Some historians have echoed this explanation, blaming the violence on frontier Indian-hating spawned by the late eighteenth-century rise of racial boundaries between "red" and "white" people. Others have focused on the durability of diplomacy and localism in early American governance, which entrenched customary practices of reciprocity, retaliation, and justifiable violence shared by Natives and white settlers alike.[6]

These accounts compellingly elucidate borderlands dynamics, but, in positing a sharp contrast between official pronouncements and popular practice, they too readily credit Knox's vision of a unified federal law. This aspiration masked the divisions and disagreements *within* that law. Two limitations particularly undercut Knox's project to construct federal sovereignty. One was jurisdictional: federal law formally recognized the existence of other sovereigns—Native nations, states, and foreign empires—who used their autonomy to thwart federal aims. The other was institutional. The crafters of federal sovereignty in the territories were military men who believed, in Knox's words, that "angry passions of the frontier Indians and whites . . . are too violent to be controlled by the feeble authority of the civil power." Civil justice in the territories did, in fact, often thwart the administration's aims, largely because the federal government had opted to recreate there the diffusion of legal power characteristic of early America. But Knox's attempted militaristic solution—"the sword of the Republic only," he argued, "is adequate to guard a due administration of Justice, and the preservation of the peace"—ensured contention rather than compliance. This controversial approach converted the question of justice for Natives into a heated struggle over the scope of federal authority in the territories, a contest in which territorial institutions of civil power offered opponents multiple sites to resist strong executive action.[7]

Yet these controversies and resistance also belie a simple story of failure. The Trade and Intercourse Acts did not end centuries of violence and discord, as their drafters hoped. But they did channel contentions over Indian affairs into federally defined legal language and fora. This, too, was federal sovereignty of a sort, and it profoundly shaped legal debates over Indian affairs for the centuries that followed.

Fixed Principles

In the American Revolution's aftermath, Natives and non-Natives in both the Ohio and Tennessee Valleys seemed trapped by violence and recrimination, as each group bitterly recalled horrors committed against them. Angry, hateful words about Indians readily came to the lips of Anglo-Americans in the territories. "I have so repeatedly been an Eye witness of the Sufferings of the people in the western country arising from the Savages," one Ohio River traveler wrote James Madison in 1790, "that when I think of an Indian, my Blood runs warm in my veins and I feel irreconcilable to those Blood thirsty miscreants." He continued: "[W]as the power in my hands they shou'd utterly be extirpated from off the face of the earth."[8]

Such vituperative, exterminatory rhetoric directed against "all bearing the name of indians" was typical of post-revolutionary political culture, as newspapers, speeches, and correspondence all luridly depicted Native atrocities in what historian Peter Silver has labeled the "anti-Indian sublime." Such narratives of white trauma at Native hands conveniently justified anti-Indian violence and dispossession, but they also reflected genuine suffering. According to "respectable evidence," between 1783 and 1790 Native raids had reportedly killed, wounded, or taken prisoner fifteen hundred U.S. citizens along the Ohio River and stolen $50,000 worth of property. Meanwhile, in the Southwest Territory, similar raids supposedly killed over four hundred territorial citizens. Nearly all the land around Nashville "has been stained with the blood of the Inhabitants since my arrival in this Country," Governor Blount reported.[9]

No less an authority than President Washington recognized, however, that such narratives of Native perfidy and Anglo-American victimhood were "one side only of a story": Natives, he observed, "have no Press thro' which their grievances are related." For their part, Native leaders insisted that if "both sides" were heard, "it would be found that the guilt of the American people would far overbalance theirs."[10]

Natives in both the Ohio and Tennessee Valleys had good reasons for this view. Although Natives and whites alike engaged in brutal violence, Natives in both regions had experienced genocidal Anglo-American attacks without parallel in Native culture. Such horrific violence increasingly led Native communities in the Ohio Country to refer to all Anglo-Americans as "Shemocteman"—which "signifies Long Knifes"—evoking a "warlike hostile people." "I know the *long knives*," one Delaware leader stated. "[T]hey are not to be trusted." This leader spoke eleven months before the Pennsylvania militia, in 1782, cold-bloodedly massacred nearly one hundred pacifist Christian Delawares in the Ohio Country.[11]

Both Natives and non-Natives, then, could point to profound sufferings at each other's hands, and both felt justified in their vengeance. To the untutored eye, this constant tit-for-tat bloodshed between non-Natives and Natives was "lawless violence." But many federal officials thought they knew better. They argued that the frontier's legal problem was, not law's absence, but the dominance of the wrong kind of law—what officials dubbed "the Savage principle of retaliation" or the "Indian Construction and Operation of the Law of Blood for Blood."[12]

Anglo-Americans regarded retaliation as the foundation of what they understood of the Native legal order. They believed that Indigenous law required that murders be avenged by killing those from the same clan, nation, or ethnic group as the killers, even if those so executed bore no personal responsibility, a practice Anglo-Americans dubbed "taking satisfaction." This interpretation was a reductive reading of diverse Native practices more focused on restoration and reciprocity than on vengeance; in practice, compensation or negotiation often mitigated further bloodshed. Yet Anglo-Americans' caricatured retribution as the core of Native law. "The passion for revenge implanted in the earliest infancy of a Savage mind, and cherished by the force of habit," Henry Knox reported, "is almost uncontroulable." Knox may have derived this understanding from Governor William Blount, who took great pains to explain to Knox the Cherokees' "Clanish Law" mandating "Blood for Blood."[13]

Federal officials distinguished this perceived Native law of retaliation from Anglo-American law, in which society adjudicated the guilt and innocence of individuals, not groups. "We do not permit an individual who has been wronged to be his own avenger," Henry Knox informed Cherokee leader Scolocutta. "This is never allowed among the whites, when the society is well regulated." An army officer similarly told gathered Anishinaabeg that "revenge is never sought for by the Whites."[14]

Such statements were mere pieties. In practice, territorial citizens eagerly adopted what they understood as the logic and the language of their Native neighbors, insisting that vengeance was the appropriate law for cross-cultural conflicts. "Let the laws of retaliation be enforced," one inhabitant of the Southwest Territory argued. Governor Blount similarly reported how victims of Native attacks "thirst[ed] for revenge, or, what is here termed, satisfaction."[15]

But, though retaliation had deep roots in borderlands law, by the 1780s and 1790s it was the subject of vigorous challenge by Native and Anglo-American leaders alike. The critique was twofold. The first was that it was indiscriminate, entirely disconnected from personal responsibility. "Let men die for their own crimes, when they commit such as are worthy of death," one *Knoxville Gazette* writer urged. John Sevier, a prominent citizen of the Southwest Territory and first governor of Tennessee, proclaimed that he held "the principle of retaliation . . . in the utmost detestation"; he sought "not the blood of the innocent, but that of the guilty."[16]

Some Native leaders reportedly espoused the same view. With his dying words, Chickasaw John Morris reportedly urged that punishment for his murder at the hands of an unknown white settler be meted out only to the guilty. And in a story related years later by federal Indian agent Silas Dinsmore, some Cherokees had plotted to kill him as "pay, and good pay" for the senseless murder of an old Cherokee man by some white hunters. Discovering the scheme, the Cherokee leader Bloody Knife berated the conspirators: "[S]uppose a mad dog should bite one of your children, would you kill all the dogs?" In Dinsmore's telling, the "logic was convincing and [the Cherokees] left, looking very sheepish."[17]

But there was an even more pressing critique of retaliation for leaders anxious to preserve peace: it created an endless and self-perpetuating cycle of violence. Under its precepts, Henry Knox observed, "the slightest offence occasions death—revenge occasions," inevitably producing a "merciless war." Knox specifically castigated whites for "exercise[ing] indiscriminate revenge against all persons bearing the name of indians, under the specious pretext of retaliation." This "practice," Knox insisted, must be "annihilated."[18]

Native leaders, too, were increasingly moving to abandon retaliation for the sake of peace. By the late 1790s, both Creek and Cherokee councils had voted to abolish aspects of retaliation; in 1797, federal Indian agent Benjamin Hawkins reported that the Creeks had publicly executed six men, including one white man, for murder, which he stated "gives a hope that the right of revenge might be transfered from private hands to a public jurisdiction." Creek and Cherokee leaders were responding to pressure from federal representatives, but they were also trying to remake their societies to abandon a principle that proved so costly.[19]

Like the Creek and Cherokee Nations, the United States was also attempting to shift the power to punish from norms of retaliation to a public jurisdiction—the federal government. "The right that each party assumes of being judges and prompt executioners in their own cause prevents all effectual interference," Knox insisted, "excepting by a legal coercive power, which shall make the necessary sacrifices to Justice, let them belong to which side they may." In both federal Indian treaties and the Trade and Intercourse Acts, largely drafted by Knox and first enacted in 1790, Knox outlined what such a legal coercive power might look like.[20]

Though brief—the original Trade and Intercourse Act contained seven sections and was barely two printed pages long—the Acts served as the foundation for federal Indian policy, codifying the two principles that Knox and other federal officials believed would secure cross-cultural peace. The first was physical separation. "[D]eep rooted prejudices," Knox argued, held both "by the Whites and Savages," would "ever prevent their being good neighbours." To end violence, the federal government had to separate Natives from whites. Government Blount was besotted with the idea of a river rather than an "immaginary line" as a boundary; for their parts, President Washington and members of Congress spoke wishfully of a "Chinese wall" to divide the two groups.[21]

The Trade and Intercourse Acts did not erect a literal wall, but they did create a sharp legal divide between what the statute labeled "the Indian country"—defined as any "territory belonging to any nation or tribe of Indians"—and regions under state and territorial control, known at the time as "ordinary jurisdiction." From 1796 on, this boundary was written into the statutory text, and crossing it was increasingly regulated. Initially focused on governing traders, later versions of the Act required that *any* person who traveled into Indian country south of the Ohio had to obtain an official passport. Crossing into Indian country to hunt, settle, or survey Native lands was criminalized. The army would enforce these provisions, as the government would establish a "chain of [federal] posts" to police the border.[22]

The Acts' second foundational principle was federal jurisdiction over cross-cultural conflicts. Multiple statutory provisions explicitly sought to prevent "private satisfaction or revenge" by barring both Natives and non-Natives who retaliated from receiving federal assistance. But the laws also went further and sought to codify Knox's leitmotif of justice for both Natives and whites, impartially and vigorously enforced by the federal government.[23]

This was clearest with respect to U.S. citizens. The law subjected them to punishment for a new federal offense consisting of "any crime upon, or trespass against" an Indian committed within "Indian country." Subsequent versions became increasingly punitive, specifying death for murder and harsh penalties, including forfeiture, for crossing onto or surveying Indian lands. They also aggrandized federal authority, providing for prosecution in federal court and authorizing the army to apprehend offenders even outside Indian country. Such provisions led many to regard the statutes as an aggressive, and controversial, assertion of federal power against its own citizens: John Sevier would later denounce the Trade and Intercourse statute as "an infamous act" that "had given more umbrage" to the citizens of the Tennessee Country "than any act ever passed since the independency of America."[24]

In contrast to the strictures applied to U.S. citizens, the Acts did not directly subject Natives within Indian country to federal criminal law. This absence likely reflected the Washington administration's view that the federal government lacked this power, since, as Henry Knox urged, "The independent nations and tribes of indians ought to be considered as foreign nations." Others in the cabinet shared this view. Federal laws were "obligatory on every person" in the United States, the U.S. attorney general opined, "except independent Nations & Tribes of Indians residing on Indian lands," a view echoed elsewhere by Thomas Jefferson. This consensus did not imply an acknowledgment that Native nations were fully foreign: their territory still lay within the United States, federal officials believed, a fact that presented complicated questions of overlapping sovereignty. But, although federal officials debated the scope and nature of federal authority in Indian country, none was so bold as to contend that these nations' presence within the United States alone authorized federal jurisdiction over Natives within this quasi-foreign territory.[25]

Yet the Acts did extend federal criminal jurisdiction over Natives as far as consistent with the nations' quasi-foreign status. They affirmed federal territorial jurisdiction over any Natives apprehended *outside* Indian country, within the states or territories, for crimes against U.S. citizens. They also codified the extradition provisions that appeared in all the era's Indian treaties that required that signatory Native nations "deliver up" Indians who committed murder or robbery against a U.S. citizen, "to be punished according to the laws of the United States." (Notably, the treaties did not similarly subject U.S. citizens to extradition for crimes committed in Indian country, promising only that the federal government would punish such offenders.)[26]

Knox minced no words in suggesting that, if Native nations failed to comply with such obligations, the United States would have just grounds to hold them responsible. Natives as well as U.S. citizens, he believed, had to be shown "the absolute necessity of submitting to the justice and mercy of the United States."[27]

Taken together, the Acts provided what federal officials regarded as a foundational charter for asserting federal supremacy over Indian affairs. Officials distributed embossed parchments of the Acts, in tin containers, to Native nations, while Washington touted the laws to Native leaders as evidence of the "fatherly care the United States intend to take of the Indians." Copies of the statutes were circulated throughout the territories, reprinted in territorial newspapers, and read verbatim by territorial judges to grand juries. The Acts' expansive "legal coercive power" reflected Knox's vision for how federal law would replace the law of retaliation, as the federal government would separate Natives from U.S. citizens and arbitrate the crimes each committed against the other. Over the ensuing decade, federal officials in the territories—governors, judges, and military officers—would struggle to implement these provisions.[28]

Promiscuous Intercourse

Knox's vision of federal sovereignty relied on an account of Natives and Euro-Americans in the territories as two sharply divided and implacably hostile groups for whom separation was the only solution—a view shared, and informed, by Governors Blount and St. Clair. Yet this supposedly hard-headed assessment of territorial realities was partial and misleading. Living alongside each other for centuries, Natives and Euro-Americans in the Ohio and Tennessee Countries had forged extensive ties of trade, debt, and sociability that the advent of U.S. sovereignty strained but did not sever. Violence between Natives and whites resulted not *despite* these relationships, but often *because* of them, as camaraderie blurred into bloodshed. This reality helped doom the federal government's quixotic efforts at separation.

Located in the Illinois Country within the Northwest Territory, the French settlement of Vincennes exemplified this long history of Native-white intermingling, which persisted into the 1790s. The town was a hub for many diverse Native communities: its immediate neighbors, the Piankeshaws, Weas, and Kaskaskias of the Illinois Confederacy, but also Potawatomis, Miamis, Kickapoos, and Delawares from across present-day Indiana and Illinois. Natives from these nations were "continually coming to and going from this place," one Vincennes resident wrote, as they brought furs and skins to trade, often remaining "eight or ten days." Court and church records suggest the close relationships that resulted, documenting cross-cultural debts, Native baptisms, and Indigenous lodgers in village homes. This free mixing of Natives and white residents shocked Anglo-American visitors. Passing through Vincennes, the traveler George Hunter stayed with a man named Smalls. "Here is a considerable resort of Indians," Hunter recorded, "they are constantly thro & about this house at all times, like as many pet Lambs, at present there is a Man, his Squa[w] & child sitting by the kitchen fire."[29]

Similar scenes occurred not only in other long-standing French settlements like Michilimackinac and Detroit (characterized by a "great Resort of Indians") but also in newly founded Anglo-American towns like Cincinnati, where

Winthrop Sargent observed "a number of Indians mixing with the Inhabitants of the Town." Knoxville, created from whole cloth as the federal administrative center of the Southwest Territory in 1791, soon rivaled Vincennes in its residents' intense relationships with neighboring Natives. Much of this conviviality surrounded what one historian described as the "court" of Governor Blount, who freely socialized with Cherokee leaders, spending entire days "devoted to eating, drinking and jocular conversation" and "unalloyed with public cares." During the Treaty of Holston, the Cherokee John Taylor "lived with Governor Blount as one of his family . . . ate and drank at his table as one of his family, and slept by his side." Though Blount's ties were especially strong, such connections characterized Knoxville more generally. Blount's successor, Tennessee governor John Sevier, reported from the town that, "as the Cherokee settlements are in our vicinity . . . they frequently resort among our inhabitants, and particularly at this place."[30]

As had long been the case, sex accompanied these commercial and social connections. Following their French predecessors, some newly arrived Anglo-American men began relationships with Native women. In one instance, an officer at Fort Finney supplied a Wyandot woman, "Young Polly," and her mother with stolen goods from the garrison; he was reportedly planning to bring his paramour to Pittsburgh once his enlistment expired. White women also allegedly became involved with Native men, as when the *Knoxville Gazette* reported that a Philadelphian woman had eloped with a Cherokee called "Young George," and, several years later, that Mrs. Abbott, a military wife, had absconded with a Cherokee after he paid her "great attention." The Cherokees, the newspaper stated, threatened to "continue to take [whites'] wives for pay" for their lands.[31]

These ties between Natives and non-Natives throughout the territories did not obviate questions of power. Rather, as a generation of scholars have emphasized, intimacy reinforced, rather than mitigated, inequalities. Commercial ties ensnared Natives in debt, while officials like William Blount sought to use their friendships with Native leaders to bolster U.S. influence. Cross-cultural sex was especially fraught. White men's relationships with Native women built on long-standing Native uses of sex to integrate and control outsiders, but they also corresponded with Anglo-American men's exploitative views of Native women as sexually available—as when William Blount wished travelers to the Lower Cherokee towns "Great plenty of Cheekamagga Squaws." Newspaper accounts of sex between Native men and white women may well have reflected fantastic projections of white men's sexual panic rather than actual relationships.[32]

But though such tense and intimate links sometimes bolstered Anglo-American power, federal officials nonetheless bemoaned what they called the "too frequent promiscuous Intercourse" between Natives and Anglo-Americans. They believed, accurately, that these connections rarely prevented conflict. If anything, the close ties between territorial citizens and their Native neighbors heightened cross-cultural tension—particularly when mixed with alcohol, which could quickly blur the boundary between conviviality and violence.[33]

Though selling alcohol to Natives was illegal in both federal territories, these statutes were openly flouted, with local officials among the culprits. Ultimately, federal officials, acknowledging that Natives would get alcohol "from some Quarter or other," sought to regulate rather than abolish liquor sales. Consequently, when Natives came to territorial towns, they traded their peltry for alcohol and went on extended benders. Vincennes residents complained that roving bands of intoxicated Natives "destroy[ed] the peace and good order of the Village." One local magistrate reported how a party of "drunken tho friendly Indians" accidentally burned down the house of one of the village's poorest residents; another house, set ablaze for the same reason three days later, was saved only by the federal soldiers from the fort. Violence, too, was common. "Our village is stained with blood every day," Vincennes missionary Jean Rivet reported, with alcohol an "inexhaustible source of quarrels . . . thefts, murders, and disorders of all kinds." Rivet offered a lengthy catalogue: the "son of a great chief" killed by a "negro"; a white man stabbed by an Indian, who was in turn stabbed by another white man; a mother shot at twice by an Indian; a village elder attacked by an Indian armed with a knife. "All these horrors," Rivet lamented, "are the sad consequences of the drunk[e]ness of the savages."[34]

Criminal cases from Vincennes underscore Rivet's link between alcohol and violence, though they demonstrate that Rivet ignored white residents' own role in the drunken mayhem. Vincennes resident Lambeir Burway, for instance, seemed to have a knack for embroiling himself in these brawls. In 1796, his home was the scene of a battery against a Potawatomi known as the brother of Grand Poo, allegedly by Leno Burway (presumably a relative). A year later, Lambeir was indicted for battery after killing another Potawatomi, a "Certain Indian Caled the Leaf." The affair began as yet another drunken tavern brawl in which the Leaf, after employing "a grate dale of insulting Language," drew his knife and stabbed a villager named Rambout. As the Leaf was about to make a second stroke, Burway intervened to separate them, at which point the Leaf attacked Burway and Burway "struk the said Indian with His Knif nere about the senter of his Brest." The Leaf collapsed and was carried to a nearby house by fellow Potawatomi, where he died.[35]

A similarly tangled skein of facts appeared in the prosecutions of James Cooney and Thomas Coulter for the death of a Delaware named George Highland a couple of years later. The alleged crime occurred at Coulter's inn in Vincennes, where a Delaware and a Frenchman had scuffled over a tomahawk. Three or four other Delawares had rushed in to help their countrymen, prompting the "white people" to push them out of the tavern. As the Delawares attacked the windows and doors of the house, Coulter and James Cooney fired into the crowd, at which point "the people cried out that an Indian was killed."[36]

Matters to the south were similar. In 1792, William Blount investigated complaints by the Cherokee leader Unacata, also known as White-Man Killer, that he had been attacked by Knoxville residents. Blount discovered that the Cherokee had been "drinking with some people, in a tavern." A drunken Unacata had insulted John White, also drunk, who struck the Cherokee. Blount concluded: "It was a drinking affair only, and I understood was so settled when the parties got sober."[37]

An incident soon after the Southwest Territory became the state of Tennessee further underscores how quickly alcohol-fueled camaraderie could turn deadly. As recounted by A.M. Hoar to federal interpreter James Carey, two Cherokees, Johny and Samy, passed by Hoar's home to return a horse to its white owner. Sammy was well-known and liked in Hoar's neighborhood, so Hoar "Got Some Whiskey and treat[ed]" the Cherokees to reward their "friendly" act. Soon, Hoar's house was full of people from the neighborhood, all "freely" drinking whisky; everyone was "friendly and in Good Humour."[38]

In the middle of this impromptu party, Barefoot Runion, a small white man, began to "Rastle or Scuffle" with Johny. Johny asked Hoar if Barefoot was not a "bad man," but Hoar told him Runion had simply had "Too Much Whiskey." The wrestling continued, and the two men frequently paused to drink together. Everything appeared to Hoar to be "in freen[d]ship and Diversion . . . Neither did I in the Least Expect Any Mischief."[39]

But, at some point, the situation turned, and the two men began to "fight in Earnest." Hoar intervened, grabbing Johny, but at the same moment Samy—who had been lying drunk on the floor—awoke and began to fight Runion, who threw the Cherokee onto the leg of a stool. Although the fight ended there, the wounded Samy began to complain of stomach pain, and, on his journey home, he died. The affair left Hoar contrite and "Much Troubled"; he particularly "Much Lament[ed] that Too Much Whiskey Was Amongst the people."[40]

The drunkenness, violence, and manslaughter at Hoar's house were not unusual in the territories. As judged by local court dockets, towns like Knoxville, Cincinnati, and Vincennes were hard-drinking, violent places where drunken men, and sometimes women, regularly slandered, assaulted, and killed one another. Alcohol-fueled camaraderie quickly turned to killing even when whites drank only amongst themselves.[41]

But, as Hoar's panicked letter to a federal official demonstrates, even if the violence that occurred between Natives and whites in territorial taverns was quotidian, the wider setting was not. Hoar understood that ordinary conflicts between neighbors took on political and diplomatic importance when set against the broader territorial background of low-level warfare, racial tension, and diplomatic negotiation between Natives and U.S. citizens. Often, it was difficult to tell whether any given death should be regarded as an ordinary crime or an act of war. In Vincennes, for instance, a local magistrate determined that a slain townsman was not a war casualty, as originally thought, but the victim of a local Piankeshaw's "personal resentment" stemming from a "dispute about a Perogue" (a canoe-like boat). The line between a "drinking affair" and warfare proved similarly blurry to the south. At Hays Station, near Nashville, two Cherokees drinking with local white residents "boasted of their war exploits," including killing two white men; both Cherokees were found shot in their camp the next morning. Depending on perspective, this seeming act of vengeance was either a murder, as territorial officials believed, or the continuation of wartime violence, as locals insisted.[42]

Relations between Native and non-Native neighbors were further complicated by the spread of anti-Indian rhetoric throughout the territories. Anglo-Americans moving to the borderlands brought with them an increasingly vituperative, racialized language that soon infected territorial print culture, particularly newspapers. Federal officials interpreted this hatred in class terms, as characteristic of impoverished "ignorant unthinking people." Yet those most likely to espouse anti-Indian rhetoric were often local elites vying for political prominence—William Cocke, the most prominent Indian hater in the Southwest Territory, was a rival of William Blount excluded from office—or recent migrants from the middling sorts: the Cincinnati citizens who offered a scalp bounty during the Northwest Indian War, for instance, or the U.S. Army officers who casually called Natives "Copper faced Sons of whores."[43]

Such views never entirely dominated the territories' political discourse. The *Knoxville Gazette*, the only newspaper in the Southwest Territory, was a battleground where many authors, often assuming Cherokee identities as pen names, rebutted anti-Indian columns; William Blount even had the paper reprint Benjamin Franklin's pamphlet from thirty years earlier condemning the Paxton Boys' massacre of peaceful Natives in Pennsylvania. This contest reflected the reality that anti-Indian views seemed to motivate political fighting—or, as explored later, mass action—more than secretive murders. But distant federal officials wrote and spoke as if all territorial citizens shared and acted on such opinions. Those who live "remote from the seat of government," Secretary of War Timothy Pickering wrote, "do not deem Indians entitled to the common rights of humanity," and so "murder & plunder Indians whenever they can."[44]

Increasingly, as outsiders who fixated on such racial divides arrived in the territories, they helped create the very tensions that fit their preconceptions. In 1797, an Indian agent to the Chickasaws recounted fondly the "long and friendly intercourse" between the nation and the white residents of Nashville. "Some years ago," he recalled, "the Indians had free access to any mans field without the least murmur." But, he lamented, that "is not now the case those that have lately imigrated will not admit of such liberties, [the Chickasaws] are now reduced to the necessity of beging or stealing."[45]

A 1791 conflict in Vincennes highlights particularly clearly how outsiders' racial hang-ups could escalate routine, local drunken arguments into full-blown diplomatic incidents. The affair began when a group of Natives became "intoxicated" at Simpson's tavern, as they reportedly often did. Simpson refused to provide more liquor without payment, "whereon some disputes arose altho' they did not understand each other, and Simpson struck the Indian." At this point Lieutenant Dirck Schuyler of the U.S. Army intervened. Schuyler—already known to his commanders as a bad egg given to "continual drunkenness" and "other base conduct"—had also been drinking at Simpson's along with some "unworthy" companions. These men seized the struck Indian and paraded him through the streets "in a riotous manner," only to have the Indian escape.[46]

The dispute might have ended as yet another drunken fight, but Schuyler and his companions pressed on. The arrival of Anglo-Americans disdainful of both Natives and French settlers had riven Vincennes with ethnic tensions, and Schuyler and his companions now uncorked these discontents. Attacking the house of local *habitant* Joseph Andre, Schuyler and company beat Andre's pregnant wife, fired a pistol into the door, seized Andre's son, and called for the death of the French, shouting, "Yes, kill them, kill them." The rioters then proceeded to the house of another *habitant* who served as a federal Indian interpreter, where they seized "an Indian and his Wife and Children" and dragged them to the guardhouse.[47]

At this point, town residents intervened, fearing Natives' reaction: "alarmed" local Natives had already begun to mass ominously opposite the village. The magistrates pleaded with Schuyler to release the Indian, emphasizing the "extreme Weakness of the Village" and the need to "conciliate as much as possible the affections of the Indians," who could "ruin" the town. After Schuyler acquiesced, villagers pleaded with neighboring Natives "to forget the whole Affair," emphasizing that Schuyler and his companions had been indicted before the local courts. In the end, Schuyler was cashiered and threatened with court martial; he opted to resign instead. A precarious peace persisted in Vincennes.[48]

The Schuyler incident illustrates why the vision of a strictly enforced separation—a "Chinese wall"—was so flawed. In the territories, Indian country and "ordinary jurisdiction" bled imperceptibly together; ostensibly Anglo-American towns like Vincennes, Nashville, and Knoxville were also central sites of Native diplomacy and trade. Natives and non-Natives in the territories did not always like each other, but they also acknowledged the commercial, social, and sexual entanglements that bound them together. They recognized that cross-cultural violence, like territorial violence more generally, often resulted from a potent mix of alcohol, personal disagreements, and happenstance, and often argued, as A.M. Hoar insisted in the death of Samy, that the ensuing deaths were inadvertent.[49]

Yet such firsthand knowledge was often lost when reports of local violence spread. Preoccupied with diplomacy and Indian affairs, federal officials fixated on divisions between opposing racial and national categories, and assumed that borderland residents did, too. Once this narrative of borderland violence as a product of racial hostility was established, it was remarkably durable. Violence became evidence of racial hatred, which then allowed intent in any cross-cultural crime to be inferred. This narrative was self-fulfilling. As more and more people like Lieutenant Schuyler—both an outsider *and* a federal officer—came into the territories, they brought with them an understanding of the territories as divided into separate and hostile racial groups. In the process, their actions helped transform the everyday violence of the borderlands *into* political violence intended to convey overt racial meaning.

Legal Coercive Power: Prosecuting Natives

Knox's second principle, the establishment of federal jurisdiction over crimes between Natives and whites, proved equally ineffective. The problem was not lack of effort. Many territorial officials shared Knox's vision of colorblind justice under federal law: "[W]e are determined to obtain the same Rule and make no Difference between Red and White People," Winthrop Sargent told Anishinaabe representatives gathered at Michilimackinac. This was not mere rhetoric, as Sargent and other officials intervened in dozens of cross-cultural crimes in the territories.[50]

Yet the federal government largely failed in its efforts to punish Natives as well as U.S. citizens for crimes committed against each other. The reasons were broadly similar, as formal as well as informal limits restricted the scope and reach of federal law. But the nature of these limits differed in the two cases. In prosecutions of Natives, jurisdiction proved the principal constraint, even as the legal infrastructure of territories itself thwarted federal efforts to hold U.S. citizens accountable for violence.[51]

On July 24, 1794, John Ish was killed and scalped while at his plow on his farm eighteen miles from Knoxville. The white settler's killing, William Blount stated, "much exasperated the Frontier People." On August 1, a territorial Court of Oyer and Terminer in Knoxville convicted Abongphohigo, a Creek Indian, for Ish's murder. He was hanged three days later. "Your Muscoga acquaintance took a civil swing," a territorial resident reported to federal Indian agent John McKee. "[H]e died with firmness."[52]

Abongphohigo's trial and execution was likely the first time in U.S. history that the federal government exercised criminal jurisdiction over an Indian. Federal officials celebrated it as "an example, worthy of imitation," of how federal authority could replace retaliation to punish Native violence. McKee argued the conviction would "spare the innocent from the rage of the exasperated frontier inhabitants." In a grand jury charge, Territorial Judge Joseph Anderson insisted that "the late punishment of the Creek Indian, for the murder of Ish," showed citizens that they must "not be your own avengers . . . but rest your hope on the due administration of the laws." And Treasury Secretary Alexander Hamilton praised the proceeding as "an example of justice and fair dealing" in urging Georgia's governor to adopt similar measures.[53]

Yet *United States v. Abongphohigo*, was also the *only* recorded prosecution of a Native in the Southwest Territory. The Northwest Territory was similar: records survive of a single capital prosecution, *United States v. Wapikinomouk*, that occurred just as Vincennes was transitioning from an outpost of the Northwest Territory to the capital of the new Indiana Territory. Understanding why events that federal officials believed so worthy of emulation occurred so rarely requires digging into the circumstances of the two cases.[54]

The accounts of Abongphohigo's trial—a brief court record and a slightly fuller newspaper report—suggest a court that adhered scrupulously to legal process. Abongphohigo was indicted by a grand jury for murdering Ish "feloniously willfully and with malice aforethought." When the indictment was translated to Abongphohigo, he reportedly "confessed," but the court, "willing to afford the prisoner the benefit of trial by a jury, (permitted him to withdraw his plea) and plead not *guilty*." A petit jury of territorial citizens was sworn, and Abongphohigo had counsel assigned by the court. After hearing the "fullest testimony" (which does not survive), the jury voted to convict. Territorial Judge Anderson then pronounced the sentence of death in the "usual form."[55]

The case's most significant legal issue was jurisdiction. The indictment stated that the Creek's crime was "contrary to the laws of the United States and Treaties of peace made with the Creek Nation and against the peace and dignity of the United States." Interpreting, James Carey explained to Abongphohigo that in the Treaty of New York "it was agreed that if any Creek Indian or Indians should commit a murder upon any citizen of the United States, he or they should be given up, and tried according to the laws of the United States." Abongphohigo replied that he was "well acquainted with the talk that was held at New York, for it was well sung in their ears by the chiefs after their return to the nation: But that the Upper Towns had thrown away that talk, and taken up the hatchet." Abongphohigo's reply was an implicit jurisdictional rebuke to the court; it suggested that the Upper Creeks, at least, had never ratified the treaty, and so it could not bind them. But this jurisdictional wrinkle did not attract any attention from the court.[56]

Federal law would likely have permitted Abongphohigo's prosecution even absent the Treaty of New York, however, since Ish's killing occurred within lands ceded at the Treaty of Holston—that is, within the Southwest Territory's "ordinary jurisdiction." International law of the time suggested that a nation's courts presumptively enjoyed jurisdiction over all persons within a nation's territorial limits regardless of nationality. Two years after Abongphohigo's execution, Section 14 of the 1796 Trade and Intercourse Act specifically affirmed the power of "legal apprehension or arresting, within the limits of any state or district, of any Indian" who had "come over or across the [] boundary line, into any state or territory" and stolen from or killed inhabitants there.[57]

Abongphohigo's trial, then, performed a triumph of federal law and jurisdiction. But this was only a facade, as Abongphohigo's subjection to federal criminal jurisdiction was due almost entirely to Cherokee law. The most important legal issue was not what happened to Abongphohigo in the Knoxville courtroom, but how he got there in the first place.

After Ish's death, two territorial militia leaders, Major King and Lieutenant Cunningham, had pursued the killers. They had followed the trail into the Cherokee Nation, but proved incompetent woodsmen and reportedly missed their chance to capture the Creeks seen with Ish's scalp. The influential Upper Cherokee leader Scolocutta, also known as Hanging Maw, offered aid, dispatching eleven Cherokee warriors, including his own son Willoe, to "overtak[e] and punish[] the Murderers of Ish." Following information from Cherokee villages, the party found and surrounded one of the Creeks—Abongphohigo.[58]

The question was what to do with the captured Creek. No one seemed to think of his apprehension in criminal-law terms—there was no warrant and no civil officer. Governor Blount himself had invoked borderland custom, not federal law, when he informed the Cherokees that they could either kill the murderers themselves or bring them Knoxville, where he would have them "put to death," not tried. It was not even clear, at the moment of Abongphohigo's capture, who should take the Creek prisoner. The Cherokees urged King to "kill or take him," likely because they considered the Creek as the enemy of the United States and so deferred to the Anglo-Americans. But King refused to do so, instead arguing the "propriety of *their* doing one or the other."[59]

King's unexplained hesitation is nonetheless revealing. Federal jurisdiction within Cherokee territory was tenuous, since, as we have seen, the federal government generally regarded Indian country as a foreign jurisdiction. Territorial citizens sometimes attempted to use this status to their own advantage. Robert Slaughter, charged with the 1798 murder of Joseph Hardin, argued that the alleged crime had occurred "on the Indian Lands, without the jurisdiction of this

Court and within the limits of another nation at the time the offence is charged to have been committed"; his success is unclear. In 1794, when Zachariah Johnson sued Charles Raygan for an assault that happened on Cherokee lands, Raygan's attorney argued that the lands where the tort occurred were "out of the protection of the United States." Raygan's argument failed, but not because the court disputed the foreign status of the Cherokee Nation. Rather, as the Trade and Intercourse Act suggested, the federal government *could* exercise jurisdiction over citizens of the United States even outside federal territory: as Johnson's attorney argued, assault and battery "is [a] personal action and always follows the person, is not local," and therefore within the scope of the territorial courts' authority over U.S. citizens.[60]

This absence of federal territorial or personal jurisdiction to apprehend Abongphohigo, a noncitizen, likely explains King's deference to the Cherokees within their own territory. Ultimately, Willoe, Scolocutta's son, bound Abongphohigo and brought him to the Tellico Blockhouse, a federal outpost within Cherokee territory. What followed further conformed to Cherokee, not Anglo-American, legal norms. Agent John McKee recorded how the Cherokee leader Middle Striker grabbed the prisoner, lifted him up "as high as he could, [then] dashed him with great violence on the ground, exclaiming, 'That is the way I shake hands with my enemy!'" When McKee managed to dissuade Scolocutta from scalping the prisoner alive, the Cherokees snatched Abongphohigo's warlock instead, "with which they danced the scalp-dance all night, and used all the ceremony of exultation commonly practiced among Indians on the death or capture of an enemy"; some of the territorial militia even came and "joined in the war dance." Only the next day, when the Cherokees escorted the prisoner to Knoxville, did the machinery of territorial law begin to operate.[61]

Abongphohigo's capture also reflected Cherokee, rather than federal, agendas. Anglo-Americans recalled the Cherokees as willing policemen "breath[ing] the keenest spirit of revenge for the death of Ish," but their eagerness likely had a different cause: the upper Cherokees were reportedly "highly exasperated" with the Creeks "on account of the many injuries [they] ha[d] received." The Cherokees also saw an opportunity to solidify their relationship with the United States. Willoe received a new rifle from McKee, while Scolocutta repeatedly cited the arrest to remind U.S. officials of Cherokee service—and his own importance within the Nation. When William Blount distributed goods, Scolocutta pointedly asked whether these items would go to Cherokees who killed whites or to those "who had given proof of their friendship to the United States by taking [a] Creek." Blount got the message, ensuring that Scolocutta and his allies received "the greatest share."[62]

The elaborate display of legal supremacy in the Knoxville courtroom sought to obscure federal dependence on Native jurisdiction and law. Yet Abongphohigo's only recorded words stripped away this veneer. Asked whether there was any reason the judgment of the court should not be pronounced upon him, the Creek replied:

> he had not any thing; that he come out with an intent of killing and stealing or being killed; that he had killed the man for which he had been tried; and that it had been his misfortune to fall into the hands of the whites; but that he should escaped them if it had not been for the Cherokees; and that if he was now put to death there was plenty of his nation remaining to revenge his death.

As Abongphohigo's statement revealed, that the real legal work had been done on the Cherokee path to Ocoee, not in Knoxville. For all the pomp of Anglo-American legal culture, it was Native law and agency that had led to Abongphohigo's trial and execution.[63]

Abongphohigo's framing of the trial also proved a more accurate harbinger of its consequences than federal officials' anticipation of a new model of federally administered justice. Mere weeks after Abongphohigo's execution, Creeks demanded that the Cherokees "deliver[] up" Middle Striker and Willoe "in satisfaction for the Creek, who they apprehended." The Cherokees had known and feared that their actions would "draw the Creeks upon them." But now, when they appealed to federal Indian agents for protection as a result of their support for the federal government, they were met with silence. This failure of the United States to adhere to Native legal norms might suggest why Abongphohigo's trial was both the first and *last* instance an Indian was prosecuted in the Southwest Territory.[64]

In *United States v. Wapikinomouk*, held in Vincennes, the defendant, a Delaware, was tried for a Court of Oyer and Terminer for murdering a white man named Harrison. The proceeding was more cursory than Abongphohigo's trial. The indictment alleged murder aforethought in violation of territorial law; although the Treaty of Greenville arguably also authorized jurisdiction, treaty law was not mentioned. Corroborating testimony came from a fellow Delaware, Johny, who was "Sworn with an uplifted hand after the Custom and manner of the Indians." It is unclear whether Wapikinomouk had counsel. The Delaware pleaded not guilty, but the jury convicted him. Wapikinomouk was hanged on Monday, November 23, 1801.[65]

Unlike in Abongphohigo's prosecution, however, extensive testimony about the crime survives, in the form of two pretrial interrogations of Johny and Wapikinomouk, conducted by two judges of the court. These statements offered a largely consistent account of the killing.[66]

According to this testimony, the crime mirrored much cross-cultural violence in territories. It began with camaraderie: Wapikinomouk, Johny, and a third Delaware, Matayhikan, had been traveling together south of the Ohio when they encountered Harrison. Harrison asked to purchase some venison, but Wapikinomouk hospitably shared the meat for free, at which point Harrison "gave them all a drink of Wiskey & then a Second & third," until they all "got drunk." The four men decided to continue together north of the river. While they waited for the ferry, Harrison and Wapikinomouk "jumped & wrestled," just as had happened at A.M. Hoar's house; Johny testified that it had been done "in good humour & [with] no Appearance of Disgust or Resentment." Once on the other side of the river, the four mounted men proceeded single file. At some point someone shouted "Let's kill him" in Delaware. Johny whipped around to hear two rifle shots and see Harrison fall from his horse.[67]

The crime was remarkable for its seeming lack of motive. Asked whether there had been any cause for "Quarrel or misunderstanding," both Johny and Wapikinomouk insisted that there was not. Wapikinomouk, perhaps self-interestedly, testified that Harrison "was killed when they were drunk and without any Cause of hatred or ill will." But Johny confirmed Wapikinomouk's account. The murder, he told the judges, was entirely unplanned. Johny had even "upraided" the other Delawares, noting that Harrison had "used them well and gave them to eat & drink with him."[68]

But it was what happened *after* the killing that explained how Wapikinomouk and Johny ended up in the Vincennes courtroom. All three Delawares had continued to Cape Giradeau, a town on the Spanish side of the Mississippi, where they told Johny's uncle, a Delaware leader, what had happened. The uncle then told the Spanish commandant, and the Spanish and the Delawares handed over Wapikinomouk for prosecution. But the third Delaware, Matayhikan, remained at Cape Girardeau, "not delivered up." The attorney general of the Northwest Territory ordered that a writ be issued for Matayhikan's arrest, but the command had no force in Spanish territory, and Matayhikan never seems to have been captured. In short, Wapikinomouk's prosecution, just like Abongphohigo's, demonstrated how much the exercise of federal criminal jurisdiction over Natives depended on the cooperation of other jurisdictions. Wapikinomouk faced federal law only because the Delawares and the Spanish decided that he should, while Matayhikan—the allegedly equally culpable—escaped punishment.[69]

Taken together, the trials of Abongphohigo and Wapikinomouk underscore what many historians have illustrated: how, proclamations of supremacy notwithstanding, federal authority in the borderlands remained tentative and dependent on Native power. But they also reveal the jurisdictional limits that federal law imposed on itself. The early federal territories were literal borderlands, in that they contained and coexisted alongside the territories of other, formally recognized sovereigns. Despite federal officials' efforts, these highly porous borders were often notional for those who freely crossed them. But they mattered in law, where they were not only real but constitutive, defining what was legally the United States and what was not. Federal law did not govern Spanish Louisiana. It also did not apply to Indians in Indian country, which the United States acknowledged as a jurisdictionally separate space outside direct federal control. As a result, even when events conspired to gift power to federal authorities, Anglo-Americans hesitated to assert jurisdiction over Natives within legally recognized Native territory.

Legal Coercive Power: Prosecuting Territorial Citizens

Prosecutions of Natives in territorial courts were rare, but prosecutions of territorial citizens for crimes committed against Natives were not: dozens occurred in both the Northwest and Southwest Territories. This surprising discrepancy reflects the jurisdictional limits described earlier—territorial courts could more readily compel territorial citizens to appear—but also the dedication of territorial officials, many of whom sincerely sought to secure what they regarded as justice for Native victims.[70]

However, few of these prosecutions produced convictions. Crime against Natives was rife in the territories: citizens of the Northwest Territory had "abused, cheated, robbed, plundered, and murdered [Indians] at pleasure," Governor St. Clair fulminated. Yet, he continued, "I have never heard that any person was ever brought to due justice and punishment"—a lament echoed by federal officials in the Southwest Territory.[71]

In explaining their inability to enforce federal law within an exclusive federal jurisdiction, officials blamed racial bias against Native peoples. "It is the prevailing opinion of the people in general upon the frontiers, that it is no harm to kill an Indian," a federal military officer informed Henry Knox. Knox himself complained that the "frontier people generally" not only "lessen the criminality" of "killing of peaceable Indians" but in fact "confer a degree of merit" on the crime. Even President Washington blamed citizens' "jealousies and prejudices" for preventing criminal punishment of crimes against Natives.[72]

Such racial animus mattered because the federal government, despite making territorial government largely independent of popular sovereignty, had retained aspects of local governance. Juries proved a particular challenge, routinely nullifying federal efforts to prosecute crimes against Natives. Yet such acquittals entangled Indian-hating with other motivations—in particular, the controversial status of federal authority in the territories. Federal officials in both the territories and Philadelphia saw securing justice for Indians as a test of federal might. When territorial citizens responded by resisting what they saw as heavy-handed federal measures, they acted as much from their contempt of federal officials as from their hatred of Indians. In fact, the questions of Native status and federal power became increasingly inseparable as territorial citizens and officials battled in the territories' diverse legal fora. These struggles subsumed Native interests and voices—or, perhaps worse still, led them to be conscripted for partisan advantage by the defenders of federal authority.

Unlike any other local government in the United States, territorial government was, as territorial citizens complained, "under governours who are in every sense independant of the people." Under the first stage of territorial governance, the president or the governor appointed every official in the territories, and, except for the appellate judges (who enjoyed lifetime tenure), could dismiss them at will, too.[73]

The territorial courts also reflected this concentration of federal power. Although they resembled the two-tier system of local and appellate courts found in most states, these courts were overseen by federally selected judges who exercised what one such judge called "federal Jurisdiction." They were the territories' ultimate legal authority, since federal law did not authorize appeal to the U.S. Supreme Court.[74]

These courts' federal nature was significant. As national institutions, federal courts were intended to transcend local bias—including, according to the Washington administration, anti-Indian sentiments. President Washington referred Senecas from upstate New York to the federal courts for justice, while St. Clair argued that Pennsylvanians who attacked Natives "should be prosecuted in the Federal Court." From 1793 onward, the Trade and Intercourse Acts codified this approach while underscoring the commonality between the territorial courts and the federal courts that scholars call Article III courts, which existed only in the states. Under the Act, territorial appellate courts and Article III federal circuit courts held jurisdiction over capital offenses, while the territorial courts and Article III federal district courts heard all other violations of the law.[75]

Many territorial judges and officials did assiduously try to punish crimes against Natives. Territorial judges charged grand juries on the need to protect Native peoples, while Governors St. Clair and Blount pressed for prosecutions. For unelected federal judges and officials, this advocacy was expedient, as it might ingratiate them with their superiors in Philadelphia. But insulation from local pressures also allowed federal officials, in their view, to assess the situation impartially. Prosecuting Indian killers was both "humane" *and* "political," in the eighteenth-century sense of good policy: by "convinc[ing] the Indians that we mean to do justice," federal punishment would "prevent retaliation upon some innocent persons."[76]

This sincere commitment to protect Native peoples partly reflected federal officials' class position: they regarded Natives through the haze of patronizing pity that the well-born felt for the weak and helpless. "As we are now powerful and more enlightened than [the Indians] are," Knox wrote, "there is a responsibility of national character, that we should treat them with kindness and even liberality." Noblesse oblige translated into a sense of official duty. As Natives "are less capable of Seeking Legal redress for wrongs don them then other people," Judge Putnam charged a Marietta grand jury, "it is the more incumbent on all officers of Government and Courts of Justice, ex oficio, to seek out and bring to punishment those who may have ben guilty of Trespasses against them." This same class prejudice also led federal officials to distance themselves from virulent anti-Indian views, which they disdained as vulgar. As part of the "dispassionate and enlightened part of mankind," officials read territorial citizens' overheated rhetoric skeptically. "[T]hough we hear much of the Injuries . . . committed by the Indians upon the Whites," St. Clair wrote, that "equal if not grate Injuries are done to the Indians by the frontier settlers of which we hear very little."[77]

If territorial law had simply reflected the will of officialdom, then, crimes against Natives might have received swift and decisive punishment. But, even where law ostensibly flowed from a single sovereign, federal officials found that checks on their authority thwarted their aims.

One challenge closely resembled the difficulties that bedeviled federal efforts to punish Native criminals: jurisdiction. Like Natives, territorial citizens readily took advantage of their borderland location to hop jurisdictions: Kentucky was an especially common destination. The U.S. Constitution bound states to extradite such criminals, yet, like Native leaders, popularly elected state governors pursued their own agendas and crafted legal theories to evade compliance. Relying on direct federal force also proved abortive. In one instance, federal soldiers entered a Kentucky town to try to apprehend a man who had allegedly murdered a Native in the Northwest Territory. The result was a near riot, with the Kentuckians' complaints prompting a court-martial for expedition's commanding officer. Such instances help explain why, despite formal requests and federal efforts, fugitives from the territories were rarely captured or punished.[78]

But the principal restrictions on prosecution came from federal, not state, law. One important barrier was the legal prohibition on Native testimony against non-Natives. Federal officials often fulminated against this restriction as though it were unalterable, but the stricture had no grounding in federal or territorial statute. It stemmed from the long-standing common-law proscription against non-Christian testimony, itself shifting during this period, and did not apply to Natives who could plausibly claim to be Christian. Yet oddly, neither Congress nor the territorial legislatures abolished this common-law rule—largely, it seemed, because of a deep and widespread veneration for the common law, described by the territorial judges as "the birth-right of the citizen."[79]

Territorial officials focused their hostility, though, on another common-law right enshrined in the Northwest Ordinance: that territorial inhabitants "shall always be entitled" to a trial by jury. In the territories, juries seemed to foil every federal effort to punish crimes against Natives. "A Jury will hardly be found" in the Southwest Territory, Blount reported, that would convict for killing an Indian. "There had never been one instance of a white man condemned and hanged by white men, on the frontier, for the murder of an Indian, since the first landing in America," one northern congressman hyperbolically informed Congress in 1795. "No jury would bring the criminal in guilty."[80]

Jurors' refusal to indict and convict criminals for such crimes was a particular bête noir for Governor Arthur St. Clair. In 1795, two Potawatomis were being transported to jail in Cahokia, in the Illinois country, escorted by a militia guard, when they were killed "in open Day Light." Two inhabitants of St. Clair County (named after the governor) were arrested, but even though the "most positive testimony was adduced," the local grand jury refused to indict. Governor St. Clair instructed the prosecutor to try again when the court moved to another location, but despite a "very pathetic charge," the second grand jury refused to indict either, even on the lesser charge of manslaughter.[81]

Informed of such failures, Secretary of War James McHenry responded with resignation: it was "deeply regretted" that such crimes were "connived at by a jury," but this was the "only medium thro' which the Culprits can be punished." St. Clair disagreed: he thought more could be done to "compel jurors to do their duties," including prosecuting them for violating their oaths and levying a "heavy" fine on counties that allowed perpetrators to go free. Such striking attacks on jury independence were evidently too bold for St. Clair's superiors, who declined to adopt them.[82]

Federal officials cited such instances as proof that local jurors were irredeemably prejudiced against Natives. But this explanation proved too much, as local courts and juries did sometimes punish offenders who harmed Indians. A Nashville jury convicted the white settler David Wallace for beating the Chickasaw chief William Glover. As discussed earlier, grand jurors in Vincennes indicted multiple white defendants for violence against Natives even in cases where the testimony supported credible claims for self-defense; the final verdicts in these cases are unknown. And in 1796, the General Court of the Northwest Territory convicted Daniel McKean, a recent arrival from New Jersey, of stealing a horse from a Delaware camp; McKean was ordered to pay a fine, receive thirty-nine lashes, and wear a sign reading, "I Stole a Horse from Indians." Usually full of screeds against St. Clair and Sargent, *The Centinel of the North-Western Territory*—the Territory's sole newspaper—approved of the conviction: it proved that "those who in future shall wantonly injure and irritate the Indians may expect to suffer the just and severe punishment which justice and sound policy demand."[83]

Such instances did not negate the sway that anti-Indian sentiments held among territorial citizens, but they do suggest that such views did not always translate straightforwardly into law. More was at work in the failures of territorial justice for Natives than racial animus alone.

Obligation to the General Government

The indignation that St. Clair and others displayed at the acquittal of Indian killers was not solely, or perhaps even primarily, about solicitude for Native peoples. These decisions so angered federal officials because they saw them an affront to them and to the federal government—and they were likely right. By eliminating elections, legislatures, and other venues for popular expression, unified federal rule in the territories had left the courts as one of the only venues to resist perceived governmental overreach—a role for judges and juries that Anglo-Americans' republican mythology valorized. The consequence was that jury verdicts became one of the only ways for territorial citizens to express their discontent with federal policy, especially in Indian affairs.[84]

That, at least, was how Governor Blount—a more astute student of public sentiment than St. Clair—explained jurors' motives in such acquittals to his superiors. "The Indians have killed in the most cruel and inhuman manner our nearest and dearest Friends," Blount ventriloquized on behalf of such jurors, "and Government has made no demand of Blood in Satisfaction." Given these facts, "why should we by our Verdict give Blood either to satisfy the Government or the [Indian] Nation[?]" Blount's linkage between federal government and Native nations suggests how readily many others in the territories similarly conjoined federal and Native interests.[85]

This conflation between federal authority and justice for Natives played out especially clearly in Cincinnati, the seat of Hamilton County. Paradoxically, the town, the capital of the Northwest Territory and U.S. Army's main hub, was also a seedbed for anti-federal sentiment. Partly, this stemmed from Cincinnatians' particular dislike for Governor St. Clair and Secretary Sargent, who found themselves in near open warfare with local juries. After multiple run-ins, Sargent complained that in Hamilton County "the great invaluable blessing of Trial by Juries . . . is perverted to a Curse." Any magistrate who attempted to enforce the law, Sargent complained, would "become the Object of their highest Displeasure"—including Sargent himself, indicted several years later on a tenuous usurpation charge.[86]

But Cincinnati's skepticism toward federal power reflected a more general hostility throughout the Ohio Valley toward a government that many westerners believed privileged eastern interests and pursued policies "calculated only to fill the purses of a few men." When, in fall 1794, many in Pittsburgh—closely linked to Cincinnati by a constant flow of people and goods along the Ohio—openly resisted the enforcement of a federal whiskey tax in the so-called Whiskey Rebellion, Cincinnatians were sympathetic. After a federal military force suppressed the Pennsylvanians, the town's residents, allegedly including federal soldiers, even helped one of the movement's ringleaders escape federal justice as he fled downriver.[87]

Cincinnati experienced its own paroxysm of populist violence against federal policy at the same moment that the Whiskey Rebellion roiled western Pennsylvania—but in the Northwest Territory, such resistance occurred, tellingly, as an anti-Indian riot. It began on the evening of September 8, 1794, toward the end of the Northwest Indian War, as yet another drinking affair. Some Choctaws and Chickasaws, having aided the U.S. Army at the behest of William Blount, were passing through Cincinnati to return to the Southwest Territory. According to subsequent testimony, some of the Choctaws were drinking whiskey and "Diverting themselves in their way," when a Mr. Findley demanded that they go away because they were disturbing a sick person. As the "intoxicated" Choctaws dispersed, one told Findley, "me Major Gen'l"—presumably alluding to his federal military service. Findley did not take this Choctaw's assertion of rank well. He responded, "you may go to hell," and then said it again. In the ensuing scuffle, knives were drawn, and Findley and his accomplices beat several of the Choctaws.[88]

In a town at war, the dispute did not end as a simple fistfight. Rather, a rumor began to spread that the Choctaws had captured a white female child, "naked, bound, and suffering." The story was poppycock; it fit so well with the tropes of anti-Indian rhetoric, and was so well calculated to appeal to Cincinnatians' racial and gender anxieties, that Sargent suspected it was concocted solely to instigate what followed—a "very general Muster of armed men." Parading through the streets firing guns, the men marched to the Choctaw camp to take a Native scalp. There, they faced off against soldiers whom Sargent had hurriedly posted; harsh words were exchanged, but the rioters ultimately left. But some rioters found other targets for their wrath, as unknown assailants fired two bullets into Sargent's house.[89]

Sargent was a whirlwind in response, demanding in person that the rioters disperse, dashing off orders to magistrates and army officers, and issuing a proclamation promising that "every legal exertion" would be used for punishment. But Sargent's hopes were disappointed. A grand jury indicted only two perpetrators for battery: one was acquitted because the principal witness was absent; the other, "by Delay of Process," escaped. In the end, Sargent concluded in a letter to the secretary of state, "the civil authority in Hamilton County is inadequate to afford protection to the Indians." The reason he ascribed was revealing. The grand jury, Sargent lamented, was neither "generally disposed (I believe) to do justice to the red people, or sufficiently sensible of their Dependence upon, and Obligation to the general Government." Hostility toward Indians, in short, was twinned with contempt for federal authority, which were increasingly coming to be seen as the same thing.[90]

Yet it was not Hamilton County's jurors alone who drew Sargent's ire in the riot's aftermath; he was equally infuriated with the county's district attorney, to whom he wrote an angry letter. This frustration was symptomatic of a larger problem that extended beyond juries: despite the formal power of appointment, territorial governors and even cabinet officials often enjoyed little effective control over the territorial judiciary. To find judges on a sparsely populated frontier, St. Clair and Blount had to scrounge among the "limited" "choice of characters" reportedly nonetheless "illiterate and ignorant of law." Often, the governors simply continued in office the same local notables who had served before.[91]

Many of these new "federal" officials proved quite hostile to federal authority. St. Clair and Sargent, for instance, got into a bitter struggle with Cincinnati judges who refused to accept appointments at pleasure. In the Southwest Territory, Governor Blount selected a rising young lawyer—Andrew Jackson—to serve as federal district attorney for the Mero District. Blount instructed Jackson to make "Examples of the first Violators" of the Treaty of Holston at the same moment that Jackson was privately fulminating about the futility of Indian treaties.[92]

Federal officials hoped for better things from territorial appellate judges—selected directly by Congress and the president—but here, too, they were often disappointed. As we shall see, Judge Campbell of the Southwest Territory bragged about living on unceded Cherokee lands in explicit violation of the Trade and Intercourse Act. In the Northwest Territory, territorial judges objected less to federal policy than to its representatives, St. Clair and Sargent. Yet these personal animosities, too, undercut federal aims. Territorial Judge John Cleves Symmes manifested his hatred for the governor and secretary by spouting republican rhetoric that challenged their authority, leading Sargent to grumble that Symmes was taking "an active part to Sedition." Symmes later tried to secure St. Clair's dismissal—an act he claimed would elate "thousands"—by attacking the governor's efforts to secure justice for Natives: the governor regarded it as "[o]utrageous, if a citizen charged with the murder of an Indian, be acquitted by a jury of the country," but he could hypocritically "calmly look on and see citizens Murdered by Indians, without one effort of the executive to bring the murderers to a trial." Although, as we have seen, Symmes elsewhere sought to distance himself from Indian haters, he proved all too ready to ride territorial citizens' favorite rhetorical hobbyhorse—the accusation that federal officials were biased in favor of Natives—to undermine his political enemy.[93]

An even more outré case was Symmes's friend and colleague, Territorial Judge George Turner. Like Symmes, Turner early feuded with Governor St. Clair over land. As a result of this bad blood, when the two Potawatomis were killed in federal custody, St. Clair was all too ready to credit allegations by Turner's political opponents that "the most Excellent Judge approved of the Deed, and took no measures to apprehend the murders." Whatever the truth of this claim, substantial evidence shows that Judge Turner used federal Indian policy to serve his own interests rather than to pursue Knox's vision of impartial justice. In summer 1794, Turner traveled to Vincennes, where he called a special, unauthorized single-judge session of the General Court. This sitting caused controversy from the moment Turner arrived on the dock on the Wabash, allegedly "so drunk he could not ascend without assistance." While in Vincennes, Turner initiated one of the few recorded prosecutions under the Trade and Intercourse Act in the Northwest Territory when he charged the operators of a barge with trading with Indians without a license. As provided under the Act, the sheriff seized the men's silver, red blankets, and knives—which Judge Turner then kept for his own use.[94]

Turner's actions caused a tremendous uproar in Vincennes, and led to the judge's indictment by the grand jury in St. Clair County, as well as complaints to Congress of his "tyranny and oppressions," including the "forfeitures" of "property of citizens quietly travelling on the Ohio." Because of the distance, the attorney general recommended that Turner be indicted before his colleagues on the General Court of the Northwest Territory rather than be impeached. Ultimately, Turner resigned. A jury, meanwhile, acquitted the defendants of the charges under the Trade and Intercourse Act.[95]

Turner's legal contretemps exemplify how intense wranglings could occur even within a polity ostensibly governed by the dictates of a single sovereign. Like his superiors, Turner seems to have envisioned law as command, albeit his own, but this view poorly understood early American legal culture. Particularly in the territories, where other avenues for politics were foreclosed, courts were less instruments of policy than arenas where diverse actors—judges, governors, juries—all jockeyed for power.

Such diffusion of power resulted from the recreation of familiar Anglo-American legal institutions in the territories, which helped secure legitimacy for federal rule. In hindsight, juries and local courts appear so fundamental to early American law that their spread to the territories seems inevitable. And yet, as territorial citizens loudly complained, Congress had excluded them from other supposedly foundational rights. There were alternatives: as we shall see, Henry Knox advocated for juryless courts martial, but this approach went too far even for the strong-fisted Trade and Intercourse Acts. Territorial citizens denounced territorial governance as "a state of such submission & slavery," yet it was arguably still too republican to punish crimes against Natives.[96]

At the same time, and paradoxically, territorial governance's perceived authoritarianism undermined Knox's paternalist efforts to secure what he regarded as justice for Native peoples. Though Knox and other officials sincerely believed in this aim, they tied this goal to the fraught project of establishing federal authority in the territories. As a result, territorial citizens conflated the question of justice for Natives with the scope of federal power. Prosecutions for crimes against Natives became referenda on other concerns: purported federal failures to adequately defend against Indian attacks, resentment over the lack of local autonomy, hatred of imperious federal officials.

Another ironic consequence of this process, also exemplified in Turner's struggles, was the near-complete erasure of the Native peoples whose interests had supposedly motivated the system to begin with. Justice in federal courts converted the traumas and violence that Natives in the territories routinely endured into power struggles among Anglo-Americans. Their testimony barred, Native voices were literally silenced.

The successive versions of the Trade and Intercourse Acts were remarkable for the power and discretion that they granted the executive: the president could craft a licensing scheme for Indian traders, select agents, supply Natives with goods and money, and even employ military force to remove intruders from Indian country. Congress enacted these robust laws with remarkably little debate. But there was one telling moment during the 1793 reauthorization, when Congressman Clark of New Jersey objected to a new provision authorizing the president to remove U.S. citizens from Native lands using "such measures, as he may judge necessary." Such robust and ill-defined executive authority, Clark argued, would "violate the solemn stipulations" in the Northwest Ordinance, which he read aloud on the House floor to remind Congress that the Ordinance governed "all civil and criminal processes" in the territories. Congress ignored him and enacted the provision anyway.[97]

This exchange is doubly revealing: it suggests at once Congress's commitment to firmly establishing federal sovereignty as well as the limits that federal law itself imposed on this effort. In governing Indian affairs in the territories, federal officials were freed from many of the constraints on federal power in the early United States, yet they still encountered substantial obstacles to achieving their goals. Some of the barriers were practical: the vision of tidy separation between Natives and non-Natives did not fit with territorial realities, and Native power forced federal officials to negotiate their authority with Native leaders. But these difficulties also derived, as Clark's comments suggest, from formal federal law. The United States could not readily seize Native criminals in part because it disclaimed jurisdiction over Indians in Indian country. And it found it hard to prosecute its own citizens because, despite rejecting Clark's suggestions, it had nonetheless recreated a governing structure in the territories in which decentralized institutions—juries, local and territorial judges—checked the reach of federal authority even in jurisdictions under ostensibly exclusive federal power.

As a result, the Trade and Intercourse Acts did not achieve what Knox had hoped—to substitute federal for private justice, ending retaliatory violence in the borderlands. But it would be too simple to label them a failure. In the long term, Knox's principles arguably succeeded, albeit in tragic ways distant from Knox's imperialist benevolence. The belief that separating Natives from whites would end interracial violence—a view that regarded "space as a solution to the problem of race," in the words of historian Nicholas Guyatt—came to justify antebellum deportations of Native nations, an expulsion advocated by states but financed and organized through federal "legal coercive power."[98]

This outcome paralleled a broader trend: Knox's vision of evenhandedly applying federal justice against both Natives and U.S. citizens increasingly became a one-sided attack against Native autonomy, as federal sovereignty morphed into the settler sovereignty recounted by historian Lisa Ford. This, too, had roots in the earlier history. As Native power waned, the formal limits on federal jurisdiction in Indian country could be, and were, readily cast aside. By contrast, the structural and institutional constraints on federal power when applied against U.S. citizens continued to doom federal efforts to secure justice for Native peoples. Knox's magisterial vision of federal sovereignty securing impartial justice gave way to a federal government that eagerly directed its power against Native peoples but rarely against its own citizens.[99]

5
Laws of War and Peace

In 1793, the Chickasaw war leader Piomingo wrote to James Robertson, a prominent Nashvillean who had co-founded the city and now served as federal Indian agent and brigadier general of the territorial militia. The two men had forged a close personal relationship—"I often go to Cumberland to see my Friends there," Piomingo boasted—alongside a political alliance. Leader of the anti-Spanish faction among the Chickasaws, Piomingo eagerly pursued ties with the United States to bolster his own status. "Never was a people more attached to a nation," a grateful Robertson observed, "than the Chickasaws are to the United States."[1]

Yet Piomingo found himself baffled by his new ally's passivity in response to what he called the "bad doings of the Creeks and Cherokees"—those nations' near-ceaseless attacks on the Cumberland District. "If we did not know you to be warriors, we should not know what to think of you calling them friends, and treating them as such, when they are continually killing your people," Piomingo told Robertson. "We, the Chickasaws, that are but as one very small house in the great city, the United States, could not bear to throw away, and let the blood of one man pass without retaliation." Another Chickasaw leader told Robertson, "The Creeks boast that your people are not men."[2]

Piomingo insisted that there was only way to end these assaults: violence, not talk. "[M]y brother, I hardly know what you mean by treating with tribes that are always at war with you, and will be, until you whip them"—an event "I hope, will not be long, my friend."[3]

Piomingo's letter encapsulated an intense territorial debate over the meaning of war and peace—ubiquitous, and yet ill-defined, terms in the early American borderlands. Violence, as we have seen, was a routine and intimate aspect of encounters between Natives and non-Natives in the territories, its specter lurking even in moments of calm. It manifested in the individual killings explored earlier, but also in the larger, more organized and overtly political forms that Piomingo described: Creek, Cherokee, and Shawnee raids resisting Anglo-American encroachments; Anglo-Americans' punitive expeditions into Indian country.

Such attacks drew from a shared yet divisive customary legal culture, one that appeared throughout Piomingo's letter and would have been well familiar to Robertson. To justify killing, Natives and non-Natives alike spun narratives of self-defense that claimed authorization from ideas of community and relied

Federal Ground. Gregory Ablavsky, Oxford University Press (2021). © Gregory Ablavsky.
DOI: 10.1093/oso/9780190905699.003.0006

on similar notions of retaliation; both Natives and territorial citizens also constructed identities around martial masculinity. When Piomingo spoke of war, then, he was referring to these borderland practices of violence, developed over decades, that blurred the boundaries between conflict and its absence, and between state and nonstate violence.[4]

Henry Knox and others in the Washington administration did not share Piomingo's definition of war. In their view, the pathological borderlands culture of violence threatened to drag an unwilling federal government into expensive, unjust, and needless conflicts with Native nations. Knox and others instead embraced the conception of war that could be found in the era's dictionaries: "the exercise of violence under sovereign command," "distinguished from robbery, and the like outrages" because it was "limited by authority"—what the influential law of nations writer Emer de Vattel defined as "public war."[5]

Just as the administration attempted to suppress cross-cultural crime, then, it also sought to transform the borderlands by imposing a definition of war that reserved war-making to sovereigns alone. In concrete terms, this meant establishing the federal government as the sole arbiter and source of legitimate organized violence against Native peoples. In this struggle, Knox and others believed they held an especially powerful tool in the newly ratified U.S. Constitution, which granted Congress alone the power to declare war while stripping this authority from states.[6]

The effects of this federal assertion of supremacy differed in the two territories. In the Northwest Territory, events pushed the Washington administration to federalize practices of borderlands violence. The resulting conflict, known as the Northwest Indian War, hugely expanded earlier ad hoc raids against Ohio Country Natives by providing federal resources and legal sanction. In the Southwest Territory, territorial citizens and officials echoed Piomingo's demands for federally authorized expeditions in response to Creek and Cherokee raid—and yet, although hotly debated in the Washington administration, Congress, and Indian country, they never ultimately came.

Much less studied than its well-known northern counterpart, the Southwest Territory's war-that-nearly-was was also arguably more revealing. While the formalization of violence in the Northwest Territory posited warfare between the "United States" and "Indians," violence in the Southwest Territory remained, like most borderlands conflicts, tangled and polyvocal, involving disparate views of territorial citizens and officials, the Washington administration, Congress, and multiple voices within the Creek, Cherokee, and Chickasaw Nations. The brutal struggles for power that followed were also legal battles, as the parties fiercely contested over the legitimacy of violence and meaning of the categories of war and peace.

At first glance, this debate pit Knox's law—the laws of war, of nations, and the U.S. Constitution—against Piomingo and Robertson's law, the customary norms of violence in the territories. Yet translation, not collision, is a more accurate description of this legal contest. The contenders in these debates, Native peoples included, did not reject federal law; instead, they sought to fit borderlands practice into federal officials' new legal vocabulary. All sides fought over who had the best claim to federal support, with territorial citizens, territorial officials, Native leaders, and even Congress strongly contesting the Washington administration's conclusions. By invoking their own interpretations of federal law, they all sought to best Knox and others at their own game.[7]

In the end, as with their efforts to entrench federal criminal law, the Washington administration did not establish federal supremacy over warfare. Despite Knox's hopes, the lines between war and peace, between violence endorsed by the national state and what officials called "unauthorized expeditions," remained unsettled on the borderlands well into the nineteenth century. But they did insinuate federal law into territorial life and Indian country. As some at the time recognized, this was a victory in its own right.

Half War

"Attacks," "depredations," "desultory operations": Anglo-Americans deployed an array of terms to describe the self-organized military campaigns that both Native peoples and territorial citizens launched against each other's towns, villages, and farms. Federal officials used another term that captured their sense of how these actions challenged sovereigns' tenuous authority in the borderlands: "irregular and unauthorized expeditions."[8]

Among Anglo-Americans, such expeditions usually began after a Native raid, when white men from the community gathered and then marched into Indian country to attack the Native communities they deemed responsible. Rarely sanctioned by the government, these expeditions nonetheless claimed quasi-official status: the participants frequently mustered as militiamen and were usually led by a prominent local leader who assumed the title of "colonel" or "general." Yet despite their military trappings, such expeditions more closely resembled the era's mobs than an army campaign. The expeditions' members were typically gangs of ill-disciplined, refractory armed men over whom their purported leaders enjoyed only nominal control. And like rioters, they enforced their own norms of justice and legality, which held Natives collectively responsible for frontier violence. Their attacks often indiscriminately selected victims, falling on whichever Native village they encountered heedless of culpability.[9]

These self-organized expeditions had a long pedigree on both the southwestern and northwestern frontiers, especially as decentralized and cash-strapped state governments relied on them to assert power in the chaotic borderlands. During the Revolution, North Carolinian and Virginian militia had destroyed British-allied Cherokee and Shawnee villages with little outside aid or oversight. But after the Treaty of Paris in 1783, such acts of violence outside the meaningful control of any state or federal government threatened the tenuous peace that officials sought to establish in the territories.[10]

Two expeditions in the 1780s—one in the Northwest Territory, one in what would become the Southwest Territory—epitomized these expeditions' weak structures of authority and brutal willingness to attack Native peoples indiscriminately. In 1786, in response to attacks purportedly committed by the Shawnees, roughly two thousand Kentucky militia under the command of General Logan crossed into the Northwest Territory. One column mutinied and retreated "in vile Disorder," but the other burned seven Shawnee towns. At one town, Melonthy, a Shawnee chief known as a "Friend to the United States," greeted the militia by raising the American flag and displaying a copy of a recent federal treaty of peace and friendship that he had signed. Defying orders, the militia tomahawked Melonthy, killed a half-dozen other Shawnee, and took several dozen women and children prisoner. When the men returned to Kentucky, they displayed Melonthy's flag as a trophy.[11]

Logan's northern campaign had its echo in a 1788 attack led by John Sevier against the Upper Cherokee. Retaliating for the alleged Cherokee killing of the local Kirk family, Sevier and his men destroyed several Cherokee towns and killed thirty people before they reached the town of Chilhowee, where the prominent Upper Town leader Old Tassel, well known to the North Carolinians, raised a white flag. When the militia demanded Tassel be killed anyway, Sevier exclaimed "Shurly Not!" and ordered that the prisoners not be hurt "by any means." But when Sevier walked away, John Kirk, son and brother of slain Kirk family members, rushed in and killed the prisoners, including Tassel. An outraged Sevier returned, denouncing the act as "disgracefull And inhuman." Yet Sevier still had to "beg" his men to spare two other Cherokee captives. Both lived, but Sevier paid a price: his plea for mercy "gave great umbridge to the whole Army, and some said it would be Well done to kill any Man that would Save an Indian." If Sevier would not uphold their norms, the militia would find other leaders who would. Mere days after Sevier's attack, another expedition, led by Alexander Outlaw, destroyed the Cherokee town of Citio, where the militia "inhumanly murdered" the "few helpless women and children" they found.[12]

Such expeditions horrified state and federal governments alike: Virginia's governor condemned the "unjust violences" committed by Logan's men, while both North Carolina and the Continental Congress denounced Sevier's "most cruel and unjustifiable attack." Yet, mere weeks later, North Carolinians defied their governor, again crossing into Cherokee country and massacring inhabitants. Such impotence infuriated Secretary of War Henry Knox: "If so direct and manifest contempt of the authority of the United States be suffered with impunity, it will be vain to attempt to extend the arm of Government to the frontiers," Knox wrote President Washington in response to Sevier's "disgraceful violation" of federal Indian treaties. "[T]he lawless whites will ridicule a government which shall, on paper only, make Indian treaties, and regulate Indian boundaries."[13]

Native communities confronted their own versions of such unauthorized expeditions. The Native raids that scarred Anglo-American settlements in the territories were smaller, handfuls of warriors quickly striking isolated outposts, but they, too, often occurred without the approval of Native leaders, who vainly strove to maintain the peace.

To understand this gap between Native assurances and reality, Anglo-Americans turned to reductive ethnography. Native communities were reportedly "not fond of waging war," yet, for over a century, colonial conflicts had ensnared the Indigenous residents of the Tennessee and Ohio Valleys in near-constant violence, producing a militarism born of necessity. Federal officials and other observers, however, did not attribute Native attacks to hard-earned experience. Some placed violence at the core of an essential Native character, in which warfare served as a primary way to achieve prominence. As long as the "scalp of an innocent white man" or "of a woman, or child" granted a Cherokee "honor," observed John McKee, a federal Indian agent in the nation, "so long there would be war." Other Anglo-Americans cast the struggle as a generational crisis of authority. Henry Knox wrote of "headlong" and "impetuous" "young savage[s]," whom Native leaders complained were "always wanting war"; such men, Knox believed, were incapable of being "restrained by the feeble advice of their Chiefs." Still others thought that the fault lay with Native statelessness. "Nations among whom the Restraints of Law & order are unknown" could not keep peace, Virginian Patrick Henry wrote. "Every Individual amongst them claims a right of gratifying his revenge, his avarice, or ambition in the time & manner he pleases."[14]

Yet in their more candid moments, Native leaders and Anglo-American officials alike acknowledged that the barriers to peace were closely parallel—that in neither society could ostensible leaders compel obedience. "I was convinced it was not the wish of them [the government officials] or my self to go to War," the Cherokee leader Kunokeski wrote, "but was afraid that the Lawless Men living on our lands & the frontiers, Would be the occation of all Mischief." Kunokeski's interlocutor was none other than John Sevier, leader of the Chilhowee raid. Sevier voiced similar sentiments when he acknowledged that it "would be as difficult for the chiefs to prevent those disorders in every instance, as it would be for the rulers in Philadelphia to restrain murders and roberies often committed within that and neighboring cities." As President Washington summarized, the United States could not demand that Native nations "will govern their own people better than we do our's."[15]

Recognizing that neither Native nor Anglo-American governments could enforce a monopoly on violence did not obviate the problem; often, it exacerbated it. Perhaps the most intense challenge it created was attribution. Both Native and Anglo-American leaders repeatedly blamed attacks on a handful of "bad men," yet neither side fully trusted such convenient excuses. After an attack, Native leaders could never be entirely sure whether the United States had secretly sanctioned the violence or if, as federal officials insisted, it stemmed from rogue actors. Native leaders grew unsurprisingly suspicious. "From all quarters, we receive speeches from the Americans, and not one is alike," the Shawnee leader Blue Jacket informed a federal emissary in 1790. "We suppose that they intend to deceive us."[16]

Anglo-Americans found it similarly hard to determine whether a given attack resulted from divisions within Native communities or demonstrated a more general hostility against the United States. "Truth in all enquiries is hard to obtain, and in none in which I have been engaged, so much so as in what respects Indians," Governor William Blount grumbled. The information that filtered to Blount from Cherokee and Creek countries, derived from a network of Native and non-Native informants, was "imperfect and contradictory." Most of what reached him was rumor: vague reports that Scolocutta opposed war, while Doublehead supported it; tales of the "bloody club"—a call to war—being offered the Creek by the Cherokee, or vice versa, and being accepted, or maybe refused; third-hand tales of traders spying white scalps in a town square. Blount was often reduced to scouring the scenes of frontier killings for clues, attempting to determine whether the weapons left behind struck him as more Cherokee or Creek.[17]

Such uncertainty cloaked all interactions between Native and federal leaders in a heavy blanket of distrust and suspicion. Most damagingly, it undercut the most promising tool to secure peace—a shared legal discourse of diplomatic negotiations and treaty-making. For the United States, written treaties, invariably containing provisions promising peace and friendship, were legally binding commitments to abjure violence. For Native nations, the final product was less legally significant than the extensive negotiations and ceremonies recommitting to "national good feelings" that were at the core of a shared law of peace among the nations of both the Native South and in the Ohio Country.[18]

But increasingly, neither Natives nor non-Natives placed much stock in the others' promises—even when formalized in a treaty. At the Treaty of Holston, Cherokee leaders responded to federal officials' assurances that they possessed full authority by observing that similarly solemn prior treaties had been freely "violated." For their part, territorial citizens mocked treaties as a mere "paper Peace." "Experience teach[es] us that Treaties answer no other Purpose," wrote Nashville's young district attorney Andrew Jackson, "than opening an Easy door for the Indians to pass through to Butcher our Citizens."[19]

Disillusioned by words and promises, both Natives and Anglo-Americans began to regard actions alone as proof of good intent. After yet another attack against an unarmed Cherokee village produced yet another federal promise to punish those responsible, the Cherokee leader Bold Hunter spoke frankly to federal officials. "We shall look to you to see it done, and not to our young warriors to say that you told them lies." Federal Indian agent John McKee made a similar demand of the Cherokee. "Peace does not consist in writing or Beads," he lectured them, "but in one and all your people leaving off to kill the Citizens of the United States and steal their property." But neither side could exercise enough control over their "people" to satisfy these demands. The ensuing inevitable failure merely reinforced the sense of both Natives and Anglo-Americans that the other group was fundamentally unreliable and untrustworthy.[20]

This unstable situation on the early American borderlands in the 1780s and 1790s was not war as most Anglo-Americans understood the term—legally sanctioned, organized violence between sovereigns. But it was not peace either, which both Natives and whites, following McKee, defined as the absence of constant bloodshed that marked the territories. It was a more confusing and ambiguous state of affairs: "half peace & half war," as William Blount termed it. Blount, observing that such a conflict had been raging in the region since the Revolution, described it as the "worst of all wars." The people "would prefer an open war to such a situation," one of Blount's correspondents wrote him. "The reason is obvious; a man would then know, when he saw an Indian he saw an enemy, and be prepared and act accordingly." Instead, with neither Native nations nor the United States able to restrain their citizens, the territories existed in a vague netherworld between war and peace marked by ambiguous, secretive, and yet organized violence outside of governmental control.[21]

Just and Lawful Wars

War had propelled both George Washington and Henry Knox to prominence and power, yet both men viewed the violence in the territories with alarm. Pursuit of a "firm peace" with "all the neighbouring tribes of Indians," would, the two men insisted, "be the leading feature of the administration of Indian affairs while [Washington] is at the head of the government." This commitment to peace was both overdetermined and instrumental: both men believed it would be easier, and cheaper, to secure federal aims through diplomacy with Native nations than through costly violence. But, particularly for Knox, insistence on diplomacy also stemmed from a near-obsession with national character. The secretary of war's great fear was that the indiscriminate assaults of territorial citizens against Natives would unwillingly drag the United States into a "general Indian war excited on principles disgraceful to the Government," for which the federal government would ultimately bear both cost and moral responsibility.[22]

This "most ardent desire" for peace did not mean that the Washington administration abjured violence against Native peoples. Knox anticipated that once the federal government had "fully impressed" his magisterial conception of federal sovereignty, justice, and moderation on Native nations, this vision would prove so compelling that "tranquility" would inevitably result. "But if the hostile Indians should, after having these intentions of the government laid fully before them still persist in their depredations," Knox continued, "it will be considered as the dictates of humanity to endeavour to punish with exemplary severity so incorrigible a race of men in order to deter other tribes in future from a like conduct." Knox's principal concern was that any such war, should it become necessary, would "be a constitutional and legislative act."[23]

Both adjectives were significant. "Constitutional," for Knox, mandated federal supremacy. The U.S. Constitution conferred significant authority on the federal government to raise and finance armies, although at the time of its adoption this power remained largely latent: the U.S. Army consisted of only a few hundred soldiers spread throughout the Northwest Territory. Just as important in the context of Indian affairs was the Constitution's restriction on *states*, which it foreclosed from maintaining troops or "engag[ing] in War." Most interpreted this language as barring federally unsanctioned militia attacks against Native peoples: Thomas Jefferson found these provisions "so explicit that no commentary can explain them further, nor can any explain them away." When residents of the Southwest Territory appealed to South Carolina for military aid against the Creeks, the state's governor rebuffed them, citing fidelity to the Constitution's prohibition on state war-making.[24]

Knox's approach was also consistent with the Washington administration's embrace of the law of nations as it sought to establish U.S. legitimacy on the world stage. The administration applied international-law principles to its relationships not just with European powers but also with Native nations, which it acknowledged as sovereign even as it sought to cabin the implications of that sovereignty. On the question of violence, the era's most influential treatise, Emer de Vattel's *Law of Nations*, was unambiguous: "the sovereign power alone is possessed of authority to make war." Vattel sharply distinguished such "[l]egitimate and formal warfare" from "predatory expeditions" that were undertaken "without lawful authority," whose perpetrators could be treated as common criminals and hanged. Knox and other officials recognized that Native nations did not look to Vattel for the law of war, but they still held the United States to this strict standard, believing it would be exemplary. By following the "custom and usage of civilized nations" in warfare, William Blount argued, "such examples must teach even savages to follow them."[25]

"Legislative" was also meaningful. The Constitution specified that the power to declare war rested with Congress, which the Washington administration interpreted to require that Congress approve any attack against Native peoples. The Northwest Ordinance seemingly codified this requirement by restricting violence against Indians to "just and lawful wars authorised by Congress."[26]

For federal officials, then, the Constitution represented a watershed. By granting the federal government alone the power to legitimate violence by deeming it "war," thereby barring the customary practices of military self-help with dubious official sanction. But this restriction was often flouted, as federal military commander John Hamtramck discovered in Vincennes in 1788. Imitating Logan, a band of Kentuckians arrived "after Indians," led by a man "who calls himself a major." When Hamtramck demanded, "by whose authority he came into the teretory of the United States to make war?," the major cited his authorization from the Kentucky assembly. "I did not know any authority but that of Congress who could order a war with the Indians," Hamtramck replied, "in co[n]sequence of which I ordered him in the name of *the United States* to depart immediatly." Yet the Kentuckians, defying Hamtramck's pitiful force of nine soldiers, killed several local Piankeshaws under federal protection and stole their horses. Under the "humiliating necessity" of passively watching this brutality, Hamtramck then had to explain to the horrified Piankeshaws that the attack was "not done by any lafull authority," hoping that this would avoid further bloodshed.[27]

The core of the Washington administration's vision was to decisively end such defiance and enshrine "lafull authority" alone. Instead of justified violence, acts like the Kentuckians' would now, legally, be crimes, subject to punishment under the Trade and Intercourse Acts like any other attack against Native peoples in Indian country. Knox explicitly instructed Governors Blount and St. Clair to prevent such expeditions and, if that failed, to prosecute the violators. In both the Northwest and Southwest Territories, the federal government would decisively assert its constitutional supremacy over war and peace.[28]

Vengeance of the Union

The process of establishing federal supremacy over organized violence played out very differently in the two territories. North of the Ohio, the federal government resolved ambiguity by transforming half-war into full war, co-opting frontier violence in the process. That was not, to be sure, Knox's original plan. Once again, the problem was attribution: Knox believed that the constant raids along the Ohio were the work of what he described as "renegade" and "banditti" Natives, whom he distinguished from the "regular tribes." He proposed a small and carefully targeted punitive "expedition" against them: "[T]he vengeance of the Union is to be pointed only against the perpetrators of the mischief," Knox stressed, "and not against the friendly nor even neutral tribes." This action, the administration believed, was consistent with its vision of the federal government as the impartial arbiter of justice on the frontier. "The [Native] aggressors should be made sensible that the Government of the Union is not less capable of punishing their crimes," President Washington informed Congress, "than it is disposed to respect their rights and reward their attachments."[29]

But the administration had other aims, too: Knox anticipated that the invasion would prove "highly satisfactory to the people of the frontiers," whose support he was eager to secure. This desire to accommodate territorial citizens' demands also extended to means. Knox authorized what he termed "desultory operations"—state militia, serving under local commanders, called into federal service—reasoning that this approach would prove "highly acceptable" to the "frontier counties," since it accorded with their "own propositions." Yet this reliance on borderlands tactics and personnel also reflected federal constraint: the United States had too few regular soldiers to undertake the campaign on its own. The ostensible congressional authorization for the invasion came when Congress authorized the president to call state militia from Pennsylvania and Virginia, including the Kentucky District, into federal service.[30]

In essence, then, what became known as the Northwest Indian War bestowed the sanction of federal law on both the aims and personnel of the earlier unauthorized expeditions. Many in the federal column that marched into the Miami Country in September 1790 under Colonel Josiah Harmar were the same men who had earlier served Logan. And, to the dismay of federal officers, the militia proved just as "totally ungovernable, and regardless of military duty or subordination" under federal command as they had been on prior expeditions. Trapped by Native resistance, Harmar sustained heavy casualties and hastily retreated.[31]

Rather than ending violence, this federal expedition escalated it, as the full-scale federal invasion removed any ambiguity about U.S. aims. Native leaders found it hard to credit Knox's claims of pacific intentions at the same moment federal soldiers were killing Miamis and destroying their towns. Emboldened by the campaign's failure, thousands of Natives stretching across the Ohio Country and Illinois Countries into the Upper Great Lakes united in opposition to the United States and its land hunger.

Knox immediately insisted on another expedition to re-establish federal sovereignty. "[T]he minds of the indians must be impressed with the power of the

United States, as the ground work of that system of justice and mercy, which it will the glory of the general government, to administer to all the indians, within its limits," he wrote as he advocated massively expanding the army to over two thousand regular soldiers. But the Ohio Country's Indigenous inhabitants were not humbled. On the contrary, the following year's larger expedition, led by Arthur St. Clair, suffered an even more ignominious defeat that remains the worst loss that the U.S. Army has ever suffered at Native hands.[32]

Ultimately, Knox's surgical expedition spawned a bitter, costly, multiyear conflict that cost at least $5 million—nearly half the federal budget during this period. Congress began to question the war's expense, with many arguing that it could be waged more cheaply and effectively by relying on militia alone. Learning that "[t]he Indian War is extremely unpopular," Knox and Washington published a self-justifying statement of the conflict's causes asserting that the federal government had been "compelled to resort" to force. Many remained unconvinced. Most in New England reportedly believed the war sprang "rather from a wish on the part of the United States to obtain lands to which they have no just claim, than as a war of necessity"—in other words, they regarded the federal government's efforts as no different from the earlier expeditions that Knox had so loudly condemned and sought to repudiate.[33]

In the end, the Washington administration felt vindicated when Anthony Wayne defeated the Native confederacy with a much expanded and better trained federal army, albeit still extensively supplemented by militia, at the 1794 Battle of Fallen Timbers. Then, even though the administration had loudly announced to Natives and non-Natives that it had no interest in claiming Native lands, the United States forced the defeated Ohio Country nations to cede it a vast chunk of the Northwest Territory—most of present-day southern Ohio—in return for federal payment at the Treaty of Greenville. Federally sanctioned war had resolved the problem of unauthorized expeditions in the Northwest Territory by accomplishing, through federal finance and support, dispossession on a much larger scale than these isolated attacks ever could. Logan and his militia could hardly have asked for more.[34]

The Northwest Indian War cast a long shadow over the Southwest Territory. By 1792, it was clear that the 1790 Treaty of New York with the Creek and the 1791 Treaty of Holston with the Cherokee had not brought peace. Reports of the "murder of some of our fellow-citizens" at Cherokee and Creek hands filled a biweekly column in the *Knoxville Gazette*. Both the Washington administration and territorial citizens looked to the northern conflict for comparison—but they interpreted it in opposing ways.[35]

The Washington administration read the conflict in the Northwest Territory as a cautionary warning: it regarded "the extension of the Northern Indian War to the Southern Tribes" with "extreme reluctance," fearing that another Indian war would be an "insupportable evil." The Northwest Indian War had shown how quickly a supposedly circumscribed conflict could expand: the president, Henry Knox reported, was "exceedingly apprehensive that the flame of War once kindled in that [southern] region upon the smallest scale, will extend itself, and become general."[36]

But Knox had moral as well as practical qualms. The United States had entered solemn treaties with the Creeks and Cherokees, which Henry Knox was loath to violate simply because tribes, like the United States, could not govern their own people. "[I]t is very questionable, while we are unable, in many cases, to execute our own laws," Knox argued, "whether we ought, in justice, to levy a general war upon the Creeks, for the criminality of an individual." Knox wanted to ensure that, if "war must inevitably ensue," it would occur under circumstances that would prove "to all the world that the government or citizens of the United States have not been the cause of bringing it on."[37]

Citizens and federal officials of the Southwest Territory, by contrast, saw the Northwest Indian War as proof that the federal government could be persuaded to allow, and even support, violence against Indians on behalf of territorial citizens. In the territorial legislature's first sitting, it drafted a memorial urging Congress to punish the "faithless and bloodthirsty nations, the Creeks and Cherokees" that argued that only exemplary violence could secure peace based on the rule of law. "Fear, not love, is the only means by which Indians can be governed," the legislators wrote. Until Natives "are made to feel the horrors of war," they insisted, "they will not know the value of peace, nor observe the treaties they may form with the United States."[38]

Territorial officials also lobbied for war. "I know how earnestly the United States wish for peace, no man can be more sincere in that wish than I am," Southwest Territorial Secretary Daniel Smith wrote to Knox. But, Smith continued, "peace is not to be had without a war to convince [the Cherokees and Creeks] of the strength and dignity of our government—that they are not to be violators of treaties with impunity." Blount, too, had become an ardent proponent for war, which, he insisted, would not be "such a bitter Pill as the War NorthWest of the Ohio." With the widespread support of territorial militia and those of the surrounding states, "the total Destruction of the two Nations" would merely be "a Party of Pleasure."[39]

In August 1793, Blount traveled to Philadelphia to make the case for war in person. But despite Blount's "great earnestness," pushing the war with extreme "ardor," the Washington administration punted. Blount was authorized to employ the militia only for defensive operations; retaliatory attacks were explicitly barred. An aggressive campaign was, the president proclaimed, out of his power: after lengthy discussion, Knox, Washington, Hamilton, and Jefferson had "unanimous[ly]" concluded that "measures of an offensive nature" could be sanctioned only by Congress, "who solely are vested with the powers of War" under the Constitution.[40]

This outcome disappointed Blount, who now had to wait while a fractious Congress deliberated. Congress, a frustrated Blount argued at one point, should be "gullatined if they do not declare war." But, perhaps because he was so dependent on the administration, he accepted its verdict and rationale. "It is Congress not the President have the power of declaring war," he told James Robertson, the Nashville militia commander and Indian agent. "Those who are bound must obey. Patience is a virtue which must yet be exercised."[41]

The Break

With their neighbors and friends dying around them, citizens of the Southwest Territory did not feel patient. The only way to end the attacks, they argued, was to destroy the Cherokee and Creek towns directly: "defensive war with Indians" was impossible when Natives were "so wolfish in their manner." With no federal aid forthcoming, territorial citizens returned to older habits of self-help. Throughout 1792 and into 1793, small claques gathered after Native raids and, spurred on by victims' relatives, proposed marching on the nearest Cherokee towns to obtain "satisfaction." Blount repeatedly intervened to stop them, in one instance by securing a warrant against the organizers to prevent a campaign. The governor was nonetheless "hourly in fear that [the people's] thirst for revenge . . . will lead them to break through the Bounds of good order and government, notwithstanding what can be said or done to prevent it."[42]

The "break" that Blount and others feared happened in the summer of 1793—at the very moment that Blount was in Philadelphia pleading the case for an offensive campaign. Before he left, Blount had authorized Captain John Beard and fifty-six militia to pursue the alleged Cherokee killers of two Nashvilleans. Blount had emphatically ordered Beard not to cross the Tennessee River, the most unambiguous boundary between the Southwest Territory and the Cherokee Nation. But, claiming to be following the murderers' track, Beard continued south of the river anyway, to Scolocutta's town.[43]

As we have seen, Scolocutta—also known as Hanging Maw—was among the most prominent Cherokee leaders, and Blount had assiduously cultivated a relationship with him. At the very moment of Beard's expedition, two emissaries from Blount were in the village, meeting Scolocutta to discuss the governor's invitation for a Cherokee deputation to visit Philadelphia. None of these facts dissuaded Beard and his men. At dawn on June 12, 1793, the militia attacked, reportedly targeting Blount's white representatives and the Cherokee indiscriminately. They killed eight or nine people, including a white man named William

Rosebury, and shot Scolocutta in the arm. Running through the hail of bullets, Blount's representatives convinced the attackers, "by hard pleading," to spare the rest of Scolocutta's family and abstain from burning his house.[44]

A much larger expedition proceeded into Cherokee territory the following summer. Led by Major James Ore, who had extensive trading ties with the Cherokee, the expedition of somewhere between 550 and 600 militia was authorized by militia commander James Robertson in Nashville. Robertson had ordered Ore and his men to intercept a rumored Cherokee invasion and, if they did not encounter the invaders, to cross the Tennessee and "destroy the Lower Cherokee towns"—a command that openly defied Blount's orders.[45]

On September 14, 1794, Ore and his men snuck up on the Cherokee town of Nickajack, on the south side of the Tennessee (Figure 5.1), surprising its residents as they ate breakfast. After briefly resisting, the Cherokee made a "precipitate retreat" to the river. Ore's men then attacked the largely abandoned neighboring town of Running Water before returning to Nashville. Ore suffered only a couple casualties, one when a militiaman fell out of a tree. By contrast, fifty Cherokee were reported killed, many of them slaughtered in the Tennessee as they fled for safety; Ore also took nineteen prisoners. Despite Robertson's explicit orders to the contrary, reports indicated that the "greatest portion of the victims were women and children"; an eyewitness reported that the first person killed in the attack was a Cherokee woman.[46]

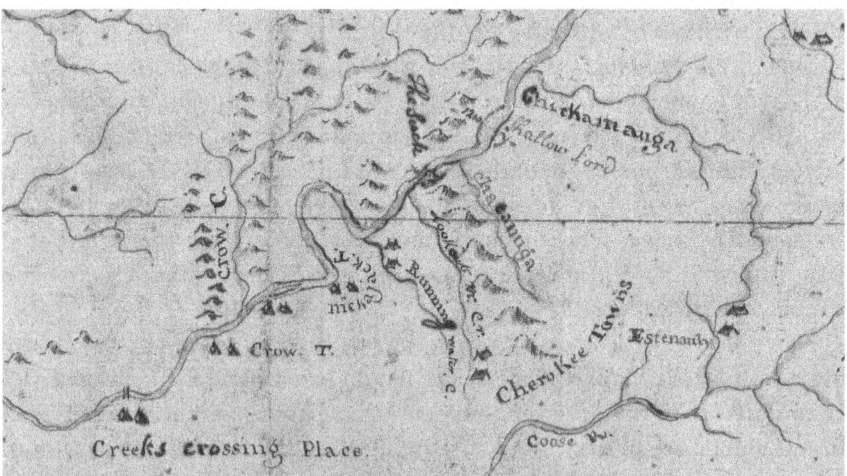

Figure 5.1: Selection from "A Map of the Tennassee Government." The map depicts the town of Nickajack, roughly 100 miles southeast of Nashville, on the Tennessee River alongside other Lower Cherokee towns.

The attacks devastated the Cherokee, whose letters to federal officials in the attacks' aftermath conveyed profoundly felt grief and despair. "I am still among my people, living in gores of blood," Cherokee leader Doublehead wrote after Beard's attack. Word of the attacks also outraged administration officials. The president expressed "extreme concern" at such "violent and lawless inroads," while Knox regarded the attack as a fundamental assault on his vision for the federal government as arbiter between Natives and Anglo-Americans. "Unless such crimes shall be punished in an exemplary manner," he told William Blount, "it will be in vain for the government to make further attempts to establish any plan or system for the administration of Indian Affairs founded on the principles of moderation and justice." He continued: "Treaties will be at an end and violence and injustice will be the Arbiters of all future disputes between the whites and the neighbouring tribes of indians; and of consequence much innocent blood will be shed, and the frontiers depopulated."[47]

Beard's and Ore's indiscriminate attacks quickly came to dominate political life in the Southwest Territory, too: "[I]n no period of my life have I seen the public mind more agitated," observed one resident. Most territorial citizens reportedly supported such measures: Ore's expedition "is spoken of by all ranks as the most brilliant thing that has happened or could have happened for this Country," one resident reported. Already, this observer claimed, attacks had abated, and the Cherokee were pleading for peace.[48]

Territorial officials—men like Blount, Secretary Daniel Smith, and James Robertson—faced the difficult challenge of mediating between these sharply divergent views. Their position was precarious: although their authority ostensibly derived from the federal government, they, unlike Knox and Washington, daily faced the consequences of attempting to enforce unpopular federal policy. "[W]hoever should attempt to preserve peace with Indians," Blount complained, "was instantly denounced as an Indian Friend and the Cry accordingly raised against him." Unsurprisingly, many territorial officers found it easier to defy a distant, and temporary, federal administration than to resist territorial citizens. Many territorial officers had allegedly actively supported the illegal expeditions, while others had remained silent, "countenancing disorder." Captain Beard himself had reportedly once been a staunch opponent of unauthorized expeditions, but had abandoned that position when he "perceive[ed] that *that* was not the [path] to popularity."[49]

Territorial citizens' views also mattered because, just as with individual crimes against Natives, they could manipulate the territorial machinery of law. Attempting to fulfill Knox's demands to bring the perpetrators to "immediate tryal," Secretary Smith sought to use "force of law against [Beard] under the 11th Art. Holston Treaty." But the secretary quickly discovered, "to my great pain," that "to punish Beard by law just now is out of the question"; he could not even prevent Beard from organizing another attack while proceedings were pending. In Philadelphia, Knox resigned himself "that the perpetrators of these violences will escape unpunished," blaming "prejudice against Indians on the frontiers." The Cherokee were understandably less forbearing. "Why do you talk of sending to the President to ask advice?" Doublehead asked Secretary Smith. "These people did not ask any advice when they came and killed our people." Scolocutta similarly mocked Smith for his impotence. "Surely you are no head-man nor warrior," he wrote. "I think you are afraid of these bad men . . . I think they are making fun of you, and won't listen to your talks."[50]

Few officials engaged in a more complicated triangulation between official duty and popularity than Governor Blount. Blount felt obligated to enforce federal law, but in ways that minimized the political cost to him. After Beard's expedition, he strategically delayed his return from Philadelphia to place responsibility for punishing the perpetrators with Secretary Smith, a lag that served, Blount reported, to "highten my Character." "I left and returned . . . in good Time," he quipped. And, though Blount did not sanction either Beard's or Ore's expeditions, he did secretly authorize another targeted expedition in his absence—even while instructing that it must seem to happen "on the Spur of the Occasion." Blount's scheming had its effect: many territorial citizens, recognizing the game the governor was playing, regarded him as a tacit supporter. "[T]he Governor is restricted to *defensive* measures, & therefore as *Governor* is bound to disapprove it," one observer wrote after Ore's expedition, "[but] as W.B. [William Blount] I dare believe that he is highly gratified."[51]

This speculation was wrong: Blount seemed genuinely and sincerely outraged when he learned of the expeditions. After receiving word of Ore's attack, for instance, Blount dashed off a blunt secret letter to Robertson expressing "surprise and mortification" that the general had "countenanced" such "lawless" actions. "No good consequences can arise from such unauthorized expeditions," Blount informed Robertson before forcing him to resign his federal positions.[52]

Why, given Blount's explicit support for war, did he condemn Ore's and Beard's expeditions, both publicly and privately? The answer lay in a roiling three-way legal and political debate—involving federal officials, Native peoples, and territorial citizens—over the U.S. Constitution, unauthorized expeditions, and war and peace in the Southwest Territory.

Constitutional Debates

Blount was the foremost of small coterie of territorial officials and others who, despite supporting formal war, condemned the unauthorized expeditions as flagrant violations of the "laws of God, of nature, and of man"—especially the newly adopted U.S. Constitution, which, a territorial judge unsubtly reminded a grand jury after Ore's expedition, "is the supreme law of the land." Judge Anderson was more explicit. The Constitution "vests Congress, with a right of making peace and war," he instructed another grand jury. "[W]e are bound as good citizens to act in conformity with their determination."[53]

Unlike Knox or Washington, these men's objections to the expeditions had little to do with humanitarianism: for Blount, the Cherokees' fate was a "a score so far as it affects the hostile part that I am quite easy on." Their concern was for their constituents. In their view, unauthorized expeditions were self-defeating because they reinforced cabinet officials' suspicions of territorial citizens and undercut their Territory's claim to federal aid. "Beard and others foolish uninformed people have done the cause of the suffering frontier people so much injury in the Eyes of the people of the Atlantic States," Blount reported from Philadelphia. Several writers in the *Gazette* similarly argued that, had territorial citizens been more obedient, they would have already obtained congressional support. Lawful conduct, Judge Anderson urged jurors, would secure the "affection of the general government, and induce them to extend . . . her kind protection."[54]

Blount and others' endorsement of the administration's legal position was thus pragmatic as well as principled. Congress's sole "right of governing this territory . . . made them the judges of when, how, and where respecting protection," in the words of one newspaper columnist, and territorial citizens could best serve their interests by accepting their judgments. Many in the Territory rejected both conclusions.[55]

One group baffled by federal actions were the neighboring Creeks and Cherokees, especially their young warriors. In both nations, a culture of martial masculinity governed violence. Tales of successful war exploits—what Anglo-Americans derisively termed "lying and exageration"—could bring acclaim, while those deficient in martial prowess were "stiled old women, which is the greatest term of reproach that can be used to them."[56]

For the Cherokees and Creeks, U.S. failure to respond to their attacks diverged from this expected legal frame and rendered Anglo-Americans fit subjects for the exaggerated and highly gendered taunts they employed to mock the cowardly. "[T]he Cherokees had eat a great quantity of the white's flesh which they were very fond of at first," some hostile warriors told James Robertson, "but they had had so much of it, had got tired and thought it too salt." (Robertson added, unnecessarily: "this they spoke in way of derision.") When eight young Creeks stopped at interpreter James Carey's house in Cherokee country, they "boasted" to him how "the Creeks did all they could to provoke the United States to war with them," offering a lengthy catalogue of humiliations: "they killed and scalped men, women, and children; that they took them prisoners, and made them slaves like negroes; that they debauched their women, they took their property." But though "they had done it for many years, yet they could not make [the Anglo-Americans] mad." The Creeks' swaggering concluded with a particularly pointed sexual jibe: "Shall we take some man and *bouger* him, and send him back to tell his people, and try if that will not rouse them to war?" Such hyperbolic braggadocio and jeering—southern nations were not cannibals, and whites commented with surprise at the rarity of rape in Native societies—underscored the humiliation of Anglo-Americans' failure to adhere to borderlands norms of violence.[57]

As the Cherokees and Creeks struggled to understand the United States' unaccountable passivity, they got an answer of sorts from white traders in Indian country. Federal officials deeply distrusted these men, seemingly loyal only to money, who nonetheless enjoyed considerable influence: "Natives," one officer wrote, "imbibe the prejudices & politicks of their traders." What the traders conveyed to their customers was a garbled version of the constitutional argument that only Congress could authorize a war—but in a highly prejudicial, incendiary form. In one story recounted to Governor Blount, a trader in Cherokee country had "with apparent exultation informed the people present that the Indians were safe; that no State could declare war against the Indians; that, let them do what they would, your Excellency could not do them any injury in return; that the people of the territory were very anxious to have a war, and that they were the cause of the past disturbances." Another trader reportedly told the Creeks, "the Congress have thrown away the people of Cumberland, 'tis w[e]ll, to kill, plunder, and commit devastations there, for Congress will not be angry at them for it."[58]

Creeks and Cherokees found the suggestion that the Southwest Territory might not be part of the United States persuasive enough to raise it with federal representatives. In 1793, a Creek delegation inquired whether "Governor Blount, and these Cumberland people . . . are under the Government of General Washington." The following year, the Cherokee leader Scolocutta, seeking to understand U.S. passivity after Creek attacks, asked, "[I]s it that this Country is not under the Protection of the U.S., or is it that the President is uninformed of the many murders & Thefts committed by the Creeks?"[59]

Such statements predictably horrified federal officials, who feared that Native leaders had "already beg[u]n to conceive . . . that the only business of Congress was to bind the hands of her citizens, whilst the Indians butchered them." And so these officials assiduously rebutted these suggestions. Not only were the Cumberland residents "citizens of the United States," William Blount assured Nenetooyah, but they were "as much under the care of the President as the people of Philadelphia are, and he is equally desirous that your people should treat them well." The governor told Scolocutta that the president had "full information of their [the Cumberland residents'] many sufferings."[60]

What struck federal officials as bizarre arguably made considerable sense. Not only had Anglo-American jurisdictions repeatedly broken apart or recombined in prior years, but the idea that Cumberland was not part of the United States explained why the United States seemed so indifferent to the fate of its own people; it also made understandable why the territorial citizens seemed to enjoy such freedom to violate what was supposedly federal law. Cherokee and Creek leaders could likely have related to, and perhaps already suspected, the true reason for both shortcomings—the complicated politics and imperfect authority that existed within the Anglo-Americans' only partly centralized polity. But federal officials, fearful of displaying weakness, admitted this reality only among themselves. In their speeches to Native leaders, they stuck to the unconvincing platitudes of federal control. The result was the perpetuation in Indian country of a garbled version of constitutional law that made the United States' odd decision to violate customary borderlands practices only partially explicable to Native observers, and that encouraged further attacks—or so territorial citizens argued.

Those territorial citizens had their own views on the constitutional meaning of war and peace, expressed by a parade of writers who took to the *Knoxville Gazette* under populist pseudonyms: "A Fellow Citizen," "A Fellow Sufferer," "A Citizen of the Frontiers of the Southwest Territory." In a territory lacking elected institutions, the *Gazette* became the principal public forum for the heated debates over law and violence. There, these self-appointed champions of the people offered the Territory's most full-throated defense of the expeditions against officials' charges of illegality.

These pieces sought to rebut federal officials within their own preferred idiom—that of law. *Which* law was uncertain: as they rummaged through early American legal pluralism, these authors often produced a grab bag of claims and sources. One author asserting a right to "seek satisfaction" cobbled together an argument from the right of assembly, the right to bear arms to defend the state, Blackstone's discussion of the right of personal security, and the preamble of the Constitution. Natural rights to self-defense—what the territorial legislature would label as "the first law of nature, self-preservation"—were a frequent trope. So too was the insistence that the authors understood the demands better than distant politicians. Like their Native counterparts, they even levied their own gendered taunts at officials like Knox: "men who are unacquainted with the savages," they alleged, were "like young women who have read romances, and have as improper an idea of the Indian character in the one case, as the female mind has of real life in the other."[61]

Yet, for all these authors' eclecticism, there was a core to their legal argument—one that challenged the Washington administration's arrogation of the right to decide war and peace to the federal government. Whether war existed, they argued, was not an abstract issue to be debated by Congress; it was a question of territorial *reality*. The citizens of the Southwest Territory were "in an actual state of war, and daily feel the effects, whatever may be said of peace elsewhere."[62]

In making this case, they pointed toward what they regarded as facts proving Native culpability. Instead of divining Native intentions from diplomacy, they pointed to supposed concrete evidence: scalps or horses discovered in Cherokee towns; assaults by large and well-organized Cherokee and Creek armies led by "the most distinguished of their warriors." These "act[s]," they insisted, could be viewed "in no other light than as positive a declaration of war as ever was or can be denounced by one nation against another."[63]

But above all, defenders of the expeditions' legality sought to rebut opponents' arguments on their own legal ground. They repurposed one of the Washington administration's favorite sources of law to insist that the "law of nations not only allows, but commands when we are attacked, either by a public or private enemy, to repel force by force." They also invoked federal statutes, especially North Carolina's cession, which stipulated federal protection. "Have we experienced a fulfilment of that promise?" one writer asked rhetorically.[64]

But the expeditions' proponents' favorite source of law was the Constitution, although they stressed a different provision from Congress's power to declare war. Secretary Daniel Smith was typical when he rejected criticism from Henry Knox's successor, Secretary of War Timothy Pickering. "Ought I not to have made use of the power understood to be lodged with me by the constitution, in the latter part of the 10th section, 1st article, where each individual state is restricted from engaging in war, unless actually *invaded*?" Smith inquired. Smith was not alone in relying on this language in Article I, Section 10: William Cocke similarly interpreted it to mean, "[W]hen an enemy invades any particular state, such state may engage in war, and Congress is bound to support her"—conveniently sidestepping the potential objection that the Territory was not a state.[65]

Such arguments demonstrate that the proponents of campaigns into Indian country were not arguing for the primacy of local law against federal supremacy. Rather than abolishing the customary law that governed borderland violence, territorial citizens' self-appointed advocates sought to codify it into forms of positive law that Knox and Washington would be bound to honor. This decision to repurpose their opponents' legal discourse to vindicate their own aims made strategic sense, but it also constrained them to fight on the terrain defined by their opponents. Even in the distant territories, federal law, and especially the Constitution, had become the primary currency of legal argument.

The Hands of Government

Ultimately, the legal debates that convulsed the Southwest Territory—over war and peace and the legal limits of defense—finally ended up in Congress, as officials had long sought. But, as Congress rehashed the same legal contentions that had divided territorial inhabitants and officials, it achieved little more consensus than they had.

One set of congressional proposals would have acceded to territorial citizens' demands and authorized "offensive operations" against the Creeks and Cherokees. In 1792, the House, rattled by the existing conflict, narrowly defeated such an authorization. "The hostilities had been authorised against the No. Western tribes almost without knowing it," one wary congressman argued, yet "this evil was deeply regretted when too late to admit of any remedy."[66]

Pro-administration New Englanders were still skeptical two years later when southern congressmen sought to empower the president to call up ten thousand militia for a southern campaign: "We have one Indian war already, which is enough at a time," one quipped. Such critics were especially dubious about employing militia, who, they claimed, would shoot "the first man, with a red skin, whom they met." In response, southerners assailed the administration's Indian policy: one Georgian alleged that federal officials betrayed "improper leanings in favor of the Indians" that made his "heart boil," and asserted he would "not give the life of one white man for those of fifty Indians." This controversy over means doomed the proposal.[67]

The administration had its own favored solution to borderland violence. Back in 1790, Henry Knox, in one of his many reports, had advocated using courts martial to punish treaty violations. Early in 1794, in response to the unauthorized expeditions in the Southwest Territory, President Washington urged Congress to codify a version of this approach. Administration allies duly introduced a bill that would extend martial law over any citizen found in arms in Indian country.[68]

Such proposals had deep roots. Even before the Revolution, imperial administrators had envisioned deploying martial law to police Anglo-American violence against Natives, and, throughout the nineteenth century, empires turned to martial law to shore up uncertain and contested authority. Particularly for military men like Knox and Washington, martial law had obvious appeal for territorial governance: it would strip jurisdiction from territorial courts and juries, where local whites so adeptly thwarted justice for Natives, and empower the territories' most unambiguously national institution, the U.S. Army, which would convene panels of officers to try offenders. Allies in Congress fully embraced the administration's vision of federal control over violence. The bill, they insisted, would achieve "one of the great objects of frontier policy"—to "restrain the right of private war, by placing the power of vengeance out of the reach of individuals, and in the hands of Government."[69]

Yet, precisely because it empowered administrators, martial law had special terror for many Anglo-Americans, who viewed it as the antithesis of the supposedly liberty-preserving verities of the common law. During and after the Revolution, many states adopted constitutions that subordinated the military to civil power. Constant clashes between military and civil jurisdiction marked the territories: in early Cincinnati, and later Detroit, territorial judges and military officers battled fiercely over the scope of their respective authority.[70]

The administration's opponents now sought to protect citizens from such supposedly arbitrary jurisdiction by amending the bill to exempt from trial any citizen "in pursuit of Indians that had committed actual hostilities on the frontier." This amendment horrified the proposal's backers: it would undermine their fundamental aim. It elevated the victim of an Indian attack into "both judge and executioner in his own case," pro-administration representatives argued; it "legalize[d] all those acts of violence and revenge, that, for a century past, have deluged the frontier with blood"; it would usher in "eternal war." The amendment "went to invert all the laws that had been made for the protection of the Indians," James Hillhouse of Connecticut insisted. "[I]nstead of being a bill to protect them from the whites, the resolutions would produce a bill to protect the whites from them."[71]

Back in the Southwest Territory, the *Knoxville Gazette*, which reprinted the debates in full, editorialized that Hillhouse's remark "let the cat out of the bag"—it confirmed their suspicions that "many members of Congress prefer the protection of the savages to that of their suffering frontier fellow citizens." The Territory's congressional defenders also responded testily. Their retort was partly legal: echoing the columns in the *Gazette*, they insisted that "a settler was, by the law of nations, authorized to pursue the [Indians] across the line and to retaliate." But they mostly appealed to outrage. In one particularly heated tirade, the Southwest Territory's newly seated nonvoting representative, the "much affected" James White, invoked the deaths of four hundred territorial citizens, insisted that Natives' "love of blood was hereditary," and lashed out so vituperatively against colleagues who had supposedly impugned the "frontier people" that he was reprimanded to confine himself to a "decent answer."[72]

In the end, both the amendment *and* the court martial proposal failed. Instead, when the Trade and Intercourse Act was renewed in 1796, it included an ambiguous provision that granted the army the power to arrest offenders within Indian country, but left jurisdiction in the regular federal courts. Congress was evidently too fixated on other controversial aspects of the bill—particularly, as we shall see, its provisions addressing property—to reopen the earlier contentions. In the end, the debates that had convulsed the Southwest Territory also paralyzed Congress, leaving the question of meaning of war and peace, and the right of private violence, to the future.[73]

Mediation

Territorial citizens were not the only people in the Southwest Territory eager to conscript federal military might against their enemies, or who spoke the language of law as they attempted to do so. Some Native leaders, it turned out, were equally keen to involve the federal government in their long-standing conflicts. As with intertribal disputes over property, officials were reluctant to entangle the federal government in these controversies. Yet some also recognized that helping resolve these conflicts—a process that, drawing from the law of nations, they called mediation—could, and did, expand federal power in Indian country.[74]

A complicated blend of violence, kinship, and diplomacy marked the Native South. Native raids did not only target Anglo-American towns: Choctaws, Creeks, Chickasaws, and Cherokees frequently fought each other, similarly fueled by practices of retaliation. But captive-taking and intermarriage also ensured that kinship and family, as well as bloodshed, bound these nations together. Such ties proved especially important for diplomacy *among* these nations. Nations, regions, and villages routinely forged alliances and made common cause against enemies. Go-betweens also played a vital role in the region's law of peace, as warring nations relied on third parties to convey messages to their adversaries and to broker an end to conflicts.[75]

The Chickasaws, southwest of Nashville in present-day northern Mississippi and western Tennessee, were especially reliant on diplomacy and alliances. They were a much smaller nation than their neighbors, with one federal report estimating that they could field only 700 warriors against the Choctaws' 3,000 and the Creeks' 4,500. Yet decades earlier, the Chickasaws and Choctaws had forged a durable peace thanks to the mediation of the Chakchiuma, descendants of a formerly autonomous people who now lived among both nations; by the 1790s, such links closely bound the two nations together. The Chickasaws had ties to the Creeks, too: a number of prominent Chickasaw leaders had reportedly married Creek wives, and vice versa. In the two matrilineal nations, such marriages integrated their children into their respective clan systems. Yet violence between the two nations nonetheless persisted, and they had been engaged in a constant, low-level war since 1787.[76]

The Chickasaws had also long used their location between Anglo-Americans and Spanish Louisiana and Florida to their advantage, with pro- and anti-Spanish factions successfully allowing the nation to both gain outside alliances and maintain its autonomy. After the Revolution, the war leader Piomingo, also known as Mountain Leader, emerged as the champion of the anti-Spanish camp, deeming the Spanish "a people we never loved."[77]

Piomingo epitomized the Native South's cosmopolitanism. Reportedly descended from the peace-making Chakchiuma, Piomingo also had close

Cherokee ties: Cherokee leader Keanetoah described him as his "nephew," while Nenetooyah called Piomingo "my old friend [who] Can Speak my tongue as well as a Cherokee." But, as noted at the chapter's outset, Piomingo pursued an especially close friendship and alliance with his neighbors in the Southwest Territory, especially James Robertson and William Blount, who returned his affection. Piomingo even twice led Chickasaw contingents to aid the U.S. Army in the Northwest Indian War.[78]

Perhaps more than any other Native leader in the post-revolutionary South, then, Piomingo gambled on the promise of U.S. power. This gamble brought him rewards. Federal officials flattered and cultivated him, leading other Chickasaw leaders to complain jealously of his perceived "pre-eminence." But these ties not only bolstered Piomingo's personal status; they also, he believed, served his nation's interest, securing them federal gunpowder, ammunition, muskets, and even cannons. The Chickasaw leader unsubtly hoped for more, continually reminding his allies that, unlike the "Rogues the Creeks," his nation had "never Shed the Blood of White People." As early as 1790, federal officials reported from Nashville that the Chickasaws were inveigling the town's residents "to join them in a War against the Common Enemy, the Creeks."[79]

In February 1793, the Creeks killed a Chickasaw, "hacking and mangling" his body as a particular "insult" to the Chickasaws. A Chickasaw council then "*unanimously* determined" on war, dispatching forty warriors to attack the Creeks. Unsurprisingly, Piomingo immediately turned to his Anglo-American friends, appealing to James Robertson for federal military assistance.[80]

The Chickasaws invoked multiple reasons why the United States owed them protection. Chickasaw leader William Glover, son of an Anglo-American trader and Chickasaw mother, cited kinship. "I received my Being from one of your nation," he told Robertson, "I am your son." But Glover adduced another reason, too: "[I]t is the friendliness of this Nation to your people that has caused this War to fall on us." The Creeks seemingly regarded Piomingo's alliance with the United States as an affront to their efforts to construct an international confederacy to resist Anglo-American encroachments. "[Y]ou said a Great Deal about me as if my loving the white people was Doing you great wrong," Piomingo wrote, in English, to Creek leaders via a federal Indian agent, recalling their earlier negotiations. Now, emboldened by U.S. defeats in the war in the Northwest Territory, the Creeks decided that federal weakness presented an opportune moment to attack the Chickasaws. "Then let the Virginians, your great friends, help you," the Creeks taunted the Chickasaws, using the state as a stand-in for all Anglo-Americans. "[Y]ou will see what they can do."[81]

But Piomingo also made a legal argument to claim federal aid, one clearly legible to federal officers: the "former promises" of the United States, he insisted, committed the federal government to defend their Chickasaw allies. Piomingo demanded that Robertson "despatch expresses to every head-man in America, particularly to General Washington, the Secretary of War, [and] Governor Blount" to "let them know that our agreement was to be as one man, in regard to our enemies and friends; that, if one was struck, the other was to feel the blow." "Let us join, to let the Creeks know what war is," he appealed.[82]

Many in the Southwest Territory would have happily done so—including William Blount, who was "glad" to learn of the conflict. Blount shared Piomingo's legal views, interpreting the Treaty of Hopewell's promise of protection as requiring the United States to aid the Chickasaws. Yet, Blount reluctantly informed Robertson, "what part the United States will act is not in my power to determine"; that authority lay with the president. When, later that year, Blount traveled to Philadelphia to make the case for federal war against the Creeks, he urged Knox and Washington that the United States' "true interest" was to "cherish and support the Chickasaws in the War."[83]

But Piomingo and Blount had competition from the Creeks, who proved as adept as the Chickasaws in exploiting federal rhetoric. "[I]f it is the wish of the President of the United States, that this people and the red people should be at peace," Creek leaders asked Washington, recalling constant federal promises, "we hope he will immediately restrain Governor Blount and his people from joining the Chickasaws."[84]

Washington thought the question of intervention significant enough to present to his cabinet. The Chickasaw war arrived at a geopolitically sensitive moment: after contentious debate, the cabinet had just embraced neutrality in the wars of the French Revolution engulfing Europe, notwithstanding the U.S.-French alliance. The cabinet members now adopted neutrality here, too. None favored military intervention: Knox and Jefferson thought that the United States might "*mediate effectually*" between the parties, but Attorney General Edmund Randolph feared this would anger the Spanish, while Treasury Secretary Alexander Hamilton worried federal involvement would commit the United States to enforce any ensuing peace through force. Ultimately, Knox forbade Blount to assist the Chickasaws directly, though he did, through some formalistic reasoning, authorize supplying the Nation with more arms.[85]

If the United States would not fulfill the role of ally or peacemaker, others would. After a meeting with the Spanish in New Orleans, Nenetooyah and other Cherokee leaders visited the Chickasaws and firmly urged them for peace. Later, the Spanish and the Choctaws similarly urged peace, arguing that the Native nations should offer a united front against U.S. encroachments. In late 1793, the war halted, supposedly through "Spanish agency," an action that reportedly secured the Chickasaws to the Spanish "interest." Several months later, the Chickasaw Nation joined other southeastern Native nations in signing the Treaty of Nogales with Spain.[86]

Despite this tenuous peace, William Blount did not abandon his plans to exploit conflict among Native nations. "[I]t is my secret wishes," Blount instructed Robertson the following year, "that you encourage in such ways as you judge best both the Chickasaws and Choctaws to fall on the Creeks." Blount got what he wanted in January 1795, when a Chickasaw raid on the Creeks renewed the fighting. Once again, Piomingo demanded help from Robertson based on their alliance. "[T]hey say, they are now people of the United States," Robertson reported to Blount, "and are commissioned by the President himself." When Robertson told them he "had no power to send men with them," Piomingo and other Chickasaws journeyed to Philadelphia to press their claim on the president directly. Meanwhile, Robertson tacitly allowed one hundred Nashvilleans to guard Chickasaw territory. "[T]he federal Government," he reasoned, "would permit a thing of the kind to be done voluntarily which they would not order." These territorial militia, along with U.S. cannons, helped defeat a Creek invasion.[87]

But in Philadelphia, the Chickasaws found their expectations sorely disappointed. Expressing "regret" at any "mistaken opinions," President Washington clarified the government's position. "It was never the design of the United States to interfere in the disputes of the Indian Nations among one another," he lectured Piomingo and the other Chickasaw leaders, "unless as friends to both parties to reconcile them." Besides, he informed them, "the power of making such a war belongs to Congress (the Great Council of the United States) exclusively. I have no power to begin such a war without their consent."[88]

The Chickasaw leaders left deeply disappointed that "the President could not gratify [their] wishes in making open war against the Creeks." The new Secretary of War Timothy Pickering blamed Blount and Territorial Judge David Campbell, reprimanding them for misleading Piomingo. Rejecting any interpretation of the language of "protection" that would commit the United States to a military alliance, Pickering expressed shock that "men in the highest offices in the territory, and men specially charged with the interests of the Indians, have so plainly encouraged the Chickasaws . . . to strike the Creeks." He concluded by reminding Campbell that he was an "officer of government" and so bound to follow federal policy.[89]

On the road back from the capital, the Chickasaw leaders, writing to Blount, despaired "that they Need not Look for help from the Secratory of War as he Denies Letting any man assist us." But there was still a possible source of federal aid: "[T]he Secratory says he will make a peace with the Creeks for us."[90]

This federal promise of mediation—more than the federal government had earlier been willing to offer—was bolstered by another source. As the Chickasaws returned from Philadelphia, Creek leader Alexander Cornell wrote to William Blount, asking the governor to help negotiate a peace with the Chickasaws and secure the return of Creek prisoners. He also enclosed a letter in English to the Chickasaws appealing for peace that he entrusted to Blount to deliver. Although the Choctaws and Spanish were reportedly once again seeking to "negociate a [Creek-Chickasaw] peace," Cornell turned instead to the United States to play the well-established role of mediator.[91]

Although it was not the military alliance he had hoped for, Governor Blount nonetheless saw opportunity in Cornell's appeal. "This is an important crisis in Indian affairs and must be embraced," Blount observed, ordering James Robertson to hurry to the Chickasaws. The key, Blount told him, was not just to secure peace but to ensure "that the Creeks should believe that peace between them and the Chickasaws [came] through your mediation."[92]

Robertson's initial efforts proved abortive. But, after the Chickasaws defeated a thousand-man Creek invasion force, reportedly mounted and equipped with siege weapons, the Creeks tired of the violence. Later that year, Blount dispatched his agent Captain Chisholm to serve "as a Mediator between those two Nations by the Authority of the United States." This time, "peace is restored," Blount crowed, thanks to Chisholm, earning "credit to himself and the United States."[93]

Blount's initial intervention helped foster Creek and Chickasaw reliance on federal mediation. When tension between the Chickasaws and Creeks resurged a couple years later, Benjamin Hawkins, the region's new agent for Indian affairs, reported that the "Chickasaws had applied to him for justice." Promising his "best endeavours," in October 1797 Hawkins presided over a Creek council where the nation agreed to reconcile with the Chickasaws; Hawkins "rejoiced that his voice, which was that of the President and the whole people of the U.S., had been listened to." To "certify the peace," the Creeks sent a transcript of the council's proceedings, which Hawkins "countersigned . . . at the request of the chiefs." This detail was revealing: Hawkins had so insinuated himself into Chickasaw-Creek negotiations that his endorsement affirmed the credibility of the Creek overtures. The gambit evidently worked: less than a year later, Hawkins's assistant had "the pleasure of seeing the Chickasaws and Creeks smoke the pipe of peace in friendship."[94]

The United States' success in resolving the Creek-Chickasaw War foreshadowed later developments. The federal government continued to avoid direct intervention in intertribal violence. "The U.S. does not wish to foment quarrels between the Indian nations," Secretary of War James McHenry summarized in 1796, "nor is it the intention of government to be a party in their quarrels or to aid one in preference to another." Rather, he continued, "[t]he *mediation of govern.* to extend only to advice." Several years later, when a war erupted between Potawatomis, Anishinaabeg, and Osage along the borders of the Northwest Territory, Governor St. Clair hewed to this position, dispatching an agent to the warring nations to "let them know explicitly that . . . the United States can take no part with either," although the agent would "endeavor to compromise their differences." The United States would serve only as arbiter, not as partisan, when violence between Native nations threatened.[95]

The history of the U.S. role in the Creek-Chickasaw War points toward two contradictory conclusions. First, it underscores, as many historians have stressed, that even as Native nations confronted U.S. colonialism, they were not defined solely, or even principally, by their relationships with Euro-American empires. Complex diplomacy between the Chickasaws and their Native neighbors still dominated the Native South; even their decision to rely on federal mediation slotted the United States into well-established roles defined by Indigenous law.[96]

At the same time, the war demonstrates the insidiousness of U.S. imperialism, as the United States was increasingly present even when seemingly absent. Despite explicitly declining to intervene in the Creek-Chickasaw War, the United States and its influence arguably both *prompted* and *ended* the conflict. For the Creeks and Chickasaws, as for many other Native peoples, their relationship with each other was now mediated through the United States. There was, it seemed, no space that the question of U.S. power did not reach.

Astute federal officials, following Blount, recognized this reality and seized it as an opportunity to insinuate federal power still further into Indian country. When the Creeks and Chickasaws gathered in 1798, Hawkins's deputy took pains to remind them that they owed their peace to U.S. efforts. "The President of the U.S. has a great regard for all his red children," he emphasized. "[I]t is his wish that you should have an unbounded confidence in the justice of the U.S." What he called confidence might also have been construed as dependence.[97]

In October 1795, as Robertson and Chisholm sought to negotiate a Creek-Chickasaw peace, Blount observed that the near-constant Creek and Cherokee raids that had plagued the Southwest Territory since long before his arrival had abruptly stopped. For the first time in eighteen years, he exulted, "Peace with the Indians exists now not only in name, or upon paper in form of treaty, but in fact."[98]

This sudden halt in violence was more mysterious than its prior stubborn persistence. It had not come as the Washington administration had hoped: through the imposition of a rigid definition of war and peace in which the federal government alone would control legitimate violence. Both Natives and whites in the territories rejected this legal straightjacket, regarding war not as a clearly delineated status between nations but as a spectrum of violence between peoples. Against this standard, federal interventions to authorize or condemn violence seemed arbitrary: Congress acknowledged raids and counterraids as "war" in the

Northwest Territory yet refused to do so in the Southwest Territory. The administration did not even succeed in defining federal law, which territorial citizens, Native leaders, and congressional representatives all plausibly reinterpreted to vindicate their actions and claim the right to federal support.

Yet peace had not come as territorial citizens expected it would, either—through decisive expeditions that, in an appalling euphemism, "chastised" Indian country. The devastating genocidal destruction of Nickajack and Scolocutta's town had nonetheless failed to halt continued attacks on Cumberland.[99]

Hindsight suggests the role of broader geopolitics in the unexpected peace. As Knox had hoped, the defeat of the Native nations in the Ohio Country had demonstrated the power of federal arms. So, too, the Washington administration's diplomatic successes in securing the Jay and Pinckney Treaties with Great Britain and Spain—both ratified in 1795—compromised the ability of Creeks, Cherokees, and others to exploit imperial tensions. Meanwhile, Native leaders, especially in the Creek Nation, began to foster their own forms of centralized authority that, like those of the United States, sought to control violence—albeit with similarly uneven results.[100]

But if the roots of violence and its absence proved difficult for anyone in the territories to fully grasp, the fights over war and peace there left important legacies. Territorial citizens, especially in the Southwest Territory, found themselves at once reliant on federal support and deeply resentful of federal authority. Native nations, too, turned to federal representatives to mediate violence between Native communities. In neither instance did the federal government enjoy the supremacy the Washington administration had sought, and yet territorial citizens and Native peoples alike increasingly oriented themselves in interpreting and repurposing federal law.

A striking example of this dynamic came in 1797, when Chickasaw leader George Colbert petitioned Congress. A political ally of Piomingo, Colbert wanted the federal government to reimburse him for provisions supplied two years earlier to the Nashvilleans who had volunteered to defend the Chickasaws against the Creeks. Congress refused, observing that "the proceeding was unauthorized by Government." Yet Colbert's petition was only one of many similar appeals for federal money that came from Natives and territorial citizens alike—many of them successful. Such claims underscored how readily fights over territorial violence turned into contests over federal finance, which, intertwined with law, became one of the most important, and contested, assets in the territories.[101]

6
Expenses of Sovereignty

In December 1796, Betty, a Cherokee woman, came to Philadelphia, where, along with a Cherokee delegation, she dined with President Washington. But her trip's principal purpose was to petition Congress. The widow of the Cherokee leader Scolocutta, who had died earlier that year, Betty asked "that some provision may be made for her" for the wounds that she and her husband received in John Beard's 1793 expedition, made "contrary to law and the good faith of Government." Betty reminded Congress that, though Beard was never punished, "instead of exciting her people to acts of retaliation, [she] has abated nothing in her friendship to the white people."[1]

The House Committee on Claims was torn. Not only did Betty's circumstances warrant a pension, but such a payment might also "influence . . . other Indians" to follow her peaceful example. "[P]olicy requires that the minds of Indians, who may be roused to hostility by acts of the settlers, should be quieted by small pecuniary interpositions," the committee concluded. Yet Natives like Betty were not the only victims of borderlands violence: "[T]here are citizens on the frontiers, who have suffered injuries as cruel and deprivations as severe, by the Indians, and who have been thereby left in situations of distress, that would equally call for assistance from the Legislature."[2]

The committee was unsure how to handle these competing claims. "Questions arise, whether both descriptions of sufferers ought to be provided for? Whether the abilities of Government would be competent to meet all possible claims of this nature? And, whether help can be extended, by law, to the one, and consistently refused to the other?"[3]

These were not abstract dilemmas. The same day it heard the report on Betty's petition, Congress received another report on a petition from Hugh Lawson White, who sought federal funds to reimburse the expenses for Beard's 1793 expedition—the same one that had wounded Betty. The secretary of war objected because, as Betty noted, Beard's expedition had violated federal law. But a select committee chaired by Andrew Jackson—now a representative from Tennessee, the erstwhile Southwest Territory—strongly urged payment.[4]

Ultimately, the federal government paid both claimants. Betty received a pension of unknown amount; White and his fellow white Tennesseans received $22,816.95 in back pay.[5]

Federal Ground. Gregory Ablavsky, Oxford University Press (2021). © Gregory Ablavsky.
DOI: 10.1093/oso/9780190905699.003.0007

These simultaneous petitions from both victim and perpetrators of Beard's massacre seeking federal funds highlight the consequences of the federal failure to staunch territorial violence through criminal law. Like Betty, Native and white claimants alike turned to the federal government to compensate them for violence suffered at each others' hands. But many expected the government to do more than just make them whole: Native leaders demanded so-called "presents," while territorial citizens, including Beard's militia, insisted that the federal government fund their "protection." As the fate of Betty's and White's petitions suggests, federal officials usually complied with these demands.

In pursuing from a new federal government with deeper pockets the "sweets of Emolument, which now offer," Natives and territorial citizens echoed the venal legislators, land speculators, and financiers further east. Contests over the distribution of government largesse, scholars have argued, were long the core of U.S. politics. Yet the vast federal sums that flowed to the territories were distinctive: they reflected less a newer democratic model in which localities competed for state-subsidized economic development than an older, hierarchical model in which distant governments sought to co-opt local elites through patronage. The federal government's goal was less to enrich itself—neither Natives nor territorial citizens were meaningfully "contributing to the [federal] revenue," which came almost entirely from Atlantic commerce—than to avoid the incredible expense of the fiscal-military state that the Northwest Indian War exemplified. Henry Knox called such peacekeeping expenditures the "unavoidabl[e]" "expenses" of "sovereignty, and an extensive territory"—the costs of empire.[6]

Ironically, funds spent to keep peace came mostly through the War Department, the government's de facto imperial bureaucracy whose principal function often seemed to be managing payments. Within the department, the Indian Department—which tellingly shared the title of its British predecessor—employed a loosely organized coterie of agents and interpreters but mostly served as an accounting category for the mounting expenses of federal civil and military officers concentrated in the territories.[7]

Similarly, the politics of federal finance in the early territories were the politics of empire, not of parties and elections. Both Native peoples and territorial citizens were political outsiders excluded from the franchise. Both groups were, in their own ways, ostensibly federal *dependents*, a richly resonant term in the early republic, associated with women, children, and people of color, that connoted subordination and "status inferiority." Native peoples were supposedly dependents because they accepted officials' convenient narrative of paternalism and Indigenous poverty that extracted federal aid all the more effectively, thereby provoking their white neighbors' ire. For their part, the territories were federal dependencies not only financially but also constitutionally, as subordinate colonies of the federal government—a status territorial citizens keenly resented.[8]

Yet neither Natives nor territorial citizens behaved as dependents were supposed to. Both regarded the national government less as a source of command to be obeyed than as a font of wealth to be mined. This attitude reflected their power, which came not from electoral mobilization but from changeable allegiances in a contested borderland where federal authority was tenuous. Competing with Britain and Spain for influence, federal officials felt they had little choice but to satisfy these groups' constant claims. Officials' beleaguered correspondence suggests a more complicated portrait of who, exactly, was dependent on whom in the early territories.

This steady flow of federal funds, in short, did not provide the authority to control territorial events that Knox sought: Native and territorial leaders could, and did, reject federal goals even as they took federal money. But it expanded federal authority in another way. Even if federal officials were thin on the ground, the national treasury made federal power ubiquitous, insinuating the national government into Cherokee councils in the form of medals and blankets and into the lives of nearly all male territorial citizens in the form of muster roles and payment vouchers. The prospect of federal payment led Natives and non-Natives alike to take their complaints to territorial officials, and even to Philadelphia, for redress. This was dependence of a different sort, as both groups came to rely on the federal largesse they so effectively extracted.

Liberal Compensation

The failure of federal criminal law to stanch frontier violence placed federal officials in a difficult position. Their treaties with Native nations implicitly permitted retaliation if the federal government could not fulfill its promises to punish offenders. When this proved impossible, federal officials hit on an ersatz solution: compensation. Instead of meting out punishment, the federal government would pay both Native and white victims for the harms they had suffered at each other's hands.[9]

Compensation played an important role in both Indigenous and Anglo-American law. Many, though not all, Native peoples of the Ohio Country and Native South rectified wrongs, including killings, through payments intended to console the aggrieved. Natives deployed this practice, which Anglo-Americans called "covering the grave," to keep peace both *within* and *among* nations. Most Native communities favored resolving disputes through compensation over employing physical punishment, which they abhorred.[10]

Under the Anglo-American common law, individuals could recover damages for injuries caused by others using writs of trespass and trespass on the case. But in practice, legislatures and executives played a more important role in making citizens whole than courts. A key part of the early republic's ubiquitous culture of petitioning was appeals to legislatures for public aid as a matter of grace, especially after disasters and wars. Moreover, under the law of nations, sovereigns sometimes bore responsibility for the harm their citizens caused other nations, culpability they could mitigate by providing "pecuniary compensation." After the Revolution, the question of national liability for purported seizures of land and enslaved Africans became a thorny diplomatic issue between the United States and Britain. Meanwhile, federal and state governments themselves compensated some U.S. citizens for their wartime losses, including through land grants in the Northwest Territory.[11]

There were precedents, then, for what the federal government routinely began to do in the 1790s: pay Natives to compensate for murders committed by U.S. citizens. Federal officials themselves recognized the parallels with Indigenous law. Was it not true, Henry Knox asked Creek leader Alexander McGillivray, that "among the Indian nations, when one Indian kills another," the aggrieved could be made whole "by pecuniary considerations?" "If this idea is just," Knox observed, then perhaps McGillivray could compensate a Creek family, with the promise of "immediate" federal repayment, in order to "prevent . . . indiscriminate retaliation."[12]

Knox may have been conforming to Native law, but not because he wanted to. He preferred that Natives receive the "same humanity and justice as [the president's] white children," as he told grieving Cherokees after Beard's massacre—which, for Knox, meant criminal punishment from the state. But in the territories, Knox lamented, "the bad escape unpunished." In that instance, "if the laws should not condemn the murderers of your friends, is there no other mode by which you could be satisfied?" Knox was unsubtly hinting at goods; he had already instructed Governor William Blount to provide items to "pacify the relations of the murdered Indians and thereby prevent future hostilities." Federal officials were grasping for any available tools to assuage Native anger after coercion failed to halt violence.[13]

Soon, federal officials were routinely doling out goods to compensate Natives for white attacks. When, for instance, unknown whites killed a group of Haudenosaunee in the Northwest Territory in early 1791, Knox, fearing that "legal process will be both slow and uncertain," ordered Arthur St. Clair to "make[] liberal compensation to the relations" of the victims, which would demonstrate the federal government's "abhorrence" of the crime. A similar process unfolded near Knoxville in 1793, when unidentified whites fired on a Cherokee and two Chickasaws, killing Chickasaw leader John Morris. Blount had Morris buried with full military honors and gave goods to the victims' families. "I considered it political nay essential that pretty liberal presents should be given," Blount reported, "the more effectually to bury their sorrows."[14]

Yet federal use of compensation to paper over the shortcomings of criminal law extended beyond unpunished murders. Such payments became especially key for suppressing "the source of much evil"—"horsestealing."[15]

After land, horses were among the most valuable forms of property in the territories, but, unlike land, thieves could nab horses. Nearly every traveler in the territories recounted losing a horse at some point in the journey. Territorial citizens routinely stole horses from each other and from Natives, sneaking into Indian camps and coming away with three or four horses. Yet territorial citizens believed horse theft a particularly Native crime, with citizens of the Southwest Territory alleging that Creeks and Cherokees had stolen two thousand horses, valued at $100,000, in the early 1790s. Both Natives and whites sold stolen horses to unscrupulous traders, who happily resold them to distant markets: horses from the Southwest Territory ended up in Savannah or Charleston, while horses taken in the Illinois Country resurfaced in Kentucky.[16]

This vast illicit trade in horse flesh threatened any tenuous peace. "Horse Stealing is the grand Source of Hostility between the white and red people in this district," William Blount opined, the cause for "almost continual" complaints to him; if unchecked, he feared, it would end in open warfare. Native horse thieves "kill[ed] in their own defence" when pursued, Blount reported, while aggrieved white victims sought "what they call Satisfaction that is . . . killing Some of the Indians." North of the Ohio, Governor St. Clair similarly believed that horse theft presaged full-fledged hostilities.[17]

One 1799 incident in the Northwest Territory underscores the link between horse theft and violence. Two Wyandots traveling on a road encountered a party of Anglo-Americans who, completely unprompted, took the horse, saddle, and bridle of one of the Wyandots. The whites justified their naked theft as compensation for their own losses: "[T]he Indians had stole horses enough, and that they would take that one in place." Continuing on, the dispossessed Wyandots encountered two other Anglo-American travelers on horseback. Employing the same logic of collective guilt as the white thieves, the Wyandots demanded a horse, "thinking it also proper having lost one of their horses." When the man refused to yield his horse, a fight ensued, and the Wyandots killed both Anglo-Americans.[18]

Territorial officials tried different approaches to halt the borderlands traffic in horses. One route was criminal law. The 1793 version of the Trade and Intercourse Act created a complicated licensing scheme for purchasing horses from Natives, and in a couple of rare instances, whites who knowingly bought stolen horses, or who stole Indian horses, were prosecuted. In another exceptional case, a Vincennes resident brought suit against a Potawatomi known as "Grand Blue" for holding a black mare that the white man claimed as his own; the two men reportedly "amicably settled the dispute." Federal agents sometimes recovered horses that Natives asserted were theirs, as Indian agent James Robertson did in Nashville in the early 1790s—thereby incurring a lawsuit from the disgruntled white claimant.[19]

Officials' most frequent approach to recovering horses, however, was to send complainants or federal representatives into Indian country equipped with letters to Native leaders that invoked treaty provisions requiring tribes return stolen horses upon application. Native leaders often seemed cooperative, especially as they rarely profited personally: Cherokee leader Towakka even promised to "procure by force or otherwise" all stolen horses in the nation. But William Blount was skeptical that such efforts would succeed. "I am very sure that the[y] [the chiefs] have not power nor influence sufficient to have [the horses] restored."[20]

In fact, even with supportive leaders, pursuing horses into Indian country often proved fruitless. One owner chased his stolen horse all over the Shawnee Nation, always seemingly one step behind, before giving up. In another instance, a federal Indian agent, with Cherokee leaders' assistance, successfully located and recovered a stolen horse. But, before the agent could leave, the horse was stolen again, recovered again, and then stolen a third and final time. "[T]herefore [I] think it is scarcely worth while to make application to the Indians for the recovery of our horses," the theft's original victim concluded.[21]

To avoid such problems, owners sometimes hired Natives to recover the horses. This solution posed its own difficulties. "I had heard the savages frequently stole horses with a view to be hired to search for them," one Illinois Country traveler reported. He retrieved his own stolen horse after he offered a local Delaware a $2 reward.[22]

Unable to retrieve horses, federal officials increasingly hit on an ad hoc solution to placate owners: money. Army officers instructed white victims of Indian horse thefts to "record their losses upon good testimony, and I am certain the Government will indemnify them sooner than have a drop of bloodshed." William Blount similarly used federal funds to compensate Chickasaws who alleged that Kentuckians had stolen their horses. "The dilemma at present is either for the United States to pay for these horses, or for the Indians to take pay (as they express it) by stealing as many other horses from some frontier people," Blount noted. "One way or the other they will have pay."[23]

Alongside the vigorous illegal trade in horses was a parallel trade in people, particularly enslaved Africans. "Negroes and Horses," Anglo-Americans repeatedly complained, were the "property" that Natives constantly stole from their settlements.[24]

Captivity and slavery had long existed among both the Native and white inhabitants of the borderlands. Most of the regions' coerced laborers were Indigenous. Native nations routinely took captives from other nations, whom whites in both territories sometimes purchased and forced to labor in their homes and fields. But by the late eighteenth century, the territories were also home to enslaved Africans held in a more rigid and racially defined form of bondage. In the Southwest Territory (as in neighboring Kentucky), chattel slavery was both legal and ever more economically central. Chattel slavery existed in the Northwest Territory, too, notwithstanding the Northwest Ordinance's formal prohibition: many Anglo-Americans either openly defied the ban or legalistically insisted did not encompass enslaved Africans already present in the Territory.[25]

Proximity between Natives and Africans seemingly bred the same familiarity and violence as it did among Natives and whites—although, because these relationships largely took place out of sight of most Anglo-Americans, sources only hint at their nature. In Vincennes in 1794, local Delawares allegedly helped a white man abduct an enslaved African asserting his freedom into the slave territory of Kentucky. In another intriguing incident northwest of Nashville in 1799, a group of Cherokee hunters well known in the neighborhood "had a dispute with a negro fellow belonging to Genl. Robertsons Iron Works and . . . killed him." No surviving testimony explains the context or cause for this fight.[26]

But Black people in the territories did not just encounter Natives in towns like Vincennes and Nashville; many lived in Native communities. Some enslaved Africans fled to Indian country to escape bondage, while others were seized in Native raids on white settlements. Native nations slotted these new arrivals into well-established captivity practices. Like numerous white captives, some Africans became full-fledged members of Native societies, while others labored in bondage, a status Native peoples defined less by race than the absence of kinship ties.[27]

Yet by the 1790s, Native attitudes toward Africans had begun to shift. Imitating their Anglo-American neighbors, some Native leaders purchased enslaved Africans to project wealth and power. Especially among southern nations, the advent of chattel slavery also led some Natives to mimic Anglo-Americans' racial ideology of African inferiority, especially as they sought to shore up their own precarious status in Anglo-Americans' racial hierarchy.[28]

The growing value of enslaved Africans both in and out of Indian country led many Natives to participate in the trade in human beings in the same ways they had joined the market for horses: through raids. One summer, the Cherokees reported, they had seized twenty-two enslaved people. The similarity, and linkage, between these illicit economies even led Tennessean John Sevier to chastise the Cherokees for taking enslaved Africans to compensate for stolen horses. "You know it is wrong to swop people for horses," he piously lectured them, "for negroes is not horses tho they are black."[29]

The bitter irony of Sevier's remark was that it was from whites like him that Natives learned to consider horses and enslaved Africans as equivalent in a crucial respect: both were a kind of commodity. Whites in the territories routinely bought, sold, and exchanged Black bodies, horses, and land, treating them as interchangeable repositories of value, a kind of currency. Moreover, as with horses, whites routinely filched slaves from each other—and from Natives. In one instance, white thieves reportedly abducted two Black slaves that belonged to a Cherokee woman.[30]

Little wonder, then, that, just like their white neighbors, Natives' actions were shaped by enslaved Africans' commodity value. When white traders offered "a ready sale for every Thing plundered from the Inhabitants of the United States, but particularly Horses and Negroes," Natives responded by seizing more enslaved Africans. "[T]he Negroes are the only ones who have a Chance of their lifes," one army officer reported of Native raids on Kentucky, "(I suppose because they sell well)."[31]

Captured African slaves paralleled horses in another way: they posed similar challenges of recovery for their erstwhile white owners. During a 1794 meeting with Cherokee leaders, William Blount "repeatedly mentioned about the delivery of Negroes." Nenetooyah recalled the location and owner of nearly every slave taken from the Southwest Territory, but lamented that he was powerless to recover them. "We are but a poor People and have no goods to purchase the Negroes from the Persons who have Possession of them, if we attempt to take them by force perhaps they might put them to death or injure them." Nenetooyah pointed toward a solution—federal finance. "[W]hen we receive out annual allowance from the U.S.," he told Blount, "then we can with those goods pay the Possessor for them & deliver them to you." Federal Indian agents, too, began to urge the federal government simply "make good the losses sustained" by slaveholders instead of attempting recovery. "The former owners of negroes would be pleased with this mode of settlement," one urged.[32]

Natives, too, turned to the federal government to recover enslaved Africans, as one long-running Chickasaw-Cherokee dispute reveals. In 1795, two enslaved Africans belonging to Chickasaw leader George Colbert—a prominent ally of Piomingo—reportedly "ran away of their own accord" and obtained refuge among the Cherokees. Now, the Cherokee leader Keanetoah (Little Turkey) complained to Governor Blount, the Chickasaws' "madness for their Negroes" was driving a rift between the two nations. Colbert did seem remarkably single-minded about the "recovery of his Negroes from the Cherokees." For the next two years, he repeatedly badgered a string of federal officials, even journeying across the entire Southwest Territory with twenty Chickasaws to discuss the matter with Blount. Just as he did for white claimants, Blount sent his errand man Captain Chisholm to recover the runaways, but to little avail.[33]

Finally, Colbert did what other claimants did—he turned to federal finance, asking new federal Indian agent Benjamin Hawkins to compensate him from the federal government's "annual present made the [Cherokee] nation." Hawkins agreed so long as the Cherokees consented in writing. According to Hawkins, the "Cherokees applied to me also to adjust this matter between the parties concerned." Ultimately, the federal government paid Colbert $750 from the Cherokee annuity. The Cherokees also finally yielded the two enslaved Africans—but to the federal government, not Colbert. Hawkins ordered them to be sold, "the proceeds to be divided among those who lost horses" in Native raids.[34]

Federal compensation for theft began as an ad hoc solution, but in 1796 Congress without debate codified the practice in the Trade and Intercourse Act. That law compensated Natives for goods stolen by whites from the federal treasury, and whites for Indian thefts from the annuities promised to Native nations. (In practice, especially early on, such funds often came from the federal treasury.) The law little altered practice toward Natives—federal officials continued to pay even supposedly dubious Native claims for stolen horses—but the formal promise of compensation enticed territorial citizens, who penned lengthy lists of horses allegedly stolen by Indians. In 1799, inhabitants of the Northwest Territory gave Arthur St. Clair a tally totaling $1,700—more than many nations' annuity.[35]

The statute provided little guidance on how to evaluate these claims, requiring only that claimants provide "necessary proofs," a term that flummoxed federal officials. Arthur St. Clair advocated repealing this provision altogether, since there was no way to get the kind of "satisfactory" evidence that would "entitle the claimants [to] recover in a Court of Justice." "[N]ot a horse will be either lost or stolen, by whomsoever it may be done," St. Clair bemoaned, "but the Indians . . . will be charged with it, and some person or other will be found to swear that they believe the Indians were guilty of it, and the United States will be called upon for all of them." Yet Winthrop Sargent saw this looseness of proof as an advantage. Compensation, he believed, was the only barrier between territorial citizens and "Lex Talonis"—the law of retaliation. So, rather than requiring "legal" evidence, Sargent made the "most liberal Construction" of the statute, offering "lavish . . . promises and assurances" of compensation to forestall violence.[36]

The uncertainty around this question outlasted St. Clair and Sargent, as the War Department struggled to articulate clearer standards. Ultimately, the compensation system was neither liberal nor stingy; it was capricious. As St. Clair predicted, claimants—many of whom petitioned Congress directly—pushed the promise of federal compensation as far as possible. Many, including Daniel Smith, the Southwest Territory's secretary, and James Ore, leader of the 1794 unauthorized expedition against Nickajack, submitted claims for harms that occurred *within* Indian country, which the statute did not authorize, or old claims tracing as far back as the Revolution. In some cases, Congress, fearful of endless claims, drew a sharp line; in others, it granted petitions with little legal basis.[37]

But, however arbitrary, the federal policy of attempting to buy peace had important consequences, as it reoriented both Natives and non-Natives toward the national government. Instead of raiding Knoxville, Nashville, or Vincennes, Native leaders arrived in these towns as supplicants seeking payment. Instead of traveling into Indian country to *take* satisfaction, white claimants forwarded petitions to Philadelphia to "obtain satisfaction." Even as the federal government became financially responsible for the acts of people it could not control, relations between Natives and non-Natives, and even *among* Native nations, were increasingly triangulated through a distant national government.[38]

Indian Presents

Compensation was only a small portion of the federal funds that flowed into Indian country. A larger proportion were so-called "Indian presents" that the federal government gave to Native nations throughout the territories. Some of these goods were symbolic—silver medals and elaborate military uniforms to be doled out to Native leaders—but most were practical: food, alcohol, gunpowder, guns, bullets, clothing, blankets, cloth, tobacco, mirrors, pots, and other household items. Native demands for these goods, and the federal willingness to satisfy them, reflected a complicated mix of dependence on both sides.

The United States was constrained because it was merely the latest in a long line of imperial powers in the borderlands. The British, Spanish, and French who preceded federal officials in the territories had all conformed to Native expectations for how an empire seeking Native support should behave. "In order to secure [Native] friendship," Major John Hamtramck observed from Vincennes, it was "necessary" to "promise them some trifling recompense. It is an old Custom and they all expect it." Native leaders were not shy about requiring federal representatives to offer material proof of their professions of goodwill. "[A] bearer of speeches should never be with empty hands," a group of Miamis informed a federal emissary as they asked for a "draught of milk" (alcohol), "some good broth," and powder and ball. Other Natives, pointing out that they were "very poor," asked for guns, clothes, liquor, and provisions "to cover me and my peoples." Such demands seemed to mark all federal interactions with Native peoples. "It is a fact that whomsoever has to see the Indians is obliged to give them [goods]," Hamtramck later complained. "[I]t is unavoidable."[39]

Such interactions made "beggar" the standard epithet that federal officials applied to Natives they encountered. They began to dread Natives' "friendly Visits," which, according to Winthrop Sargent, "they generally eke out while you have any thing to give them, & this may be applied to their whole Colour, who are beggarly past Description." A federal military officer reported that Natives visited "almost every day to eat and drink with us, by way of brightning the chain of friendship curse them."[40]

As historians have demonstrated, such contempt fundamentally misunderstood Native peoples' expectations. For Native communities, gift-giving served a critical diplomatic role in cementing relationships—a view that Native leaders forcefully articulated as they rejected Anglo-American portrayals. "I am no beggar," Piomingo insisted as he appealed for powder and bullets, for which he would pay using fur, skins, or horses. Natives routinely showed up to diplomatic meetings with their own gifts, often maple sugar or wampum.[41]

But there was an important difference between the diplomatic goods offered by Native nations and those supplied by the United States. Federal officials had little direct use for the wampum they dismissively called "beads," while Native peoples needed, often urgently, federal presents. After centuries of trade, the European-made blankets, pots, and especially guns and gunpowder that Natives demanded had become essentials that, as Cherokee leader Keanetoah articulated, "we could not make . . . ourselves."[42]

Native needs were especially pressing in the 1790s. In thirty years of war, Anglo-Americans had destroyed Native villages, leveled cornfields, and pillaged Native goods. Federal officials sought to exploit the resulting economic inequality. "[W]hen your Houses [and] Cornfields are destroyed you have no provisions made to replace them, but are thrown into the greatest distress and Missary," a U.S. Army commander told Anishinaabeg assembled in the Northwest Territory in 1799: "[I]n short it's the W[hite] people that you have to depend on and to apply too [*sic*] for all your wants."[43]

Native leaders and federal officials alike interpreted these gifts through shared and yet differently understood narratives—what Richard White has described as "creative misunderstanding"—that served both their interests. Both groups, for instance, framed Native poverty through gender and age. "The white People cloath their women and children," a leader of the Wabash Confederacy told a federal representative at a treaty session in Vincennes in 1792. "[O]urs are running naked. Take pity on them & send something every spring to make them glad." Embracing this rhetoric, federal officials promised to supply goods for "your women and children." U.S. representatives also found themselves literally providing for "old [Native] men, Women, and Children, who seem to have no relations to afford them support." Such gendered statements reflected a mutual discourse associating masculinity with autonomy, but they served antithetical goals. For male Native leaders, appealing for goods on behalf of women and children preserved their masculine independence. For federal officials, such rhetoric had the opposite effect: it heightened their association between Indians and Anglo-Americans' well-worn gendered tropes of dependency.[44]

Shared kinship metaphors also shaped the meaning of federal "presents." By providing for Native peoples, the United States was stepping into a well-established diplomatic role as Indians' "father." Federal officials eagerly adopted this rhetoric: when William Blount doled out gifts to the Cherokees, he spoke of "the good things which our father, the President, ha[s] done for you." Yet, as scholars have traced, the two groups interpreted such language differently: fathers played a more benevolent role in predominantly matriarchal Native societies than the patriarchal authority figures envisioned by Anglo-Americans. By the 1790s, though, Natives grasped Anglo-Americans' paternalistic implications—and inverted them. "[Y]ou have grown up on our land," Cherokee leaders observed at Holston. "[N]ow taking it away from us it is just like an ungrateful child robbing his father."[45]

Both Natives and federal officials largely agreed on a shared story of a benevolent federal government dispensing its largesse to an impoverished people. For both, this was an expedient account, bolstering federal pretensions to power even as it extracted goods for Native communities. But, although it contained elements of truth, this paternalistic narrative was mostly a fiction. In practice, federal compliance with Native demands for material support reflected, not federal authority and Native dependence, but the reverse: a recognition that Native power obliged the federal government to send goods westward.

Notwithstanding its liberal self-presentation, the early federal government had little desire to serve as a conduit for food, weapons, and goods to Native peoples. Burdened by an enormous war debt, the new nation sought to spend as little on Indian affairs as possible, with Henry Knox constantly urging "the most rigid oeconomy." Yet presents flowed anyway, accompanied by a stream of excuses from federal officers that offered a very different view of federal authority than the one offered for Native consumption. In this correspondence, officials described *themselves* as the constrained supplicants as they confronted Natives confident of their own strength, writing of "the impossibility of resisting the applications of Indians for rations, and presents." Generosity was required, they acknowledged in their more candid moments, because of the federal government's tenuous hold on the territories: the "constant Practice" of feeding and clothing Natives was necessary "on Account of the weak Situation of the Country," one group of Northwest Territory magistrates wrote.[46]

Native power and federal acquiescence had several sources. For one, the United States could ill afford a war with Native peoples. As we have seen, when, despite what Knox regarded as the nation's best efforts, the United States engaged in the four-year Northwest Indian War, the conflict nearly bankrupted the federal government. Little wonder, then, that federal officials concluded that buying Native loyalties would be far cheaper than a "system of coercion and oppression." "The most economical as well as the most humane conduct towards [Indians],"

Thomas Jefferson argued, "is to bribe them into peace, and to retain them in peace by eternal bribes." For the price of a single military expedition, Jefferson believed, the United States could supply Natives with "presents on the most liberal scale" for a century.[47]

Satisfying Native demands was also important because, as every territorial official was well aware, the British and Spanish, perched on the borders of the new United States, continued to compete for Native loyalties, freely doling out goods to the Native peoples of the Ohio, Illinois, and Tennessee Countries. "[I]f our Government does not make [Natives] presents," Major Hamtramck wrote Henry Knox, "they will go to the British, who will be glad to see them and who will supply them amply." Wabash chiefs told Hamtramck that the British had given them "Goods . . . in large heaps like stacks of Hay"; travelers to New Orleans reported entire warehouses of goods intended for the Cherokees, Chickasaws, and Choctaws. Native leaders were only too happy to pit the bidding powers against each other. When a federal Indian agent offered the influential Cherokee leader White Owl's Son a laced scarlet coat, ruffled shirt, and handkerchief, he disdained the gifts: he had received more "valuable presents," he noted, from "the British in Detroit." Native leaders also told federal officials that the British and Spanish were bad-mouthing the United States, informing Natives that the "Americans were poor."[48]

This competition produced an expensive arms—or rather presents—race, as federal officials sought to outgift the British and Spanish. To wean the Chickasaws and Choctaws from foreign influence, Governor Blount gave them "ten beaves [cattle] a day and what Rum thay wanted and tobaco to smoak after thay get home and every other thay could say," the Chickasaws bragged. Reportedly, the strategy was working, with the feted Natives "bo[a]st[ing] they never met with so good treatment from the british as from your Exelncy." Nenetooyah similarly praised American liberality, asking his fellow Cherokees when they had ever gone to the British and "brought home the like of this?" In the Chickasaw Nation, Piomingo's pro-Spanish rival Ugalayacabe complained that the "delusory presents of the Americans [] unhappily blinds too many of my color."[49]

Federal gifts to Natives thus mostly reflected the weakness, not the strength, of the United States. Federal officials sought to mask this reality through rhetoric of Native dependence, yet many Anglo-Americans believed Natives could readily perceive the true motive for such "large presents and annuities." Native nations, the legislature of the Southwest Territory informed Congress, perceived such payments not as "an evidence of friendship" but "as an evidence of fear, or as a tribute paid to their superior prowess in war."[50]

Though these legislators had their own agenda in urging diplomacy's abandonment, they were right: judging from their behavior, many Native leaders understood all too well the bargaining power they held. Federal officials frequently complained that Native leaders, rather than acting like supplicants, expected federal goods as a "Matter of Right." The entourage of Cherokee leader Kunokeski, for instance, reportedly burned their government-supplied beds on a diplomatic visit after officials refused to permit them to take the beds with them. In 1795, Secretary of War Timothy Pickering wooed Chickasaw leader George Colbert with $400, a considerable amount of money, to purchase "an elegant Stallion." But Colbert "seemed to consider this sum hardly sufficient"; the Chickasaw, Pickering complained, "was singularly difficult to please."[51]

Such hauteur was not limited to leaders. Benjamin Hawkins, in charge of Indian affairs throughout the Southeast, described the Creeks and Cherokees he encountered as "spoiled," accustomed to goods "sufficient to clothe all the Idlers in the Nation." Natives, he complained, "demand any thing they want, from a whiteman, and feel themselves insulted, when refused, they think they confer a favour on the donor if they accept of clothes from him when naked or provisions when hungry."[52]

Worst of all for officials like Hawkins, the one thing that the federal government's extravagance was supposed to purchase—Native allegiance—proved fickle. "The very Indians, who no longer ago than the last autumn were prevented from suffering the extremes of hunger by the bounties of the United States," an official in the Southwest Territory reported to Henry Knox, "have recently been either stealing horses, or murdering defenceless women and children." Native leaders whom whites had feted and dined—men like Nenetooyah and Kunokeski (John Watts), who had always received "the attention [of] Governor Blount and the White People . . . whenever he came among them"—were reportedly among the first to push for war. Rather than buying loyalty, federal gifts merely puffed the leaders up: "[T]he Whites had given him (Watts) a great many fine Clothes and he had grown saucy," Kunokeski's own brother Unacata stated, mocking Kunokeski's changeable allegiances.[53]

Such complaints of Native entitlement should be read critically. Federal officials' accounts of haughty and spoiled Natives represented the converse of the tropes of Native poverty and dependency; when they refused to mouth the requisite supplications, Native leaders were violating the diplomatic script. In condemning Natives for insufficient gratitude, federal officials echoed the era's wider denunciations of the unworthy poor.[54]

But, just as Native poverty was more than a rhetorical artifact, so too the entitled behavior of Native leaders reflected more than federal officials' biases. Native leaders recognized that the federal government was more dependent on them than vice versa. Like the federal officials they encountered, Natives were leveraging the power they had to pursue their own aims.

Half the Wealth of the Union

How successful Native leaders were at extracting money from the federal government is a matter of perspective. In one sense, the federal government got off cheap, particularly when it came to land: it bought Native title for much less than the land was worth on the Anglo-American market. Between 1790 and 1800, the federal government paid Native nations roughly one cent per acre for their lands in annuities, the recurring payments that the federal government promised in return for land cessions. The government then sought to resell that same land for prices ranging from thirty cents to $2 per acre. Even Henry Knox acknowledged that the federal government was "taking away [Native] lands" for "pitiful considerations."[55]

Yet Knox did not feel that the federal government spent too little on Indians. On the contrary, Knox was the most vocal of a bevy of federal officials bemoaning what they regarded as the Indian Department's inordinate expenses. Though these protestations reflected the standard carping of public officials during the cash-strapped early republic, the assertion that Indian affairs cost the federal government a great deal of money, particularly during the 1790s, rang true.

For one, despite rosy-eyed expectations about sales of western lands, there was tremendous uncertainty over the public domain's future. In the 1790s, income from federal lands was hypothetical—it did not even cover the government's expenditures on treaty annuities—and many feared it would never materialize.[56]

More broadly, fixating on federal annuities as consideration for Native lands ironically construed treaties to be what federal officials wished: straightforward land sale contracts. But, though they concluded in written documents, treaty sessions were also grand diplomatic affairs where Natives reaffirmed their relationship with the United States. These elaborate weeks- or months-long conventions in the woods, usually held in the borderlands distant from Anglo-American settlements, were attended by scores of federal officials, soldiers, interpreters, and clerks, as well as hundreds or even thousands of Natives.[57]

All these aspects of treaty sessions cost money, leading one treaty commissioner to bemoan "the great expence attending Indian Treatyes." Federal officials had to feed, clothe, and house all the Natives who showed up, as well as supply them with gifts, while paying and feeding their own staff. Natives also had a frustrating habit of failing to stick to federal timelines: Blount complained that the Chickasaws and Choctaws showed up "many days" early to 1792 treaty session, "which made expenses much higher." Treaty commissioners futilely tried to keep down costs by limiting attendees only to "headmen," but what officials called "common Indians" came in enormous numbers anyway, expecting to be housed and fed.[58]

Despite officials' best efforts, then, treaty negotiations were elaborate affairs that literally ate up public resources. At the small treaty that Rufus Putnam held at Vincennes in 1792, attended by only seven hundred Natives, Putnam thought forty thousand rations was a "moderate calculation"; he also brought coats, coats, hats, suits, kettles, blankets, shirts, hatchets, knives, and ribbons to the meeting. For a proposed meeting with the Cherokees, federal officials purchased eight thousand pounds of flour, nine hundred gallons of whiskey, and a ton of lead. Most of these items were transported from Philadelphia, requiring salaries for wagoneers, boatmen, and storekeepers.[59]

Consequently, a single treaty session usually cost many times more than the federal annuities that resulted. One conference with the Chickasaws and Choctaws—a peace conference where no lands were to be purchased—ran an estimated $6,754.50, while the goods alone for a proposed treaty with the Cherokees cost $4,743.25. In 1789, Arthur St. Clair estimated that a treaty along the Mississippi would cost an estimated $10,250 in goods, transportation, and salaries, with another $5,000 for thirty thousand rations. St. Clair would know: the Treaty of Fort Harmar that he had just concluded had cost over $18,000. One congressman's extreme estimate put the cost of the 1790 Treaty of New York with the Creeks at $61,000 in presents and priced a subsequent meeting at $150,000. Little wonder that the white residents of Cumberland feared that supporting an Indian treaty from their own coffers would "reduce them to the Greatest Poverty and Distress."[60]

Yet treaties were merely the most concentrated instances when federal moneys went to house, clothe, and feed Natives. Because treaties represented a relationship rather than a single transaction, the underlying logic—that the federal government had to supply Native peoples to secure their allegiance—meant that most of the federal government's Indian Department expenditures went to maintain Native goodwill, not buy lands. For instance, neither the Chickasaws nor the Choctaws sold the federal government land in the 1790s, but their strategic location, coupled with U.S. fear of Spanish influence, nonetheless directed federal money their way. In 1793, William Blount, who hoped to use the Chickasaws to counter the Creeks, proposed that a staggering $97,500 in goods be supplied to the Chickasaws and Choctaws annually—including sixteen thousand blankets, seventy thousand yards of cloth, and fifteen thousand pounds of ammunition. The actual amount they received, though less dramatic, was still significant: $16,000 in goods and the salary for a hired white blacksmith. Another $3,000 worth in goods followed a few years later.[61]

And it was not just goods. Throughout the 1790s, Native people constantly showed up at federal forts throughout the territories demanding to be fed. Reluctant to allow these visitors to leave empty-handed—officers feared they would then report, "We have nothing to expect from the United States"—the officers issued the rations these Natives expected: 3,154 pounds of flour, 2,196 pounds of beef, 220 gills (5 ounces) of salt, and 294 gills of whiskey at Fort Defiance in 1798; 2,556 pounds of beef in a single month of 1796 to support ninety Indians at Fort Wayne; 688 rations of liquor in October 1801 at Fort Washington. Costs mounted. One officer in Vincennes spent $1,600 in a single year on the Indian Department, while other officers decried the "incredible expence to government" of feeding Natives. Complaining that the "provisions to Indians distributed at military posts far exceed in value the amount of their annual Stipends [and] encourage the Indians in idleness," the secretary of war attempted to have the practice "absolutely terminated." But the "incidental expenses" of the Indian Department—including the "rations issued to Indians"—only continued to rise, going from thousands to tens of thousands of dollars every year.[62]

Nor were such demands limited to frontier outposts. Cherokees, Choctaws, Chickasaws, and Native leaders of many other nations could routinely be found strolling the streets of Philadelphia, bedecked in federally provided attire. On these "Indian visits," Native leaders journeyed thousands of miles to meet directly with the president and the secretary of war in the capital, with some representatives like the Cherokees Kunokeski and Nenetooyah making the trip nearly annually. One week in 1796, President Washington reportedly dined with four different "Setts of Indians"; a congressman joked that Henry Knox would soon learn Cherokee "by keeping continually whole tribes of indians at this place."[63]

Both cabinet officials and Native leaders saw advantages in such visits. Successive secretaries of war encouraged trips as an opportunity to impress Native leaders with the size, power, and goodwill of the United States. For their part, Natives embraced the visits as an opportunity to conduct diplomacy unmediated by lower officials. "Indian visits to this place [Philadelphia] ought to be prevented," one associate of William Blount complained. "[A]fter the agreement made in Treaty the Indians had only to say we are dissatisfied with the Superintendant we will go to Congress, this they do and get what they want." This complaint helps explain why so many Natives eagerly made the long and occasionally dangerous journey.[64]

Indian visits, too, were expensive: the federal government bore all expenses, including the accompanying translators and agents. Once in Philadelphia, Native leaders were further "abundantly supplied with goods" so that they could report back on U.S. generosity. William Blount, who accompanied the Chickasaws on a 1793 visit to Philadelphia, hoped that Piomingo would "give occular demonstration of the liberality of the United States" upon his return. The consequence was that such visits cost as much as a treaty: Blount estimated that a single Cherokee visit in 1792 ran about $10,000.[65]

Satisfying Native demands through elaborate treaty sessions, provisions, "presents," and Indian visits was costly. Tallying up the precise figures is difficult given the poor state of early federal recordkeeping, but one bureaucratic calculation—pieced together from various records in 1820 and likely an underestimate—stated that the federal government spent $722,393 in the Indian Department throughout the 1790s, nearly 2 percent of the federal government's nondebt expenditures during the period. Expenditures continued to rise, precipitously, in the following decades: by the early 1800s, Indian Department expenditures routinely exceeded $100,000 a year.[66]

These sums vindicated those who saw placating Native wants as cheaper than warfare, which consumed most of the federal budget: between 1789 and 1800, over 70 percent of the federal government's nondebt budget went to military spending. (The rest went largely to civil salaries and foreign affairs, with much smaller amounts to run the mint and lighthouses.) Yet the cost of Indian affairs dramatically exceeded earlier guesses of how much generous presents would cost—usually estimated at $15,0000 to $20,000 annually. The Indian Department expenditures look quite large, for instance, when set against the $972,000 the federal government spent on compensation and pensions for Revolutionary War veterans during the same period. They were especially enormous sums of money in the territories, with fledgling economies and scarce currency: the Northwest Territory, for instance, brought in a little less than $40,000 in federal taxes in 1798–1799, when Tennessee supplied the treasury merely $13,000.[67]

More revealing than the absolute numbers, though, were Anglo-Americans' perceptions of these expenditures. Whites in the territories believed that huge amounts of federal money went to Native nations—and deeply resented it. "[H]alf the wealth of the union [is] presented to the enemy," one *Knoxville Gazette* writer observed; a Georgian citizen similarly bemoaned the "enormous sums of money" expended "yearly" on Indian "presents." Some explicitly contrasted federal expenditures on Natives with spending on veterans. If Congress "has any bounty to spare," Tennessee's first governor John Sevier argued, it should grant its "charity" to "the lame, the halt, and the blind soldier" who sacrificed for their nation, rather than "giving thousands to those who dispise it."[68]

In the Northwest Territory, resentment of federal funding of Natives fueled calls for their extermination. In Vincennes, residents began arguing that instead of "receiv[ing] any Indians into the Village, [] we ought to kill them." During the 1794 Cincinnati riot described in Chapter Four, inhabitants invoked federal finance to justify their genocidal fury against Choctaws aiding the U.S. Army: bystanders testified that the rioters "Observed that those Indians were a Considerable Expence to the US—that it would be Serviceable totaly to destroy them (*and that Instantly*) than that they should receive any further Support."[69]

Underlying this rage was a sense of betrayal—a belief that the federal government was coddling Natives at the same moment that the nation's own citizens were left to suffer the fury of Native attacks unaided. "While [the Cherokee chief] Double Head . . . and his sanguinary Brothers are received and caressed at Philadelphia," residents of the Southwest Territory complained, "we are daily Suffering at the Hands of their Associates in Iniquity." Few complaints were more common among territorial citizens than that the federal government, biased in favor of Indians, had forgotten its obligation to its own citizens. The "present measures of the Federal Government," one observer reported, led many people to believe "they are neglected, and the interest of the indians only consulted." Returning to the paternalist metaphors that dominated Indian affairs, one citizen of the Southwest Territory complained that Congress "are more favourable to their savage, adopted, and illegitimate, than to us their legitimate children."[70]

Allegiance and Protection

Territorial citizens' self-serving narrative of federal neglect in favor of Native interests was nonetheless partially right: their relationship with the federal government paralleled Native nations' status in key respects. The subject of a similar debate over the meaning of dependence, territorial citizens exploited the same source of power as the territories' Native peoples—uncertain allegiances in a contested borderland—toward the same aim: wringing resources from the federal government. But territorial citizens' self-pitying insistence that they were the losers in this contest for federal support was both strategic and wrong. Territorial citizens easily outcompeted their Native neighbors in this shared endeavor to extract federal aid.

In vocally attacking Native peoples as federal dependents, territorial citizens were, perhaps, projecting anxiety over their own status. A clear-eyed view suggests that territorial citizens better merited the title of federal dependents than their Native neighbors.

Citizens' claims that Natives were enriching themselves at federal expense, for instance, ignored how much Indian Department money ended up in whites' pockets. Some white residents of Vincennes, Detroit, Knoxville, and Nashville were department employees, working as interpreters and agents. Many more were department contractors: merchants who sold the department overpriced goods; wagoneers and boatmen who transported those goods into Indian country; craftsmen who constructed trading posts and warehouses to store the goods. Minimal oversight made it easy to exploit these opportunities. One army officer, proclaiming himself an Indian agent, used his supposed position to operate a "system of job-making" for the "sole benefit" of him and his confederates, at "very Enormous" expense. In Nashville, legitimate Indian agent James Robertson allegedly organized a cartel of local merchants, to whom he directed department business in return for kickbacks—while only delivering Natives half the goods contracted for. Little wonder that Secretary of War Timothy Pickering bemoaned the "great abuses existing in the conduct of [Indian] affairs in the Southwestern Territory."[71]

This blindness to how Indian Department spending benefited whites reflected a broader dynamic. The territories were federal dependencies in multiple senses, even as territorial citizens contested or mitigated these meanings.

"Dependency" was, in fact, a term of art to describe the territories' legal and constitutional status. Unlike Native nations—whom federal law defined as autonomous, "independent" sovereigns, albeit amorphously under U.S. territorial sovereignty—the Northwest Ordinance unambiguously subjected the territories to federal power and control, rendering them, in Governor St. Clair's words, "dependent colon[ies] of the United States." Territorial citizens were well aware of, and keenly resented, their disempowerment. Territorial newspapers seethed with pseudonymous denunciations of the Ordinance as "oppressive impolitical, and altogether improper." "We have no suffrage at all," one typical grievance from Cincinnati read. "We are obliged to be subjects to [the national government]; & yet without redress of our grievances."[72]

The territorial governors rejected such complaints. The imperious St. Clair thought territorial citizens lacked meaningful rights and should be "put in Mind that they are not yet a part of the Union, but dependent upon it." Blount, by contrast, conceded the Ordinance's imperfections. "But if certain liberties are given up temporarily," he noted, "temporary benefits are given in lieu, that is the expense of government, of which the people bear no part, not even the tax of an excise, for it is borne by the federal government."[73]

Blount was right: although Congress later extended the excise, the federal government still heavily subsidized territorial governance. Territorial citizens paid some local taxes, but, thanks to the federal treasury, their tax obligation was considerably less than in most states. As one Southwest Territory judge observed, "We experience all the Advantages of Government without feeling any of its burdens." Dependence, in short, conveyed financial advantages alongside political costs.[74]

As with Native peoples, federal officials used paternalistic rhetoric to naturalize the territories' dependency. No metaphor for the territories was more common in the early United States than depictions of the regions as the growing children of a benevolent federal father. The Northwest Territory was a "Child . . . Nursed with such tenderness by the United States," one set of petitioners wrote Congress, while the territorial legislature later thanked "the federal Government for the paternal care which they have exercised over the colony." As such statements suggest, territorial citizens no less than Natives could repurpose federal paternalism to assert claims: in both instances, this language prefaced requests for federal aid on behalf of its territorial infants.[75]

Yet as in the case of Native nations, such shared and even obsequious language often masked federal impotence and the boldness of territorial citizens, who, if they were children, were remarkably disobedient—or so federal officials felt. In fact, most territorial citizens couched their relationship with the United States differently. For one, male citizens rejected accounts that portrayed them as helpless infants, which smacked uncomfortably of the feminized dependence they associated with Natives. So, like their male Native counterparts, Anglo-American men in the territories displaced their suffering. The true victims of federal neglect, they insisted, were the "poor women and children" sacrificed to violent (yet coddled) Natives. Territorial citizens ritually invoked this gendered trope as part of the lurid language of the anti-Indian sublime to demand federal aid.[76]

For their own relationship with the federal government, male territorial citizens rejected the feminized metaphor of family in favor of the masculine language of contract and citizenship: their loyalty to the government, they insisted, was contingent on its fulfillment of certain obligations. Above all, the bargain between citizen and state required the government to provide "protection."

"Protection" was a resonant word in the late eighteenth-century borderlands. Under the law of nations, the term had an imperial connotation that federal officials exploited when they forced Native nations to acknowledge the "protection" of the United States. But the protection that territorial citizens demanded from the federal government had a different meaning: it was a governmental duty, not a power, and connoted organized force and violence directed against enemies. "[P]rotection is the best & grand object of social compact," Virginian Patrick Henry observed of this state obligation. "[I]f it is found that no relyance can be placed in Congress for protection, are not all the Western people driven into a separation from us?" One writer in the *Knoxville Gazette* put it baldly. "Allegiance and protection are reciprocal in their nature," the pseudonymous "Fellow Citizen" wrote, "and the one *may* of right be refused when the other is withdrawn."[77]

Many, especially in the Southwest Territory, believed federal protection *had* been withheld, describing themselves as the "most easy prey & the most out of protection" of anywhere in the United States. To explain why the federal government neglected them in favor of other citizens, they blamed their remoteness and political powerlessness. "[C]itizens who live in poverty on the extreme frontier are as much entitled to [be] procted [*sic*] in their lives, their families, and their little property," the territorial legislature reminded Congress after it funded a navy against Barbary pirates, "as those who roll in luxury, ease, and affluence, in the great and opulent Atlantic cities." An author in the *Knoxville Gazette* expressed this sense of neglected grievance when writing of recent Creek attacks: "Had THESE DEPREDATIONS been committed in PHILADELPHIA the reader can fill in the blank." One anonymous reader actually did so, scrawling: "there would have been provisions made to punish those savages."[78]

If the federal government would not satisfy its obligation of protection, many concluded, they could find a sovereign that would. Throughout the 1780s and 1790s, the western United States was aflame with secessionist sentiments, with the vision of a "separate, independent Govrnment" as a "maggot . . . in the heads of some people." The allegiances of the regions' white residents seemed as fickle as those of their Native neighbors, and, like their neighbors, territorial citizens used their strategic borderlands location to flirt with Spanish and British patronage. The most elaborate intrigues sprang from local elites—often the very men whom the federal government relied on to implement its policies, like U.S. General James Wilkinson or federal Indian agent James Robertson.[79]

Similarly to Indian country intelligence, belated and imperfect accounts of such plotting trickled back to Philadelphia, where alarmed cabinet officials regularly panicked over rumors of foreign agents working their way through the territories. Those officials were, in fact, arguably the principal audience for such scheming. Westerners' secessionist dalliances never amounted to much, but their posturing powerfully reminded the federal government of its tenuous hold on the region. Territorial citizens had built their own playoff system, born of frustration and supposed neglect, in which they used the prospect of disloyalty to wring resources from a reluctant federal government.[80]

The message was clear: "Does not Congress consider the lives of their people of more value than money?" wrote one western settler pleading for military action. And federal policymakers heard. "[A]cts of protections," one Massachusetts congressman concluded, would be "the most successful way to banish the ruinous idea of the future independency of the western country" since it would "gain [settlers'] hearts." Henry Knox similarly determined that military spending was the means most likely "to attach the people of the frontiers to the government of the United States."[81]

In the Northwest Territory, such rhetoric helped drag the reluctant national government into its lengthy and costly war against the Northwest Indian Confederacy. "A frontier citizen possesses as strong claims to protection as any other citizen," Henry Knox wrote in his public justification of the conflict. Privately, he urged Arthur St. Clair to tout the ongoing "expensive arrangements for the protections of the frontiers" so as to "impress the frontier Citizens, of the entire good dispositions of the General government towards them." This effort seemed to work: citizens of the Northwest Territory now prefaced complaints about territorial governance with "our acknowledgments and gratitude" to Congress for "having expended the whole revenue of the union for several years, in order to afford us ample protection."[82]

This spending not only encouraged settlement but fueled the Northwest Territory's economy, as money cascaded westward with the U.S. Army. The Northwest Indian War proved a particular boon for Cincinnati, its population doubling in nine months of 1790, a transformation one observer attributed to "the residence of the army here." An inhabitant of Marietta later recalled how all "the Yong & interpriseing men follow[ed] the Armey to catch the Government's money & Make to themselves Fourtains [fortunes]." Embittered, he complained, "The Indian War Built up Cincinaty & the adjacent Countrey at the expence of the Ohio Companeys Settlement."[83]

Other parts of the Northwest Territory benefited from military spending, too. When the United States took possession of Detroit in 1796, long-standing fur-trade firms began a lucrative sideline in supplying the army with enormous quantities of alcohol, beef, and especially flour, while the town received "the benefit of the free circulation of Cash" from soldiers' pay. The military kept the flour mills of the Illinois Country similarly busy, with one officer estimating that his soldiers consumed one-third of all the flour in Vincennes. Little wonder that William Blount observed that the Northwest Territory was "more full of Money arising from . . . the army North of Ohio than any other Part of America."[84]

As Blount's jealousy indicates, the Southwest Territory ostensibly fared differently, since, as we have seen, Congress refused to authorize similar punitive expeditions. Many historians have followed Andrew Cayton in concluding that this failure soured the Territory against the federal government, creating long-standing regional divergences in attitudes toward national authority. But the claim that the federal government neglected the Southwest Territory too readily credits the self-serving statements of its most vocal citizens. Their complaints were not neutral descriptions of reality but strategic efforts to shape federal policy—and they proved remarkably effective.[85]

Paying the Militia

The militia was a paradoxical institution in the early United States. On the one hand, it was deeply local. The militia had long been the instantiation of the community in arms, requiring the service of all able-bodied young white men. Officers were usually prominent locals, often selected by the militiamen themselves. Yet on the other hand, the militia was key to national defense, even for those who, like Henry Knox, favored the regular army. The Constitution itself empowered Congress to oversee local militias, yet Knox's initial attempt at national militia regulations failed in the First Congress amidst intense controversy. Only after St. Clair's disastrous 1791 defeat did Congress enact two militia statutes. One empowered the president to call the militia into national service whenever the United States was in "imminent danger of invasion from any foreign nation or Indian tribe," and the other governed the organization and equipment of the militia while leaving enforcement to the states.[86]

The territorial militia was especially ambiguous. Like all aspects of governance in the territories, it was formally a federal institution. The president appointed the territorial militia's generals, while Governors Blount and St. Clair chose all other officers and determined when, and how, to call out the militia. Yet, as elsewhere in the territories, this paper federal power yielded only nominal authority. St. Clair and Blount largely maintained local notables as officers and, because of distance, gave them discretion to mobilize their soldiers in response to threats. "[T]eazed to death by rumours of persons killed" in Native raids, these commanders routinely called up more militia than Blount or St. Clair thought necessary. The militia officers, St. Clair grumbled, did "not ma[k]e a very discreet use of the powers they were invested with, as to numbers."[87]

But, if the federal government exercised little control over the militia's personnel or service, it did provide the finance. The territorial militia received the same pay as regular army soldiers, as well as reimbursement for subsistence and supplies, from the national treasury. They proved unsurprisingly free with other people's money, with Henry Knox lamenting that the militia made "unlimited expences" and were "exceedingly inattentive to public Stores of every kind." Knox found especially outrageous the pay afforded to the mounted rangers favored by frontier whites. "Were it carried to a considerable extent," Knox grumbled, "no Government on earth could support it."[88]

The numbers supported Knox's critiques. As Native attacks escalated in the early 1790s, the federal government expended tens of thousands of dollars *monthly* on territorial militia defense. By 1792, with a white population of thirty-five thousand, the Southwest Territory had an estimated fifteen hundred militia under arms, at the cost of $20,000 for three months' service. In October and November 1793 alone, the Territory spent $37,517.69 on militia; Henry Knox feared that costs would top $100,000 by February of the next year. Expenses around isolated Nashville were especially heavy, purportedly four times greater than elsewhere in the Territory. To pay these claims, literal chests filled with tens of thousands of dollars made their way to the office of David Henley, the War Department's Knoxville paymaster. Henley later recounted being completely overwhelmed as he single-handedly processed claims worth hundreds of thousands of dollars.[89]

Though many territorial inhabitants regarded these measures as inadequate to defend them against Native attacks, others, such as the writer L.M. in the *Knoxville Gazette*, acknowledged that the Southwest Territory received a double benefit from these expenditures. For one, "the citizens have been protected." For another, "for these services they are and will be paid, in money, a medium of trade, general and efficacious." Thanks to the federal government, "a medium of commerce, viz. gold and silver, has been introduced," replacing the earlier near-worthless North Carolina paper currency and contributing to the "rise and growth of every little town."[90]

The promise of payment in specie made the militia claims themselves a form of currency, as "the [militia] Certificates became as it were a circulating Medium thro' out the Territory." Like title claims, these pieces of potentially valuable paper became the subjects of both outright fraud and elaborate speculation. In one instance, a muster master allegedly skimmed $4 from the pay of every officer; in another, a commander reportedly mustered more men than actually served, redistributing these phantom soldiers' pay among the actual militia. More commonly, militiamen treated their vouchers akin to bounty land rights, routinely assigning them informally and at a discount to other parties, who then passed them along as currency to shopkeepers and others.[91]

Militia claims, in short, were another form of federal security, with territorial citizens, no less than eastern financiers, trading and gambling on federal credit. Yet cabinet members in Philadelphia viewed this repurposing of federal debt differently from financiers' speculations on the national debt. Secretary of War Timothy Pickering feared that this "unauthorized" trade in militia rights would facilitate "unjust emolument" for a few even as "discontents . . . have been excited among the Citizens." Rather than bolstering federal authority, he worried, such speculation stripped federal control while leaving federal officials both responsibility and blame.[92]

Yet the seemingly ceaseless flow of federal funds to pay the militia bolstered federal power in one way. Because federal officials could, and did, refuse to pay expenses they had not authorized, federal finance seemingly provided a tool to control an otherwise ungovernable militia.

A particularly fierce controversy raged around the Beard and Ore expeditions of 1793 and 1794. As discussed in Chapter Five, these expeditions flagrantly violated federal law, but the perpetrators escaped punishment. Territorial citizens now brazenly argued that not only were the expeditions legal, but that "equitable" grounds obligated Congress to repay their expenses. William Blount was shocked when James Robertson signed off on the muster rolls needed for federal reimbursement. There was not "the most distant hope that the Perpetrators of such lawless unauthorized acts could expect the least Pecuniary Reward for their trouble, for services I cannot call them," Blount told Robertson. "I know not the price I would take to report such an order to the War office."[93]

Initially, Blount was right. Successive secretaries of war refused to pay for these offensive military operations, causing "great Disappointment" to many speculators in the Southwest Territory, who were "deeply interested . . . holding many of the claims." Because of this refusal, one resident reported, the inhabitants'

"Confidence in the General Government [was] lost." When a Hamilton District grand jury presented grievances in 1795, two of its four complaints related to the federal government's unwillingness to repay the expeditions' expenses under the "*pretence*" that they were unauthorized.[94]

To explain this supposed mistreatment, the grand jury noted that states that had congressional representatives had received both federal payment and protection. Many citizens similarly concluded that the Territory's apparent neglect stemmed from its constitutional status: as one writer observed in the *Knoxville Gazette*, "All dependent governments are deficient as to form." Were the Territory represented in Congress, another *Gazette* author opined, the citizens' sufferings would wring tears from the walls themselves, while William Blount surmised that Ore's expedition would have been authorized in "states who have Senators and Representatives in the Public Councils."[95]

Yet territorial governance offered a remedy to this deficiency: once it had sixty thousand free inhabitants, the Territory could assume statehood and gain representation. Anxiety over Native attacks led many to argue that the Territory should seek admission as a "member state of the federal union" as "speedily as possible." Blount, too, embraced this position. After the secretary of war refused to reimburse another territorial militia expedition, the governor wrote: "Every day's experience points out in stronger Terms the Necessity for a *New* State in preference of a territorial Government."[96]

What might seem a naïve hope in the power of representation proved prescient. After Tennessee's statehood, disgruntled militiamen once again sent Congress petitions appealing for reimbursement for Beard's 1793 expedition and Ore's 1794 attack, including Hugh Lawson White's petition. The secretary of war argued against payment, but Tennessee's newly elected congressman, Andrew Jackson—who had served as a private in Ore's expedition—championed the militiamen's cause. Serving as chairman of the committee to which Congress referred the petition, Jackson insisted that the attacks were legal, bolstering his argument with melodramatic descriptions of how "the knife and the tomahawk were held over the heads of women and children." Without much discussion, Congress authorized payment for Beard's expedition in its yearly military appropriation, an action that a Tennessean told Jackson "has hightened the esteem of the people, for the General Government, and secured to yourself a permanent interest." Jackson's successor, William Claiborne, accomplished the same feat with Ore's even more dubious expedition the next year. The cause of congressional silence is unclear: perhaps the earlier debates on unauthorized expeditions had exhausted them, or they were indifferent to what seemed a local issue. Jackson and Claiborne, in contrast, were far from apathetic, and their passion prevailed.[97]

That the newly "independent" state of Tennessee proved its autonomy by lapping at the federal trough reflected the territories' creation and development.

For years, territorial citizens had been even more effective than their Native neighbors at using similar sources of leverage—changeable allegiances in a competitive and precarious borderland—to extract cash from the federal government. These expenditures buoyed an often-marginal economy. "All the Stirrings of Industry" had been "set in Motion by the circulation of [federal] Money," Arthur St. Clair reported from the Northwest Territory. Such money "like a gentle stream fertilize[d] and beautif[ied] the whole Country through which it flowed."[98]

Yet all this federal money did not alter the belief of territorial citizens, especially in the Southwest Territory, that distant, unfeeling politicians had abandoned them to destruction. The money, after all, was but an inadequate recognition of their right as citizens to federal protection, and their survival stemmed from self-reliance rather than government beneficence. Native peoples might be federal wards, but territorial citizens were among that "class of men, that earn their scanty living by hard labour, and who do not seek in the sweets of the general Government, to their aid."[99]

Betty, Scolocutta's widow, made one more appearance in whites' written records. In 1799, two years after Betty's Philadelphia visit, two Moravian brethren, members of a proselytizing German Protestant faith, scouted Upper Cherokee country for a possible mission. On the road to Chota, they stopped at the prosperous farm where Betty supported her extended family, partly through her federal pension. "The old woman is called 'Grandmother Maw' by the white people," the missionaries reported, "and is honored as an industrious and intelligent woman." They tried to talk to her, but she was "not much interested."[100]

The brethren had more luck with others. Befriending several federal officials, they had a long dinner with War Department Paymaster David Henley, who supplied the requisite federal pass to enter Cherokee land. Henley "regretted that we had not come two or three weeks earlier when all the chiefs and more than four thousand Indians had been at Tellico Blockhouse to receive their annual gifts [annuity], which consisted of about $6,000 worth of goods"—a time when, the missionaries recorded, "the Indians are fed by the United States, drawing daily rations." Henley also warned the pair that the Cherokees were "much given to horse-stealing"—although the practice was "gradually decreased," he assured them, because "according to the treaty, $50 for each stolen horse was taken from the annual gift to recompense those who claimed it."[101]

Once within the Cherokee Nation, the missionaries encountered other visitors. Three Chickasaws en route to David Henley to get compensation for stolen horses "greeted us with a nod and friendly smile." Less agreeable was a white trader named Tooker who trafficked in such horses; the brethren watched as the Indian agent expelled him from the Nation. The Moravians also chanced upon Creeks bringing cattle north to sell to the federal garrison, noting that the Cherokees, too, fed the fort by selling "butter, eggs, and fruit."[102]

Of course, the missionaries also spoke with Cherokees. Aarcowce, "beloved man of Chota," presented his white visitors the sole book he owned: a printed copy of Washington's 1796 address to the Cherokees "wrapped in thick paper." Another evening, the Moravians chatted at length with the "half Indian" Dick Fields, who worked as the federal agent's interpreter, receiving $300 annually; several nights later, they slept on feather beds at the home of Mrs. Martin, the Cherokee wife of a former Indian agent. The Moravians admired her "fine plantation," with extensive furniture, livestock, and "Negro slaves," and, though the owner was away, conversed with her cousin Walker. Yet Walker, they feared, was "too civilized" to accept the Gospel: at the age of thirty, he had traveled to Detroit, Philadelphia, New York, and Augusta, and "knew how to talk about many things, including trade, knew the value of money in the different states and the articles which could be brought from Charleston or Philadelphia with most profit."[103]

What the Moravians encountered in the Cherokee Nation, in short, was a complex commercial society significantly shaped by the fledgling Indian Department and its money. Finance continued to be a crude tool for purchasing Native allegiance—like Grandmother Maw, many Cherokees remained skeptical of what whites had to offer—but its reach had made federal authority seemingly inescapable in Indian country. But the Cherokees that the Moravians encountered were neither poor nor dependent as a result; on the contrary, many had savvily profited from federal largesse. The extensive federal presence mostly demonstrated the ability of the Cherokees—as well as Shawnees, Delawares, Chickasaws, and Choctaws—to extract expensive aid from a reluctant United States.

Of course, that was not how the Cherokees' white neighbors understood matters. Mistaking mutually convenient rhetoric for reality, they cast Native peoples as dependents on federal funding motivated by a supposedly misplaced humanitarianism—akin to the government-provided veterans' pensions, poor relief, and disaster aid that other scholars have described as the antecedents of the national welfare state. This perception only grew: as the British and Spanish retreated, federal authority increasingly became Native peoples' principal weapon to counter their neighbors' rapacity, until, in 1831, the U.S. Supreme Court wrote Native dependence into federal law. "They look to our government for protection; rely upon its kindness and its power; appeal to it for relief against their wants; and address the president as their great father," Chief Justice John Marshall claimed in *Cherokee Nation v. Georgia*, which famously declared the Cherokee a "domestic dependent nation." Erasing the history of empowered

Natives and conciliatory, even obsequious, federal officials, Marshall offered a narrative in which the continued flow of hundreds of thousands of federal dollars into Indian country demonstrated Native weakness rather than strength.[104]

Marshall's decision came in the midst of national crisis over Cherokee persistence in which Hugh Lawson White—the *other* 1796 petitioner—played a key role. At the time of the Moravian brethren's visit, White had recently left his job as William Blount's private secretary to become an attorney in rapidly growing Knoxville, the capital of a newly independent Tennessee only thirty miles from Betty's homestead. White might even have encountered the Moravians when they passed through town, recording the construction of an imposing two-story limestone courthouse. The prosperity that the brethren observed here and in Nashville owed much to federal funds. Nonetheless, as we shall see, white Tennesseans remained strikingly hostile to the federal government. Prefiguring a later discourse that differentiated "needs" from "rights"—one that contrasted pitiable dependents of state aid, often women and people of color, from those "entitled" to governmental benefits—they distinguished themselves from Natives by defining the enormous sums of federal money that flowed to them as merely their due.[105]

Two years later, White was presiding over Knoxville's impressive new courthouse—now as a judge on Tennessee's highest court. The appointment marked the beginning of White's ascent through Tennessee politics until, in 1825, he returned to the body that had approved his youthful petition—now as a U.S. Senator. There, he became chairman of the Committee on Indian Affairs, which drafted the Indian Removal Act that proposed that Native nations "exchange" their treaty-guaranteed lands for federal lands beyond the Mississippi. White's committee report dismissed the Cherokee leadership's vociferous objections to this project as the cavils of a tiny minority who "have acquired considerable property . . . through the annuities paid by the United States"; the mass of Cherokees, White insisted, were "as poor and degraded as well can be imagined."[106]

And so White once again successfully directed federal funds toward Cherokee destruction—only this time, the sum was in the millions. The ensuing federally financed deportation ripped Native peoples from their homelands, seizing the prosperity that Betty and other Natives had carefully amassed over generations to bestow upon their "independent" white neighbors.

PART III
STATEHOOD

7
Equal Footing

In 1796, the Southwest Territory became the first federal territory to seek statehood. The Northwest Ordinance provided some guidance on this process—territories would be entitled to statehood once they had sixty thousand free (non-Native) inhabitants, or earlier at Congress's discretion—but it left many other questions unresolved. This uncertainty prompted a lengthy debate over the Territory's admission focused less on the new state of "Tennessee" than on the future. "Other States would be rising up in the Western wilderness, and claiming their right to admission," one congressman observed, "and therefore the precedent now to be established, was of very considerable importance."[1]

What followed was one of the most significant, if less studied, federalist controversies in the early United States. Statehood's key question was whether the end of direct federal rule would similarly unspool the federal government's deep involvement in the region's governance. Having long chafed at federal control, newly minted Tennesseans pressed for expansive autonomy. Pointing to the Northwest Ordinance's promise that new states would enjoy "an equal footing with the original States in all respects whatsoever," they insisted that Tennessee now enjoyed all rights of sovereignty and property previously enjoyed by the federal government. Federal officials resisted this interpretation, seeking to preserve the authority accrued under territorial governance.[2]

Framed in the high rhetoric of federalism, these controversies nonetheless centered on concrete disputes. Unlike later contests over admission, the legality of chattel slavery was barely discussed: with over ten thousand enslaved Africans already in Tennessee, white politicians simply assumed the institution's persistence. Rather, Tennessee's admission reopened contentions over the two intertwined areas of governance that had dominated the Southwest Territory: land and Indian affairs. Under territorial rule, federal officials had built land and Indian Department bureaucracies that remained outside state control, a potent symbol of federal power's persistence. Challenging that supremacy, Tennessee asserted its own authority over both the public domain and Native diplomacy. The two issues swirled together in a series of collisions—over ownership of public lands, Zachariah Cox's Yazoo speculations, former Governor Blount's borderland scheming—that culminated in the new state's most heated confrontation, an at-times violent showdown over Cherokee land rights under the Treaty of Holston.[3]

Federal Ground. Gregory Ablavsky, Oxford University Press (2021). © Gregory Ablavsky.
DOI: 10.1093/oso/9780190905699.003.0008

Tennessee and the federal government disagreed not only about the merits of these claims but also about how they should be resolved. With judicial review still tentative and contested, neither turned to courts. Instead, Tennessee, emphasizing its equality, pressed for state-federal negotiation, while Congress insisted on its sole authority to adjudicate. In the end, the federal government won a seemingly Pyrrhic victory: Congress resolved the dispute by giving Tennessee the power and land that the state sought, leaving the Cherokee Nation to bear the costs of federal capitulation. But, because of the precedential stakes, even this limited federal success had important consequences—especially when, in 1802, the eastern portion of the Northwest Territory sought to become the new state of Ohio.[4]

Ohio's admission demonstrated that the federal government had learned the lessons of Tennessee. For the first time, Congress conditioned a new state's admission, requiring Ohio to disclaim rights to the expansive public domain within its borders. The politics of Ohio's statehood led the state to acquiesce, entrenching a practice that quickly became a constitutional norm. Ohio also tacitly accepted continued federal authority over the state's Native peoples, seemingly because it regarded federal jurisdiction in Indian country as a boon rather than a harm. The federal government's brief moment of sovereignty over the Northwest Territory—also bitterly resented by many citizens there, even if, just as to the south, it had brought concrete benefits—nonetheless resulted in a durable expansion of federal power.

The dominant federalist frame for these contests over new state admissions, however, obscures as well as illuminates. The highly personal, polyvocal and pluralist politics of the borderlands that had marked the territories persisted after statehood; diverse claimants still asserted rights. But the dual structure of the emerging U.S. constitutional order meant that claimants could now invoke state as well as federal sovereignty. Federalist struggles became proxy battles for the borderlands' competing interests: white settlers with inchoate title turned to a sympathetic Tennessee while the Cherokees sought vindication from the federal government.

Such disputes demonstrated the stakes in determining *which* sovereign arbitrated conflicts over ownership and jurisdiction. Tennessee aimed not just to displace the federal government but to suppress any challenger to state authority altogether. The state raged against federal authority because the federal government was the most visible and, however half-hearted, most influential defender of the earlier, multipolar order. Ironically, then, the survival of the borderlands' prior pluralism, however tenuous, increasingly depended on the federal government's persistent power to adjudicate.

Right of Soil

In the Southwest Territory, frustration with federal rule prompted widespread support for statehood. "People here almost without Exception are for a State," Governor William Blount wrote. In late 1795, Blount commissioned a census that reported that the Territory had 66,650 free inhabitants: 36,123 free white men, 29,554 free white women, and 973 "other free persons." Concluding that this population in excess of the stipulated 60,000 free inhabitants made the Territory "a State of Right," Blount called a constitutional convention.[5]

The convention met for two and a half weeks in January 1796 in one of the only public buildings in Knoxville, the office of War Department paymaster David Henley. The constitution it drafted for the new state—to be called "Tennessee" after the river, itself named for the Upper Cherokee town of Tănăsĭ'—closely resembled other states' constitutions except in one important respect: the attention it devoted to land. One proposed article specifically guaranteed settlers south of the French Broad River the right of preemption; others defined the boundaries of the new state and proclaimed the state's "Sovereignty and right of Soil" within those borders.[6]

Those few words—"right of Soil"—aggressively asserted state land ownership against competing claimants, including the United States, Native nations, and North Carolina; they also directly challenged the Northwest Ordinance, which stated that "new States shall never interfere with the primary disposal of the soil by the United States in Congress assembled." This was too bold for the delegates, who tempered this statement to claim ownership only "so far" as consistent with the U.S. Constitution, the Northwest Ordinance, and North Carolina's constitution and act of cession—thereby merely acknowledging the confusing muddle of land claims that had long characterized the Southwest Territory. Native rights went unmentioned, even though federal treaties guaranteed that over two-thirds of the new state's land would legally remain Indian country.[7]

When Congress received a copy of Tennessee's constitution, many were astonished by the would-be state's effrontery: Tennessee had drafted its constitution on its authority alone, without any congressional authorization. An intense debate followed over the quasi-metaphysical question of when, exactly, Tennessee became a state, and whether Congress had a role in deciding that question. But another line of debate focused on the seeming deficiencies of Tennessee's constitution, particularly around the question of land. The House's leading defender of Native title, James Hillhouse of Connecticut, advocated redrawing the state's borders to exclude all Indian lands, a call that other northern congressmen supported.[8]

Proponents of Tennessean statehood insisted that such a move was unnecessary. The Northwest Ordinance would remain "paramount," they soothed, the

Trade and Intercourse Act would guard Native title, and North Carolina's cession would ensure that unappropriated lands still belonged to the United States. These blandishments ultimately carried the day. Congress retroactively authorized Tennessee's actions but accepted Tennessee's constitution as written.[9]

But, with statehood was secured, newly minted Tennesseans quickly challenged the federal laws that supposedly settled title, spawning what one congressman had accurately predicted would be "disagreeable discussions." Weeks into its first sitting, the Tennessee Assembly remonstrated to Congress on the land question, stressing the state's "equal footing" and emphasizing constitutional guarantees of each state's "right of soil and sovereignty."[10]

State officials soon expanded on the Assembly's legal argument. Most of Tennessee's newly elected officers had been politically prominent in the Southwest Territory, often through their attacks on federal policy. Tennessee's first governor, John Sevier, was already a former governor—of the abortive state of Franklin; from retirement, George Washington grumbled that Sevier was distinguished only for "the murder of Indians." Now-Governor Sevier insisted that "the state of Tennessee is reinvested with all the right of domain"—that is, ownership—that North Carolina had held prior to cession. Otherwise, the promise that Tennessee was admitted to the Union on an equal footing would be violated, since Tennessee would "not equally stand possessed of those free and independant rights the original States enjoy." Sevier made these observations while forwarding the Assembly's petition to Tennessee's sole congressman: former U.S. Attorney Andrew Jackson. Jackson strongly concurred. "[T]he right to the Soil," he responded, "is so firmly invested in the sovereignty of the State, both by Constitutional principles and by the law of nations . . . that nothing but the act of the Strong hand of power itself, can divest us of that right."[11]

Jackson and Sevier similarly attacked federal authority over Indian affairs. Jackson endorsed Sevier's plans for Tennessee to prosecute Native crimes against white citizens, arguing that such jurisdiction fell within "the powers, that Consistant, With the Sovereignty retaind. by the States, properly belong to Each Individual State, which never ought on any account to be Surrender[ed] to the General Government." Jackson attacked the Adams administration's Indian policy for threatening to "overwhelm[]" the "Sovereignty of the Individual States," singling out the federal officer David Henley, who remained in Tennessee as army paymaster and was now invested with authority to "superintend[] the Indian affairs." This position, Jackson complained, was unsanctioned by "any law that I can find."[12]

Acting on this theory, Sevier conducted his own Indian policy: he corresponded with Native leaders, dispatched representatives into Indian country, and arrogated to Tennessee the right to determine whether it would honor federal Indian treaties. As he lectured Secretary of War James McHenry, "notwithstanding the [federal] Agents resident among them," most of the Cherokee nation lay "within our territorial limits," which mandated that the state be "constantly engaged, and much time taken up, in the transaction of indian business."[13]

In attacking federal power, Jackson and Sevier spoke the abstract language of state sovereignty, yet their targets were more immediate political controversies. Chief among these was the issue of the property rights of white Tennesseans living on Cherokee lands. These would-be settlers claimed title based on North Carolina's land grants, valid under the act of cession, but their presence on land that the Treaty of Holston guaranteed to the Cherokee Nation violated the federal Trade and Intercourse Act. These claimants' legally tenuous position dominated early Tennessee politics: their petitions preoccupied the state legislature's first sessions; their plight featured in Governor Sevier's inaugural addresses; securing their relief was the "chief[]" and "grand object" for the new state's congressional delegation.[14]

At stake in the debates over federal and state authority in Tennessee, then, was *which* sovereign would weigh the respective title claims of the Cherokees and the land grant holders. White Tennesseans already knew, and feared, the federal government's views. In early 1796, mere months after Tennessee drafted its constitution, the Washington administration had urged Congress, in renewing the Trade and Intercourse Act, to enact harsher penalties for settlement on Native land. Although the Act applied nationwide, the intense, freewheeling debate over Native property that ensued focused nearly exclusively on settlers claiming under North Carolina's grants in what was still the Southwest Territory. Though North Carolina's representatives strenuously insisted that Native peoples lacked ownership rights, most in Congress, especially New England Federalists, disagreed. They argued North Carolina's grants provided a right to take possession only once the federal government had purchased the land from its Native owners—a *prospective* ownership right entirely consistent with Native title.[15]

The law's final version largely reflected the New Englanders' wishes: it bolstered the penalties for illegal settlement, authorized the president to expel intruders with military force, and mandated that any claimant who settled or surveyed Native lands would forfeit any property claim in these lands. This controversial provision specifically targeted the Tennessee settlers; its proponents hoped that stripping claimants' property rights would discourage them from invading Cherokee lands.[16]

The Tennessee Assembly assessed the merits of the competing title claims very differently from Congress. Its remonstrance to Congress argued that Native peoples were mere "tenants at will" whom the state could simply expel. The claimants under North Carolina's grants, by contrast, deserved "every right, privilege, and advantage, which they are entitled to by constitutional laws."[17]

As the Southwest Territory passed from federal dependency to sovereign state, then, there was substantial doubt as to whether the authority that the federal government had accumulated over property and Indian affairs could survive. Congress insisted on its supremacy, but Sevier and Jackson found state sovereignty a powerful tool to argue that they, and not federal officials, should now adjudicate the conflicting claims to ownership and jurisdiction that dogged the new state.

Leader of the Ecunnaunuxulgee

As Sevier and Jackson crafted theories to justify why the state rather than the federal government should determine the merits of Tennessee land claims, two men arrived in Knoxville, the new state's capital, in early 1797, each with his own view on federal power and ownership.

One was Benjamin Hawkins, William Blount's successor as the federal official in charge of Indian affairs south of the Ohio. A former U.S. senator from North Carolina, Hawkins differed from Knox, Pickering, and other Washington administration officials: he was not a consistent defender of federal power and had at times fought the administration's policies. Yet, based on his early experiences as a federal treaty commissioner, Hawkins had long advocated a robust federal role in defending what he repeatedly called "Indian rights."[18]

Now, in his new role crafting federal Indian policy for half the nation, Hawkins became one of the foremost proponents of the Knoxian vision of federal sovereignty. For the next twenty years, Hawkins would earnestly urge civilization on the Native peoples within his jurisdiction, especially the Creeks, where Hawkins enjoyed particular "influence." But Hawkins was equally committed to Knox's conception of the federal government as impartial arbiter between Natives and U.S. citizens. "You may depend on my taking great care of your interests and those of the white people," Hawkins wrote to Cherokee leaders Keanetoh (Little Turkey) and Ocunna (the Badger). "I know no difference between you; you live on the same land are intitled to equal rights, and must live as friends and brothers, and it is my particular duty to see justice equally distributed among you."[19]

The other Knoxville arrival was Zachariah Cox. Georgia's 1795 grant to the Tennessee Company in hand, the Georgia speculator returned to once again attempt to settle the Company's land at Muscle Shoals, reportedly building a large boat and purchasing twenty-two cannons. Despite the dubious legality of his enterprise, Cox insisted that he would "not proceed until authorized by the laws of his country." He even met Hawkins, confident that he could secure the necessary federal license for his journey downriver.[20]

Cox was disappointed. Hawkins learned from leaders throughout the four southeastern Native nations that word of Cox's plans had already spread throughout Indian country and had much "alarmed" the nations. The Creeks, having heard "all about" the project from Keanetoh, labeled Cox "leader of the Ecunnaunuxulgee"—a word Hawkins translated as "those greedily grasping after land regardless of governmental disapproval." Chickasaw leader Ugalayacabe wrote James Robertson to convey "notise" that Cox should not "Attempt to Settel" since he lacked "the consent of the Chickasaw Nation": the Chickasaws, he threatened, would immediately "strike" any such settlement. And the Cherokee National Council appealed for President Adams to "fulfill his promises" by thwarting Cox's plan: if that failed, Cherokee warriors reportedly had "their moccasins ready" to resist.[21]

Citing his "duty" to protect Native interests, Hawkins sided with these nations and "unequivocally" rejected Cox's application for federal approval. The plan sought "with the aid of the officers of government, to trepass on the Indian rights," he lectured Cox; "it would "destroy that confidence which the Indians have in the justice of the United States." Hawkins urged his superior, Secretary of War McHenry, that Cox be "brought to condign punishment" if he proceeded. McHenry, fearing "an extensive Indian war," strongly agreed, and ordered the army not to allow Cox to pass federal posts. "Tennesee and Cox have a good deal disturbed me," McHenry confided to a colleague.[22]

Yet this unambiguous federal refusal did not stop Cox. Instead, the speculator turned to another source of law and authority: state officials. Writing Congressman Andrew Jackson, Cox abandoned his feigned allegiance to federal aims to argue that the project would benefit Tennessee: "Government will find it a better policy to people a country with their own citizens," he told Jackson, "than to reserve it as an asylum for savages." Cox also met Governor Sevier and the Tennessee Assembly, where he found a receptive audience. Sevier—who had been involved in Cox's earlier 1791 scheme—became a Tennessee Company shareholder and praised Cox's endeavor: the federal government's "prevention of a settlement at or near the muscle shoals," he alleged, was "a manifest injury done the whole western country." Sevier's sentiment was reportedly widely shared: "Coxes expedition," one observer wrote from Tennessee, "is supported by almost every man of influence in the Country."[23]

Invoking the "approbation of the executive of the state of Tennessee," Cox set out in January 1798. But, because of federal opposition, Cox went not to the Shoals but across Kentucky to the confluence of the Tennessee and Ohio Rivers, where he and his men established a town called Smithland as base for further settlement. Cox ran the town as his own fiefdom, enacting "laws of Smithland" and creating his own courts to enforce them—"tribunals . . . unknown to the nation," one federal official fulminated. When a passing trader punished under these laws questioned Cox's authority, Cox insisted that "every man has a right to make himself laws of his own house, and that the houses there were his." The trader's threat to involve the local army commander incensed Cox. "By God we are not to be threatened with the Federal Officers," Cox thundered, expelling the trader from the settlement.[24]

Federal officials closely monitored Cox's "usurpation[s] . . . of the rights of sovereignty," but were powerless to intervene: Smithland lay in a remote corner of Kentucky, whose governor had sanctioned Cox's settlement. This stalemate ended in July 1798, when Cox and a number of his men attempted to pass nearby federal Fort Massac, allegedly en route to New Orleans. The fort's commander threatened to fire, leading Cox to rant against this exercise of "military prerogative" in violation of the "constitution and laws of the United States." The commander finally allowed Cox to pass with a few men if he submitted to inspection. Cox complied—but then secretly dispatched the rest of his men overland to rejoin him.[25]

Cox and his men proceeded down the Mississippi River, perhaps actually headed to New Orleans. If so, they never made it. Cox got as far as Natchez, capital of the newly created Mississippi Territory, where he recalled waking surrounded by "battalion of federal troops, with fixed bayonets." He was then held in a nearby fort, without access to letters or visitors. Cox appealed to the territorial governor for the right of the writ of habeas corpus guaranteed "by the federal constitution." But the new territory's governor was Winthrop Sargent, freshly promoted from his prior role as Northwest Territorial Secretary. As steadfast a defender of federal power as ever, Sargent refused to aid Cox; Cox's appeals to a territorial judge were similarly unavailing. Finally, after a month in captivity, Cox climbed over the fort wall, fleeing first to New Orleans, then through Choctaw Country back to Tennessee, supposedly pursued by Natives offered a federal reward for his capture (this measure especially angered Cox, smacking of "savage or military prerogative" rather than "impartial laws").[26]

When he finally arrived in Nashville, Cox was arrested on a federal warrant and hauled into Tennessee's new federal court. But although the U.S. attorney general opined that Cox's actions amounted to treason, Cox was released after three months' detention, evidently for lack of evidence. The arrest nonetheless represented the "end to this troublesome man's career," in one newspaper's words. Plagued by lawsuits, Cox lost control over the Tennessee Company, and Muscle Shoals remained Indian country until after the War of 1812.[27]

Like many property controversies in the early republic, Cox's speculation ended in appeals to Congress for compensation. One came from Cox himself. In 1803, he petitioned Congress for $9,000 in goods—merchandise, a boat, and an enslaved person—purportedly lost in his arrest. Congress referred him to the courts for relief; there is no evidence he received any. Cox moved to Virginia, where died in the 1830s.[28]

The other appeal came from the Yazoo claimants. Deeds for the Tennessee and other Yazoo Companies had floated through Tennessee and elsewhere, regarded as "of little Value" by locals but snapped up by investors, who promptly resold them to unsuspecting northerners, especially in New England. An ironic reversal ensued: Federalists who had castigated Cox as a profound threat now transformed into staunch defenders of the "vested rights" that the Yazoo sale had conferred, even as critics of federal authority lined up to argue that Georgia had lacked the title it purported to sell.[29]

In 1802, Congress finally persuaded Georgia to cede its western title to the federal government—the last state to do so. Georgia transferred its claim to western lands in return for $1.25 million and a federal promise to extinguish Native title. To investigate the Yazoo claims to this newly federal land, Congress appointed commissioners who concluded that, although the claimants lacked legal title, Congress should recognize their moral claim to the land.[30]

A lengthy and vitriolic debate over compensation ensued, both in Congress and, ultimately, in the courts. In 1810, in *Fletcher v. Peck*, the U.S. Supreme Court for the first time invalidated a state law: in a decision implicating federalism, Indian affairs, and land policy, the Court held that Georgia's repeal of the Yazoo land sale violated the U.S. Constitution's Contract Clause. Yet few conceded that the Court's decision resolved the question. Arguments continued, even as Republicans in Congress slowly shifted in favor of compensation. Finally, in 1814, Congress agreed to compensate Yazoo shareholders with the promise of $5 million from future federal land sales. Cox's scheme had finally profited—thanks to the largesse of the federal government he had so consistently antagonized.[31]

Blount's Scheme

Cox's defiant plan to settle Muscle Shoals in the teeth of Native and federal opposition reflected his long-standing aspirations. But his borderlands scheming found a near-simultaneous parallel in an unlikely source: former Governor William Blount.

As Tennessee gained statehood, Blount's complex maneuvering to maintain popular support seemingly paid off: transitioning seamlessly from federal to state office, he became one of the new state's U.S. senators. Yet Blount still nursed the resentments of his prior office, especially his acrimonious relationship with former Secretary of War Timothy Pickering. "[H]e had taken great pains to settle that state, and to render it important," one person recalled of a conversation with Blount soon after Tennessee's statehood. Yet "he been treated very ill by the

President . . . [and] the executive officers of the United States. The conversation indeed became so affecting to him, that he wept."[32]

The lachrymose Blount sought to reclaim his former preeminence in the wake of statehood. "[P]eople about here thought it was all over with Governor Blount," one correspondent reported back in Tennessee, "but he would rise yet." Blount became involved with a dubious scheme hatched by John Chisholm, long Blount's lackey and errand man in Indian country. Chisholm, apparently an errant boaster— a "windy blasty fellow," as Blount himself once described him—concocted a plan to attack and capture Spanish Pensacola. Blount expanded the proposal into an ambitious, if vague, project to seize all of Spanish Louisiana and transfer it to the British. Betraying his motives, Blount expressed "high expectations of emolument and command" if successful.[33]

Blount believed his triumph depended on the influence he had cultivated among the regions' Native peoples while governor; his nebulous plans seemed to envision leading a Native army into Spanish territory. He accordingly obsessed about his reputation among Native nations, which he feared was waning now that he was no longer superintendent of Indian affairs; he needed, he insisted, to "hold[] his importance among them." To that end, Blount wrote to the federal Indian interpreter James Carey to involve him in the conspiracy. "If I attempt this plan," Blount told Carey, "I shall expect to have you and all my Indian country and Indian friends with me."[34]

Blount was particularly concerned that Native leaders' attachments be to *him* personally rather than to the federal government. Receiving flattering accounts that the Cherokees, "much dissatisfied" with the new regime, "were calling out for their old friend Gov. Blount," he worked hard to undermine his successors. When the Cherokee leader Kunokeski complained that the secretary of war refused to provide alcohol, Blount mocked the secretary and promised the Cherokee leader two kegs of whiskey in Knoxville. He even told Carey that any Native dissatisfaction with Blount's past actions should be blamed on former President Washington.[35]

Blount saw an even greater obstacle in his successor Benjamin Hawkins. The two men were, in fact, "old friend[s]," longtime political allies and correspondents with a shared background in North Carolina politics. They had traveled a similar ideological path—initially hopeful backers of the new federal government who grew increasingly skeptical of the Washington administration—but their opposing views on federal authority over Indian affairs now divided them. Blount instructed Carey that he should seek to undermine Hawkins's influence among the Creeks, even suggesting that the Creek Nation could get President Adams to recall the superintendent.[36]

Blount's letter to Carey proved his undoing. Rather than following Blount's instructions to burn the letter, Carey gave it to Hawkins. Hawkins, shocked at this betrayal from an "unexpected quarter," passed it along to his superiors. The ensuing political scandal convulsed Philadelphia, although most there focused on the implications for foreign relations: suspicious Anglo-Americans viewed British officials' brief flirtation with Chisholm's proposal as proof of British perfidy. The Senate expelled Blount, but the House of Representatives impeached him nonetheless, for violating, among other laws, the Trade and Intercourse Act and the Treaty of Holston that he himself had negotiated. In the first impeachment trial under the U.S. Constitution, the Senate ultimately determined it lacked jurisdiction over now ex-Senator Blount.[37]

For most observers then and now, Blount's Conspiracy, as it became known, was a parable about international intrigue, constitutional law, and betrayal: from retirement, George Washington lamented that "a man in high trust, and a responsible station, should be found, so debased in his principles." But, like many in the borderlands, Blount's allegiances had always been fickle: he had viewed his role as federal official instrumentally, and happily discarded his duties once power shifted. As for his cockamamie plan, it epitomized the grandiose and nebulous dreams of sovereignty that had long marked the borderlands. Not only did Blount's Conspiracy prefigure Aaron Burr's later western plotting, it closely resembled the simultaneous effort of Blount's former political opponent Cox. Many in Tennessee even speculated that the two men's schemes were linked, with Cox serving as "an advanced corps" for Blount. There may have been something behind the rumor: in a telling reversal, Blount reported that the two were now "upon the best of Terms."[38]

Yet Tennessee's statehood had altered the context for both men's borderlands scheming. Neither was a particular proponent of state autonomy; both Blount and Cox sought to benefit themselves, not Tennessee. Yet their challenge to federal authority, especially when federal officers defended Native sovereignty and title, endeared them to the people of a state where a "very general defection prevails . . . towards the federal government." Blount found much to admire in the "Uneasyness" that Cox caused the federal "*Military Gentry*." Similarly, a state visitor reported that the "people generally of Tennessee [showed] a strong attachment to Govr. Blount and to [his] plan" because they regarded the ex-governor as a martyr "persecuted by the *tools of Administration*."[39]

There was special irony in Blount's continued popularity. As we have seen, the federal government had poured money into the Southwest Territory in a bid to secure citizens' allegiance to the United States. Yet, in the end, these funds attached white Tennesseans less to the federal government than to *Blount*—influence which the ex-governor now deployed to flout federal law: "[T]hey speak of him as having always been the means of drawing large sums of money into the Country," a visitor reported of Tennesseans, "and that the expedition against the Spaniards of which Blount was the chief would have brought them much wealth and that it would go on yet."[40]

Unlike Cox, Blount did not vanish from Tennessee politics after his scheme failed. Rather, warming to the new role that his downfall had thrust upon him, he readily adopted his new compatriots' anti-federal rhetoric of state sovereignty. "The State of Tenessee is affected to the federal Government as it ought to be," he later wrote, "alive to their Duties & their Rights, ready to perform one and defend the other." National disgrace notwithstanding, Blount found room for advancement serving yet another sovereign, the state government, where he became speaker of the state senate and made common cause with Governor Sevier's struggle against the federal government. As Blount's transformation as well as Cox's machinations suggest, state sovereignty now offered a flag of convenience for all those who, whether for reasons of principle or personal animosity, had soured on federal authority.[41]

Hawkins's Line

Cox and Blount kept Benjamin Hawkins busy throughout 1797, but they were not his principal business in Tennessee. The federal government had sent him to the state to mark the boundary with the Cherokee Nation delineated in the 1791 Treaty of Holston. This project quickly made Hawkins one of the most controversial figures in Tennessee; it also precipitated the new state's most heated constitutional confrontation.

There were conflicting explanations as to why the Holston boundary had so long gone unmarked. Blount and the Cherokees had agreed to send commissioners to run the line in late 1792. Blount's commissioners reported that the Cherokees never arrived, and so they had run an informal boundary, later known as the "line of experiment." But in another account, the white commissioners had sought to run the line "secretly" to their own advantage and, when they met the Cherokee representatives, attempted to conceal their surveying equipment.[42]

The new Adams administration now appointed Hawkins and two other federal commissioners to survey the boundary at last. This explicit and unambiguous division between Cherokee "Indian country" and Tennessee's "ordinary jurisdiction" would, it hoped, forestall disputes. In fact, the new boundary transformed Tennessee's simmering conflict over state and federal authority into an open confrontation.

The Holston boundary worried many in Tennessee. The contested Treaty of Holston remained a sore subject in the Cherokee Nation: when, on April 25, Hawkins met 147 leaders from across the Cherokee Nation to explain his purpose, the Cherokees continued to insist that they "never did assent" to it. "They lamented that their efforts, thrice repeated, had been unsuccessful in obtaining an alteration in the treaty to correspond with what they intended when they made it," Hawkins recorded. "They lamented that from the language of the agent of the four nations [Hawkins], the treaty could not be altered after the President had signed it." But finally, the Cherokees agreed to cooperate in Hawkins's project and appoint commissioners to accompany Hawkins. Nenetooyah (Bloody Fellow), the central Cherokee representative at the original Holston negotiations, played a key role here, too: not only would he serve as commissioner, but he successfully negotiated for eight commissioners instead of four to ensure full representation for Lower Town Cherokees like himself.[43]

At the end of the Cherokees' discussions, they presented Hawkins a written "Talk of the Chiefs and Warriors of all the Cherokees to the President of the United States." Signed by Keanetoh (Little Turkey), the ostensible head of the entire Cherokee Nation, the talk suggests that the Cherokees acquiesced in Hawkins's project because they saw a chance to hold the federal government to its promise to arbitrate. Praising Hawkins as a man "who respects our rights," they expressed faith that he would "see justice done to the red and whites." They concluded with the gendered invocations for aid that so often accompanied Native appeals for federal assistance: "[W]e now hope things are so arranged that we may go into our own woods and hunt to cloathe our naked women and children," they wrote. "We now hope to have some rest and that no one will be permitted to disturb us again by intrusions on our rights."[44]

Once again, it seemed, federal adjudication offered the Cherokees the least bad choice among a series of unappealing options. When Hawkins had arrived, he reported that the Cherokees were "apprehensive [that] the object in inviting them, under pretence of runing their line, is to obtain more land from them to accommodate the intruders on their lands." But Hawkins's speeches suggested that he might actually uphold the "solemn guarantee of the government" against white Tennesseans' relentless land hunger. This prospect gave the Cherokee Nation some cause for hope: as the Upper Town leader Neeka-anneah told Hawkins, "[H]e and all the Cherokees rejoiced at the expectation of having their line closed."[45]

What gave the Cherokees joy panicked their white neighbors. For the past six years, white Tennesseans had settled on Cherokee lands, asserting title under North Carolinian land grants that simply disregarded Cherokee ownership. With the creation of the clear boundary line, these settlers would be unambiguously labeled intruders in violation of the Trade and Intercourse Act, notwithstanding rights under state law. Anxious claimants now thronged Hawkins. Although there were rumors of violence and even death threats against Hawkins, the intruders were determinedly civil, pleading their case using the mixture of supplication, legal entitlement, and obedience routinely offered governments by claimants with threatened title. "[T]hey were a plain, industrious people who lived by their labour," they stressed, and "were not opposed to Law." This was likely because law, as they interpreted it, vindicated their claims. Not only had their farms been "obtained by fair purchase from North Carolina, under the land laws of that State," but, they argued, the long-standing practice of honoring preemption rights bolster their claim: "Heretofore intrusions were always countenanced by the government in the provision made to give them a preference in all the land laws," they told Hawkins. "They wished much that what had heretofore been usual as to persons in their situation, might apply to them."[46]

Yet Hawkins was unyielding, emphasizing the sanctity of the federal treaty promise and his sworn duty to enforce it. Hawkins offered only to help the residents draft a petition to the president. One delegation acquiesced, although not eagerly: "They saw clearly they being a small people, could not make head against the government." They nonetheless clung to the hope that federal officials might succor them if evicted, appealing for land elsewhere as compensation.[47]

In adjudicating between the conflicting land claims of Natives and purported intruders, Hawkins's role echoed earlier federal interventions along the Ohio River and in the French Broad Valley. Yet there was an important difference between this Holston boundary controversy and earlier struggles. Alongside Cherokees and intruders, a third group was "materially and essentially interested" in the dispute, in the words of Governor Sevier: Tennessee state officials.[48]

Unlike the Cherokees or the intruders, who both hoped to win Hawkins's favor, officials like Sevier saw little to gain from cooperation: they regarded Hawkins and his fellow commissioners as "inveterate enemies to this country." Soon, Hawkins began to hear whispers of Sevier's "rude remarks" and "warmth" against federal policy, as well as rumors that white Tennesseans planned to attack the Cherokees to provoke a war; Sevier even wrote to Hawkins threatening to call out the state's militia. Hawkins had anticipated resistance but still found this hostility "more powerful than I expected." "A something crept into the State of Tennessee," he reported, "which leaped over the bounds of decency and law, and determined to put the [federal] government to defiance."[49]

Confronted with such opposition, one commissioner proposed a delay, but Hawkins refused: "The Indians comprehend well . . . their rights, and expect justice from the Government." In mid-May, the three federal commissioners, accompanied by two surveyors, several packhorse men, and a military escort, set out from Nashville to trace the line. The first four Cherokee commissioners met them in late May, led by Nenetooyah. The Cherokee leader initially balked, concerned that the current course would "deprive them of much more than the Nation ever had the idea they should loose." Hawkins offered reassuring words. "[I]t was particularly his duty to attend to the rights of the Indians," he insisted, and "particularly necessary to their [the Cherokees'] preservation that the lines should be closed." He also agreed to supply the Cherokee commissioners with horses and food and provide them an additional federal allowance, a promise that, at Nenetooyah's request, he put in writing. "After some little reflection," one observer reported, Nenetooyah "replied he was satisfied with the explanations given, He gave his hand and said he would go on to the end of the line."[50]

Yet even with these commissioners and three Cherokee guides, the party made slow progress. Struggling to impose the treaty's abstract language onto the twisting waterways and endless mountains of eastern Tennessee, the party covered only fifty-nine miles in two months. Each mile, the surveyors carved "C.I." onto a tree on the Cherokee side of the line and "U.S." on the Tennessee side, and then had horses beat the ground to make the boundary still clearer. It was difficult, exhausting work. Despite Hawkins's promises, the army rations failed to reach the expedition; instead, Cherokee hunters fed the entire party with freshly caught bear and fish.[51]

In late June, the party reached mountains too difficult to pass in the summer heat. Hawkins paid the Cherokee commissioners for their assistance—a dollar a day apiece, amounting to nearly $300 in total. The line was not completed until the cool of fall, when a federal commissioner, joined by the next set of Cherokee commissioners, returned. The party reached the boundary's end, the Cumberland River, in late October, marking it by carving a portrait of Cherokee commissioner Silliqoughe onto the final tree.[52]

By this point, Hawkins was gone: he had traveled on to Georgia to assume his duties among the Creek Nation. But the controversy over the boundary widely known as Hawkins's Line was just beginning.

A Shew of Force

Even before surveying finished, the Adams administration moved to enforce the newly surveyed line against U.S. citizens illegally settled on Cherokee lands. On August 19, 1797, Colonel Thomas Butler, commander of the several companies of federal soldiers stationed in Tennessee, ordered that all such intruders—an estimated 2,500 to 3,000 people—remove by October 25 or face military expulsion. "[E]very attempt to occupy these lands, under colour of grants, or otherwise," Butler warned, "will be a violation of law, and must be resisted."[53]

Butler's proclamation prompted a constitutional crisis that, like prior controversies, swirled together disagreements over federal law, Native ownership, and inchoate land rights. But statehood had altered the context. Now, the core of the disagreement was a "dispute . . . betwixt the general and state governments" over which law—federal or state—would govern the new state's territory.[54]

The Supremacy Clause of the U.S. Constitution ostensibly resolved this question, mandating that the Trade and Intercourse Act prevail over North Carolina's land grants. Only the previous year, the U.S. Supreme Court had held that federal treaties trumped contrary state law, even when that law vested property rights. But Tennessee rejected that conclusion. Appointing its own boundary commissioners, who unsurprisingly concluded that Hawkins's route was wrong, the state legislature drafted a defiant remonstrance to Congress sharply at odds with the intruders' obedient supplications. Tennesseans, it thundered, had "less confidence" in Hawkins "than in the Indians themselves." Should the federal government attempt to enforce the new boundary by military force, the legislature warned, they would regard it as an "act of violent oppression."[55]

The ghostwriter of the state's fire-breathing complaint was none other than William Blount, despite being out of office. Blount's hatred for Hawkins was palpable: "Never was Man more execrated in any Country than Hawkins in this," Blount scrawled across his personal copy, accusing Hawkins of weeping "Crocodile tears" over the intruders' situation.[56]

Blount was not alone in his passionate anger. In a replay of the earlier controversies over unauthorized military expeditions, "repeated publications in the newspaper printed in Knoxville" sought to persuade the intruders "that all force that might be applied to expel them would be illegal, and that the United States alone were wrong in every proceeding that respected them," in the words of Secretary of War James McHenry. What McHenry regarded as tendentious pleading the pseudonymous writers cast as the vigorous defense of constitutional rights. The purported intruders, they pressed, held vested rights to the lands: "[T]he constitution of the United States," one author argued, "does not authorize military force, or diplomatic authority to decide the right of property." But these authors found an even more powerful line of constitutional attack in Tennessean statehood. "Whence does the Federal Government derive the power to exercise legal jurisdiction over the land on which we are settled," one author queried, "in any other than the general mode in which other states of the union are governed[?]"[57]

The most legally sophisticated version of the federalist argument came from the writer "Campbell." Promiscuously citing eclectic provisions—Article III's provision extending the judicial power of the United States over cases and controversies, the Guarantee Clause of Article IV, the Enclave Clause of Article I—Campbell concluded that, because the Treaty of Holston "dismember[ed] the state of Tennessee," it invalidly attempted to "arrogate" to the federal government "the barbarous right of alienating . . . any part of an individual state."[58]

"Campbell" was the barely disguised David Campbell, a former federal territorial judge who now served as state judge on Tennessee's highest court. Campbell played a paradoxical role in this controversy. As a territorial judge, he had urged upholding the Treaty of Holston, and had served on the abortive 1792 surveying commission. But privately, he defended what he called the "right of intrusion," and boasted of having lived illegally on Cherokee lands for ten years in what he dubbed his "intrusion castle." Campbell, Hawkins wrote of another of his "old friend[s]" from North Carolinian politics, was incapable of acknowledging that Natives "possess any rights at all."[59]

Tennessee's arguments failed to sway Congress—which rejected the state's remonstrance—or the Adams administration. Convinced that, in Hawkins's words, a "shew of Force only" would protect Cherokee title, in early 1798 federal officers ordered the army to remove intruders from Cherokee land. Violence ensued, as the settlers killed several army horses and wounded a soldier. Predictably, federal actions also outraged state officials. "[S]urely there never was an instance of such mistaken policy, in any other government, since governments had an existence," Governor Sevier excitedly exclaimed.[60]

The conflict reached its climax when, at 10 p.m. on the evening of February 3, 1798, two army officers arrested Judge Campbell at his "castle" and detained him in a military camp overnight. Campbell offered a pathetic account of his and similar removals, focused on the trauma inflicted not only on his wife and children but also on women with newborn infants who had been "driven into the fields or woods, with as little ceremony, as if they were wild beasts." He was especially indignant at the mistreatment of his enslaved African Jenny, who, despite having just given birth, was summarily expelled into wet weather. Campbell suspected that she had then been seized under the Trade and Intercourse Act's provision forfeiting intruders' property.[61]

Campbell's account echoed narratives of suffering at Native hands ubiquitous in the Southwest Territory. Campbell similarly fixated on women and children as victims; he also opportunistically paraded Black people's suffering while simultaneously emphasizing harm to his enslaved property. Above all, Campbell sought to persuade readers that the perpetrators of such atrocities were "savage barbarians" deserving of punishment. But, unlike in the past, the "authors of those cruel inhuman acts" were not Native; they were U.S. soldiers. To underline the savagery of this "military despotism," Campbell asserted he would rather live alongside Indians than regulars, and ventriloquized that the Lower Cherokee leader "Col. John Watts will be ashamed of this transaction when he hears of it."[62]

While Campbell repurposed familiar anti-Indian tropes against federal power, Tennessee's congressional delegation found leverage in the new language of statehood. They shared Campbell's outrage, but they focused on the federal insult to the dignity not of women and children but to the abstract entity of Tennessee. "Representing as we do, the Sovereignty of the State of Tennesee," the state's congressional representatives wrote President Adams, "[we] Consider[] that Sovereignty as haveing been Outra[g]'d, by the Conduct of Colonel Butler, on the person of one of the Supreme Judges of the State." The congressmen demanded an investigation into this "Military Tyranny," which they received: the secretary of war promised to explore Butler's conduct.[63]

The representatives' letter underscored the key difference between the fight over the Holston boundary and prior controversies over federal power in the Southwest Territory: the presence of voting congressional representatives made defying the region's interests much more politically costly. With the state's entire congressional delegation constantly agitating on the subject, the Adams administration decided that abandoning Cherokee land rights was the easier course. Congress authorized another treaty with the Cherokees, one that would "give a more convenient form to the State of Tennessee," as Secretary of War McHenry instructed the federal treaty commissioners. The right for the intruders to return, he told them, was to be the treaty's "first stipulation."[64]

Proclaiming with his usual melodrama that "[t]he state of Tennessee perhaps will never be more interested in any event than in the present intended treaty," Governor Sevier sprang to action. He secretly dispatched James Ore—the trader who had led the brutal 1794 Nickajack expedition—to suss out Cherokee intentions and persuade the Nation that selling was in its best interest. Ore met a number of influential Lower Town leaders, including John Watts and Nenetooyah, at a Cherokee ball game, but found them "very tacit and reserved" on the question of land sales. Ore nonetheless believed an "advantageous purchase" was possible, in part because many Cherokees had reportedly moved west across the Mississippi.[65]

The Treaty of Tellico

Ore's prediction proved wrong. Soon after the treaty session between federal commissioners and Cherokee representatives began in July 1798 at Tellico Blockhouse, Nenetooyah reportedly presented a paper "which he stated to contain their [Cherokees'] final resolutions, which were a preemptory refusal to sell, and an absolute denial to permit the inhabitants to return to their homes."[66]

Nenetooyah's refusal to yield "one inch of land" played out against a backdrop of intense confrontation among white officials. Not content to rely on federal officers to protect the state's interests, Sevier had appointed three Tennessee representatives to the treaty, and even made a brief cameo himself. Sevier told the state's agents to challenge both Cherokee title and the "constitutionality" of the Treaty of Holston as a measure "that prostrated the guaranteed rights of the whole state." The commissioners obeyed and, like Nenetooyah, presented a written declaration to the federal officers. Their eight-page screed rejected both

Cherokee land rights and any federal power to overrule North Carolina's land grants.[67]

Recriminations persisted after treaty negotiations broke off, as white Tennesseans, unable to credit Cherokee autonomy, publicly blamed each other for the treaty's "failure." Elisha Hall, the secretary of the federal commission, publicly alleged that William Blount had said he hoped the treaty would fail. Another accusation came from a surprising source: David Campbell. Bitter that Sevier had not done enough to protect him against federal arrest—the governor, Campbell thought, should have used his supposed authority to "command" the U.S. soldiers "not to intermeddle with the internal police of the state of Tennessee"—the judge now turned on Sevier. Not only had the presence of state agents had "throw[n] the Indians into confusion," he alleged, but they were unconstitutional: in a bizarre reversal, this robust defender of Tennessean sovereignty now argued that the state had lacked any power to intervene in the federal treaty proceeding. Campbell provoked a heated response from Sevier and his allies. "Certainly Campbell is the most medling blockhead that ever crept into such high office in any Country," William Blount opined.[68]

Amidst this bickering, federal officials managed to lure Cherokee leaders back to the treaty ground in September 1798. This time, the commissioners succeeded, aided by a speech from Governor Sevier promising that the United States would supply the Cherokee Nation "everything" that "your wants may require": thirty-five Cherokee leaders agreed to cede the contested territory for an immediate payment of $5,000 in goods and an additional $1,000 annuity. First among the Cherokee signatories of the resulting Treaty of Tellico was the previously defiant Nenetooyah.[69]

No treaty record survives to help explain the Cherokee reversal, but another document sheds some light. After the first treaty session, the Cherokees finally received a response from President Adams to their message a year earlier. Adams's "talk" recited all the ways that the federal government had aided the Cherokees: guarding their lands, providing trade, teaching them farming. But, Adams continued, just "as I have looked upon it as a part of my duty to attend to your interests, I am also under the strongest obligations to hear the complaints, and relieve, as far as is in my power, the distresses of my white children, citizens of the United States." Here, he described how he had been forced to remove "worthy and well-intentioned settlers," whose "representation of their sufferings induced the Senate of the United States to advise a new purchase of land." Surely, he believed, his "Cherokee children, when they come to consider the whole subject, will agree with me in opinion, that a sale of such lands as they can spare, without injury. . . will be a proper and wise measure upon their part."[70]

Adams's talk both exemplified and highlighted the flaws of the Knoxian vision of the federal government as impartial arbiter. Adams cast himself as the protector of both Cherokees and U.S. citizens, yet the president's "children" were not similarly situated. Nenetooyah, Keanetoh, and other Cherokees had repeatedly voiced their grievances over the Treaty of Holston to the federal government, but Congress had only heard whites' suffering; their "representation" enjoyed privileged access to federal power. The Cherokees had their federal allies, too, and the sincere commitment of people like Hawkins to "Indian rights" had led the federal government to fight hard to defend Cherokee title. But in the end, even raw military power could not overcome the political influence that white Tennesseans now wielded.

Federal law had seemingly offered the Cherokees an alternative to the unpalatable choices of violence or acquiescence. Now, after Hawkins's promises proved illusory, Nenetooyah and his fellow leaders—having lived through decades of fruitless bloodshed—evidently chose the latter.

Tennessee's politicians crowed about the outcome of the Treaty of Tellico: they had forced a reluctant federal government to pursue the state's aims at federal expense. Yet this triumph failed to quell the debates over federal authority prompted by Hawkins's line, even as contentions shifted from treaty ground to courtroom.[71]

With Tennessee's statehood, a dual system of state and federal courts replaced the unitary territorial courts. In early 1797, the president appointed John McNairy—a Nashvillean who had previously served as both territorial and, briefly, state judge—as the state's sole federal judge. In mid-1798, McNairy heard his first case in the federal court's Nashville District: a prosecution against Archibald Lackey and Robert Trimble for violating the Trade and Intercourse Act by crossing into Cherokee territory without a passport.[72]

U.S. soldiers had arrested Lackey and Trimble at the same time as Judge Campbell and thrown them into a "fetid" military prison. Their trial became a cause célèbre, reportedly attracting "serious attention" from the "people in general," who felt that their "civil rights" were at stake. Their defense attorney, Lachlan McIntosh, was a Georgian closely tied to Tennessee's many critics of federal authority: an attorney for Zachariah Cox, McIntosh had been appointed by Sevier as one of the state commissioners at Tellico; he also lived for months in William Blount's Knoxville house during his sojourn in Tennessee.[73]

Lackey and Trimble would escape punishment, Blount predicted, based on his "thorough knowledge" of the law. He was wrong. Despite McIntosh's insistence that "it is not among the [U.S. Constitution's] Delegated powers to dismember the empire," the jury convicted both men, fining Lackey $25 and Trimble $10.[74]

Blount soon turned to the courts himself: he sued Elisha Hall in state court for defamation over Hall's claim that Blount wanted the treaty to fail. But Blount's new opponent Judge David Campbell dismissed the complaint. Campbell concluded that Hall, as a federal ambassador, was immune from suit under the law of nations and the federal Judiciary Act—reasoning his critics labeled "fiat quackery."[75]

Blount now turned his ire from Hall to Campbell: newly empowered as Speaker of the Tennessee Senate, Blount initiated impeachment proceedings. Among other things, the opportunistic charges alleged that Campbell had been too zealous in defending the white settlers and too vociferous in his attacks on the federal government. Assisted by Lachlan McIntosh, Blount both presided over and prosecuted the ensuing impeachment trial. But Campbell managed to escape removal from office by a single vote.[76]

Campbell's impeachment proved William Blount's last major political act. On March 15, 1800, Blount sat outside reading newspapers late into the night when he reportedly caught bilious fever; he died the next day. His half-brother Willie—a future governor of Tennessee—later eulogized William as a man devoted to his country's "best interests, from pure motives; free from ignoble vices, or selfishness."[77]

The swirling legal controversies that followed the Treaty of Tellico demonstrated how thoroughly the personal animosities and unpredictable alignments that had marked politics in the Southwest Territory persisted into statehood. They underscored, too, how, just as under territorial rule, Indian affairs could be the state's principal source of political contention even as Anglo-Americans erased actual Native people and their voices. Seemingly the sole organizing principle of the state's chaotic politics was resistance to federal control, as the persistence of the infrastructure of federal rule developed under the Southwest Territory frustrated white Tennesseans' aspirations of complete autonomy.

Yet the Holston controversy demonstrated that the state also possessed a powerful new weapon in this struggle: political representation. As the Adams administration's hasty retreat from enforcement of the Trade and Intercourse Act in favor of placating Tennessee's white settlers demonstrated, the state's newfound influence functioned just as many advocates for statehood had hoped.

Judging Their Own Cause

Yet political representation did not always allow white Tennesseans to prevail against the federal government. As Tennessee pressed its claim to own all public lands within the state, it ultimately gained much of what it wanted—but only after a hard-fought debate, and only by depending on the federal power it sought to defy.

Tennessee's leaders renewed their argument that statehood entitled Tennessee to all public land within state borders after their success at the Treaty of Tellico. "It is time for this government to assert her just rights & claim of domain of country included in her chartered limits," Governor Sevier told the state legislature, which duly enacted a statute to open state land offices on the North Carolinian model.[78]

Yet, unlike the Holston controversy, Congress did not back down. Instead, a Senate committee that included Senator Anderson of Tennessee investigated the Tennessee's claim, only to vindicate federal title. The committee thoroughly rebuffed the core of Jackson and Sevier's argument: "the principle that a grant of jurisdiction over territory possesses the right of soil therein." This reasoning had a strong basis in prior law and practice—colonial charters and state cessions alike had conjoined sovereignty and property—but the committee rejected this linkage. "The right of jurisdiction, and the right of soil, are distinct rights, and may be severed," the committee insisted. Thus, when the Southwest Territory attained statehood, "in the opinion of the committee, the State of Tennessee acquired jurisdiction over, but not the right of soil, within the said territory." By virtue of North Carolina's cession, "the right of soil remained in the United States."[79]

The committee's recommendations, however, did not match the firmness of its legal conclusions, which perhaps explains Senator Anderson's endorsement. It urged opening a federal land office, but only for the contested French Broad lands, even as it proposed codifying existing settlers' preemption rights. It also requested that the attorney general gather all laws related to state land claims in preparation for a further report.[80]

Congress did none of these things: it dithered, perhaps because it was preoccupied with simultaneously resolving the exceedingly complicated Yazoo claims. Over the next few years, a near-unanimous Congress—with the sole exception of Tennessee's delegation—created new committees to gather evidence and deferred the alarmist petitions it received recounting ongoing conflicts in Tennessee between Cherokee land and North Carolina grants.[81]

The delay alarmed Tennesseans, who followed the debate "with some concern." A group of Nashvilleans pressed Governor Sevier to act lest the state's silence be read as a "virtual acknowledgement of the right of the General government." This outcome, they feared, would be disastrous for their property: the federal government would likely not make "necessary provision for individual claims"—their preemption and land grant rights—"thereby involv[ing] us in lasting difficulties."[82]

Yet seemingly no neutral arbiter could resolve this state-federal property dispute. Unlike the U.S. Constitution's Federalist proponents, Sevier did not trust the federal courts to play that role: any resolution by the "supreme judiciary of the united States," he believed, would prove "very problematical." The issue was not the merits but the principle: allowing federal courts to decide the controversy would concede the federal government's authority to adjudicate.[83]

Instead, Tennessee opted for an approach more befitting an independent sovereign: negotiation. The state legislature appointed Tennessee's congressional delegation as "agents" with "full power and authority" to assert the state's "absolute right of disposing of [its] vacant and unappropriated soil" and to secure "relinquishment of [the U.S.] claim." This negotiated approach mirrored how prior disputes over land and sovereignty had been resolved, including Georgia's 1802 cession, and implied formal equality between the parties.[84]

Yet many outside Tennessee had begun to question this practice. Because the U.S. Constitution recognized federal authority over land and territory, they argued, any resolution of the dispute had to come from the federal government alone. In this sense, as one congressman put it in an earlier debate over Tennessee lands, the "United States were, in this case, made a judge in their own cause," because Congress would ultimately decide Tennessee's claims.[85]

In the end, Congress *did* resolve the dispute—largely because, even as Tennessee rejected federal title, the state needed federal authority to protect its claim against yet another claimant: North Carolina. Citing its cession, Tennessee's parent state still granted military bounty lands *within* Tennessee, infuriating Tennesseans. Governor Sevier redirected his equal footing argument to insist that North Carolina's claim to govern the "most important business in the state of Tennessee" grossly violated Tennessee's right to "every power, privilege, sovereignty and jurisdiction that any of the original states in the union enjoy." This interstate dispute produced a bizarre tussle in which some Tennesseans attempted to seize a chest with North Carolina's land records from an armed North Carolinian escort. In 1804, the two states reached a compromise: North Carolina would issue military land warrants that Tennessee would fulfill. But under the U.S. Constitution, such a compact was valid only with congressional approval.[86]

Finally, in 1806—a decade after Tennessee's admission—Congress codified a three-way agreement between the federal government, Tennessee, and North Carolina over the state's land. The law ratified the interstate compact and split the difference between federal government and Tennessee. Drawing a line across west-central Tennessee, the statute declared lands *west* of the boundary a "congressional reserve . . . at the sole and entire disposition of the United States," to which Tennessee relinquished all "right, title, or claim." Lands *east* of the line Congress gave to the state, ceding it the same power to issue "perfect titles" there "as Congress now have." The law guaranteed the preemptive rights of settlers south of the French Broad, but it also mandated that nothing in the statute "shall be construed to affect the Indian title, or to subject the United States to the expense of extinguishing the same"; it further stipulated that Tennessee use some of its public lands to support education.[87]

The 1806 statute largely settled the contested question of whether the state or the federal government owned Tennessee's public lands. In one sense, the outcome reflected federal weakness when confronted with state intransigence. Ostensibly enshrined in both the U.S. Constitution and the Northwest Ordinance, federal title in practice proved limited by the intricacies of North Carolina's cession, by federal officials' political inability to use raw force to enforce federal law, and by the rhetorical power of state sovereignty.

Yet reading the 1806 statute as solely a Tennessean victory misinterprets the federal government's goals. Clotted with conflicting claims, Tennessee's public lands were as much an administrative burden as an asset. What Congress sought to vindicate was its authority to decide the conflicting claims, and here, it succeeded. The 1806 resolution came through federal statute, not a contract; state representatives filed their vestigial, and seemingly legally meaningless, "consent" a year after its enactment. In the end, Congress *was* the sole judge in its own cause.[88]

Subsequent events only further entrenched the supremacy of Congress's 1806 statute. When, years later, North Carolina again claimed ownership of Tennessee lands, the U.S. Supreme Court cited the 1806 compact to rebuff these efforts. Like other land claimants, Tennessee had come to rely on the federal government as the arbiter and guarantor of its rights to ownership.[89]

Conditional Admission

After Tennessee, the next state admitted to the union was Ohio, carved from the eastern portion of the Northwest Territory; its admission came in 1802, right in the midst of the controversies over Tennessee's public lands. But Ohio's statehood unfolded very differently from Tennessee's. While statehood offered Tennessee a weapon to resist federal authority, Ohio's new status actually helped entrench federal power over the state's future development—in part because, in the wake of Tennessee's resistance, the federal government sought to forestall future attacks on its authority.

The politics of statehood in Ohio were quite different from in Tennessee: while white Tennesseans had largely united behind statehood, Ohio's admission was, from start to finish, a partisan affair that divided both territorial citizens and Congress into antagonistic camps based on affiliation with clearly defined political parties. Yet Ohio's statehood shared a key aspect with Tennessee's contentions—the controversial status of federal authority.[90]

In the Northwest Territory, nearly everyone conflated federal power with its most visible and controversial representative, Governor Arthur St. Clair. By the late 1790s, long-standing resistance to St. Clair's self-important leadership coalesced around the "Chillicothe Junto," transplanted Virginians named after the new county seat at the center of the Virginia Military District. These men had grown rich from the District's property chaos: St. Clair despised them as having "suddenly raised fortunes by speculations in lands, and many of those not the most honorably." Led by Thomas Worthington, the Junto's members were ideologically "democrats," in St. Clair's view, but they also resented the governor for his stranglehold on territorial patronage.[91]

The election of 1800 and the ascendance of the Jefferson administration significantly shaped Worthington and St. Clair's contest for power. As scholars have traced, the Jeffersonians retained preexisting federal institutions to govern land and Indian affairs, but they were hostile to St. Clair, Sargent, and other Federalist loyalists who had long dominated territorial offices. Worthington offered an alternative. The Harrison Land Act of 1800 had established federal land offices at Cincinnati, Marietta, Steubenville, and Chillicothe, all in the Northwest Territory. In its waning days, the Adams administration had chosen Worthington, as a prominent local, to serve as superintendent of public land sales and the registrar of the Chillicothe office. But Worthington had never been a Federalist, and now, with the new administration, Worthington quickly became the Northwest Territory's most prominent Jeffersonian.[92]

As a result of Worthington's office, the emerging federal land system became the center for the Northwest Territory's political contentions. After Worthington oversaw the first auctions under the Harrison Land Act, Governor St. Clair alleged that his political opponent had levied unlawful fees. Angered by this attack by a man he thought had "no concern Whatever in the regulation of My Office," Worthington sought absolution from the new secretary of treasury, Albert Gallatin—yet Jefferson's attorney general sided with St. Clair. A lawsuit proceeded against Worthington in the territorial courts, which ultimately vindicated him. Undissuaded, St. Clair now insinuated to Gallatin that Worthington was tamping down bidding on choice lands in return for kickbacks.[93]

The bitter antagonism between St. Clair and the Chillicothe Junto led Worthington and his allies first to attempt to secure the governor's removal and, when that failed, to press for the Northwest Territory's admission as a separate state. But St. Clair and his Federalist backers forestalled statehood, at least temporarily, by dividing the Territory in the waning days of the Adams administration. In 1800, the western portion of the Territory, containing the Illinois and Wabash Countries, became the Indiana Territory. Redefined to encompass only its former eastern portion, the shrunken Northwest Territory now contained fewer than the sixty thousand free inhabitants stipulated by the Northwest Ordinance for admission.[94]

This demographic reality significantly shaped the struggle over statehood. Tennessee had controversially claimed that its population automatically entitled it to statehood, but the Northwest Territory had too few inhabitants to make this argument; even statehood's proponents conceded that admission could come only through act of Congress. Eager to admit a politically friendly state, a majority Republican committee duly crafted a bill that would authorize the Northwest Territory to draft a constitution and seek admission.[95]

Yet many in Congress, still in throes of controversies over Tennessee's public lands, feared admission would repeat those contentions. They fretted that "the Territory, when formed into a State, actuated by the inordinate possession of power, will be likely grasp at our lands"—concerns fanned by Federalist opponents eager to forestall Ohio's statehood. Unlike in Tennessee, the public domain in the Northwest Territory was vast and potentially lucrative, as the federal government's enormous expenditure on the Northwest Indian War had "extinguished" Native title from much of the would-be state.[96]

Secretary of the Treasury Albert Gallatin proposed a solution to forestall state claims to ownership. A staunch Republican, Gallatin wanted to ensure Ohio's admission. But he also was a strong defender of the federal land system, and "fervently" argued for "effectual provisions" to "secure to the United States the proceeds of the sales of the Western lands." He proposed a constitutional innovation: Congress could attach conditions to the state's admission to ensure the new state would not "interfere with the regulations adopted by Congress for the 'primary disposal of the soil.'" The committee accepted, and the Enabling Act not only required the new state to follow the Northwest Ordinance but also mandated that all lands sold by the federal government be immune from state taxes for five years—on the grounds, Gallatin claimed, that state foreclosure proceedings might impede federal authority over the land system. The bill attempted to sweeten this sweeping restriction on state power by promising the new state 5 percent of the proceeds of federal land sales for internal improvements (Congress having rejected the Territory's delegate's competing proposal for 50 percent).[97]

Formally, conditional admission followed the model of negotiated federalism earlier embraced by Tennessee: the conditions, Gallatin insisted, were mere proposals to the Territory's constitutional convention for their "free acceptance or rejection." Yet Gallatin's view ignored the vast disparity in bargaining power: because Ohio could only become a state with Congress's approval, the conditions were more akin to mandates. But, with the Jeffersonians eager for statehood, it fell to the Federalists to point out this legal fiction and defend state sovereignty.[98]

The most sustained version of this attack came from an especially improbable source: the Territory's staunchest advocate of submission to federal authority, Arthur St. Clair. Reluctantly permitted to speak before Ohio's Constitutional Convention in late 1802, the governor, in a striking about-face, offered a defense of local autonomy that echoed Sevier and Jackson. The enabling act, he insisted, was a "nullity," because Congress could not regulate the Territory's internal affairs. As for the attachment of conditions to a "right which is ours by nature and by compact," it was, he thundered, unprecedented, an "odious distinction" reserved for the Territory alone: "Were conditions imposed upon Vermont, or upon Tennessee, before they could be admitted into the Union? There was none attempted." The whole reason that Congress had hurried the Territory toward statehood, he argued, was that it was the "only time to saddle us with conditions," since, once they had the requisite numbers, "it would be no longer in their power."[99]

Eager to escape St. Clair's rule, the Convention ignored the governor and approved a constitution for the new state of Ohio that accepted Congress's stipulations. "The poor old man has made his last speech and will very soon die politically," Worthington gleefully reported. Yet the speech touched a nerve in the Jefferson administration. Even though St. Clair's post would expire in mere weeks with statehood, President Jefferson peremptorily dismissed St. Clair, citing his "intemperance and indecorum of language towards the Legislature of the United States." St. Clair thanked the president for "discharge[ing] me from an office I was heartily tired of" six weeks sooner than planned.[100]

The Jefferson administration's touchy response to St. Clair's speech perhaps reflected unease over their political position. In conditioning admission, the Republicans had jettisoned their ideological commitment to state autonomy for expediency's sake. Perhaps uncomfortable with Gallatin's legal fiction, many Republicans adopted another defense of conditional statehood: the conditions were merely "explanatory" of Northwest Ordinance's preexisting protections and "additional securities for the national property," the enabling act's drafter argued to Congress. Federal power's skeptics had come to embrace the supremacy of federal title.[101]

Ultimately, the Republicans' gambit paid off. After Congress accepted Ohio's constitution, the new state promptly selected Thomas Worthington as one of its first U.S. senators. As for St. Clair, "after the sacrifice of my best days and the dissipation of my fortune in the public service," the former governor retreated to his home in Pennsylvania, where, nearly bankrupt, he spent the rest of life fruitlessly seeking compensation for his expenses in office.[102]

The political contortions over Ohio's admission nonetheless left an important legacy. Ohio could have easily followed Tennessee's lead and claimed ownership of the state's substantial public lands. Gallatin's solution—to condition state entry into the union—was uncertain and contested, yet the partisan alignments over Ohio's statehood mitigated any constitutional controversy. The politics that rendered the toothless St. Clair an implausible defender of local sovereignty also led the party of Sevier and Jackson to embrace congressional authority over both statehood and federal land. As a result, federal title and the congressional right to condition state admission—both long subject to constitutional challenge from federal authority's skeptics —ripened into precedent.

No Collisions

Congress worked hard to ensure that Ohio's statehood did not repeat the intense fights over public lands in Tennessee. But another hotly contested issue in Tennessee's admission went almost entirely undiscussed in Ohio: federal authority over Indian affairs. When a jurisdictional dispute over Ohio's Indian country finally reached federal court three decades later, the judge observed that, unlike to the south, "Within this state no collisions on this important subject have occurred."[103]

This absence of contention had several causes. One concerned land. While federal law labeled over two-thirds of Tennessee as Indian country at the time of statehood, the proportion in Ohio was closer to a third—a consequence of the Northwest Indian War and the 1795 Treaty of Greenville, where the government had forced the signatory nations to cede title to most of what became Ohio. Supposedly free of Native claims, this land could now be purchased through the federal land system—abating the demand for Native title, at least for a while.[104]

Another important consequence of the Northwest Indian War was Native peoples' persistent mobility. After the Treaty of Greenville, many Shawnees, Delawares, and others continued their long-standing migrations, resettling to the west along the White River. Yet this movement unintentionally took these Native communities out of the new state of Ohio and *into* the federally run Indiana Territory. In other words, as Native peoples moved westward to avoid Anglo-American settlement, they were inadvertently reversing the Northwest Ordinance's demographic trajectory: in an inversion of their white neighbors' actions, Natives' quest for autonomy led them out of *state* jurisdiction and back into *federal* jurisdiction.[105]

There, within the new Indiana Territory, the complicated interplay between federal and Native authority persisted. The Territory's new governor and superintendent of Indian affairs, William Henry Harrison, had deep roots in the Northwest Territory. He had first come to the region as an officer during the Northwest Indian War, and he briefly served as the Territory's secretary as well as its first representative to Congress. Now, governing from Vincennes, Harrison found maintaining peace between the town's Natives and whites just as difficult as St. Clair and Blount had. Yet Harrison ultimately became a much more central figure in Indian affairs than either of his predecessors. Like them, he acted as both treaty negotiator and military commander for campaigns into Indian country, but with far more success. His time in territorial governance propelled him to the presidency rather than the ignominy that ultimately befell both St. Clair and Blount.[106]

But, while many Native peoples moved westward after Greenville, over two thousand Shawnees, Delawares, Senecas, and Wyandots remained within the new state. The region's most influential leaders, especially the Shawnee leader Black Hoof in the village of Wapakoneta, made the strategic decision to accept, and even welcome, U.S. authority. Ohio's Indian Country accordingly became a center of federal efforts to "civilize" Native peoples, as federally funded Indian agents, Quaker missionaries, storeowners, and mill keepers poured in and built infrastructure. Like the federal presence in Cherokee country to the south, the resulting federally underwritten "mission complex," as one historian has labeled it, became a linchpin for the regional economy. But, as in the Southwest Territory, this flow of federal funds did not obviate conflicts between Anglo-Americans and their Native neighbors. Rather, proximity continued to breed interconnection and violence, which the federal government still sought to staunch through finance: "[N]othing was so embarrassing," Ohio's Indian agent complained in the early nineteenth century, "as the conflicting claims of the whites and Indians for depredations."[107]

Yet, unlike Tennesseans, the Ohio state government seemed content to allow the federal government to manage Indian affairs within the state. This was partly because, in Indian affairs, state and federal officials were the same people: among the federal treaty commissioners selected to negotiate with Ohio's Native communities were the state's governor and one of its U.S. senators, Thomas Worthington. State officials felt little need to assert state sovereignty against a federal government they constituted. From the perspective of most Ohioans, the federal government was already accomplishing much of what the state could have wanted in Indian country and at its own expense.[108]

The United States created the Southwest and Northwest Territories in large part to resolve the seemingly interminable struggles over sovereignty, jurisdiction, and property in the early American West. Rather than settling these questions, territorial governance had channeled them into the politics of federal administration. However overstated territorial citizens' rhetoric of powerlessness, the territories' formal dependence had forced citizens, as well as many other territorial residents, into a constant, unwelcome encounter with federal law and authority.

Tennessee and Ohio's statehood reopened these issues, but with an important difference. Contentions in the territories had been polyvocal, as secessionist movements, Native nations, land companies, and multiple states jockeyed alongside the federal government for jurisdiction and ownership. As Tennessee's statehood particularly underscored, such multipolar borderlands confrontations persisted, but Anglo-Americans increasingly interpreted them as clashes between national power and newly sovereign states. Cox's speculation, Blount's scheming, Cherokee land rights, Ohio's vituperative politics—all were now read through the newly emergent lens of federalism.

As a result, in both Tennessee and Ohio, statehood's fundamental question was how much of federal authority would endure now that they were no longer federal dependencies but independent states. The territorial system's foundational premise was that the federal government would temporarily control all aspects of governance but that, once the territory became a sovereign state on "equal footing," this authority would recede. But in practice, Jackson and Sevier were right: the former territories were not equal to preexisting states. Instead of vanishing, federal authority accreted under territorial governance endured, especially over land and Indian affairs. This reality produced sharply different responses in Tennessee and Ohio. Tennessee's citizens fought fiercely against federal persistence, at once achieving their goals while pushing the federal government to resist future state recalcitrance. White Ohioans, by contrast, accepted continued federal authority out of political expediency, establishing a precedent that entrenched federal power within the newly independent states.

Federal authority, as manifested in much of the territories, was ad hoc and improvisational, differing sharply from the power of command that Knox and others envisioned. Yet, when challenged, federal officials and Congress, even those generally sympathetic to state power, had fought fiercely to guard the authority they had eked out during territorial rule. The result was that, promises of equal footing notwithstanding, the federal government retained an outsized presence in the West even after former territories ascended to statehood.[109]

Epilogue

Three Systems

In 1798, Congress established the Mississippi Territory in the disputed lands south of the Southwest Territory—the first of the thirty-five federal territories that have followed the Northwest and Southwest Territories to date. The Territory's first governor was well versed in territorial governance: the president tapped erstwhile Secretary of the Northwest Territory Winthrop Sargent, whose continued insistence on federal supremacy soon made him as loathed among his new constituents as among his old. What Sargent called "the whole tribe of *land squatters*"—deploying a new term for those occupying federal lands without formal title—appealed to Congress to remove the governor.[1]

Newly inaugurated President Jefferson acted first, replacing Sargent with William Claiborne. A prominent lawyer in the Southwest Territory, Claiborne had helped draft Tennessee's constitution and succeeded Andrew Jackson as the state's congressional representative. But Claiborne was not in Mississippi long. Only months after Ohio's statehood, the United States concluded the Louisiana Purchase, the first expansion of the nation's international borders since the Treaty of Paris. Jefferson tapped Claiborne to serve as governor of the new Orleans Territory carved from this vast expanse.[2]

This flow of personnel from old territories to new exemplified a broader process. As laboratories for a new, federally administered colonialism, the Northwest and Southwest Territories now became models and precedents for their successors. This result did not occur as most Anglo-Americans had anticipated. As Jefferson's 1791 report underscored, the federal government had bumbled into the territories largely ignorant of the work that would confront it there. Territorial officials quickly discovered that the vague and grandiose plans earlier crafted in Philadelphia offered little guidance for daily governance. Attempting to keep order and avoid violence, they instead fashioned ad hoc efforts to placate residents' demands. But over time, Congress codified these experiments, and people increasingly began to speak of these formerly ersatz solutions as "systems"—"a scheme which unites many things in order," per one contemporary dictionary. Reclad in routinized garb as simply the way the federal government did things, these past practices, like territorial personnel, were transplanted into

Federal Ground. Gregory Ablavsky, Oxford University Press (2021). © Gregory Ablavsky.
DOI: 10.1093/oso/9780190905699.003.0009

new territories. What had developed almost by accident had become a new repertoire of federal governance.[3]

CONGRESS FIRST REFERRED TO the "land system" in 1806. The context was telling. No emptier than the Northwest or Southwest Territories, the Mississippi Territory had existing residents who petitioned Congress, yet again, to recognize preemption rights. Congress's Committee on Public Lands urged rejection: acknowledgment, it feared, might lead to the "entire abandonment of the existing land system." This now-sacrosanct "system" was only a few years old. The Harrison Land Act of 1800 had settled its basic principles—prior survey, rectangular grid, land offices, and auctions and prior sales—only after a decade of intense disagreement and experimentation in the first territories. Yet these hard-won resolutions had become the foundation for a system that endured through the Civil War and beyond.[4]

The earliest territories supplied the land system another equally durable precedent. Alongside "squatters," many in the Mississippi Territory claimed ownership based on prior Spanish or British grants. Their demands for recognition of their title led Congress in 1803 to extend and codify the ad hoc adjudications of prior property rights first adopted almost unthinkingly in the Illinois Country. Now, just as St. Clair and Sargent had done, three-person presidentially appointed commissions (usually consisting of territorial officials) would hear these prior land rights and make rulings that, Congress mandated, "shall be final."[5]

Such adjudicatory land commissions became a core part of the federal land system as Congress extended them into the newly acquired lands of the Louisiana Purchase, and then still further into formerly Mexican territories seized in the Treaty of Guadalupe Hidalgo. The work that confronted federal commissioners in Louisiana, Missouri, and Arkansas—let alone California, Arizona, and New Mexico—far eclipsed the already onerous burden that had fallen on St. Clair and Sargent. No land problem of the nineteenth century caused "more difficulty or took up as much time," historian Paul Gates observed, as resolving these prior land rights. Gates estimated that, by century's end, the federal government had ruled on 30,000 to 35,000 of these so-called private land claims covering forty-five million acres of land.[6]

Tellingly, no equivalent "system" emerged for Native title. Throughout the nineteenth century, officials adjudicated Native property rights in the same ad hoc manner as in the first territories—with federal treaty commissioners determining which nations owned what based on their own assessments and the representations of Native leaders. Native title remained the wellspring for ownership within the new land system, but Congress did not establish a formal forum for Native title akin to those it offered private land claims until 1946, when it created the Indian Claims Commission. Like the private claims commissions, this body consisted of three presidentially appointed commissioners, but, unlike those past commissions, it could award only money damages, not title. Because of the long delay and this limitation, Native nations' arguments that they were stripped of their property in the 1780s and 1790s in violation of federal law endure and remain unsettled.[7]

FEDERAL NEGLECT OF NATIVE TITLE did not mean the absence of "system" in Indian affairs. On the contrary, as early as 1800, Secretary of War James McHenry spoke of his desire to achieve "a more perfect controul over the Indians by an uniform System to be acted upon by one and the same authority." Over time, the nascent Indian Department expanded as it sought to obtain this "controul." The 1796 establishment of federally run trading posts, explicitly intended to foster Native dependency, institutionalized the federal distribution of goods in Indian country. Federal annuities paid for Native lands grew into what historian Emilie Connolly has called "fiduciary colonialism," in which the Indian Department itself managed these funds for Native beneficiaries, forcing them into greater reliance on federal authority. And, as the federal government's ability to reach into Indian country grew, the federal government's early, abortive efforts to prosecute Native crimes became increasingly successful. In 1817, Congress broke with prior versions of the Trade and Intercourse Act and asserted federal jurisdiction over crimes committed by Indians in Indian country.[8]

The growth of federal administration over Indian affairs was not a simple story of imposition. Native peoples—including the Cherokees, Wyandots, Shawnees, and Chickasaws who found themselves within the new states of Tennessee and Ohio—still found opportunities for enrichment within this expanded bureaucracy. These communities' leaders milked federal largesse for the same trappings of success that their white neighbors displayed: houses, livestock, enslaved Africans. This wealth came at a cost for Native nations: it insinuated federal power ever further into their politics and daily existence. But it came at a literal cost for the federal government, too. By 1824, when diverse federal efforts in Indian country were reorganized into the Office of Indian Affairs, the federal government was routinely spending over a half million dollars annually on the budget category "Indians," a figure that climbed as high as three or four million in the subsequent decade of deportations. In the 1820s, "Indians" cost as much as 60 percent of the total salaries for *all* federal civil officers; in 1836, a particularly expensive year, the equivalent figure was 251 percent.[9]

Of course, just as in the first territories, much of the money spent on "Indians" went not to Native peoples but to U.S. citizens—even though, also as before, such expenditures offered little federal "controul." The federal government still compensated its citizens for harms suffered at Native hands, a practice increasingly formalized under the title of Indian depredation claims. When this system finally ended, in 1920, the federal government had adjudicated tens of thousands of claims and paid out millions of dollars, ostensibly from the annuities promised to Native nations. (In practice, one study found, most of these payments came directly from the federal treasury.) Yet these payments never established the monopoly on violence that the federal government sought.[10]

But the federal treasury did not only "insure conquest," as K-Sue Park has described the payment of depredation claims; it also paid for it directly. The Ore and Beard expeditions were merely the first of many instances of violence against Native peoples outside federal control, and at odds with federal policy, nonetheless funded from federal coffers. When Andrew Jackson led Tennessee's militia against the Creeks in 1813, and again against the Seminoles in 1819, he displayed little regard for federal law or diplomacy. Instead, explicitly reminding white Tennesseans that their earlier attack on Nickajack had been a "secret movement on the part of the people," he acted in the confidence—correct, as it turned out—that the federal government would ultimately foot the bill. An even more extreme echo came in the 1850s, when California's militia committed genocide against the state's Native peoples. Over the objections of the secretary of war, the state successfully secured federal arms and repayment for its butchery, thanks largely to the agitation of its congressional delegation.[11]

ALONGSIDE LAND AND INDIAN AFFAIRS, the first territories helped establish the "territorial system" itself, a phrase bandied about in Congress as both territories sought to become states. Ironically, the particulars of this system as established in the Northwest Ordinance proved among the first territories' least durable legacies: already by the 1820s, Congress had begun to tweak the Ordinance to democratize territorial governance, seeking to placate some of the vociferous complaints of the earliest territories.[12]

But other legal and constitutional technologies developed haphazardly in the first territories persisted and grew—none more so than the practice of conditional admission. After hitting on this method to safeguard federal title, Congress eagerly embraced the practice as the surest method to guard federal authority past statehood. Congress subsequently attached conditions every time it admitted a former territory to the union. These limitations on states quickly expanded beyond issues of land to include English language mandates, polygamy bans, and, most significantly and controversially of all, prohibitions on chattel slavery. From the 1820 Missouri Crisis through *Dred Scott*, arguably the most heated political and legal fights of the antebellum United States centered on whether the federal government could mandate states' free status in the same way it had earlier protected federal land title.[13]

But the early territorial system's most significant and enduring legacy was more abstract. The persistence in popular imagination of Frederick Jackson Turner's epic of frontier closure has frustrated historians eager to displace its celebration of the foreordained passing of the borderlands' pluralism. Yet the territorial system gave this tenacious account an institutional reality by writing it into federal law and governance; to invert historian Patricia Limerick, the territories codified the West as process, not place. Like the allied federal land system and its rectangular grid, the federal territories willfully defied geography and difference, transplanting near-identical institutions across the continent. The territorial system was also literally processual, establishing a universal procedure through which the territories would supposedly inevitably pass. The territorial system thus entrenched Anglo-Americans' widely held sense that, when it came to the West, they already knew how the story would end.[14]

That end, symbolically as well as legally, was statehood. By tying governance directly to demographics, race, and gender, the Northwest Ordinance and the system it created codified the expectation that white male U.S. citizens would, over time, supplant Native peoples, French *habitants*, and other existing territorial residents. Statehood became the capstone of a process of transition, signifying the moment when the pluralism of the borderlands—which the territorial system inextricably tied, in Anglo-Americans' minds, to the temporary period of federal rule—had faded away.[15]

Newly minted white Tennesseans and Ohioans quickly discovered that reality did not match their fantasies of complete authority. Nearly 70 percent of the new state of Tennessee and one-third of Ohio legally remained Indian country, even as the federal government owned millions more acres of state land. This discrepancy between ideology and reality infuriated these new states. "[A]fter conquering the savages and supporting our independence without the aid of the parent," Governor Sevier told Tennessee's legislature in 1804, the state should be able to enjoy "our own justly acquired rights" and "convert[] the fruits of our labour to our own Emolument," just as other states had. He was deeply angered that "so many obstacles" still barred the state's citizens "from procuring their just and legal Titles."[16]

But, however inaccurate, the belief and demand that statehood extinguished competing sovereignties helped call that reality into being. That outcome owed much to the territorial system and, in particular, its culmination. Proclamations of independence notwithstanding, statehood actually offered citizens of the former territories the most effective way yet to demand federal support.

Knox's vision that the federal government would serve as neutral arbiter, particularly between Natives and U.S. citizens, was always fundamentally flawed: it paternalistically assumed that supposedly enlightened federal officials—who nonetheless shared their society's bedrock belief in the superiority of "white people"—were best positioned to secure what Native nations would acknowledge as justice. Yet there were times when Native and federal goals aligned. In those moments, territorial citizens' self-interested complaints proved true: federal officials disregarded their demands to advance what officialdom saw as the national interest.[17]

But such instances were few and increasingly fewer—a result that reflected the territorial system itself. By bestowing statehood on the former territories, the system ensured that erstwhile territorial citizens were no longer supplicating the federal government as outsiders, as they had done under territorial rule. Rather, their political participation increasingly placed them among federal decision makers. They had become the federal government.

This dynamic played out across multiple domains. One was public lands, where antebellum debates continued the fierce arguments of the 1790s about who should benefit from the public domain. But by the 1820s and 1830s, growing numbers of representatives from the former territories challenged the priority of revenue long insisted by eastern congressmen. Initially, these states revived demands that all federal lands be ceded to states, reiterating Tennessee's equal footing arguments. Conditional admission, however, had made this argument difficult: the only state that ultimately won outright cession was, appropriately, Tennessee, gaining ownership of its western lands in a statute signed by President James K. Polk, a Tennessean. But the larger aim of these demands was to loosen federal law, and here, western states' vocal representatives succeeded. First, they successfully pushed Congress to liberally grant states huge blocks of public land to subsidize internal improvements, support public education, and drain swamps. Then, in 1830, after forty years of contestation, Congress finally enacted a temporary statute providing general recognition for preemption rights—one that it made permanent in 1841.[18]

A similar process unfolded nearly simultaneously in Indian affairs, especially in states' long antebellum struggle to expel Native sovereignty from within their borders. Although Georgia served as the symbolic center of this fight, euphemistically called Removal, much of it played out in former territories: Tennessee, Alabama, and Mississippi to the south, and Ohio, Illinois, and Indiana to the north.[19]

Legally and politically, Removal continued the contest between Native nations and erstwhile territorial citizens over their respective claims to federal protection and support, underscoring the long legacy of those earlier fights. In 1835, the Tennessee Supreme Court rejected federal restrictions on Tennessee's jurisdiction over Indian country. In the opinion, Justice John Catron——soon to be elevated to the U.S. Supreme Court by now-President Andrew Jackson—rehearsed at length Tennessee's forty-year-old anti-federal grudge for supposed failure to protect the Southwest Territory against the Cherokees: "We were not permitted to enter their country, and punish them there by an offensive war, although the work of death was daily doing upon us," Catron complained. Catron's constitutional reasoning, meanwhile, repeated near-verbatim Jackson and Sevier's earlier arguments about statehood. "Tennessee was admitted with all the rights of the original States," Catron wrote. "[H]er constitution, of 1796, expressly declaring the power of exercising sovereignty, within limits accurately described by the instrument, and on which condition she was accepted as one of the United States by congress."[20]

Tennessee's Cherokees and other Native leaders made claims on the federal government, too, just as they had under territorial rule, invoking treaty rights and their own language of sovereignty. Partly because they played so adeptly on the persistent Knoxian strain of paternalism and anxiety over national character, these efforts proved effective. Winning allies and publicity, Native nations persuaded the U.S. Supreme Court to endorse the Cherokees' legal position against that of the states.[21]

But this victory was not enough, as states ultimately prevailed in this hard-fought, remarkably close contest for federal support. It was not a fair fight. Natives' appeals for federal protection came before President Andrew Jackson and his secretary of war, fellow Tennessean John Eaton, who unsurprisingly sided with their home state against Native claims: "the sovereignty of the states must be preserved," Jackson supposedly fulminated. Just as important was Congress, which, for decades, had slowly filled with representatives from the former territories, who, like Hugh Lawson White, were committed to deploying federal authority to further their states' agendas. This was political power that Native nations, appealing for federal assistance from the outside, could not match.[22]

As territorial citizens had foreseen decades earlier and as Tennessee's early history underscored, statehood, and particularly representation, had given new state citizens a significant edge in exploiting federal authority for their own ends. In the process, they successfully transformed the federal government from a purportedly neutral arbiter into their most potent ally.

IN THE END, IT took legislatures and courts nearly a century to unspool the tangle of title and authority created in Tennessee and Ohio in the 1780s and 1790s. Yet the history of the first two territories obscured this long and difficult process: both appeared striking successes when measured against the aims of the territorial system and their citizens' aspirations. Both had passed quickly from territory to state (the Southwest Territory's six-year existence was the second-shortest territorial period in U.S. history, exceeded only by silver-mad Nevada during the Civil War). And in both, federal colonialism's key work—defining, then confining and extinguishing, prior rights to ownership and sovereignty inherited from a long and complicated past—was well underway by the time of statehood.[23]

Commentators then and now explained these territories' apparent success in divergent ways. Some adopted Sevier's narrative that territorial citizens, neglected by an indifferent federal government, pulled themselves up by their own bootstraps. Others, taking the opposite tack, attributed the territories' rapid transformation to a cruelly effective scheme of dispossession engineered and executed by the federal government, which moved peoples around the continent like so many chess pieces.[24]

Both accounts overlook what was arguably the more accurate explanation: that the early territories fulfilled Anglo-Americans' long-standing settler colonial aspirations due less to self-help or the unfolding of a careful federal plan than to territorial citizens' skill at exploiting federal power for their own ends. This reality had important consequences for subsequent territories. In Illinois, Indiana, Alabama, and Mississippi, the chief industry was the land office business, just it had been in the Northwest and Southwest Territories. As a result, the chief demand of these territories' citizens remained federal dispossession of Native peoples and other longtime residents. But in the upper Great Lakes, or in much of the trans-Mississippian West, territorial rule outpaced the demographic transformation that drove the booming trade in title. Residents there instead expanded on a different facet of the early territorial experience: federal money as resource. They farmed the federal government itself, with the result that the federal government found itself managing rather than supplanting pluralism. The supposedly temporary federal role became increasingly permanent.[25]

Yet the mistaken narratives about the earliest territories mattered. Assumptions about the first territories became the yardsticks against which subsequent territories were measured. Evaluating later territories against the myth of a rapid transition, Congress concluded that these newer territories were too diverse and pluralist to have earned the symbolic marker of statehood. Congress consequently extended their territorial infancy for decades—and, as the U.S. empire extended to insular possessions, abandoned the promise of statehood altogether. Former territories that did attain statehood immediately clamored for what they thought the earlier states had gotten; many of them are clamoring still. They, too, wanted pluralism erased, title to public lands secured, and Native sovereignty extinguished. To achieve these ends, they repurposed the constitutional language of state sovereignty and equal footing advanced decades and centuries earlier, although not always successfully.[26]

And so, just as in the first territories, these states turned in anger at the institution they perceived as the most visible impediment to these goals—the federal government. Even more than the first territories had been, these "independent" states remained economically and politically dependent on federal authority. But this irony was less a paradox than one of the oldest patterns of U.S. governance, with the understudied Southwest Territory as a particularly strong harbinger of later history. The Territory's many successors have uncannily echoed its dual history as effective exploiter of federal largesse and seedbed for anti-federal resentment.[27]

THESE OVERLAPPING SYSTEMS—over land, Indian affairs, and the territories—long lay at the core of what historians have described as federal power over the West. All three initially grew out of the contradictory demands that territorial residents made on the federal government. Only later did these haphazard structures coalesce into the more formalized bureaucracies that led historian Richard White, repurposing the language of infancy so prevalent in the first territories, to describe the West as "the kindergarten of the modern American state."[28]

Of course, like all children, the federal government changed as it aged. Even as the federal practice of resolving claims not only persisted but expanded over the nineteenth century, the source and nature of federal authority increasingly diverged from its early American origins. Many accounts identify the late nineteenth century as a particularly important inflection point when the federal government shed its earlier passivity before citizens' demands and began to actively craft and pursue its own policy agenda.[29]

Yet this grown-up federal government still bore traces of its youth. Its adjudicatory roots appear in accounts identifying nineteenth-century pensions to widows and veterans as key sources of federal authority; in arguments that the modern administrative state is a formalized outgrowth of antebellum petitioning practices; and in narratives that place a stubborn legalism and rights-consciousness at the center of the modern federal government's accumulation of authority. These origins are perhaps most obvious in the dockets of federal courts and administrative agencies. Especially, although hardly only, in the American West, these institutions still arbitrate competing claims to property, jurisdiction, and sovereignty advanced by Native nations, states, descendants of Anglo-American settlers and European colonists, and others with conflicting views about how land should be owned and governed.[30]

In this sense, the work of colonialism, to extinguish preexisting claims, never fully succeeded: as every court decision or congressional statute wading into this thorny history demonstrates anew, the United States remains a borderland where boundaries and authority are still up for grabs. But, as these acts also reiterate, the role of federal adjudication—sometimes vindicating, although all too frequently quashing, the claims of owners and sovereigns predating the United States—also endures.

IN 1940, TENNESSEE marked the sesquicentennial of the Southwest Territory. It was a respectable affair, as two thousand attendees gathered in eastern Tennessee to hear an address. But it was far outshone by the Northwest Territory's sesquicentennial three years earlier. For those celebrations, a "pioneer caravan" of re-enactors retraced Rufus Putnam's 1787–1788 route to found the Ohio Company's settlement. Everywhere it went, the caravan caused a tremendous sensation. National radio programs broadcast updates on its progress; an estimated two million people watched the caravan pass through Ohio alone.[31]

The contrast between the two celebrations reflected how central the Northwest Territory had become to national and regional identity, even as Tennessee's territorial history had become mere stage setting for the brief first scene in the life of the state's most illustrious citizen, Andrew Jackson. Yet the figure of Jackson arguably offered a stronger case for territorial governance's enduring national legacy than Putnam's arrival or even the Northwest Ordinance. Far from a mere interlude, Jackson's years in the Southwest Territory were formative for his subsequent politics, which reflected the struggles that had dominated the Territory. Betrayed, in his view, by a federal government that territorial citizens thought biased against them, Jackson spent his career attacking federal authority and law while also serving as a federal official, directing federal power and wealth toward those he deemed deserving, particularly states. It proved an ideology with remarkable power in the era that would ultimately bear Jackson's name.[32]

Jackson was not alone in effacing the federal role in the territories. The 1937 Northwest Territory Celebration focused not on those in Congress who had crafted the Ordinance, nor on the leaders of the Ohio Company, but on the "plain American citizens . . . who pushed [democratic] government westward across a continent and to eminence among the nations of the earth," as one speaker at the culminating Marietta commemoration put it. This celebration of the common people reflected the politics of the 1930s, but it also correctly assessed who had built the federal government in the territories—territorial citizens as much as federal officials. Of course, the celebration, in valorizing the Ohio Company "pioneers," elided all the people already there: Shawnees, Wyandots, Delawares, Miamis, German-speaking Moravian missionaries,

French *habitants*, English traders, and restless Virginians. Just as much as the late-arriving New Englanders, these people, too, had helped construct the federal government in the territories. That government was not democratic in the way that the Marietta celebration—which invoked the Northwest Ordinance as harbinger of Abraham Lincoln—meant. Thanks to both racial barriers and the Ordinance's heavy-handed federal control, territorial rule was not a government of or by the people, as territorial citizens loudly complained. But it was a government *for* the people, in effect if not by design, as all these myriad groups eagerly laid claim to federal power amidst the general scramble for property and authority.[33]

This was not the memory of territorial rule advanced in Marietta in 1937. Amidst the speechifying that day was an appeal to return to the frontier ethic of local pioneer self-sufficiency set against federal bureaucracy's encroaching reach in the New Deal. Then again, these critics of federal power were perhaps already closer to the spirit of that earlier age than they acknowledged. Their sesquicentennial celebration of autonomous, democratic expansion, after all, was organized by the Northwest Territory Celebration Commission, an ad hoc body authorized through congressional resolution after lobbying by Marietta residents. Congress also foot the bill, appropriating $100,000.[34]

Acknowledgments

Writing this book has unexpectedly paralleled its central thesis. Even as I discovered that the federal government in the territories was a product not just of federal officials but also of the regions' residents, I similarly learned that a book is the collective work of many people who make it possible.

I owe a great debt to librarians and archivists at many institutions, including the American Antiquarian Society; the American Philosophical Society; the Archives of Michigan; the Beinecke Rare Book Library, Yale University; the Connecticut Historical Society; the Burton Historical Collection, Detroit Public Library; the Historical Society of Pennsylvania; the Indiana Historical Society; the Indiana State Archives; the Indiana State Library; the Knox County, Indiana, Public Library; the Knox County, Tennessee, County Archives; Special Collections, University of Tennessee–Knoxville; the Manuscript Division, Library of Congress; the Library of Virginia; the McClung Historical Collection, Knoxville Public Library; the U.S. National Archives; the North Carolina State Archives; the Newberry Library; Special Collections, Northwestern University; the Ohio History Center; the Rubenstein Library, Duke University; Rauner Special Collections, Dartmouth College; Special Collections, University of Chicago Library; Special Collections, Vanderbilt University. Thanks to Richard King at the Byron R. Lewis Historical Collection Library at Vincennes University for assembling materials for my visit, and to Tom Kanon and the staff at the Tennessee State Library and Archives for their kind welcome and assistance. I am particularly grateful to Linda Showalter and the staff at Special Collections at the Marietta College Library, who opened the collection for me just before the winter holidays. This extensive research was possible only through financial support from Penn Law School, Stanford Law School, and a Price Fellowship from the Clements Library.

I have also been fortunate to call home institutions with outstanding libraries and staff. Thanks to Merle Slyhoff and Alvin Dong at the Biddle Law Library and to the staff at Crown Law Library, where Sonia Moss in particular did outstanding work to help me obtain the sources I needed. I benefited from the outstanding research assistance of my students: thanks to Michael Abrams, Tanner Allread, Alison Gocke, and Adam Mendel. Ginny Smith has always offered me both fantastic logistical support and a good excuse to discuss southern food.

This work was much improved by the feedback I received in many fora. Thanks to the Clark Legal History Series at Boston University, the Legal History

Workshop at Harvard Law School, the Legal History Forum at Yale Law School, the American Society for Legal History, the Stanford Law School faculty workshop, the University of Minnesota Public Law Workshop, CalTech, and the University at Buffalo School of Law for opportunities to present. The students in my 2020 Law and Empire seminar kindly permitted me to inflict a draft chapter on them.

This book is also the product of conversations, discussions, and support from an outstanding group of friends, colleagues, and mentors. I was fortunate to begin graduate school with a highly talented group of fellow historians, including Beatrice Wayne, Cassie Good, Zain Lakhani, Brian Rouleau, and Karen Tani. Special thanks to Justin Simard, who helped push me toward Penn's dual degree program and has been a stalwart friend and sounding board ever since, and to my McNeil hallmate Sarah Gronningsater, who read much of the original dissertation and has been a constant source of encouragement and support.

I did not realize when I began my studies at Penn Law that I was joining such a supportive scholarly community. Cathie Struve and Bill Ewald have been enthusiastic backers and mentors since the moment I took their classes. Judge Anthony Scirica provided a model of deep intelligence accompanied by unparalleled thoughtfulness and kindness. I owe a tremendous debt to all the members of the Writers' Bloc(k), who read multiple chapters of this work, and especially Serena Mayeri and Sophia Lee. I cannot imagine two kinder, more generous, more thoughtful scholars, who welcomed me as a colleague and friend from the beginning, and freely gave their time to a budding legal historian. I was also very lucky the day I started law school in Steve Burbank's civil procedure class. Since then, as I journeyed from student to research assistant to co-author to friend and colleague, I have gained immensely from his support and mentorship.

This book began as a dissertation that benefited hugely from the wisdom of three exceptional scholars. Mike Zuckerman's infectious passion for history made working with him a joy, and his astute critical eye always made my work stronger. His appreciation for the absurdities and foibles of the past, and his impatience with the abstractions that historians often fall back on as explanations, made me a more incisive and careful scholar. Dan Richter has always exemplified for me the scholarly virtues: collegiality, an outstanding attention to craft, and deeply reflective practice. He exemplifies the human virtues, too: despite my partial defection to law early on, he has remained an outstanding and loyal mentor, finding time while managing one of the fullest plates of anyone I know. I aspire to pay Dan's model forward to my students. Sally Gordon welcomed me into her home days after we first met—the first of many visits. At every step of the way, she has been at once a mentor, cheerleader, confidant, fixer, and advocate. Along with everyone who has met her, I am in awe of her dynamism, dauntlessness, and fierce commitment to her students.

In moving to Stanford Law School, I joined a vibrant group of scholars who gave generously of their time. I am deeply appreciative of feedback from my legal history fellow travelers Rabia Belt, Lawrence Friedman, Bob Gordon, Amalia Kessler, and Bernie Meyler, all of whom read the original manuscript. Jacob Goldin, David Hayes, Lisa Ouellette, David Sklansky, and Norm Spaulding helpfully talked through ideas with me. Colleagues in Stanford's history department thoughtfully allowed me to share parts of the work with them: particular thanks to Jonathan Gienapp and Kathryn Olivarius for support and advice.

I am fortunate to be part of supportive communities of both historians and legal scholars. Although not directly a work of Indian law scholarship, the book reflects the insights I've gained over many years of conversations with those who've made huge contributions to the field: thanks to Judge Abby Abinanti, Dawn Baum, Bethany Berger, Kristen Carpenter, Amy Cordalis, Matthew Fletcher, Riyaz Kanji, and Angela Riley. Friends at other institutions graciously read portions of the manuscript and offered helpful suggestions, including Michael Blaakman, Maggie Blackhawk, Dan Carpenter, Colin Calloway, Peter Onuf, K-Sue Park, and Jess Roney. I benefited tremendously from a manuscript workshop organized by Bernie Meyler and funded by Stanford Law School. Huge thanks to Kevin Arlyck, Molly Brady, Greg Dowd, Rachel St. John, and Richard White for sacrificing their time to engage with the work; thanks to Nancy Gallman for participating from afar.

I already knew that Dan Hulsebosch was an outstanding scholar before starting this project with him; I have now learned he is a great editor, too, offering exemplary feedback and advice.

I would be hard-pressed to draw a straight line between my family and this book; I don't think my parents have even been to either Ohio or Tennessee. But their patient support and encouragement throughout the project, as well as a considerate refusal to press me as to when, exactly, it would be finished, helped see me through to the end.

The origins of this book perhaps lie in my time teaching in Zuni, New Mexico, where I witnessed firsthand the complexities of federal power in Indian country. That was also where I met my wife, Stephanie. Completing this academic project that grew from that time gives me considerable satisfaction; continuing the lifelong journey she and I began then fills me with joy and happiness.

Abbreviations

ASCP	Arthur St. Clair Papers (microfilm), MIC 96, Ohio Historical Society, Columbus, Ohio.
ASP:IA	Walter Lowrie and Matthew St. Clair Clarke eds., *American State Papers: Indian Affairs*, vol. 1 (Washington: Gales and Seaton, 1832).
ASP:PL	Walter Lowrie ed., *American State Papers: Public Lands*, vol. 1 (Washington: Printed by Duff Green, 1834).
CJCS	Beverley Waugh Bond ed., *The Correspondence of John Cleves Symmes: Founder of the Miami Purchase, Chiefly from the Collection of Peter G. Thomson* (New York: Pub. for the Historical and Philosophical Society of Ohio by the Macmillan Co., 1926).
CJR	"The Correspondence of Gen. James Robertson," Pts. 1–18, *The American Historical Magazine* 1, no. 1 (Jan. 1896): 71–91; no. 2 (Apr. 1896): 189–94; no. 3 (July 1896): 280–91; no. 4 (Oct. 1896): 390–96; 2, no. 1 (Jan. 1897): 59–86; 2, no. 2 (Apr. 1897): 172–77; 2, no. 3 (July 1897): 278–79; 2, no. 4 (Oct. 1897): 355–75; 3, no. 1 (Jan. 1898): 74–83; 3, no. 3 (July 1898): 267–98; 3, no. 4 (Oct. 1898): 348–94; 4, no. 1 (Jan. 1899): 66–96; 4, no. 2 (Apr. 1899): 163–92; 4, no. 3 (July 1899): 247–86; 4, no. 4 (Oct. 1899): 336–81; 5, no. 1 (Jan. 1900): 67–96; 5, no. 2 (Apr. 1900): 162–90; 5, no. 3 (July 1900): 252–86.
JCC	Worthington Chauncey Ford ed., *Journals of the Continental Congress 1774–1789*, 34 vols. (Washington: Government Printing Office, 1904–1937).
JGBP	Alice Barnwell Keith ed., *The John Gray Blount Papers*, 3 vols. (Raleigh [N.C.] State Dept. of Archives and History, 1952–1965).
JHP	Josiah Harmar Papers, William L. Clements Library, University of Michigan.
MRP	Rowena Buell ed., *The Memoirs of Rufus Putnam and Certain Official Papers and Correspondence* (Boston and New York: Houghton, Mifflin, 1903).
NWTC	Northwest Territory Collection, M367, Indiana Historical Society, Indianapolis, Ind.
PAJ	Sam B. Smith and Harriet Fason Chappell Owsley eds., *The Papers of Andrew Jackson*, 10 vols. (Knoxville: University of Tennessee Press, 1980–2013).
PGW:PS	W.W. Abbot and Dorothy Twohig eds., *The Papers of George Washington, Presidential Series*, 19 vols. (Charlottesville: University Press of Virginia, 1987–2013).
PTJ:MS	Julian P. Boyd ed., *The Papers of Thomas Jefferson: Main Series*, 44 vols. (Princeton, N.J.: Princeton University Press, 1950–2014).
RPP	Rufus Putnam Papers, Special Collections, Marietta College Library, Marietta, Ohio.

SCP	William Henry Smith ed., *The St. Clair Papers: The Life and Public Services of Arthur St. Clair* (Cincinnati: R. Clarke & Co., 1881).
TP: Vol. II	Clarence Edward Carter ed., *The Territorial Papers of the United States, Vol. II, The Territory Northwest of the River Ohio, 1787–1803* (Washington, D.C.: Government Printing Office, 1934).
TP: Vol. III	Clarence Edward Carter ed., *The Territorial Papers of the United States, Vol. III, The Territory Northwest of the River Ohio, 1787–1803, Continued,* (Washington, D.C.: Government Printing Office, 1934).
TP: Vol. IV	Clarence Edward Carter ed., *The Territorial Papers of the United States, Vol. IV, The Territory South of the River Ohio, 1790–1796* (Washington, D.C.: Government Printing Office, 1936).
WBP:LC	William Blount Papers (microfilm), MMC-0163, Manuscript Division, Library of Congress.
WSP	Winthrop Sargent Papers (microfilm), Massachusetts Historical Society, Boston, Mass.

Notes

Note on Terminology

1. "At a Meeting of a Number of the Inhabitants of Columbia at the House of Mr. William Stanley, on Monday the 25th of Jan. 1796, Pursuant to Public Notice," *Centinel of the North-Western Territory*, Feb. 20, 1796.
2. George Strather to David Henley, Jan. 28, 1797, David Henley Papers, Rubenstein Rare Book and Manuscript Library, Duke University. I have written on the historical debates on whether to call Native peoples "tribes" or "nations" elsewhere: *see* Gregory Ablavsky, "'With the Indian Tribes': Race, Citizenship, and Original Constitutional Meanings," *Stanford Law Review* 70 (2018): 1025.

Introduction

1. Thomas Jefferson, "Report on Public Lands," Nov. 8, 1791, in *PTJ:MS*, 22: 274–86.
2. The literature on these subjects is enormous. For an introduction to the Northwest Ordinance, *see* Peter S. Onuf, *Statehood and Union: A History of the Northwest Ordinance* (Bloomington: Indiana University Press, 1987); R. Douglas Hurt, "Historians and the Northwest Ordinance," *Western Historical Quarterly* 20, no. 3 (1989): 261–80; Frederick D. Williams ed., *The Northwest Ordinance: Essays on Its Formulation, Provisions, and Legacy* (East Lansing, Mich.: Michigan State University Press, 1989). On the significance of the 1785 Land Ordinance, *see* George W. Geib, "The Land Ordinance of 1785: A Bicentennial Review," *Indiana Magazine of History* 81, no. 1 (March 1, 1985): 1–13; Paul W. Gates, *History of Public Land Law Development* (Washington: [For sale by the Supt. of Docs., U.S. Govt. Print. Off.], 1968), 59–74; Robert V. Hine and John Mack Faragher, *Frontiers: A Short History of the American West* (Yale University Press, 2007), 41–43; Payson J. Treat, *The National Land System, 1785–1820* (New York: E.B. Treat & Co, 1910), 15–40; Bill Hubbard, *American Boundaries: The Nation, the States, the Rectangular Survey* (Chicago: University of Chicago Press, 2009), 192–202; Malcolm J. Rohrbough, *The Land Office Business: The Settlement and Administration of American Public Lands, 1789–1837* (New York: Oxford University Press, 1968), 5–10. For works that emphasize the settler-colonial nature of these foundational documents, *see* Michael Witgen, "Seeing Red: Race, Citizenship, and Indigeneity in the Old Northwest," *Journal of the Early Republic* 38, no. 4 (Dec. 3, 2018): 581–611; Bethel Saler, *The Settlers' Empire: Colonialism and State Formation in America's Old Northwest* (Philadelphia: University of Pennsylvania Press, 2014), 25–29; Robert F. Berkhofer,

"Americans versus Indians: The Northwest Ordinance, Territory Making, and Native Americans," *Indiana Magazine of History* 84, no. 1 (1988): 90–108.

3. Jefferson, "Report on Public Lands." For the non-Native population of the territories at the time Jefferson wrote, *see* "Population of the Northwest Territory," Jan. 31, 1791, in *PTJ:MS*, 18:217; William Blount to Secretary of State, Sept. 19, 1791, in *TP: Vol. IV*, 80–81.
4. U.S. CONST. art. VI. For key entries in the vast literature on the U.S. Constitution's drafting, *see* Gordon S. Wood, *The Creation of the American Republic, 1776–1787* (Chapel Hill: University of North Carolina Press, 1998); Jonathan Gienapp, *The Second Creation: Fixing the American Constitution in the Founding Era* (Cambridge, Mass.: Belknap Press, 2018); Jack N. Rakove, *Original Meanings: Politics and Ideas in the Making of the Constitution* (New York: A.A. Knopf, 1996).
5. On the federal government's waterfront presence, *see* Gautham Rao, *National Duties: Custom Houses and the Making of the American State* (Chicago: University of Chicago Press, 2016); Hannah Farber, "State-Building After War's End: A Government Financier Adjusts His Portfolio for Peace," *Journal of the Early Republic* 38, no. 1 (Mar. 3, 2018): 67–76; Kevin Arlyck, "Forged by War: The Federal Courts and Foreign Affairs in the Age of Revolution" (Ph.D. dissertation, New York University, 2014). On the federal government as an "imperial state," *see* Saler, *The Settlers' Empire*; Gautham Rao, "The New Historiography of the Early Federal Government: Institutions, Contexts, and the Imperial State," *William and Mary Quarterly* 77, no. 1 (2020): 97–128. On debates over the meaning of sovereignty in this era, *see* Wood, *Creation of the American Republic, 1776–1787*, 345–89; Gregory Ablavsky, "Species of Sovereignty: Native Nationhood, the United States, and International Law, 1783–1795," *Journal of American History* 106, no. 3 (Dec. 1, 2019): 591–613.
6. Secretary of State to David Campbell, Mar. 27, 1792, in *TP: Vol. IV*, 130–31. For instances of discussion of the national character, *see* "Report of the Secretary at War: Indian Affairs," May 2, 1788, in *TP: Vol. II*, 103–05; George Washington to United States Senate and House of Representatives, Jan. 30, 1794, in *PGW:PS*, 15:157–58. On this vision for the West, which has usually been labeled as "Federalist," *see* Peter S. Onuf, "Liberty, Development, and Union: Visions of the West in the 1780s," *William and Mary Quarterly*, 43, no. 2 (Apr. 1, 1986): 179–213; Andrew R.L. Cayton, *The Frontier Republic: Ideology and Politics in the Ohio Country, 1780–1825* (Kent, Ohio: Kent State University Press, 1986); David Andrew Nichols, *Red Gentlemen & White Savages: Indians, Federalists, and the Search for Order on the American Frontier* (Charlottesville: University of Virginia Press, 2008); Kristopher Maulden, *The Federalist Frontier: Settler Politics in the Old Northwest, 1783–1840* (Columbia: University of Missouri, 2019). Other scholars have noted continuity between the Republican and Federalist projects for the early American West. Brian Balogh, *A Government Out of Sight: The Mystery of National Authority in Nineteenth-Century America* (Cambridge; New York: Cambridge University Press, 2009), 190–97; Bethel Saler, "An Empire for Liberty, a State for Empire: the U.S. National State before and after the Revolution of 1800," in James P.P. Horn, Jan Lewis, and Peter S. Onuf eds., *The Revolution of 1800: Democracy, Race, and the New Republic* (Charlottesville: University of Virginia Press, 2002), 360–78.

7. For background on the federalist struggles in early New York, *see* Laurence M. Hauptman, *Conspiracy of Interests: Iroquois Dispossession and the Rise of New York State* (Syracuse, N.Y.: Syracuse University Press, 1999); Alan Taylor, *The Divided Ground: Indians, Settlers and the Northern Borderland of the American Revolution* (New York: Alfred A. Knopf, 2006); on Georgia, *see* Lisa Ford, *Settler Sovereignty: Jurisdiction and Indigenous People in America and Australia, 1788–1836* (Cambridge, Mass.: Harvard University Press, 2010); Gregory Ablavsky, "Beyond the Indian Commerce Clause," *Yale Law Journal* 124, no. 4 (2015): 1012–90; on Kentucky, *see* Stephen Aron, *How the West Was Lost: The Transformation of Kentucky from Daniel Boone to Henry Clay* (Baltimore: Johns Hopkins University Press, 1996); Patrick Griffin, *American Leviathan: Empire, Nation, and Revolutionary Frontier* (New York: Hill and Wang, 2007), 185–210.
8. "A Statement of the Troops in the Service of the United States," Aug. 10, 1789, in Walter Lowrie and Matthew St. Clair Clarke eds., *American State Papers: Military Affairs* (Washington: Published by Gales and Seaton, 1832), 1: 5–6. Henry Knox estimated that in 1788 the actual effective force averaged 350 soldiers. "Report of the Secretary at War: Indian Affairs," Mar. 31, 1788, in *TP: Vol. II*, 101–02.
9. *JCC*, 32:334–43. The Ordinance was re-enacted after the adoption of the Constitution with minor alterations to conform to the new constitutional system. Act of Aug. 7, 1789, ch. 8, 1 Stat. 50, 51–53.
10. Benjamin Hawkins to William Blount, Apr. 24, 1792, Folder 4: 1792, WBP:LC; Vitrivius, "Cincinnati, Sept. 27," *Centinel of the North-Western Territory*, Sept. 27, 1794; Balogh, *A Government Out of Sight*, 153. For additional histories of territorial governance, John Porter Bloom ed., *The American Territorial System* (Athens: Ohio University Press, 1973); Jack Ericson Eblen, *The First and Second United States Empires; Governors and Territorial Government, 1784–1912* ([Pittsburgh]: University of Pittsburgh Press, 1968); Gary Lawson and Guy Seidman, *The Constitution of Empire: Territorial Expansion and American Legal History* (New Haven, Conn.: Yale University Press, 2004); Stefan Heumann, "The Tutelary Empire: State- and Nation-Building in the 19th Century United States" (Ph.D. dissertation, University of Pennsylvania, 2009). The District of Columbia, also outside state control, held similar constitutional status to the territories; it, too, was subject to direct federal rule. Act of Feb. 27, 1801, ch. 15, 2 Stat. 103.
11. "Volume 63: An Account of Dr. Cutler's Work for the Ordinance of 1787," July 13–Aug. 4, 1787, Vol. 63, Manasseh Cutler Papers, Special Collections, Northwestern University Library. On the forward-looking nature of U.S. territorial governance, *see* Onuf, *Statehood and Union*, 44–66.
12. Jonathan Heart to William Judd, Oct. 14, 1787 (typescript copy), Jonathan Heart Papers, VFM 5748, Ohio Historical Society. For an introduction to the large literature on the peoples of the Native South in this period, *see* Gregory D. Smithers, *Native Southerners: Indigenous History from Origins to Removal* (Norman: University of Oklahoma Press, 2019); Tim Alan Garrison and Greg O'Brien eds., *The Native South: New Histories and Enduring Legacies* (Lincoln: University of Nebraska Press, 2017). On particular Native nations, *see* James R. Atkinson, *Splendid Land,*

Splendid People: The Chickasaw Indians to Removal (Tuscaloosa: University of Alabama Press, 2004); Greg O'Brien, *Choctaws in a Revolutionary Age, 1750–1830* (Lincoln: University of Nebraska Press, 2002); Robbie Franklyn Ethridge, *Creek Country: The Creek Indians and Their World* (Chapel Hill: University of North Carolina Press, 2003); William Gerald McLoughlin, *Cherokee Renascence in the New Republic* (Princeton, N.J.: Princeton University Press, 1986); Claudio Saunt, *A New Order of Things: Property, Power, and the Transformation of the Creek Indians, 1733–1816* (Cambridge, U.K.: Cambridge University Press, 1999); Angela Pulley Hudson, *Creek Paths and Federal Roads: Indians, Settlers, and Slaves and the Making of the American South* (Chapel Hill: University of North Carolina Press, 2010). On the Native peoples of the Ohio and Illinois Countries, *see* Michael N. McConnell, *A Country Between: The Upper Ohio Valley and Its Peoples, 1724–1774* (Lincoln: University of Nebraska Press, 1992); David Andrew Nichols, *Peoples of the Inland Sea: Native Americans and Newcomers in the Great Lakes Region, 1600–1870* (Athens: Ohio University Press, 2018); Eric Hinderaker, *Elusive Empires: Constructing Colonialism in the Ohio Valley, 1673–1800* (New York: Cambridge University Press, 1997); James H. O'Donnell, *Ohio's First Peoples* (Athens: Ohio University Press, 2004); Sami Lakomäki, *Gathering Together: The Shawnee People through Diaspora and Nationhood, 1600–1870* (New Haven, Conn.: Yale University Press, 2014); Stephen Warren, *The Worlds the Shawnees Made: Migration and Violence in Early America* (Chapel Hill: University of North Carolina, 2014); Amy C. Schutt, *Peoples of the River Valleys: The Odyssey of the Delaware Indians* (Philadelphia: University of Pennsylvania Press, 2007); Stewart Rafert, *The Miami Indians of Indiana: A Persistent People, 1654–1994* (Indianapolis: Indiana Historical Society, 1996); Jacob F. Lee, *Masters of the Middle Waters: Indian Nations and Colonial Ambitions along the Mississippi* (Cambridge, Mass.: Belknap Press, 2019). On the transformation of Native governance in this era, *see* Rennard Strickland, *Fire and the Spirits: Cherokee Law from Clan to Court* (Norman: University of Oklahoma Press, 1975); Steven C. Hahn, *The Invention of the Creek Nation, 1670–1763* (Lincoln: University of Nebraska Press, 2004); Kevin Kokomoor, *Of One Mind and of One Government: The Rise and Fall of the Creek Nation in the Early Republic* (Lincoln: University of Nebraska Press, 2019).

13. On the Illinois Country, *see* Carl J. Ekberg, *French Roots in the Illinois Country: The Mississippi Frontier in Colonial Times* (Urbana: University of Illinois Press, 1998); Robert Michael Morrissey, *Empire by Collaboration: Indians, Colonists, and Governments in Colonial Illinois Country* (Philadelphia: University of Pennsylvania Press, 2015); John Reda, *From Furs to Farms: The Transformation of the Mississippi Valley, 1762–1825* (Dekalb: Northern Illinois University Press, 2016); Sophie White, *Wild Frenchmen and Frenchified Indians: Material Culture and Race in Colonial Louisiana* (Philadelphia: University of Pennsylvania Press, 2012), 21–142. On settlements in eastern Tennessee, *see* Kevin T. Barksdale, *The Lost State of Franklin: America's First Secession* (Lexington: University Press of Kentucky, 2008); Jessica Choppin Roney, "1776, Viewed from the West," *Journal of the Early Republic* 37, no. 4 (Oct. 31, 2017): 655–700; on Cumberland, *see* Kristofer Ray,

Middle Tennessee, 1775–1825: Progress and Popular Democracy on the Southwestern Frontier (Knoxville: University of Tennessee Press, 2007); on both regions, *see* John R. Finger, *Tennessee Frontiers: Three Regions in Transition* (Bloomington: Indiana University Press, 2001); Cynthia Cumfer, *Separate Peoples, One Land: The Minds of Cherokees, Blacks, and Whites on the Tennessee Frontier* (Chapel Hill: University of North Carolina Press, 2007). On borderlands, *see* Pekka Hämäläinen and Samuel Truett, "On Borderlands," *Journal of American History* 98, no. 2 (Sept. 1, 2011): 338–61; Juliana Barr and Edward Countryman eds., *Contested Spaces of Early America* (Philadelphia: University of Pennsylvania Press, 2014).

14. On the contest between the British, Spanish, and the United States in this period, *see* Kathleen DuVal, *Independence Lost: Lives on the Edge of the American Revolution* (New York: Random House, 2015); J.C.A. Stagg, *Borderlines in Borderlands: James Madison and the Spanish-American Frontier, 1776–1821* (New Haven, Conn.: Yale University Press, 2009); Taylor, *The Divided Ground*; Gene Allen Smith and Sylvia L. Hilton eds., *Nexus of Empire: Negotiating Loyalty and Identity in the Revolutionary Borderlands, 1760s–1820s* (Gainesville: University Press of Florida, 2011); David Narrett, *Adventurism and Empire: The Struggle for Mastery in the Louisiana-Florida Borderlands, 1762–1803* (Chapel Hill: The University of North Carolina Press, 2015); Arthur Preston Whitaker, *The Spanish-American Frontier: 1783–1795: The Westward Movement and the Spanish Retreat in the Mississippi Valley* (Boston: Houghton Mifflin, 1927).
15. On earlier imperial struggles over these regions, *see* Eric Hinderaker, *Elusive Empires: Constructing Colonialism in the Ohio Valley, 1673–1800* (New York: Cambridge University Press, 1997); Rob Harper, *Unsettling the West: Violence and State Building in the Ohio Valley* (Philadelphia: University of Pennsylvania Press, 2018); Kristofer Ray ed., *Before the Volunteer State: New Thoughts on Early Tennessee, 1540–1800*, 1st ed. (Knoxville: University of Tennessee Press, 2015).
16. As Rachel St. John aptly notes, "the antebellum West was both the region where the federal government was most active and where the limitations of federal power were most evident." Rachel St. John, "State Power in the West in the Early American Republic," *Journal of the Early Republic* 38, no. 1 (Mar. 3, 2018): 87–94.
17. On the cabinet officials' responsibilities, *see* Act of July 27, 1789, ch. 4, 1 Stat. 28; Act of Aug. 5, 1789, ch. 7, 1 Stat. 49; Act of Sept. 2, 1789, ch. 12, 1 Stat. 65; Thomas Jefferson "Notes on Executive Departments," [after Mar. 21, 1790], in *PTJ:MS*, 27:780.
18. Attorney General to Secretary of State, Aug. 22, 1799, in *TP: Vol. III*, 66–67. One scholar of territorial governance has stressed "how little control the governors really exercised over their appointments," emphasizing the dominance of "local oligarchy rather than executive autocracy." Eblen, *The First and Second United States Empires*, 114–36.
19. On territorial governors, *see* Leonard Dupee White, *The Federalists: A Study in Administrative History* (New York: Macmillan, 1956), 366–78; Elben, *The First and Second United States Empires*. Eblen observes of the governors, "In law they held the key positions of power in every essential respect. As federal officials, they were the liaisons between the federal and territorial governments." *Id.*, 11.

20. Journal of Ichabod Nye (typescript), Folder 2, Box 3, Marietta, Ohio Collection, Ohio Historical Society, 62; "Governour St. Clair before a Committee of Congress upon W.S. as Adjt. Genl," Apr. 1792, Reel 3, WSP; Griffin Greene to "Peter," n.d., Northwest Territory Collection, Clements Library, University of Michigan; Secretary of State to President, Jan. 4, 1794, in *TP: Vol. II*, 472–73. On St. Clair's biography, *see SCP*, vol. 1; on Sargent, *see* Benjamin Harrison Pershing, "Winthrop Sargent: A Builder in the Old Northwest" (Ph.D. dissertation, University of Chicago, 1927).
21. "Recommendations for Federal Offices in North Carolina and the Southwestern Government," [before June 7, 1790], *PTJ:MS*, 16:476–48; Benjamin Hawkins, "Journal," Nov. 24, 1797, in C.L. Grant ed., *Letters, Journals, and Writings of Benjamin Hawkins* (Savannah, Ga.: Beehive Press, 1980), 220–22. On Blount, *see* William H. Masterson, *William Blount* (Baton Rouge: Louisiana State University Press, 1954); on Smith, *see* Walter T. Durham, *Daniel Smith: Frontier Statesman* (Gallatin, Tenn.: Sumner County Library Board, 1976) .
22. "Deposition of William Davy," July 13, 1797, in *Report of the Committee of the House of Representatives of the United States, Appointed to Prepare and Report Articles of Impeachment against William Blount, a Senator of the United States . . .* (Philadelphi a: Printed by John Fenno, 1797), lxxii–lxxx; Robert Buntin to Arthur St. Clair, Oct. 28, 1790, Reel 3, ASCP; John Sevier to Andrew Jackson, Jan. 29, 1797, Jackson Papers, 1:120–21; "Report of Committee on Conduct of General Joseph Martin, Indian Agent (Depositions, Letters, and Messages Only)," Dec. 15, 1789, Joint Select Comm., Reports & papers, Dec. 15–21, GASR Nov.–Dec. 1789, Box 2, North Carolina State Archives; Turner Williams to William Blount, Nov. 25, 1792, Folder 4: 1792, Manuscript Division, Library of Congress. On Indian agents in the early republic, *see* Saler, *Settlers' Empire*, 71–73; Francis Paul Prucha, *American Indian Policy in the Formative Years: The Indian Trade and Intercourse Acts, 1780–1834* (Cambridge, Mass.: Harvard University Press, 1962), 51–63.
23. This paper network resembled what Dan Hulsebosch has helpfully identified as the "epistolary constitution of empire" under prerevolutionary British rule. Daniel Joseph Hulsebosch, *Constituting Empire: New York and the Transformation of Constitutionalism in the Atlantic World, 1664–1830* (Chapel Hill: University of North Carolina Press, 2005), 77–83.
24. As Bethel Saler notes, "More often, congressional policymakers and government officials reacted rather than initiating actions or new policies on their own." Saler, *Settlers' Empire*, 39–40. This approach to state-building heeds Bill Novak's call to recount the history of the state not as a story of a "cadre of state builders" or "self-governing bureaucratic institutions" but through what he terms the "state in society." William J. Novak, "The Concept of the State in American History," in James T. Sparrow, William J. Novak, and Stephen W. Sawyer eds., *Boundaries of the State in US History* (Chicago: University of Chicago Press, 2015), 325–49. Gautham Rao has recently called for reconstructing federal authority by looking beyond institutions "to explain how people distant from the nation's capital—of different backgrounds, races, and ethnicities, with varying cultural understandings of government—confronted, contested, and legitimated federal authority and the state in the early republic." Rao,

"The New Historiography of the Early Federal Government," 98. On the multifaceted nature of early American political culture, *see* Jeffrey L. Pasley, Andrew W. Robertson, and David Waldstreicher eds., *Beyond the Founders: New Approaches to the Political History of the Early American Republic* (Chapel Hill: University of North Carolina Press, 2004).

25. Report of the Secretary at War to Congress, July 10, 1787, in *TP: Vol. II*, 31–35. On the role of federal perceptions of Native peoples in shaping policy, *see* Robert F. Berkhofer, *The White Man's Indian: Images of the American Indian from Columbus to the Present* (New York: Knopf, 1978), 113–94. On Indigenous law and complications of defining the category, *see* Saliha Belmessous ed., *Native Claims: Indigenous Law Against Empire, 1500–1920* (Oxford: Oxford University Press, 2012); Gregory Ablavsky, Sarah Deer, and Justin Richland, "Indigenous Law," in Simon Stern et al. eds., *The Oxford Handbook of Law and Humanities* (Oxford: Oxford University Press, 2019), 516–30.
26. The debate on how to measure state power is voluminous. For influential entries in debates over the early federal government, *see* Michael Mann, "The Autonomous Power of the State: Its Origins, Mechanisms and Results," *European Journal of Sociology* 25, no. 2 (1984): 185–213; Theda Skocpol, "Bringing the State Back In: Strategies of Analysis in Current Research," in Peter B. Evans, Dietrich Rueschemeyer, and Theda Skocpol eds., *Bringing the State Back In* (Cambridge, U.K.: Cambridge University Press, 1985), 3–38; Laura S. Jensen, "Government, the State, and Governance," *Polity* 40, no. 3 (2008): 379–85. On the distinctiveness of the early federal state, and the desire to move beyond the weak/strong dichotomy, *see* Peter Baldwin, "Beyond Weak and Strong: Rethinking the State in Comparative Policy History," *Journal of Policy History* 17, no. 1 (Jan. 2005): 12–33; Desmond King and Robert C. Lieberman, "Finding the American State: Transcending the 'Statelessness' Account," *Polity* 40, no. 3 (2008): 368–78; Balogh, *A Government Out of Sight*; William J. Novak, "The Myth of the 'Weak' American State," *American Historical Review* 113, no. 3 (June 2008): 752–72; Stephen Skowronek, "Present at the Creation: The State in Early American Political History," *Journal of the Early Republic* 38, no. 1 (Mar. 3, 2018): 95–103.
27. Thomas Jefferson to James Madison, Jan. 30 1787, in *PTJ:MS*, 11:92–97; David Zeisberger, *David Zeisberger's History of Northern American Indians* (Columbus, Ohio: Press of F.J. Heer, 1910), 90; Max M. Edling, *A Revolution in Favor of Government: Origins of the U.S. Constitution and the Making of the American State* (Oxford; New York: Oxford University Press, 2003); Max M. Edling, *A Hercules in the Cradle: War, Money, and the American State, 1783–1867* (Chicago: University of Chicago Press, 2014). On the U.S. military in the early territories, *see* Richard H. Kohn, *Eagle and Sword: The Federalists and the Creation of the Military Establishment in America, 1783–1802* (New York: Free Press, 1975); William H. Bergmann, *The American National State and the Early West* (Cambridge; New York: Cambridge University Press, 2012); Ira Katznelson, "Flexible Capacity: The Military and Early American Statebuilding," in Ira Katznelson and Martin Shefter eds., *Shaped by War and Trade: International Influences on American Political Development* (Princeton, N.J.: Princeton University Press, 2002), 82–110. On the fiscal-military state in

Europe, *see* M.J. Braddick, *State Formation in Early Modern England, C. 1550–1700* (Cambridge, U.K.: Cambridge University Press, 2000); John Brewer, *The Sinews of Power: War, Money, and the English State, 1688–1783* (Cambridge, Mass.: Harvard University Press, 1990).

28. James Madison, "Vices of the Political System of the United States," Apr. 1787, in William T. Hutchinson and William M.E. Rachal eds., *Papers of James Madison: Congressional Series* (Chicago: University of Chicago Press, 1962–), 9: 345–58; Publius, "The Federalist 80," May 28, 1788, in Merrill Jensen ed., *The Documentary History of the Ratification of the Constitution* (Madison: State Historical Society of Wisconsin, 1976–), 6: 96–102; Arthur St. Clair to Secretary of State, Dec. 15, 1794, in *TP: Vol. II*, 499–500. On Madison's vision of the federal government as arbiter, albeit with a libertarian inflection, *see* Gordon S. Wood, *Empire of Liberty: A History of the Early Republic, 1789–1815* (Oxford: Oxford University Press, 2009), 91, 103, 148. On role of jurisdictional conflicts in early modern European state formation, *see* Michael P. Breen, "Law, Society, and the State in Early Modern France," *Journal of Modern History* 83, no. 2 (2011): 346–86; Lauren A. Benton, *Law and Colonial Cultures: Legal Regimes in World History, 1400–1900* (Cambridge, U.K.: Cambridge University Press, 2002). On contests over jurisdiction in the creation of early modern states, *see* Ulrike Müßig, "Jurisdiction, Political Authority, and Territory," in Heikki Pihlajamäki, Markus Dirk Dubber, and Mark Godfrey eds., *The Oxford Handbook of European Legal History* (Oxford: Oxford University Press, 2018), 678–704; Tamar Herzog, *A Short History of European Law: The Last Two and a Half Millennia* (Cambridge, Mass.: Harvard University Press, 2018). One of the scholars who emphasized the rise of "fiscal military state" in early modern England also described the simultaneous rise of state authority grounded in courts and other jurisdictional conflicts. Braddick, *State Formation in Early Modern England*, 9–172.

29. As one scholar observed of a slightly later period, "'Policy' was little more than the accumulation of isolated, individual choices, usually of a distributive nature." Richard L. McCormick, *The Party Period and Public Policy: American Politics from the Age of Jackson to the Progressive Era* (New York: Oxford University Press, 1986), 206. On law as a zone of contestation, *see* Hendrik Hartog, "Pigs and Positivism," *Wisconsin Law Review* (1985): 899–936. For examples of policy histories, *see* Francis Paul Prucha, *The Great Father: The United States Government and the American Indians*, 2 vols. (Lincoln: University of Nebraska Press, 1984); Reginald Horsman, *Expansion and American Indian Policy, 1783–1812* (East Lansing: Michigan State University Press, 1967); Rohrbough, *The Land Office Business*.

30. For a few of the numerous examples of such language in the territories, *see* Jonathan Heart to [Unknown], May 1, 1786, Folder 1: 1786–87, William Judd Papers, Connecticut Historical Society; "No. 57: Sales of Lands Acquired by the Cession of North Carolina," May 9, 1800, in *ASP:PL*, 1:97–99; Arthur St. Clair to Gen'l Wilkinson, July 16, 1798, in *SCP*, 1:427–28. For a Native use of rights talk, *see* "Reply of the Indian Council to the Commissioners of the United States," Aug. 16, 1793, in *ASP:IA*, 356–57.

Literature on rights and rights-talk is enormous. For an overview on rights in the early United States, *see* Jud Campbell, "Republicanism and Natural Rights at the Founding," *Constitutional Commentary* 32, no. 1 (2017): 85–112; Gordon S. Wood, "The Origins of Vested Rights in the Early Republic," *Virginia Law Review* 85, no. 7 (1999): 1421–45. On rights and American state-building, *see* Karen M. Tani, "Welfare and Rights Before the Movement: Rights as a Language of the State," *Yale Law Journal* 122, no. 2 (2012): 314; Karen Orren and Stephen Skowronek, *The Policy State: An American Predicament* (Cambridge, Mass.: Harvard University Press, 2019). Because Skowronek and Orren focus on "the extent to which rights constrain official discretion," they contrast rights with what they call the policy motive—the forward-looking commitment to a governmental goal. *Id.*, 27–32. But control over the distribution of rights, particularly property, was arguably the paradigmatic form of policymaking in the early United States: *see* Hendrik Hartog, *Public Property and Private Power: The Corporation of the City of New York in American Law, 1730–1870* (Chapel Hill: University of North Carolina Press, 1983).

31. For a rare work comparing the two territories, *see* Walter T. Durham, "The Southwest and Northwest Territories, a Comparison, 1787–1796," *Tennessee Historical Quarterly* 49, no. 3 (Oct. 1, 1990): 188–96.
32. Act of May 26, 1790, ch. 14, 1 Stat. 123. For the existence of slavery in the Northwest Territory notwithstanding the Northwest Ordinance, *see* M. Scott Heerman, *The Alchemy of Slavery: Human Bondage and Emancipation in the Illinois Country, 1730–1865* (Philadelphia: University of Pennsylvania Press, 2018); John Craig Hammond, *Slavery, Freedom, and Expansion in the Early American West* (Charlottesville: University of Virginia Press, 2007); Matthew Salafia, *Slavery's Borderland: Freedom and Bondage Along the Ohio River* (Philadelphia: University of Pennsylvania Press, 2013); Paul Finkelman, "Slavery and the Northwest Ordinance: A Study in Ambiguity," *Journal of the Early Republic* 6, no. 4 (1986): 343–70. For studies of enslaved Natives in the Northwest and Southwest Territories, *see* Carl J. Ekberg, *Stealing Indian Women: Native Slavery in the Illinois Country* (Urbana: University of Illinois Press, 2007); Brett Rushforth, *Bonds of Alliance: Indigenous and Atlantic Slaveries in New France* (Chapel Hill: The University of North Carolina Press, 2012); Christina Snyder, *Slavery in Indian Country: The Changing Face of Captivity in Early America* (Cambridge, Mass.: Harvard University Press, 2010), 152–81.
33. Historian Andrew Cayton was the strongest proponent of this view, arguing that the Southwest Territory was a largely stateless realm where white settlers "initiated and completed the conquest of the southern flank of the American republic largely on their own . . . because they had no other choice . . . . [T]hey filled a vacuum left by the government of the United States." Andrew R.L. Cayton, "'Separate Interests' and the Nation-State: The Washington Administration and the Origins of Regionalism in the Trans-Appalachian West," *Journal of American History* 79, no. 1 (June 1, 1992): 39–67; *see also* Andrew R.L. Cayton, "'When Shall We Cease to Have Judases?' The Blount Conspiracy and the Limits of the 'Extended Republic,'" in Ronald Hoffman and Peter J. Albert eds., *Launching the "Extended Republic": The Federalist Era* (Charlottesville: Published for the United States Capitol Historical Society by the

University Press of Virginia, 1996), 157–89. Cayton's argument has become conventional wisdom: for other instances, *see* Wood, *Empire of Liberty*, 133; Kristofer Ray, "Land Speculation, Popular Democracy, and Political Transformation on the Tennessee Frontier, 1780–1800," *Tennessee Historical Quarterly* 61, no. 3 (Oct. 1, 2002): 171–81; Roney, "1776, Viewed from the West," 694–95.

34. On early American land obsession, *see* Michael Albert Blaakman, "Speculation Nation: Land and Mania in the Revolutionary American Republic, 1776–1803" (Mar. 2016) (unpublished Ph.D. dissertation, Yale University); Reeve Huston, "Land Conflict and Land Policy in the United States, 1785–1841," in Andrew Shankman ed., *The World of the Revolutionary American Republic: Land, Labor, and the Conflict for a Continent* (New York: Routledge, 2014), 324–45; Aaron Morton Sakolski, *The Great American Land Bubble; the Amazing Story of Land-Grabbing, Speculations, and Booms from Colonial Days to the Present Time* (New York: Harper & Brothers, 1932).
35. Francois Furstenberg, "The Significance of the Trans-Appalachian Frontier in Atlantic History," *American Historical Review* 113, no. 3 (2008): 647–77.

Chapter 1

1. "Report of the Secretary of State to the President," 85–100.
2. In using the term "property pluralism," I seek to echo, and mirror, the analytic concept of legal pluralism. For scholarly introductions to the concept as applied to legal history, *see* Lauren A. Benton, *Law and Colonial Cultures: Legal Regimes in World History, 1400–1900* (Cambridge, U.K.: Cambridge University Press, 2002); Richard J. Ross and Lauren A. Benton, "Empires and Legal Pluralism: Jurisdiction, Sovereignty, and Political Imagination in the Early Modern World," in Richard J. Ross and Lauren Benton eds., *Legal Pluralism and Empires, 1500–1850* (New York: NYU Press, 2013).
3. Allan Greer, *Property and Dispossession: Natives, Empires and Land in Early Modern North America* (Cambridge, U.K.; New York: Cambridge University Press, 2018), 389–436. On post-revolutionary debates over property and its remaking, *see* Gregory S. Alexander, *Commodity & Propriety: Competing Visions of Property in American Legal Thought, 1776–1970* (Chicago: University of Chicago Press, 1997), 27–88; Claire Priest, "The End of Entail: Information, Institutions, and Slavery in the American Revolutionary Period," *Law and History Review* 33 (2015): 277; Stanley N. Katz, "Republicanism and the Law of Inheritance in the American Revolutionary Era," *Michigan Law Review* 76, no. 1 (Nov. 1977): 1–29. The most recent and best account of early American land mania is Blaakman, *Speculation Nation*; an older account appears in Sakolski, *The Great American Land Bubble*. For an attack on "land jobbing," *see* George Washington to Alexander Hamilton, Apr. 4, 1791, in *PGW:PS*, 8:57–58.
4. Samuel Holden Parsons to His Children, Jan. 7, 1786, Folder 6, Samuel Holden Parsons Papers, Connecticut Historical Society, Hartford, Conn. For background on Iroquoia, *see* Laurence M. Hauptman, *Conspiracy of Interests Iroquois Dispossession and the Rise of New York State* (Syracuse, N.Y.: Syracuse University Press, 1999); Alan

Taylor, *William Cooper's Town: Power and Persuasion on the Frontier of the Early American Republic* (New York: Alfred A. Knopf, 1995); Taylor, *The Divided Ground*; on Maine, *see* Alan Taylor, *Liberty Men and Great Proprietors: The Revolutionary Settlement on the Maine Frontier, 1760–1820* (Chapel Hill: University of North Carolina Press, 1990); on Kentucky, *see* Frederika Teute, "Land, Liberty, and Labor in the Post-Revolutionary Era: Kentucky as the Promised Land" (Ph.D. dissertation, The Johns Hopkins University, 1988); Mary K. Bonsteel Tachau, *Federal Courts in the Early Republic: Kentucky, 1789–1816* (Princeton, N.J.: Princeton University Press, 1978), 167–90; Stephen Aron, *How the West Was Lost: The Transformation of Kentucky from Daniel Boone to Henry Clay* (Baltimore: Johns Hopkins University Press, 1996), 58–123.

5. 1 Annals of Cong. 411–16 (1789). On state cessions, *see* Onuf, *Origins of the Federal Republic*.
6. Historians and scholars from other disciplines have both interpreted early American land conflict as a struggle between squatters and formal law. For examples, *see* Andrew R.L. Cayton, *The Frontier Republic: Ideology and Politics in the Ohio Country, 1780–1825* (Kent, Ohio: Kent State University Press, 1986), 1–11; Onuf, *Statehood and Union*, 28–33; Huston, "Land Conflict and Land Policy in the United States, 1785–1841," 324–45; Eduardo Moisés Peñalver and Sonia Katyal, *Property Outlaws: How Squatters, Pirates, and Protesters Improve the Law of Ownership* (New Haven: Yale University Press, 2010); Hernando de Soto, *The Mystery of Capital: Why Capitalism Triumphs in the West and Fails Everywhere Else* (New York: Basic Books, 2000).
7. *JCC*, 32:334–43.
8. William Wirt, "Virginia Land Warrants," Oct. 8, 1819, in *Official Opinions of the Attorneys General of the United States* (Washington: Robert Farnham, 1852), 1:311. On the law of property in the early United States, *see* Gregory S. Alexander, *Commodity & Propriety: Competing Visions of Property in American Legal Thought, 1776–1970* (Chicago: University of Chicago Press, 1997); Claire Priest, "Creating an American Property Law: Alienability and Its Limits in American History," *Harvard Law Review* 120, no. 2 (Dec. 2006): 386–459. For debates over Native ownership rights in this period, *see* Banner, *How the Indians Lost Their Land*, 150–89; Blake A. Watson, *Buying America from the Indians: Johnson v. McIntosh and the History of Native Land Rights* (Norman: University of Oklahoma Press, 2012).
9. On the rise of consent in Anglo-American governance and law, *see* Holly Brewer, *By Birth or Consent: Children, Law, and the Anglo-American Revolution in Authority* (Chapel Hill: University of North Carolina Press, 2005); Hulsebosch, *Constituting Empire*, 229; James H. Kettner, *The Development of American Citizenship, 1608–1870* (Chapel Hill: University of North Carolina Press, 1978). For an example of Native invocation of consent, *see* Old Tassel to Governor of Virginia, June 12, 1787, Cherokee Collection, Reel 1, Box 1, Item 20, Tennessee State Library and Archives. On Native consent in Anglo-American law more generally, *see* Matthew L.M. Fletcher, "Tribal Consent," *Stanford Journal of Civil Rights & Civil Liberties* 8 (2012): 45.
10. Indian Land Sale Contract, May 20, 1786, Doc. I.214, Lasselle Family Papers, L127, Indiana State Library, Manuscripts & Rare Books Division, Indianapolis, Ind.

For other examples of such purchases, *see Records of Washington County Court of Pleas and Quarter Sessions, Volume Book 1, 1778–1798* (Nashville, Tenn.: Historical Records Survey, Works Progress Administration, 1938), 20; "Report of Governor St. Clair to the Secretary of State," Feb. 10, 1791, in *TP: Vol. II*, 352–53. On the prevalence of purchasing land from the Indians from the seventeenth century onward, *see* Banner, *How the Indians Lost Their Land*, 10–48.

11. James Ross to Winthrop Sargent, Dec. 22, 1797, Reel 4, *WSP*. On fraud in Indian land purchases throughout the eighteenth century, *see* Banner, 62–68. Francis Jennings famously referred to such dubious land practices as the "deed game." Francis Jennings, *The Invasion of America: Indians, Colonialism, and the Cant of Conquest* (New York: Norton, 1976), 128–45.
12. By the King, a Proclamation, Oct. 7, 1763, in W. Walter Lowrie, ed., *Documents Legislative and Executive of the Congress of the United States in Relation to the Public Lands, From the First Session of the First Congress to the First Session of the Twenty-Third Congress: March 4, 1789 to June 15, 1834*, 1:30–31 (Washington: Printed by Duff Green, 1834) [hereinafter *ASP:PL*]. A very large literature discusses the Proclamation; for recent entries, *see* Colin G. Calloway, *The Scratch of a Pen: 1763 and the Transformation of North America* (Oxford: Oxford University Press, 2006); Daniel K Richter, "Native Americans, the Plan of 1764, and a British Empire That Never Was," in Robert Olwell and Alan Tully eds., *Cultures and Identities in Colonial British America* (Baltimore: JHU Press, 2005), 269–92.
13. "Memorial of the Surviving Partners of the Henderson Company," 30 Dec. 1791, Petitions (re real estate and confiscated property), GASR Dec. 1791–Jan. 1792, Box 3, North Carolina State Archives, Raleigh, N.C. For additional background on the Henderson purchase, *see West of the Revolution: An Uncommon History of 1776* (New York: W.W. Norton & Company, 2015), 17–26; Samuel C. Williams, "Henderson and Company's Purchase Within the Limits of Tennessee," *Tennessee Historical Magazine* 5, no. 1 (Apr. 1, 1919): 5–27; William Pitt Palmer ed., *Calendar of Virginia State Papers and Other Manuscripts* (Richmond, Va.: R.F. Walker, Superintendent of Public Printing, 1875), 1:271–311. On the history of the Illinois & Wabash purchases, *see* Watson, *Buying America from the Indians*, 66–92; Lindsay Gordon Robertson, *Conquest by Law: How the Discovery of America Dispossessed Indigenous Peoples of Their Lands* (Oxford: Oxford University Press, 2005), 3–29.
14. "Memorial of the Surviving Partners of the Henderson Company"; William Blount to John Steele, May 5, 1789, Box 1, Folder 4, John Steele Papers, Southern Historical Collection, University of North Carolina, Chapel Hill; Illinois and Wabash Companies to the Senate, 12 Dec. 1791, in *TP: Vol. II*, 333.
15. Report of Committee, June 27, 1788, in *TP: Vol. II*, 115–17; Act of July 22, 1790, § 4, 1 Stat. 137; Act of Mar. 1, 1793, § 5, 1 Stat. 329; *Papers of James Madison: Congressional Series*, 14:441–42.
16. Jonathan Heart to William Judd, July 29, 1790, Folder 2, William Judd Papers, Connecticut Historical Society, Hartford, Conn; Ross to Sargent, Dec. 22, 1797; Peter Audrain to Winthrop Sargent, Mar. 23, 1797, Reel 4, *WSP*.

17. "Journal of Bishop Francis Asbury (1788–1800)," in Samuel Cole Williams, ed., *Early Travels in the Tennessee Country, 1540–1800* (Johnson City, Tenn.: Watauga Press, 1928), 312; John Edgar to Arthur St. Clair, Aug. 25, 1797, Reel 4, *WSP*.
18. Richard Butler, "Journal of General Richard Butler," Sept. 9, 1785, Codex 33, Durrett Collection, Special Collections, University of Chicago Library; John Francis Hamtramck to Secretary of War, Mar. 31, 1792, in *TP: Vol. II*, 38–83.
19. Timothy Pickering to Anthony Wayne, Apr. 8, 1795, *NWTC*; Henry Knox to Joseph Brant, June 27, 1792, Henry and Lucy Knox Collection, Clements Library, University of Michigan, Ann Arbor, Mich. On the retreat from claims of conquest, *see* James H. Merrell, "Declarations of Independence: Indian-White Relations in the New Nation," in Jack P. Greene ed., *The American Revolution: Its Character and Limits* (New York: New York University Press, 1987), 197–218.
20. Henry Knox to William Blount, Aug. 27, 1790, *NWTC*; Pickering to Wayne, Apr. 8, 1795.
21. James Adair, *The History of the American Indians*, ed. Kathryn E. Holland Braund (Tuscaloosa: University of Alabama Press, 2005), 427; Rufus Putnam to Henry Knox, Aug. 16, 1792, in *MRP*, 321. On the contrast between civil and military leaders within Native societies, *see* Zeisberger, *History of Northern American Indians*, 96–104; Shoemaker, *Strange Likeness*, 46.
22. Putnam to Knox, Aug. 16, 1792; "Report of the Secretary at War: Indian Affairs," May 2, 1788, in *TP: Vol. II*, 103–05.
23. Timothy Pickering to Anthony Wayne, Apr. 8, 1795, Northwest Territory Collection, M367, Indiana Historical Society, Indianapolis, Ind.; Taylor, *The Divided Ground*, 404. Eric Kades employed economic models and game theory to argue, similarly to Taylor, that federal policy served to dispossess Native lands "efficiently." "Dark Side of Efficiency: Johnson v. M'Intosh and the Expropriation of American Indian Lands," *University of Pennsylvania Law Review* 148 (2000): 1065.
24. Knox to Blount, Aug. 27, 1790; Pickering to Wayne, Apr. 8, 1795.
25. The official record of the treaty negotiations at Houston was destroyed, but Daniel Smith's copy of the proceedings survives. "Treaty of Holston—June & July, 1791. Between Gov. Wm. Blount & the Cherokees," 15U1-59, Draper Manuscripts, Reel 58, Wisconsin Historical Society, Madison, Wis. For a discussion of Holston, *see* Cynthia Cumfer, *Separate Peoples, One Land: The Minds of Cherokees, Blacks, and Whites on the Tennessee Frontier* (Chapel Hill: University of North Carolina Press, 2007), 57–63.
26. Treaty of Holston, Cherokee Nation–U.S., July 2, 1791, 7 Stat. 39; "Conference at Tellico Blockhouse," Nov. 7, 1794, in *CJR*, 367–72; William Blount to David Henley, Dec. 17, 1795, 1/6, William Blount Papers, Ayer MS 74, Newberry Library, Chicago, Ill. On the regional divides within the Cherokee Nation, *see* Tyler Boulware, *Deconstructing the Cherokee Nation: Town, Region, and Nation Among Eighteenth-Century Cherokees* (Gainesville: University Press of Florida, 2011).
27. Treaty of Holston; Conference at Tellico Blockhouse," Nov. 7, 1794. On the Chickamaugas, *see* Gregory D. Smithers, *The Cherokee Diaspora: An Indigenous History of Migration, Resettlement, and Identity* (New Haven, Conn.: Yale University Press, 2015), 37–44; Boulware, *Deconstructing the Cherokee Nation*, 152–76;

McLoughlin, *Cherokee Renascence*, 33–57; John Sevier to William Blount, Sept. 13, 1792, in *ASP:IA*, 277–78.

28. "Report of Committee on Treaty of Holston," Nov. 9, 1791, *ASP:IA*, 135; Henry Knox to William Blount, Nov. 19, 1791, in *CJR*, 194.
29. Juan de Villebeuvre to Baron de Carondelet, Feb. 7, 1793, in Roberta Corbitt and D.C. Corbitt, "Papers from the Spanish Archives Relating to Tennessee and the Old Southwest, 1783–1800," *East Tennessee Historical Society's Publications* 29 (1957): 141, 151–53; Baron de Carondelet to Conde de Aranda, Nov. 28, 1792, in Roberta Corbitt and D.C. Corbitt, "Papers from the Spanish Archives Relating to Tennessee and the Old Southwest, 1783–1800," *East Tennessee Historical Society's Publications* 28 (1956): 127, 139–40. Additional accounts of Nenetooyah appear in Arturo O'Neill to Conde de Galvez, May 20, 1786, in Roberta Corbitt and D.C. Corbitt, "Papers from the Spanish Archives Relating to Tennessee and the Old Southwest, 1783–1800," *East Tennessee Historical Society's Publications* 10 (1938): 128–55. On Nenetooyah (Bloody Fellow) and the rise of the Lower Towns, *see* William Gerald McLoughlin, *Cherokee Renascence in the New Republic* (Princeton, N.J.: Princeton University Press, 1986), 58–92; Boulware, *Deconstructing the Cherokee Nation*, 152–78.
30. "Journal Extract about George Welbank's Information," Aug. 13, 1793, in *PGW:PS*, 14:147–52; John Parrish, "Journal 1793 No. 2 Indian Treaty" [6], Aug. 25, 1793, John Parrish Journals, Clements Library, University of Michigan; Cherokee Nation to Baron de Carondelet, Apr. 5, 1793, in *PTJ:MS*, 26:316–17.
31. "Conference of the Chiefs of the Cherokee Nation with the Secretary of War," Jan. 3–11, 1792, in *ASP:IA*, 1:203–06.
32. *Id.*
33. *Id.* Daniel Smith's treaty journal confirms many of Nenetooyah's allegations, including the debate over price terms that occurred between Blount and the Cherokees, and the suggestion that a generally amicable initial discussion quickly became heated and acrimonious. By the end, the Cherokees were clearly upset with Blount, complaining that he "only ask'd more and more"; "If your heart was straight," the Cherokee leader Nontuaka told him, "you would have accepted our offers." Treaty of Holston—June & July, 1791. Between Gov. Wm. Blount & the Cherokees.

    The journal is less forthcoming on why the Cherokees, who had grown increasingly contemptuous of Blount and his offers, suddenly reversed course and acceded to Blount's demands; Cynthia Cumfer describes the reversal as "inexplicabl[e]." Cynthia Cumfer, "Local Origins of National Indian Policy: Cherokee and Tennessean Ideas about Sovereignty and Nationhood, 1790–1811," *Journal of the Early Republic* 23, no. 1 (Apr. 1, 2003): 27. But the treaty record also acknowledges frequent private meetings between the Cherokee leaders and Blount—Blount spoke of routinely having dinner with the Cherokee delegates—where Nenetooyah alleged that many of his conversations with Blount occurred.
34. "Conference of the Chiefs," Jan. 3–11, 1792.
35. *Id.* On the law of nations principles articulated to the British, *see* Gould, *Among the Powers of the Earth*, 112–40.

36. Cherokee Nation to Baron de Carondelet, Apr. 5, 1793; Heckewelder, *History, Manner, and Customs*, 186. An alternate version of the Carondelet letter appears in Roberta Corbitt and D.C. Corbitt, "Papers from the Spanish Archives Relating to Tennessee and the Old Southwest, 1783–1800," *East Tennessee Historical Society's Publications* 32 (1960): 72, 72–73.
37. "Journal of the Grand Cherokee National Council," June 26, 1792, in *ASP:IA*, 1:271–74. On Native interpretations of treaties in this period, *see* Robert A. Williams, *Linking Arms Together: American Indian Treaty Visions of Law and Peace, 1600–1800* (New York: Oxford University Press, 1997).
38. Treaty with the Cherokees, July 2, 1791, 7 Stat. 39; William Blount to Secretary of War, Jan. 14, 1793, in *TP: Vol. IV*, 226–34; "Minutes of Information given Governor Blount by James Carey, One of the Interpreters of the United States, in the Nation," Nov. 3, 1792, in *ASP:IA*, 327–29.
39. James Madison, Jr. to James Madison, Sr., July 28, 1787, in *Papers of James Madison: Congressional Series*, 10:119; Secretary of War to President, July 28, 1792, in *TP: Vol. IV*, 159–61; Treaty with the Cherokees, June 26, 1794, 7 Stat. 43. On the transformation of the era's law of nations, *see* Jennifer Pitts, *Boundaries of the International: Law and Empire* (Cambridge, Mass.: Harvard University Press, 2018), 118–46.
40. "Conference of the Chiefs of the Cherokee Nation with the Secretary of War," Jan. 3–11, 1792; Journal Extract about George Welbank's Information, Aug. 13, 1793; William Blount to Secretary of War, Dec. 26, 1793, Reel 2: Territory Southwest of the River Ohio, Senate Territorial Papers (microfilm), M200, U.S. National Archives.
41. "Conference of the Chiefs of the Cherokee Nation with the Secretary of War," Jan. 3–11, 1792; "Treaty of Holston—June & July, 1791. Between Gov. Wm. Blount & the Cherokees."
42. "Report of the Secretary of State to the President," 85–100.
43. "Virginia: Cession of Western Claims," Mar. 1, 1784, in *TP: Vol. II*, 6–9.; "North Carolina: Cession of Western Land Claims," Dec. 22, 1789, in *TP: Vol. IV*, 3–9.
44. Act of Apr. 18, 1783, ch. 2, in *The Public Acts of the General Assembly of North-Carolina* (Newbern, N.C.: Martin & Ogden, 1804), 1:322–25; Act of May 3, 1779, in William Waller Hening ed., *The Statutes at Large: Being a Collection of All the Laws of Virginia: Vol. 10: 1779* (New York: R & W & G. Bartow, 1823), 35–50.
45. 2 Annals of Cong. 1829–30 (1790). Scholars have generally condemned indiscriminate location, especially in contrast with the later rectangular grid. Paul Gates's verdict is typical: "Nothing contributed more to raising the cost of land to actual settlers and to litigation than the system of indiscriminate location and subsequent survey which had characterized Virginia from the beginning." Gates, *Public Land Laws*, 47. For a contrary view focused on colonial New England, *see* Maureen E. Brady, "The Forgotten History of Metes and Bounds," *Yale Law Journal* 128 (2019): 782.
46. "Report of the Secretary of State to the President," 85–100. On this vision of juries as expressions of localism, albeit in very different locales, *see* William Edward Nelson, *Americanization of the Common Law: The Impact of Legal Change on Massachusetts Society, 1760–1830* (Cambridge, Mass.: Harvard University Press, 1975), 19–31;

Bruce H. Mann, *Neighbors and Strangers: Law and Community in Early Connecticut* (Chapel Hill: University of North Carolina Press, 1987), 68–79.

47. Walter Clark ed., *The State Records of North Carolina: Vol. XVIII—1786* (Goldsboro, N.C.: Nash Brothers, 1900), 456; Thomas B. Jones, "The Public Lands of Tennessee," *Tennessee Historical Quarterly* 27, no. 1 (Apr. 1, 1968): 17. As Jones notes, this result was hardly inadvertent; he describes the statute as a "shrewdly laid and masterful example of land speculation," and the statute became known as the "Land Grab Act of 1783." *Id.* 15–17. On the discovery of land frauds and the resulting scandal, *see* Russell S. Koonts, "'An Angel Has Fallen!': The Glasgow Land Frauds and the Emergence of the North Carolina Supreme Court," *North Carolina Historical Review* 72, no. 3 (July 1, 1995): 301–28; Albert Bruce Pruitt, *Glasgow Land Fraud Papers: 1783–1800* (Rocky Mount, N.C.: A.B. Pruitt, 1988).
48. Jones, "Public Lands," 17; Andrew Jackson, "Statement Regarding Land Frauds," Dec. 6, 1797, *PAJ*, 1:157–58.
49. William Starling to Lucas Sullivant, Feb. 28, 1796, Box 1, Sullivant-Starling Collection, MSS 459, Ohio Historical Society, Columbus, Ohio; David Jones to Lucas Sullivant, Aug. 14, 1796, Box 1, Sullivant-Starling Collection. On land holdings in the Virginia Military District, *see* Gates, *Public Land Laws*, 255–56.
50. "Land Warrants"; "An Estimate of the Lands Granted by the State of North Carolina within the Western Territory Ceded by the Said State of the United States," July 30, 1791, M068, List of North Carolina Land Grants in Tennessee, 1778–1791, U.S. National Archives; "Geo. Doherty's Certificate from the Entry Office Respecting Lands by William Blount Entered for Micajah Thomas &c &c," 1790, Box 193.28, John Gray Blount Papers, North Carolina State Archives; "Land Warrants" Nov. 31, 1793, Box 193.28, John Gray Blount Papers, North Carolina State Archives; Masterson, 171; William Blount to John Steele, July 10, 1790, at 36, vol. 1, John Steele Papers, North Carolina State Archives.
51. "Grand Jury Presentment, Fayetteville Dist. Superior Ct.," Oct. 1794, Box 193.28, John Gray Blount Papers; "Virginia: Cession of Western Claims," Mar. 1, 1784; "North Carolina: Cession of Western Land Claims," Dec. 22, 1789, in *TP: Vol. IV*, 309.
52. Land Warrants, Nov. 31, 1793, Box 193.28, Business/Legal/Land/Miscellaneous Records, John Gray Blount Papers, North Carolina State Archives, Raleigh, N.C. On North Carolinians' ignorance of western geography in this period, *see* Saunt, *West of the Revolution*, 23–28.
53. On the growth of what became the Southwest Territory in the 1780s, *see* Finger, *Tennessee Frontiers*, 99–124.
54. For the history of the writ of ejectment, *see* A.W. Brian Simpson, *A History of the Land Law* (Oxford: Oxford University Press, 1986), 15–46, 144–72.
55. On the court system in early North Carolina, *see* Walter F. Pratt, "The Struggle for Judicial Independence in Antebellum North Carolina: The Story of Two Judges," *Law and History Review* 4, no. 1 (1986): 129–59; in the Southwest Territory and early Tennessee, *see* William Michael Toomey, "Prelude to Statehood: The Southwest Territory, 1790–1796" (Ph.D. dissertation, University of Tennessee, 1991), 22–85; Theodore Brown Jr., "The Formative Period in the History of the Supreme Court of

Tennessee, 1796–1835," in James W. Ely ed., *A History of the Tennessee Supreme Court* (Knoxville: University of Tennessee Press, 2002), 24–26.

56. On the history of equity, *see* Amalia D. Kessler, *Inventing American Exceptionalism: The Origins of American Adversarial Legal Culture, 1800–1877* (New Haven, Conn.: Yale University Press, 2017), 19–111. On early American equity practice, *see* Stanley N. Katz, "The Politics of Law: Controversies over Chancery Courts and Equity Law in the Eighteenth Century," *Perspectives in American History* 5 (1971), 257.
57. On equity practice in early North Carolina, *see* William E. Nelson, "Politicizing the Courts and Undermining the Law: A Legal History of Colonial North Carolina, 1660–1775," *North Carolina Law Review* 88 (2010): 2133–97; Brown, "The Formative Period in the History of the Supreme Court of Tennessee, 1796–1835," 6–7.
58. James Miller v. James White (Hamilton District Superior Court of Law and Equity 1804), in Historical Records Survey, Transcription Unit, Division of Women's and Professional Projects, Works Progress Administration, *Records of Knox County, Superior Court Record Book "B", 1797–1804* (Nashville, Tenn.: Historical Records Survey, 1939), 444–51.
59. James Berry v. Elisha Wallen (Hamilton District Superior Court of Equity 1801), in Historical Records Survey, *Records of Knox County*, 186–202; Newman v. Jones & Haworth (Hamilton District Court of Equity 1800), in Historical Records Survey, *Records of Knox County*, 91–91.
60. King v. Daniel (Washington District Superior Court of Law and Equity 1799), in *Records of Washington County, Superior Court Minutes, Book B, 1791–1804*, 57–65.
61. Dillon to McHenry, May 22, 1796; Cuthbert v. Dotson (Washington District Superior Court of Law and Equity Sept. 1799), in *Records of Washington County, Superior Court Minutes, Book B, 1791–1804*, 65, 103.
62. On the history of adverse possession, *see* Henry W. Ballantine, "Title by Adverse Possession," *Harvard Law Review*, no. 2 (1919): 135–59. For cases limiting adverse possession in North Carolina, *see* Baker v. Webb, 2 N.C. (1 Hayw.) 43 (1794); Anonymous, 2 N.C. (1 Hayw.) 466 (1797); Young v. Irwin, 3 N.C. (2 Hayw.) 9 (1797). On the history of adverse possession in the Southwest Territory and Tennessee, *see* R.D. Cox, "History of the Adverse Possession Statutes of Tennessee," *Memphis State University Law Review*, no. 4 (1976): 673–700; Brown, "The Formative Period in the History of the Supreme Court of Tennessee, 1796–1835," 24–26.
63. "Petition from Inhabitants of TN, Miro District," 1796, Petitions (Concerning Land), GASR Nov. 1796–Dec. 1796, Box 3, North Carolina State Archives. This conflict arose in court cases as well: *Ross v. Vance*, for instance, involved competing land patents from 1783 and 1790. Historical Records Survey, Transcription Unit, Division of Women's and Professional Projects, Works Progress Administration, *Records of Washington County, Superior Court Minutes, Book B, 1791–1804* (Nashville, Tenn.: Copying Historical Records Project, Works Progress Administration, 1938), 205. On supernumerary warrants, *see* "Proclamation by the Governor of North Carolina," Oct. 1, 1792, in *TP: Vol. IV*, 191–92.
64. James Criswell v. Stockley Donalson et al. (Hamilton District Court of Equity 1800), in *Records of Knox County, Superior Court Record Book "B,"* 72–78.

65. William Thomas Hutchinson, *The Bounty Lands of the American Revolution in Ohio* (New York: Arno Press, 1979), 51–192; "Virginia Military Bounty Lands," July 31, 1789, in *ASP:PL*, 1:1–3; Act of Aug. 10, 1790, ch. 40, 1 Stat. 182; Annals of Cong. 4:133–34 (1794).
66. "Virginia Military Bounty Lands," Jan. 17, 1791, in *ASP:PL*, 1:12–13; Hutchinson, *Bounty Lands*, 51–123; Jackson v. Clark, 26 U.S. (1 Pet.) 628 (1828).
67. Act of June 9, 1794, ch. 62, 1 Stat. 394; Hutchinson, 51–123; Gary D. Libecap and Dean Lueck, "The Demarcation of Land and the Role of Coordinating Property Institutions," *Journal of Political Economy* 119, no. 3 (June 1, 2011): 426, 453; Wills v. Cowper, 2 Ohio 124 (1825); Galt v. Galloway, 29 U.S. (4 Pet.) 332, 337 (1830). The county court records from Ross and other Virginia Military District counties are incomplete, but the Ohio Supreme Court decisions from later in the nineteenth century demonstrate how many of the same issues that plagued Tennessee lands also arose within the district: contradictory surveys, Kerr v. Mack, 1 Ohio 161 (1823); disputes between junior and senior entries, McArthur v. Phoebus, 2 Ohio 415 (1826); ambiguous boundaries, McArthur v. Nevill, 3 Ohio 178 (1827); lengthy delays of twenty-five years or more between survey and patent, which the court described as a "not very uncommon," Wallace's Lessee v. Minor, 7 Ohio 249 (1835); overlapping entries due to original entries being withdrawn and applied to new lands, Wallace v. Patten, 14 Ohio 272 (1846). Libecap and Lueck find that 1.25% of parcels in the district resulted in litigation that reached the Ohio Supreme Court, the vast majority of which related to validity of title. Libecap and Lueck, "Demarcation of Land."
68. On this conception of property, *see* Felix S. Cohen, "Dialogue on Private Property," *Rutgers Law Review* 9 (1954): 357.
69. St. George Tucker, "Note D: The Manner of Obtaining Grants of Land, Under the Commonwealth of Virginia; and from the United States," in *Blackstone's Commentaries: With Notes of Reference to the Constitution and Laws of the Federal Government of the United States and of the Commonwealth of Virginia* (Philadelphia: William Young Birch and Abraham Small, 1803), 3:66–72.
70. Tucker, "Note D." On the role of local influence in the selection of territorial officials in the Southw st Territory, *see* "Recommendations for Federal Offices in North Carolina and the Southwestern Government," in *TJP:MS*, 16:476–78;
71. Most scholars have focused on the struggle over preemption rights in *federal* law, although they emerged first within state land schemes. For background, *see* Weaver, *Great Land Rush*, 46–87; De Soto, *The Mystery of Capital*, 107–36; Gates, *History of Public Land Law*, 219–48; Ford, *Colonial Precedents*, 112–42.
72. John Armstrong to Josiah Harmar, Apr. 13, 1785, 56, Vol. 2, JHP; Gov. Johnston to Dr. Williamson, 22 Sept. 1788, in Walter Clark ed., *The State Records of North Carolina, Vol. XXI:1788–90* (Goldsboro, N.C.: Nash Brothers, 1903), 500–01. Jefferson's report three years later made a more modest guess of three hundred families south of French Broad. "Report of the Secretary of State to the President," 85–100.
73. *Minutes of Superior Court of Law & Equity of Washington County, 1791–1799*, 38–39; William Irvine to Josiah Harmar, May 31, 1785, 77, vol. 2, JHP. For discussions of the role of improvement in Anglo-American claims to land, *see* Christopher Tomlins,

Freedom Bound: Law, Labor, and Civic Identity in Colonizing English America, 1580–1865 (Cambridge, [U.K.]: Cambridge University Press, 2010), 133–90; Joyce E. Chaplin, *Subject Matter: Technology, the Body, and Science on the Anglo-American Frontier, 1500–1676* (Cambridge, Mass.: Harvard University Press, 2001), 202–42; Patricia Seed, *Ceremonies of Possession in Europe's Conquest of the New World, 1492–1640* (New York: Cambridge University Press, 1995), 18–39.

74. On earlier fights over preemption rights, *see* Ford, *Colonial Precedents*, 112–40.
75. Arthur Lee to John Adams, May 11, 1784, in Paul Hubert Smith ed., *Letters of Delegates to Congress, 1774–1789* (Washington: U.S. Government Printing Office, 1976), 21:607–08; Jonathan Heart to William Judd, Jan. 8, 1786, William Judd Papers; Jonathan Heart to William Judd, Feb. 7, 1786, in Jonathan Heart Papers; Arthur St. Clair to Robert Buntin, Sept. 19, 1796, in *SCP*, 198. Emphasis on federal lands as an asset for debt repayment was ubiquitous among the early American political elite. For a small sample, *see* William Ellery to Francis Dana, Dec. 3, 1783, in Smith, *Letters of Delegates*, 21:173; David Howell to Jabez Bowen, Mar. 23, 1784, in *id.*, 21:453–54; William Grayson to James Monroe, Oct. 22, 1787, in *id.*, 24:489–90; James Madison to George Nicholas, May 17, 1788, Box 1, Folder 6, Durrett Collection, Special Collections, University of Chicago Library.
76. Benjamin Hawkins to William Blount, Mar. 10, 1791, Folder 3: 1791, WBP:LC.
77. George Washington to Jacob Read, Nov. 3, 1784, in *PGW:PS*, 2:119–20; Secretary of State to David Campbell, Mar. 27, 1792, in *TP: Vol. IV*, 130–31.
78. Josiah Harmar to Henry Knox, May 14, 1787, in *SCP*, 2:19–22. For a few of the many instances when "intruders" were described as "lawless," *see* Henry Knox to Josiah Harmar, May 12, 1786, 38, Vol. 3, JHP; Richard Butler, "Journal," Sept. 9, 1785, at 189, Codex 33, Durrett Collection, Special Collections, University of Chicago Library.
79. "Memorial of the Inhabitants on the West Side of the Ohio," Apr. 5, 1785, Vol. 2, JHP. The classic statement interpreting supposed instances of "lawlessness" as examples of legal pluralism appears in Hendrik Hartog, "Pigs and Positivism," *Wisconsin Law Review* (1985): 899–936. For examples from the early American borderlands, *see* Hulsebosch, *Constituting Empire*, 98–104; Ford, *Settler Sovereignty*, 85–107.
80. Act of Nov. 15, 1777, ch. 1, *The Acts of Assembly of the State of North Carolina* (Newbern: Printed by James Davis, printer to the Honourable the General Assembly, 1778), 3–7; Act of May 3, 1779.
81. Josiah Harmar to Henry Knox, Aug. 4, 1786, Vol. 28, Letterbook A, JHP; "Report on the Petition of Persons Settled on the Lands of the Cherokee Indians," Nov. 25, 1788, Committee of Propositions & Grievances, GASR Nov.–Dec. 1788, Box 2, North Carolina State Archives; "Petition of Sundry Inhabitants South of the French Broad River" Nov. 14, 1788, Committee on Ind. Affairs Folder, GASR Nov.–Dec. 1788, Box 1, North Carolina State Archives.
82. "Report on the Petition of Persons Settled on the Lands of the Cherokee Indians"; "Petition of Inhabitants of Greene Co. & south of French Broad River," Nov. 20, 1788, Committee on Indian Affairs, Box 1, GASR Nov.–Dec. 1788, North Carolina State Archives, Raleigh, N.C.; "Petition of Sundry Inhabitants South of the French Broad River"; Obediah Robins to Josiah Harmar, Oct. 4, 1785, 127, vol. 2, JHP.

83. "Memorial of the Inhabitants on the West Side of the Ohio," Apr. 5, 1785, Vol. 2, JHP; "Petition of the Inhabitants on the Western Side of the Ohio, Aug. 30, 1785, vol. 2, Harmar Papers; "Petition from the Inhabitants of the Indian Territory," Petitions—Rejected or Not Acted On, Box 1, GASR Nov.–Dec. 1789, North Carolina State Archives, Raleigh, N.C. On self-sovereignty, *see* Griffin, *American Leviathan*, 125–50; Fritz, *American Sovereigns*, 11–47.
84. [Northwest Territory. Land Laws], n.d., Northwest Territory Collection, Clements Library, University of Michigan, Ann Arbor, Mich; John Emerson, Advertisement, Mar. 12, 1785, in *SCP*, 5; Armstrong to Harmar, Apr. 12, 1785. Although the provenance of the pamphlet is unknown, the archive indicates that the item probably originates in the Josiah Harmar Papers. The references to the Articles of Confederation demonstrate that the document predates 1788.
85. "Talk Delivered to Col. Joseph Martin by Old Corn Tassel," Sept. 19, 1785, Cherokee Collection. For additional background on Franklin, *see* Kevin T. Barksdale, *The Lost State of Franklin: America's First Secession* (Lexington: University Press of Kentucky, 2008); Samuel Cole Williams, *History of the Lost State of Franklin* (Philadelphia: Porcupine Press, 1974).
86. Joseph Martin to [William] Russell, Aug. 1, 1785, 2XX5, Reel 116, Draper Manuscripts, Wisconsin Historical Society, Madison, Wis.; "A Talk from the Head Men Warriers of the Cherokey Nation at a Meeting Held at Ustinare," Nov. 20, 1788, Ayer MS 157, Ayer Collection, Newberry Library; Joseph Martin to Edmund Randolph, Mar. 16, 1787, Cherokee Collection; Joseph Martin to Edmund Randolph, Mar. 25, 1787, Cherokee Collection; Martin to Russell, Aug. 1, 1785.
87. "Articles of Association [of French Broad Settlers]," c. 1788, in J.G.M. Ramsey, *The Annals of Tennessee to the End of the Eighteenth Century* (Charleston [S.C.]: J. Russell, 1853), 435–36; Joseph Martin to Henry Knox, Jan. 15, 1789, in *ASP:IA*, 48. On the treaty of Dumplin Creek, *see* "Memorial of John Sevier," Nov. 20, 1789, Joint Standing Comm., Committee on Indian Affairs, GASR Nov.–Dec. 1789, Box 1, North Carolina State Archives.
88. Arthur St. Clair to Henry Knox, Aug. 17, 1791, Arthur St. Clair Papers, Burton Historical Collection, Detroit Public Library.
89. Josiah Harmar to Henry Knox, June 1, 1785, in *SCP*, 6–7; Henry Knox to Josiah Harmar, May 12, 1786, 38, Vol. 3, JHP; Josiah Harmar to Henry Knox, Aug. 4, 1786, at 144–45, Letterbook A, Vol. 28, JHP.
90. John Armstrong to Josiah Harmar, Apr. 12, 1785, Vol. 2, JHP; John Armstrong to Josiah Harmar, Apr. 13, 1785, Vol. 2, JHP.
91. William Irvine to Josiah Harmar, May 31, 1785, 77, Vol. 2, JHP; Annals of Cong. 1:411–12 (1789).
92. "Report on the Petition of Persons Settled on the Lands of the Cherokee Indians"; Act of Apr. 2, 1790, ch. 6, 1 Stat. 106, 108.
93. "Report of the Secretary of State to the President," Nov. 8, 1791. North Carolina was willing to concede this right, at least in abstract: the state's governor stated he was "well satisfied with the claim the United States have to these lands [south of French Broad] since the treaty of Holston." Governor of North Carolina to Secretary of State, Oct. 4, 1792, *TP: Vol. IV*, 192–93.

94. Attorney General to Secretary of State, Nov. 12, 1792, in *TP: Vol. IV*, 217; Secretary of State to William Blount, Nov. 14, 1792, in *TP: Vol. IV*, 218.
95. Secretary of State to Blount, Nov. 14, 1792.
96. William Blount to Secretary of State, Apr. 23, 1792, in *TP: Vol. IV*, 142–43; William Blount to Alexander Martin, Jan. 22, 1791, in *JGBP*, 2:163–64; William Blount to John Gray Blount, Nov. 10, 1790, in *JGBP*, 2:135–40.
97. Secretary of State to Governor of North Carolina, June 6, 1792, *TP: Vol. IV*, 156–57; Governor of North Carolina to Secretary of State, Aug. 24, 1792, *TP: Vol. IV*, 164–66. Blount observed that the settlers "found[ed] their right" for settling the French Broad lands "on the latter part of the second condition of the Act of Cession." Blount to Secretary of State, Apr. 23, 1792.
98. "Memorial of the French Broad Settlers," Sept. 12, 1794, in Ramsey, *The Annals of Tennessee*, 631.
99. Robert King v. Robert Wilson (Hamilton District Superior Court of Law and Equity 1803), in *Records of Knox County, Superior Court Record Book "B," 1797–1804*, at 316–27.
100. *King v. Wilson*.
101. Samuel Holden Parsons to His Children, Jan. 7, 1786, Folder 6, Samuel Parsons Papers, Connecticut Historical Society, Hartford, Conn. (Emphasis in original).
102. 1 Annals of Cong. 1067–72, 1829–42 (1790). The Land Ordinance of 1785 was largely forgotten in in these congressional debates: it was mentioned only once, in an offhand remark by New Jersey congressman Elias Boudinot: "The late Congress, he was informed, had adopted a method to obviate the inconvinences of the former mode [of indiscriminate location]." *Id.*
103. Act of July 22, 1790, ch. 33, 1 Stat. 137; Johnson v. M'Intosh, 21 U.S. (8 Wheat.) 543 (1823).
104. Land Office Bill [HR-114], Feb. 16, 1791, in Linda Grant De Pauw et al. eds., *Documentary History of the First Federal Congress of the United States of America* (Baltimore: Johns Hopkins University Press, 1972), 5:1239–42; Resolution on Unclaimed Western Lands, Mar. 3, 1791, in *id.*, 6:2127–28.
105. George Beckwith, "Notes of Conversations with Different Persons," Apr. 30, 1790, in *id.*, 19:1377–88.

Chapter 2

1. Few of the broad-scale histories of the federal land system spend considerable time on the sales to the land companies: Paul Gates, for instance, discusses them in two pages, Gates, *History of Public Land Law Development*, 70–72, while Malcolm Rohrbough devotes a page and a half, Rohrbough, *The Land Office Business*, 11v12. One except is John Weaver, who stresses Symmes's role alongside other large-scale speculations. Weaver, *The Great Land Rush*, 194–202.

2. "Indenture Between the Board of Treasury and the Agents of the Ohio Company," Oct. 27, 1787, *TP: Vol. II*, 80–84; "Indenture Between the Board of Treasury and Manassah Cutler and Winthrop Sargent," Oct. 27, 1787, *TP: Vol. II*, 85–88; John Cleves Symmes, *To the Respectable Public* (Trenton, N.J.: Printed by Isaac Collins, 1787); "Volume 63: An Account of Dr. Cutler's Work for the Ordinance of 1787" (July 13, 1787), Vol. 63, Manasseh Cutler Papers, Special Collections, Northwestern University Library; *JCC*, 34:564–65. On state land sales, *see* Thomas Perkins Abernethy, *Western Lands and the American Revolution* (New York: D. Appleton-Century Company, 1937); Shaw Livermore, *Early American Land Companies: Their Influence on Corporate Development* (New York: The Commonwealth Fund, 1939), 133–73; Blaakman, "Speculation Nation"; Laurence M. Hauptman, *Conspiracy of Interests: Iroquois Dispossession and the Rise of New York State* (Syracuse, N.Y.: Syracuse University Press, 1999). On Yazoo, *see* C. Peter Magrath, *Yazoo: Law and Politics in the New Republic: The Case of Fletcher v. Peck* (Providence, R.I.: Brown University Press, 1966); Charles F. Hobson, *The Great Yazoo Lands Sale: The Case of Fletcher v. Peck* (Lawrence: University Press of Kansas, 2016).
3. 1 Annals of Cong. 411–16 (1789). On federal land still available to be sold, *see* "Report of the Secretary of State to the President," 85–100.
4. For an introduction to the large literature on corporations in early America, *see* Pauline Maier, "The Revolutionary Origins of the American Corporation," *William and Mary Quarterly* 50, no. 1 (1993): 51–84; Naomi R. Lamoreaux and William J. Novak eds., *Corporations and American Democracy* (Cambridge, Mass.: Harvard University Press, 2017). On the East India Company, *see* Philip J. Stern, *The Company-State: Corporate Sovereignty and the Early Modern Foundation of the British Empire in India* (New York: Oxford University Press, 2011); on states' corporate origins, *see* Mary Sarah Bilder, "The Corporate Origins of Judicial Review," *Yale Law Journal* 116, no. 3 (Dec. 1, 2006): 502; on municipal corporations and title, *see* Hendrik Hartog, *Public Property and Private Power: The Corporation of the City of New York in American Law, 1730–1870* (Chapel Hill: University of North Carolina Press, 1983), 43.
5. "An Account of Dr. Cutler's Work for the Ordinance of 1787"; Manasseh Cutler, *An Explanation of the Map Which Delineates That Part of the Federal Lands* (Printed by John Dabney, Dabney, 1787), 13–14.
6. On Cox's biography, *see* "Foreword," in Isaac Joslin Cox and Reginald Charles McGrane eds., *Documents Relating to Zachariah Cox* (Cincinnati: Press of Jennings and Graham, 1913), 31–32; David M. Robb, "Zachariah Cox," in *Encyclopedia of Alabama*, Alabama Humanities Foundation, last modified Mar. 22, 2011, http://www.encyclopediaofalabama.org/article/h-1915.
7. A.P. Whitaker, "The Muscle Shoals Speculation, 1783–1789," *The Mississippi Valley Historical Review* 13, no. 3 (Dec. 1, 1926): 365–86; William H. Masterson, *William Blount* (Baton Rouge: Louisiana State University Press, 1954), 71–73, 91, 108, 119.
8. "[Virginia; South Carolina]," *Georgia Gazette*, Dec. 31, 1789; Act of Dec. 21, 1789, in [Laws] (Augusta, Ga.: Printed by John E. Smith, 1790), 27–28.
9. The current literature on Yazoo focuses almost exclusively on the legal, financial, and partisan wranglings that followed the sale, especially in the early nineteenth century.

For examples, *see* Magrath, *Yazoo*; Hobson, *The Great Yazoo Lands Sale*; George R. Lamplugh, *Politics on the Periphery: Factions and Parties in Georgia, 1783–1806* (Newark, Del.: University of Delaware Press, 1986).

10. "New-York, Monday, July 18," *Daily Advertiser*, July 18, 1791; "Extract of a Letter from Zachariah Cox, Esq. to His Correspondent in Maryland, Dated Fredericksburg," *Daily Advertiser*, Aug. 12, 1791; Acting Governor Smith to Secretary of State, Oct. 4, 1791, in *TP: Vol. IV*, 83–84.
11. Henry Knox to Anthony Wayne, Apr. 10, 1790, 27, Reel 26, Henry Knox Papers; Thomas Jefferson, "Opinion on Certain Georgia Land Grants," May 3, 1790, in *PTJ:MS*, 16:406–07; George Washington to Edmund Randolph, Oct. 10, 1791, in *PGW:PS*, 9:68–70; Secretary of State to William Blount, Aug. 12, 1791, in *PTJ:MS*, 22:29–30; Cox's activities had a parallel in the actions of James O'Fallon, the supposed "general agent" for the South Carolina Company. Thomas Jefferson instructed the U.S. attorney in Kentucky to initiate a prosecution against O'Fallon, warning, "a well ordered government [cannot] tolerate such an assumption of it's sovereignty by unauthorised individuals." Thomas Jefferson to William Murray, Mar. 22, 1791, in *PTJ:MS*, 19:598. President Washington issued a proclamation against O'Fallon for violation of the Trade and Intercourse Act. "Proclamation," Mar. 19, 1791, in *PGW: PS*, 7:605–06. For more background, *see* John C. Parish, "The Intrigues of Doctor James O'Fallon," *Mississippi Valley Historical Review* 17, no. 2 (Sept. 1930): 230–63.
12. Holstonian to Mr. Claypoole, Aug. 16, 1791; "Report of the Secretary of War to the President," Jan. 17, 1792, in *TP: Vol. IV*, 111–15.
13. Alexander McGillivray to William Panton, May 8, 1790, in John Walton Caughey, *McGillivray of the Creeks* (Columbia: University of South Carolina Press, 2007), 259–63.
14. *Id.* 259–63.
15. Holstonian to Mr. Claypoole, Aug. 16, 1791; "New-York, Monday, July 18," *Daily Advertiser*, July 18, 1791; Alexander McGillivray to Esteban Miro, June 8, 1791, in Caughey, *McGillivray*, 291–92.
16. William Blount to James Robertson, Sept. 3, 1791, in *TP: Vol. IV*, 79; Holstonian to Mr. Claypoole, Aug. 16, 1791; Smith to Secretary of State, Oct. 4, 1791.
17. "Extract of a Letter from Zachariah Cox," *Daily Advertiser*, Aug. 12, 1791; David Campbell to Secretary of State, Feb. 25, 1792, in *TP: Vol. IV*, 121–28; George Ogg to William Blount, Apr. 16, 1792, Folder 4: 1792, *WBP:LC*.
18. Holstonian to Mr. Claypoole, Aug. 16, 1791; Ogg to Blount, Apr. 16, 1792.
19. St. Clair to Wilkinson, July 16, 1798.
20. Act of Jan. 7, 1795, in *Acts of the State of Georgia: Passed at Aug.a, Dec., 1794, and Jan., 1795* (Augusta, Ga.: Printed by John E. Smith, 1795), 3–6. On the reaction to the statute, *see* Hobson, 37–56.
21. "Petition for the Ohio Country," May 7, 1783, in *MRP*, 215; "Information," Jan. 25, 1786, in *The Records of the Original Proceedings of the Ohio Company: Ohio Company Series* (Marietta, Ohio: Marietta Historical Commission, 1917), 1:1–4. On Putnam's life, *see* his autobiography, "Rufus Putnam's Memorandum Book of Family Concerns," in *MRP*, 39–126.

22. *Articles of an Association by the Name of the Ohio Company* (Worcester, Mass.: Isaiah Thomas, 1786), 3; Rufus Putnam to George Washington, June 16, 1783, in *MRP*, 216; "Petition for the Ohio Country," May 7, 1783.
23. "An Account of Dr. Cutler's Work for the Ordinance of 1787."
24. *Id.* A fuller account of the motivations for the agreement between Congress and the Ohio Company appears in Blaakman, "Speculation Nation," 215–50. On Cutler's successful lobbying, *see* Jeff Pasley, "Private Access and Public Power: Gentility and Lobbying in the Early Congress," in Kenneth R. Bowling and Donald R. Kennon eds., *The House and Senate in the 1790s: Petitioning, Lobbying, and Institutional Development* (Athens: Ohio University Press, 2002), 57–99.
25. "An Account of Dr. Cutler's Work for the Ordinance of 1787"; Manasseh Cutler, *An Explanation of the Map Which Delineates That Part of the Federal Lands* (Salem, Mass.: Printed by Dabney & Cushing, 1787), 13–14.
26. Worthington Chauncey Ford ed., *JCC*, 32:334–43; Rufus Putnam to [John Heckewelder], Feb. 29, 1788, Box 1, Folder 9, Rufus Putnam Papers.
27. Cutler, *An Explanation of the Map*; Rufus Putnam to Heckinwilder [*sic*], Feb. 27, 1788, Box 1, Folder 9, Rufus Putnam Papers; Jonathan Heart to William Judd, July 8, 1787, Jonathan Heart Papers.
28. "An Account of Dr. Cutler's Work for the Ordinance of 1787" (July 13, 1787); "Indenture Between the Board of Treasury and the Agents of the Ohio Company"; Gates, *Public Land Law Development*, 70.
29. "Indenture Between the Board of Treasury and Manassah Cutler and Winthrop Sargent," Oct. 27, 1787, in *TP: Vol. II*, 85–88; Rufus Putnam to Winthrop Sargent, Oct. 8, 1787, Reel 2, *WSP*; "Securities Received from the Agents," Oct. 27, 1787, Reel 2, *WSP*.
30. Congress authorized the Board of Treasury to enter into contracts for the sale of lands to private companies in excess of one million acres. "Resolution of Congress: The Sale of Lands," Oct. 23, 1787, in *TP: Vol. II*, at 78.
31. On Symmes's biography, *see* R. Douglas Hurt, "John Cleves Symmes and the Miami Purchase," in Warren R. Van Tine and Michael Dale Pierce eds., *Builders of Ohio: A Biographical History* (Columbus: Ohio State University Press, 2003), 14–25; Beverley Bond, Introduction, in *CJCS*, 1–24; Charles H. Winfield, "Life and Public Services of John Cleves Symmes," *New Jersey Historical Society Proceedings*, ser. 2, 5 (1879): 22–43.
32. Symmes, *To the Respectable Public*, 19; "Miami Lands for Sale," in *CJCS*, 281.
33. John Cleves Symmes to Jonathan Dayton, May 18–20, 1789, in *CJCS*, 77.
34. Solomon Drown to Rufus Putnam, Sept. 3, 1790, Box 1, Folder 10, Rufus Putnam Papers; Manasseh Cutler to Rufus Putnam, Apr. 21, 1788, Series II, Box 1, Folder 1, Manuscripts and Documents of the Ohio Company of Associates, Special Collections, Marietta College Library, Marietta, Ohio; "Treatise on the Ohio Phobia," vol. 74, Manasseh Cutler Papers. For examples of the diverse subscribers to the Ohio Company, *see* Ledger "A" and Ledger "B," Vols. 59–60, Manasseh Cutler Papers.
35. "Meeting of the Agents of the Ohio Company," Mar. 2–July 6, 1789, in *Records of the Original Proceedings of the Ohio Company*, 100–06; "Meeting of Ohio Company [in

Marietta]," July 2–Aug. 14, 1788, in *id.*, 44–58; "Lands in the Ohio Company Purchas Drawn in the Name of Arthur St. Clair Esq.," Sept. 10, 1790, Reel 7, *ASCP*; "Journal of a Journey from Boston, Mass. to the Mouth of Muskingum, Ohio, Kept by John May," Box 4, Marietta, Ohio Collection, MS 210, Ohio Historical Society, Columbus, Ohio, at 19, 36; "Governor St. Clair's Address at Marietta," July 15, 1788, in *SCP*, 2:54–55.

36. William Kersey to Josiah Harmar, Apr. 17, 1789, 20, Vol. 10, *JHP*; "Journal of a Tour to the Ohio and Muskingum," July 21, 1788; Josiah Harmar to John Cleves Symmes, Nov. 28, 1788, Letterbook D, Vol. 28, *JHP*.
37. Rufus Putnam to Thomas May, May 17, 1788, Series II, Box 1, Folder 1, Manuscripts and Documents of the Ohio Company of Associates; Samuel H. Parsons to Unknown, July 16, 1788, Vol. 69, Manasseh Cutler Papers.
38. Rufus Putnam to Manasseh Cutler, May 16, 1788, Box 1, Folder 9, Rufus Putnam Papers; "Extracts from the Journal of Manassah Cutler," Box 2, Marietta, Ohio Collection, 22–23; "Copy From a Manuscript in the Hand Writing of Major Horace Nye (son of Ichabod) of Putnam Ohio prepared about 1847 for Dr. Hildreth," Marietta, Ohio Collection; "Journal of a Journey," 23, 25, 34.
39. Symmes to Dayton, May 18, 1788, 58–60; John Heckewelder, *Thirty Thousand Miles with John Heckewelder*, ed. Paul A.W. Wallace ([Pittsburgh]: University of Pittsburgh Press, 1958), 275.
40. Manasseh Cutler to Rufus Putnam, Dec. 19, 1787, Box 1, Folder 7, Rufus Putnam Papers; Manasseh Cutler to Rufus Putnam, Apr. 21, 1788, Series II, Box 1, Folder 1, Manuscripts and Documents of the Ohio Company of Associates; Minerva Nye to Mrs. Stone, Sept. 19, 1788, Box 2, Marietta, Ohio Collection; Elnathan Haskell to Winthrop Sargent, May 9, 1788, Reel 2, *WSP*; Samuel H Parsons to Unknown, July 16, 1788, Vol. 69, Manasseh Cutler Papers; John Cleves Symmes to Jonathan Dayton, July 17, 1789, in *CJCS*, 100–07; John Cleves Symmes to Jonathan Dayton, May 22, 1789, in *CJCS*, 96–97. U.S. Army officers similarly reported that Symmes's settlement suffered because of reports of Native threats. *See* Joseph Asheton to Josiah Harmar, June 26, 1789, 90, Vol. 10, *JHP*.
41. Symmes to Dayton, May 18, 1788. On Pipe's ties to federal officers, *see* Josiah Harmar to Henry Knox, Mar. 9, 1788, Vol. 28, Letterbook C, *JHP*, 25–32. For another account of the encounter between Symmes and Blackbeard, *see* Heckewelder, *Thirty Thousand*, 275.
42. Symmes to Dayton, May 18, 1788; John Cleves Symmes to Jonathan Dayton, July 17, 1789, in *CJCS*, 100–07.
43. "Journal of a Journey," 22; Rowena Tupper to Mrs Stone, Nov. 11, 1788, Box 2, Marietta, Ohio Collection; Arthur St. Clair to Secretary at War, Sept. 14, 1788, in *TP: Vol. II*, 156–59; Putnam to May, May 17, 1788; Symmes to Dayton, May 18, 1788.
44. On the origins of this conflict, *see* Colin Calloway, *The Victory with No Name: The Native American Defeat of the First American Army* (Oxford: Oxford University Press, 2014), 61–68; *see also* the discussion in Chapter Five.
45. Meeting of Ohio Company [in Marietta], July 2–Aug. 14, 1788; Parsons to Unknown, July 16, 1788.

46. For accounts of the Big Bottom Massacre, *see* "Narrative of the captivity of Daniel Converse & massacre at Big Bottom block house," Vol. 1, at 316, Hildreth Papers; "Rufus Putnam's Memorandum Book," 112.
47. Rufus Putnam to Unknown, Jan. 6, 1791, Box 1, Folder 10, Rufus Putnam Papers; "A Biographical Sketch of the Origen & Descent of Gen'l Benjamin Tupper Connected with his Military Life," 65–76, 98.
48. Patrick Griffin, "Reconsidering the Ideological Origins of Indian Removal: The Case of the Big Bottom 'Massacre,'" in Andrew R.L. Cayton and Stuart D. Hobbs eds., *The Center of a Great Empire: The Ohio Country in the Early American Republic* (Athens: Ohio University Press, 2005), 11–31; Putnam to Unknown, Jan. 6, 1791.
49. "Rufus Putnam's Memorandum Book," 113; Rufus Putnam to President Washington, Feb. 28, 1791, in *TP: Vol. II*, 337; Rufus Putnam to Unknown, Jan. 6, 1791; Rufus Putnam to Henry Knox, Mar. 8, 1791, Box 1, Folder 10, Rufus Putnam Papers.
50. "At a Special Meeting of the Agents & Proprietors of the Ohio Company on the 7th Day of Jan.," Jan. 7, 1791, Reel 6, *ASCP*; "Names of the Men Hireed [*sic*] by the Ohio Company . . . & Arrived at Marietta 7th of April 1788," Box 1, Folder 9, Rufus Putnam Papers; Return Jonathan Meigs, Jr. to Nehemiah Hubbard, Jr., Aug. 30, 1792, Northwest Territory Collection; David Zeigler to Directors of the Ohio Company, Jan. 8, 1791, Series II, Box 1, Folder 2, Manuscripts and Documents of the Ohio Company of Associates.
51. Griffin Greene to "Peter", [1791]; Arthur St. Clair to John Cleves Symmes, Dec. 7, 1790, Reel 3, *ASCP*.
52. Arthur St. Clair to John Cleves Symmes, May 23, 1791, in *TP: Vol. II*, 342–43; Arthur St. Clair to Secretary of Treasury, May 25, 1791, in *TP: Vol. II*, 347–48.
53. Arthur St. Clair to John Cleves Symmes, July 12, 1791, Reel 3, *ASCP*; "Proclamation by His Excellency, Arthur St. Clair," Aug. 23, 1791, in *SCP*, 2:211–12; John Cleves Symmes to Arthur St. Clair, Aug. 24, 1791, Reel 3, *ASCP*; John Cleves Symmes to Jonathan Dayton, Aug. 15, 1791, in *CJCS*, 146–54.
54. "Rufus Putnam's Memorandum Book," 117; Symmes to Dayton, Aug. 15, 1791.
55. "Meeting of the Ohio Company" Nov. 10, 1787, in *Records of the Original Proceedings of the Ohio Company*, 19–21; Griffin Greene to "Peter", c. 1791, Northwest Territory Collection, Clements Library, Univ. of Michigan, Ann Arbor, Mich.
56. Jonathan Heart to William Judd, Sept. 9, 1790, Jonathan Heart Papers; Benjamin Gilman to Josiah Harmar, Dec. 27, 1789, 125, Vol. 11, *JHP*.
57. Rufus Putnam to [Dwight Foster], June 30, 1788, Box 1, Folder 1, Manuscripts and Documents of the Ohio Company of Associates; Gilman to Harmar, Dec. 27, 1789; "Meeting of the Agents of the Ohio Company," Dec. 3, 1788, in *Records of the Original Proceedings of the Ohio Company*, 1:70–89; Heart to Judd, Sept. 9, 1790; Benjamin Haywood to Rufus Putnam, Dec. 23, 1790, Vol. 69, Manasseh Cutler Papers. For an example of litigation resulting from surveying confusion, *see* Solomon Sibley, "D6: Docket Book," 1797–99, at 8–13, Box 58, Solomon Sibley Papers, Barton Historical Collection, Detroit, Mich.
58. Heart to Judd, Sept. 9, 1790; Manasseh Cutler to Rufus Putnam, Nov. 18, 1788, Box 1, Folder 1, Manuscripts and Documents of the Ohio Company of Associates, Special

Collections, Marietta College Library, Marietta, Ohio; Joseph May to Winthrop Sargent, Apr. 29, 1789, Reel 3, *WSP*; Manasseh Cutler to Rufus Putnam, Aug. 23, 1791, Vol. 70, Manasseh Cutler Papers.

59. Joel Barlow to Benjamin Walker, Dec. 21, 1790, Vol. 69, Manasseh Cutler Papers.
60. Barlow to Walker, Dec. 21, 1790. On Scioto's financial machinations, *see* Shannon, "The Ohio Company and the Meaning of Opportunity in the American West, 1786–1795"; Archer Butler Hulbert, "The Methods and Operations of the Scioto Group of Speculators," *Mississippi Valley Historical Review* 1, no. 4 (1915): 502–15.
61. "Petition of the French Inhabitants of Gallipolis," Dec. 22, 1792, in *TP: Vol. II*, 422–28; Gov. Arthur St. Clair to Secretary of War, Nov. 26, 1790, in *SCP*, 2:192v97. On the sensation Scioto prompted in France, *see* François Furstenberg, *When the United States Spoke French: Five Refugees Who Shaped a Nation* (New York: Penguin Press, 2014), 247–52; Suzanne Desan, "Transatlantic Spaces of Revolution: The French Revolution, Sciotomanie, and American Lands," *Journal of Early Modern History* 12, no. 6 (Dec. 2008): 467–505. For additional background on the history of Gallipolis, *see* Jocelyne Moreau-Zanelli, *Gallipolis: Histoire D'un Mirage Américain Au Xviiie Siècle* (Paris: l'Harmattan, 2000);George Henry Allen, Joseph Edward Harry, and Theodore Thomas Belote, *The Scioto Speculation and the French Settlement at Gallipolis: A Study in Ohio Valley History* (Cincinnati: University of Cincinnati Press, 1907).
62. Cutler to Putnam, Nov. 18, 1788.
63. "Rufus Putnam's Memorandum Book," 116.
64. "Petition of the Directors of the Ohio Company to Congress," Mar. 2, 1792, Series I, Manuscripts and Documents of the Ohio Company of Associates.
65. "Rufus Putnam's Memorandum Book," 117; Act of Apr. 21, 1792, ch. 25, 1 Stat. 257. For the history of the bill's passage in the House and Senate, *see* 3 Annals of Cong. 123–26, 433, 486, 494, 540, 558 (1792).
66. Richard Platt to Winthrop Sargent, Mar. 25, 1792, Reel 3, *WSP*; J. Gilman to Winthrop Sargent, Apr. 20, 1792, Reel 3, *WSP*. On Duer and his subsequent biography, *see* Robert Francis Jones, *"The King of the Alley": William Duer: Politician, Entrepreneur, and Speculator, 1768–1799* (Philadelphia: American Philosophical Society, 1992).
67. Winthrop Sargent to Inhabitants of Gallipolis, Nov. 23, 1792, in *TP: Vol. II*, 417–20; Heckewelder, *Thirty Thousand Miles*, 289; "Petition of the French Inhabitants of Gallipolis," Dec. 22, 1792; John Rome to Attorney General, Apr. 14, 1793, in *TP: Vol. II*, 450–51; "No. 15: French Settlers at Galliopolis," Mar. 24, 1794, in *ASP:PL*, 23–24; "Extract from the Journal of the Senate of the United States," May 13, 1794, Box 2, Folder 6, Rufus Putnam Papers.
68. Act of Mar. 3, 1795, ch. 49, 1 Stat. 442; *Records of the Original Proceedings of the Ohio Company*, 2:171, 191, 231–32.
69. For land distributions, *see* "Ohio Company Land Records," 1787–1796, at 182–222, Series I, Box 2, Folder 1, Manuscripts and Documents of the Ohio Company of Associates. On the dividends, *see* Benjamin Tallmadge to Rufus Putnam, Oct. 1, 1796, Vol. 69, Manasseh Cutler Papers; "Ledger 'A' of the Ohio Company" n.d., Vol. 59, Manasseh Cutler Papers.

70. Benjamin Tallmadge to Rufus Putnam, Feb. 27, 1796, Series II, Box 1, Folder 4, Manuscripts and Documents of the Ohio Company of Associates; Edward Harris to William Parker, Oct. 23, 1795, Box 1, Folder 7, Paul Fearing Papers, Marietta College Library.
71. Symmes to Dayton, May 18, 1789; John Cleves Symmes to Jonathan Dayton, Nov. 25, 1788, in *CJCS*, 48–53.
72. Act of May 5, 1792, ch. 30, 1 Stat. 266; "Patent Issued to John Cleves Symmes," Sept. 30, 1794, in *TP: Vol. II*, 496–98.
73. "No. 33: Contract with John Cleves Symmes," Feb. 9, 1797, in *ASP:PL*, 67–68; "No. 72: Contract with John Cleves Symmes," Jan. 28, 1803, in *ASP:PL*, 115–19; John Cleves Symmes to Peyton Short, Apr. 28, 1797, Folder 1, Short-Harrison-Symmes Papers; John Cleves Symmes to Peyton Short, Aug. 10, 1797, Folder 1, Short-Harrison-Symmes Papers.
74. "No. 23: Contract with John Cleves Symmes," May 5, 1796, in *ASP:PL*, 59–60; "No. 33: Contract with John Cleves Symmes," 7; John Cleves Symmes to Peyton Short, Apr. 22, 1798, Folder 1, Short-Harrison-Symmes Papers; Act of Mar. 2, 1799, ch. 34, 1 Stat. 728. For Gallatin's role, *see* 6 Annals of Cong. 2247–48, 2367–38 (1797).
75. Unknown to Arthur St. Clair, Nov. 1799, Reel 4, *ASCP*.
76. "At a Meeting of a Number of the Inhabitants of Columbia at the House of Mr. William Stanley, on Monday the 25th of Jan. 1796, Pursuant to Public Notice," *Centinel of the North-Western Territory*, Feb. 20, 1796; Gov. Arthur St. Clair to President, Aug. 1789, in *TP: Vol. II*, 204–12; Gov. Arthur St. Clair to Secretary of State, Dec. 15, 1794, in *TP: Vol. II*, 499–500.
77. Arthur St. Clair to Secretary of State, Dec. 2, 1799, Reel 4, *ASCP*.
78. "Deposition of James McCushen," Aug. 13, 1799, Box 7, Folder 5, *ASCP*; Arthur St. Clair to Secretary of State, July 15, 1799, Reel 4, *ASCP*.
79. John Cleves Symmes to Jonathan Dayton, Mar. 5, 1804, in *CJCS*, 189–90; John Cleves Symmes to Jonathan Dayton, Feb. 13, 1800, in *CJCS*, 183–88; "No. 70: Contract with John Cleves Symmes," Apr. 29, 1802, in *ASP:PL*, 115; "No. 72: Contract with John Cleves Symmes," Jan. 28, 1803, *CJCS*, 19–24.
80. "Report of Arthur St. Clair on Western Lands," Feb. 21, 1799, Senate Territorial Papers, M200, Reel 1; Arthur St. Clair to Joseph Parks, Dec. 13, 1798, in *SCP*, 2:436–38; Israel Ludlow to Paul Fearing, Jan. 8, 1802, Box 2, Folder 11, Paul Fearing Papers; Arthur St. Clair to Secretary of State, July 1799, in *SCP*, 2:443–45; Act of Mar. 2, 1799. When the initial statute proved inadequate—only three people had taken advantage of the statute by December 1800—Congress lengthened the terms and extended credit. Oliver Wolcott, "Statement of What Has Been Done, since the Establishment of the Present Government, Respecting the Lands of the United States in the Territory North-West of the Ohio," Dec. 1800, Box 5, Folder 12, Oliver Wolcott Papers, Conn. Historical Soc'y, Hartford, Conn; "No. 55: Claimants Under John Cleves Symmes," Apr. 16, 1800, in *ASP:PL*, 93–95.
81. 1 Annals of Cong. 621–22 (1789); Abraham Baldwin to Joel Barlow, Apr. 7, 1790, in Linda Grant De Pauw et al. eds., *Documentary History of the First Federal Congress of the United States of America, March 4, 1789–March 3, 1791* (Baltimore: Johns Hopkins University Press, 1972–), 19:1160–65.

82. "Plan for Disposing of the Public Lands," July 22, 1790, in *ASP:PL*, 1:4–5; Alexander Hamilton, "Statement of My Property and Debts July 1, 1804," Harold C. Syrett ed., *Papers of Alexander Hamilton*, 27 vols. (New York: Columbia University Press, 1961–1987), 26:283–85.
83. 1 Annals of Cong. 1865–66, 1973 (1791); Land Office Bill, Feb. 2, 1791, in *Documentary History of the First Federal Congress*, 5:1239–42.
84. 5 Annals of Cong. 166–70 (1795). Scholars have discussed Randall's plan largely in the context of Congress's contempt power. Zephyr Teachout, *Corruption in America* (Cambridge, Mass.: Harvard University Press, 2014), 107; Josh Chafetz, "Executive Branch Contempt of Congress," *University of Chicago Law Review* 76, no. 3 (2009): 1083, 1128–29.
85. John Steele to John Haywood, Feb. 28, 1796, Box 2, Folder 14, Ernest Haywood Collection, Southern Historical Collection.
86. 5 Annals of Cong. 337–55, 402–23 (1796).
87. *Id.*
88. *Id.*
89. Act of May 18, 1796, ch. 29, 1 Stat. 464.
90. Over 43,000 acres sold for a little over $100,000 at the Pittsburgh auction. Oliver Wolcott, "Statement of What Has Been Done, Since the Establishment of the Present Government, Respecting the Lands of the United States in the Territory North-West of the Ohio, Dec. 1800" (Dec. 1800), Box 5, Folder 12, Oliver Wolcott Papers, CT Historical Soc'y.
91. Rufus Putnam to Oliver Wolcott, July 12, 1800, Reel 1, Letters Sent by the General Land Office to Surveyors General, 1796–1816 (microfilm). I derived the cost of surveying by adding the sums expended over the year. *See* Rufus Putnam to Oliver Wolcott, Mar. 9, 1798, Box 2, Folder 10, Rufus Putnam Papers, Marietta College Library, Marietta, Ohio [hereinafter Putnam Papers]; "John Mathews, Deputy Surveyor, Copy of Account and Receipt to Rufus Putnam for Surveying Military Lands," Dec. 30, 1797, Box 2, Folder 9, Putnam Papers; "Jonathan Stone and Jeffery Mathewson, Copy of Account to Rufus Putnam, for Surveys Mad[e]," Jan. 20, 1798, Box 2, Folder 10, Putnam Papers; Rufus Putnam to Joseph Nourse, Oct. 20, 1798, Box 2, Folder 12, Putnam Papers.

Chapter 3

1. Act of May 17, 1796, 6 Stat. 27. For scholarly work on the military bounty lands, *see* Laura Jensen, *Patriots, Settlers, and the Origins of American Social Policy* (Cambridge, U.K.; Cambridge University Press, 2003), 128–52; Rohrbough, *Land Office Business*, 71–88; Gates, *Military Bounty Land Policies*, 249–84.
2. Box No. 1, Letters Received by the Secretary of the Treasury, 1796–1851, Entry 179, RG 49, Bureau of Land Management, U.S. National Archives. On the land systems of Virginia and North Carolina, *see* Chapter One.

3. For public acts, *see* Act of Mar. 2, 1799, ch. 34, 1 Stat. 728; Act of Mar. 2, 1799, ch. 29, 1 Stat. 724; Act of Mar. 3, 1797, ch. 14, 1 Stat. 507; Act of June 1, 1796, ch. 46, 1 Stat. 490; Act of Mar. 3, 1795, ch. 49, 1 Stat. 442; Act of June 9, 1794, ch. 62, 1 Stat. 394; Act of Feb. 21, 1793, ch. 10, 1 Stat. 318; Act of May 5, 1792, ch. 30, 1 Stat. 266; Act of Apr. 21, 1792, ch. 25, 1 Stat. 257; Act of Mar. 3, 1791, ch. 27, 1 Stat. 221; Act of Aug. 8, 1790, ch. 40, 1 Stat. 182; Act of July 16, 1798. For private acts, *see* ch. 87, 6 Stat. 36; Act of June 25, 1798, ch. 59, 6 Stat. 35; Act of May 17, 1796, ch. 28, 6 Stat. 27; Act of Apr. 12, 1792, ch. 19, 6 Stat. 7.
4. On relativity of title, *see* Larissa Katz, "The Concept of Ownership and the Relativity of Title," *Jurisprudence* 2, no. 1 (2011): 191–204.
5. Citizens of the Mero District to George Washington, Nov. 30, 1789, in *PGW:PS*, 4:345–47; Northwest Ordinance, in *JCC*, 33:337. On the rise of such exterminatory rhetoric, *see* Silver, *Our Savage Neighbors*; Jeffrey Ostler, *Surviving Genocide: Native Nations and the United States from the American Revolution to Bleeding Kansas* (New Haven, Conn.: Yale University Press, 2019). For an example of officials' pathos, *see* "Report of Henry Knox to President Washington" Dec. 29, 1794, Reel 2: Territory SW of the Ohio River, M200, Senate Territorial Papers, U.S. National Archive.
6. Samuel Holden Parsons and James Davenport to His Excellency Governor [Samuel] Huntington, Apr. 6, 1789, Ayer MS 687, Newberry Library. Patrick Wolfe's work elaborated the "logic of elimination" as the central core of what he called settler colonialism: *see, for instance*, Patrick Wolfe, "Land, Labor, and Difference: Elementary Structures of Race," *American Historical Review* 106, no. 3 (2001): 866–905. For invocations of *nemo dat*, *see* Joseph Murray, *Mr. Murray's Opinion Relating to the Courts of Justice in the Colony of New-York* (New York: printed by William Bradford, 1734), 14; *Letters of Verus, Addressed to the Native American* (Philadelphia: Printed by Benjamin Franklin Bache, 1797), 34.
7. A growing literature has stressed the significance of Native conceptions of territory: *see* Juliana Barr, "Geographies of Power: Mapping Indian Borders in the 'Borderlands' of the Early Southwest," *William and Mary Quarterly* 68, no. 1 (Jan. 1, 2011); Matthew Babcock, "Territoriality and the Historiography of Early North America," *Journal of American Studies* 50, no. 3 (Aug. 2016): 515–36. However, this literature has largely ignored federal officials' efforts, albeit grudging and partial, to grasp these concepts—a reflection of Native success in forcing federal officials to recognize Native territory. Another literature focuses on the federal government's half-hearted efforts to understand Native property rights much later, mostly in the twentieth century: *see* Christian W. McMillen, *Making Indian Law: The Hualapai Land Case and the Birth of Ethnohistory* (New Haven, Conn.: Yale University Press, 2007); David E. Wilkins, *Hollow Justice: A History of Indigenous Claims in the United States* (New Haven, Conn.: Yale University Press, 2013).
8. Timothy Pickering to Anthony Wayne, Apr. 4, 1795, *NWTC*; Henry Knox to George Washington, July 21, 1794, in *PGW:PS*, 16:402; Timothy Pickering to David Campbell, Aug. 28, 1795, Folder 2, Timothy Pickering Letters, Ayers 926, Newberry Library; Hopewell Commissioners to John Hancock, Jan. 14, 1786, Item No. 138, Henry Knox Papers (microfilm), Reel/Vol. 47, Massachusetts Historical Society.

9. Hopewell Commissioners to John Hancock, Jan. 14, 1786.
10. Piomingo's role is strongly suggested by his later statement, "I am the man who laid off the boundary on that map." "Record of the Conference with the Choctaws and Chickasaws," Aug. 7, 1792, in *ASP:IA*, 284–88.
11. *Id.*
12. *Id.*
13. Timothy Pickering to David Henley, Mar. 23, 1795, Folder 4, Timothy Pickering Letters, Ayers 926, Newberry Library; Timothy Pickering to David Campbell, Aug. 28, 1795, Folder 2, Timothy Pickering Letters, Ayers 926, Newberry Library. For Washington's proclamation, *see* Henry Knox to George Washington, July 21, 1794, in *PGW:PS*, 16:40.
14. William Blackstone, *Commentaries on the Laws of England* (Philadelphia: Printed by Robert Bell, 1771), 2:3. For an introduction to the large literature on this topic, *see* Andrew Fitzmaurice, *Sovereignty, Property and Empire, 1500–2000* (New York: Cambridge University Press, 2017); Robert A. Williams, *The American Indian in Western Legal Thought: The Discourses of Conquest* (New York: Oxford University Press, 1990). On early European ethnography, *see* Joyce E. Chaplin, *Subject Matter: Technology, the Body, and Science on the Anglo-American Frontier, 1500–1676* (Cambridge, Mass.: Harvard University Press, 2001); Anthony Pagden, *The Fall of Natural Man: The American Indian and the Origins of Comparative Ethnology* (Cambridge, U.K.: Cambridge University Press, 1982).
15. "Some Hints & Observations, Concerning the Civilization of the Indians, or Aborigines of America," Reel 47, Henry Knox Papers; John Gottlieb Ernestus Heckewelder, *Thirty Thousand Miles with John Heckewelder*, ed. Paul A.W. Wallace (Pittsburgh: University of Pittsburgh Press, 1958), 260–92; William Blount to Secretary of War, Nov. 10, 1794, in *TP: Vol. IV*, 364–70; William Blount to Secretary of War, Mar. 20, 1793, in *TP: Vol. IV*, 244–47.
16. Henry Knox, "Instructions to Major General Anthony Wayne Relatively to a Proposed Treaty with the Indians North West of the Ohio," Apr. 4, 1794, *NWTC* (emphasis added); President [Washington] to Attorney General, Feb. 12, 1793, in *TP: Vol. II*, 435.
17. [Washington] to Attorney General, Feb. 12, 1793; Pickering to Wayne, Apr. 8, 1795.
18. "Minutes of a Treaty with the tribes of Indians called the Wyandots, Delawares, Shawanese, Ottawas, Chippewas, Pattawatamies, Miamies, Eel River, Kickapoos, Piankeshaws, and Kaskaskias, begun at Greenville, on the 16th day of June, and ended on the 10th day of Aug., 1795," in *ASP:IA*, 1:564.
19. On Native methods of marking territory, *see* Barr, "Geographies of Power"; on the reading of wampum, *see* John Gottlieb Ernestus Heckewelder, *History, Manners, and Customs of the Indian Nations Who Once Inhabited Pennsylvania and the Neighboring States* (Philadelphia: Historical Society of Pennsylvania, 1881), 109; Calloway, *Pen and Ink Witchcraft*, 27–37.
20. David Zeisberger, *David Zeisberger's History of Northern American Indians* ([Columbus, Ohio]: Press of F.J. Heer, 1910), 94; John Parrish, "Book Relative to Indian Affairs Journals to Treaties," June 12, 1791, Ayer MS 3146, Newberry Library,

Chicago, Ill.; James McHenry to Maj. H. LeButts, Dec. 15, 1797, Box 2, James McHenry Papers, Clements Library, University of Michigan. On the role of writing among Native communities during this period, *see* Shoemaker, *Strange Likeness*, 61–81; Phillip H. Round, *Removable Type: Histories of the Book in Indian Country, 1663–1880* (Chapel Hill: University of North Carolina Press, 2010).

21. William Bartram, "Observations on the Creek and Cherokee Indians," in Gregory A. Waselkov and Kathryn E. Holland Braund eds., *William Bartram on the Southeastern Indians* (Lincoln: University of Nebraska Press, 1995), 156–60; "Conference of the Chiefs of the Cherokee Nation with the Secretary of War," Jan. 3–11, 1792, in *ASP:IA*, 1:204; Benjamin Hawkins to William Blount, Mar. 10, 1791, Folder 3, WBP:LC.
22. White, *Middle Ground*, 11–49; Boulware, *Deconstructing the Cherokee Nation*, 152–78; Nichols, *Peoples of the Inland Sea*, 24–40.
23. Arthur Camp[bell] to Arthur St. Clair, Jan. 8, 1791, Reel 3, *ASCP*; "Report of Antoine Gamelin," May 17, 1790, in *SCP*, 155–60. On these histories of mobility, *see* Amy C. Schutt, *Peoples of the River Valleys: The Odyssey of the Delaware Indians* (Philadelphia: University of Pennsylvania Press, 2007); Stephen Warren, *The Worlds the Shawnees Made: Migration and Violence in Early America*, reprint ed. (Chapel Hill: University of North Carolina Press, 2016); Gregory D. Smithers, *The Cherokee Diaspora: An Indigenous History of Migration, Resettlement, and Identity* (New Haven: Yale University Press, 2015).
24. Josiah Harmar to Henry Knox, Nov. 24, 1787, in *SCP*, 30–35; Richard Butler, "Journal of General Richard Butler," Codex 33, Durrett Collection, Special Collections, University of Chicago Library, at 187; on women's roles within Cherokee society and their transformation during this period, *see* Theda Perdue, *Cherokee Women: Gender and Culture Change, 1700–1835* (Lincoln: University of Nebraska Press, 1998); among the Creeks, *see* Ethridge, *Creek Country*, 93–117; Saunt, *A New Order of Things*, 139–62; among some of the Ohio Country nations, *see* Susan Sleeper-Smith, *Indigenous Prosperity and American Conquest: Indian Women of the Ohio River Valley, 1690–1792* (Chapel Hill: University of North Carolina Press, 2018).
25. "Narrative of Colonel Thomas Procter," July 9, 1791, in *ASP:IA*, 149; "Speech of Farmers Brother New King of the Six Nations," May 13, 1791, Reel 3, *ASCP*. According to subsequent accounts, Silas Dinsmore, federal agent among the Cherokees, was especially assiduous in seeking to transform gender roles within the nation: *see* Silas Dinsmore to Messrs. Inteligencers, [1828], Box 4, Dinsmoor Family Papers, Rauner Special Collections, Dartmouth College; "John Ridge on Cherokee Civilization in 1826," ed. William C. Sturveant, *Journal of Cherokee Studies* 7 (1981): 79–91. On the history of such efforts, *see* Gregory Evans Dowd, "The Spinning Wheel Revolution," in James P.P Horn, Jan Lewis, and Peter S. Onuf eds., *The Revolution of 1800: Democracy, Race, and the New Republic* (Charlottesville: University of Virginia Press, 2002), 267–83.
26. On the congruence, rather than divergence, between European and Native property concepts, particularly concerning common ownership, *see* Greer, 365–86; Shoemaker, *A Strange Likeness*, 13–34. On the more expansive property rights that women occasionally enjoyed in the early American West, *see* Honor Sachs, *Home*

Rule: Households, Manhood, and National Expansion on the Eighteenth-Century Kentucky Frontier (New Haven, Conn.: Yale University Press, 2015), 58–64.

27. On Cumberland, *see* White to Monroe, Aug. 9, 1792; Kristofer Ray, *Middle Tennessee, 1775–1825: Progress and Popular Democracy on the Southwestern Frontier* (Knoxville: University of Tennessee Press, 2007); Finger, *Tennessee Frontiers*, 75–151.
28. William Blount to Secretary of War [Henry Knox], Jan. 14, 1793, in *TP: Vol. IV*, 226–34; William Blount to Secretary of War [Henry Knox], Nov. 8, 1792, in *id.*, 114.
29. Blount to Secretary of War, Nov. 8, 1792; "Conference at Tellico Blockhouse," Nov. 7, 1794, in "The Correspondence of Gen. James Robertson," *American Historical Magazine* 3, no. 4 (Oct. 1, 1898): 367–72.
30. Pickering to Campbell, Aug. 28, 1795.
31. Knox, "Instructions to Major General Anthony Wayne," Apr. 4, 1794. On the 1768 Treaty of Fort Stanwix, *see* William J. Campbell, *Speculators in Empire: Iroquoia and the 1768 Treaty of Fort Stanwix* (Norman: University of Oklahoma Press, 2012); Calloway, *Pen and Ink Witchcraft*, 49–95.
32. *JCC*, 34:95–101 (emphasis added); Samuel Holden Parsons to Samuel Johnson, Dec. 3, 1785, Folder 5, Samuel Holden Parsons Papers, Connecticut Historical Society; David Duncan to Josiah Harmar, Mar. 28, 1786, Vol. 3, *JHP*.
33. Henry Knox, "Instructions to Major General Anthony Wayne," Apr. 4, 1794; Jonathan Heart to William Judd, Aug. 20, 1789, Jonathan Heart Papers, VFM 5748, Ohio Historical Society, Columbus, Ohio.
34. Pickering to Wayne, Apr. 8, 1795.
35. For histories that consider later Native land claims advanced before federal officials, *see* W. McMillen, *Making Indian Law*; Wilkins, *Hollow Justice*. The history presented here suggests that the more explicit role for ethnohistorical sources in Native land claims that McMillen traces in the twentieth century had important precursors in late eighteenth-century federal officials' informal ethnographies.
36. *JCC*, 34:247–52; "Resolution of Congress: The Inhabitants of Vincennes," Aug. 29, 1788, in *TP: Vol. II*, 145–47; "Report of Committee: Petition from Post Vincennes and the Illinois Country," May 5, 1788, in *TP: Vol. II*, 105–09; George Washington to Arthur St. Clair, Oct. 6, 1789, Reel 2, *ASCP*.
37. On the history of French settlements in the Illinois country and their relations with Natives, *see* Robert Michael Morrissey, *Empire by Collaboration: Indians, Colonists, and Governments in Colonial Illinois Country* (Philadelphia: University of Pennsylvania Press, 2015); Carl J. Ekberg, *French Roots in the Illinois Country: The Mississippi Frontier in Colonial Times* (Urbana: University of Illinois Press, 1998). On Vincennes in particular, *see* Andrew R.L. Cayton, *Frontier Indiana* (Bloomington: Indiana University Press, 1998), 1–97; Denise Marie Wilson, "Vincennes: From French Colonial Village to American Frontier Town, 1730–1820" (Ph.D. dissertation, West Virginia University, 1997). Detroit, formally part of the United States under the terms of the Treaty of Paris, remained under British control until 1796, when the British ceded sovereignty. Catherine Cangany, *Frontier Seaport: Detroit's Transformation into an Atlantic Entrepôt* (Chicago; London: University of Chicago Press, 2014). As discussed later, after cession Detroit presented many of the same land claims challenges as the Illinois Country.

38. On the Revolutionary War in the Illinois Country, *see* George Rogers Clark, *The Conquest of the Illinois*, ed. Milo Milton Quaife (Carbondale: Southern Illinois University Press, 2001); Cayton, *Frontier Indiana*, 70–97.
39. John Cleves Symmes to Robert Morris, June 22, 1790, in *CJCS*, 287; William Clark, "Journal," Aug. 20, 1797, *NWTC*; John Armstrong to Richard Anderson, Aug. 8, 1787, Box 1, Folder 20, Armstrong Papers, M6, Indiana Historical Society. On Anglo-American views of the habitants—which sometimes romanticized them as premodern peasants—*see* Edward Watts, *In This Remote Country: French Colonial Culture in the Anglo-American Imagination, 1780–1860* (Chapel Hill: University of North Carolina Press, 2006).
40. The foremost work on land tenure in the Illinois Country is Carl J. Ekberg, *French Roots in the Illinois Country*. Ekberg observes that "the system of land tenure in the early Illinois Country was variegated and complex," but notes that, throughout the region, nearly all the towns employed the same land use pattern, what he terms the "iron triad" of "nuclear village, compound of arable fields, pasture commons." *Id.*, 31–110. For an examination of the *Coutumes de Paris* in the region, *see* Carl J. Ekberg and Sharon Person, *St. Louis Rising: The French Regime of Louis St. Ange de Bellerive* (Urbana: University of Illinois Press, 2015).
41. "Petition of the Inhabitants of Post Vincennes," July 26, 1787, in *TP: Vol. II*, 58–59; "Journal Kept by George Hunter of a Tour from Philada. to Kentucky by the Illinois Country," July 14–Oct. 15, 1796, American Philosophical Society, Philadelphia, Penn.
42. "Land Sale Contract Btw/Dominque Burguant and Josete Poirier and Vital Bouche," (typescript translation), Dec. 24, 1782, Translation, I.164, Lasselle Family Papers, L127, Indiana State Library, Indianapolis, Ind.; "Land Contract" (typescript translation), Feb. 28, 1792, I.291, Lasselle Family Papers.
43. "Petition to Congress from the Illinois Country," Sept. 15, 1787, in *TP: Vol. II*, 72–73.
44. "Cession of Western Land Claims," Mar. 1, 1784, in *TP: Vol. II*, 6–9; *JCC*, 32:334–43. For a codification of the requirement of honoring the land rights of conquered peoples in the era's most influential international-law treatise, *see* Emer de Vattel, *The Law of Nations*, Book III, Chapter XIII, § 200, at 598 (Indianapolis, Ind.: Liberty Fund, 2008).
45. *JCC*, 34:247–52; "Resolution of Congress: The Inhabitants of Vincennes," Aug. 29, 1788, in *TP: Vol. II*, 145–47; "Report of Committee: Petition from Post Vincennes and the Illinois Country," May 5, 1788, in *TP: Vol. II*, 105–09.
46. "Report of the Proceedings of Winthrop Sargent Upon the Land Claims of the Settlers of Vincennes," July 31, 1790, in *TP: Vol. III*, 323–32.
47. "Report of the Proceedings," July 31, 1790; Gates, *History of Public Land Law Development*, 90; Symmes to Morris, June 22, 1790.
48. Symmes to Morris, June 22, 1790; "Petition of the Inhabitants of Post Vincennes," July 26, 1787, in *TP: Vol. II*, 58–60.
49. On gender and community property in French law in the Illinois Country, *see* Susan C. Boyle, "Did She Generally Decide? Women in Ste. Genevieve, 1750–1805," *William and Mary Quarterly* 44, no. 4 (1987): 775–89;
50. "Report of the Proceedings of Winthrop Sargent," 323–32.

51. "List of Lots at Kaskaskia," Mar. 17, 1790, Reel 7, *ASCP*; "Report of Governor St. Clair to the Secretary of State," Feb. 10, 1791, in *TP: Vol. II*, 323–37.
52. "Report of the Secretary of State to the President," Dec. 14, 1790, in *TP: Vol. II*, 315–17; "F. Bosseron and Others to Acting Governor Sargent," July 3, 1790, in *TP: Vol. II*, 282–83; Gabriel Legrand, clerk of the court, "Land Grant to Thomas James" (typescript translation), Feb. 22, 1782, I.157, Lasselle Family Papers.
53. "List of Lots," Mar. 17, 1790; Arthur St. Clair to Winthrop Sargent, July 6, 1790, in *TP: Vol. II*, 283–84.
54. "Report of Governor St. Clair to the Secretary of State," Feb. 10, 1791.
55. Act of Mar. 3, 1791, 1 Stat. 221. Congress responded to further complaints from the villagers in another statute two years later, promising to pay for surveying at public expense. Act of Feb. 21, 1793, 1 Stat. 318.
56. "Report of Arthur St. Clair on Western Lands," Feb. 21, 1799, Reel 1: Territory Northwest of the Ohio River, Senate Territorial Papers, M200, U.S. National Archives; William Bradford to Secretary of State, Mar. 25, 1794, Northwest Territory Archives, Burton Historical Collection, Detroit, Mich.; Winthrop Sargent to Secretary of State, Apr. 19, 1794, in *id.*
57. "Journal Kept by George Hunter," July 14–Oct. 15, 1796; Judge Turner to Gov. Arthur St. Clair, June 14, 1794, in *TP: Vol. II*, 325–26; Francis S. Philbrick, *The Laws of Indiana Territory 1801–1809* (Springfield, Ill.: Trustees of the Illinois State Historical Library, 1930), lxxiii. For examples of residents selling their lands, *see* "Land Contract" (typescript translation), Apr. 15, 1791, I.293; "Land Contract," Aug. 24, 1791, translation, I.298, Lasselle Family Papers.
58. Gov. Arthur St. Clair to Secretary of State, Jan. 1796, *TP: Vol. II*, 542; "Report of Arthur St. Clair on Western Lands," Feb. 21, 1799.
59. *ASP:PL*, 1:539, 2:176. Tracing the incredible tangled history of the land claims in the Illinois Country and Vincennes—described by a chronicler as "tedious in its details"—is beyond the scope of this study. An overview appears in Francis S. Philbrick, "Introduction," in *The Laws of Indiana Territory 1801–1809* (Springfield, Ill.: Trustees of the Illinois State Historical Library, 1930), lxv–c, and Leonard Lux, *Vincennes Donation Lands* (Vincennes, Ind.: Vincennes Historical and Antiquarian Society, 1977). Some of the lengthy reports considering the subsequent history of land claims in the region appear in *ASP:PL*, 1:146, 237, 264, 267, 508; 2:101, 220, 389; 3:1, 249, 341, 359, 379, 381, 409.
60. *ASP:PL*, 1:539.
61. Winthrop Sargent to Secretary of State, Sept. 30, 1796, *TP: Vol. III*, 456–68. A consideration of these claims appears in Gates, *History of Public Land Law*, 87–120.
62. Henry Knox, "List of Soldiers Entitled to Bounty Lands," Nov. 14, 1787, Reel 2, *WSP*; *JCC*, 33:226; Act of June 1, 1796, 1 Stat. 490.
63. For veterans' claims, *see* Kristin A. Collins, "Petitions without Number: Widows' Petitions and the Early Nineteenth-Century Origins of Public Marriage-Based Entitlements," *Law and History Review* 31 (2013): 1–60; Jensen, *Patriots, Settlers, and the Origins of American Social Policy*; John Phillips Resch, *Suffering Soldiers: Revolutionary War Veterans, Moral Sentiment, and Political Culture in the Early*

Republic (Amherst: University of Massachusetts Press, 1999); Theda Skocpol, *Protecting Soldiers and Mothers: The Political Origins of Social Policy in the United States* (Cambridge, Mass.: Belknap Press of Harvard University Press, 1992).

64. Act of June 1, 1796, 1 Stat. 490.
65. 5 Annals of Cong. 402–23 (1796); John Armstrong to Mathey McConnel, Francis Johnston, and William Alexander, Sept. 5, 1788, Box 1, Folder 21, Armstrong Papers, M6, Indiana Historical Society, Indianapolis, Ind.; Mathey McConnel to John Armstrong, Oct. 29, 1788, Box 1, Armstrong Papers; Indenture to John Armstrong, Jan. 1, 1789, Box 2, Folder 1, Armstrong Papers. One study found that about two-thirds of the 9,900 land warrants issued had changed hands, at an average price of ten cents per acre, far below the federal minimum price as established in the 1796 act. Hutchinson, *Bounty Lands*, 251.
66. *JCC*, 34:95–101.
67. Indenture to John Armstrong, Mar. 2, 1789, Box 2, Folder 1, Armstrong Papers; "List of the Men for Whom I Have Not Drawn Lands with the Reasons Annexed to Each Name," 1789, Box 2, Folder 3, Armstrong Papers; Jonathan Story to Ebenezer Sproat, Oct. 12, 1789, Solomon Sibley Papers, Burton Historical Collection, Detroit Public Library; John Cleves Symmes to Jonathan Dayton, May 16, 1789, in *CJCS*, 213–18.
68. Henry Hill to Secretary of Treasury, Dec. 29, 1798; Judah Alden to Secretary of Treasury, Jan. 18, 1800; Benjamin Walker to Secretary of Treasury, Feb. 6, 1797, in Box No. 1, Letters Received by the Secretary of the Treasury, 1796–1851, Entry 179, RG 49, Bureau of Land Management, U.S. National Archives.
69. "Printed Broadside in Re: Military Bounty Lands," May 4, 1796, Box 1, McHenry Papers; James McHenry to [Congress], Apr. 15, 1800, McHenry Papers.
70. McHenry to [Congress], Apr. 15, 1800; "Plan for Disposing of the Public Lands," July 22, 1790, *ASP:PL*, 4–5; Secretary of State to John Cleves Symmes, Dec. 4, 1791, in *TP: Vol. II*, 352–53.
71. McHenry to [Congress], Apr. 15, 1800; Charles Lee, "Patents for Virginia Lands," Dec. 21, 1797, in Benjamin F. Hall ed., *Official Opinions of the Attorneys General of the United States* (Washington, D.C.: Robert Farnham, 1852), 1:79.
72. McHenry to [Congress], Apr. 15, 1800.
73. Oliver Wolcott, Secretary of Treasury, to Joseph Nourse, Registrar of the Treasury, Jan. 9, 1800, Letters Received by the Secretary of the Treasury, 1796–1851. On the role of courts in resolving disputes that arose in the land office, *see* Secretary of the Treasury to Thomas Worthington, June 10, 1801, in *TP: Vol. III*, 139–44; Secretary of the Treasury to Judge of Court of Common Pleas of Ross County, Aug. 7, 1802, in *TP: Vol. III*, 240–42.
74. "Military Bounty Land Warrants Fraudulently Obtained," Feb. 27, 1809, in *ASP:PL* 827. For the number of warrants issued versus claims rejected, *see* Hutchinson, *Bounty Lands*, 151. On the War of 1812 bounty lands, *see* Act of May 6, 1812, ch. 77, 2 Stat. 728; Gates, *Public Land Law*, 262–63.
75. William Henry Harrison, "Circular," May 14, 1800, Series 1, General Correspondence, 1734–1939, William Henry Harrison Papers, Manuscript Division, Library of Congress. On Congress's many land issues at this moment, *see* Annals of Cong. 10:185–721.

76. Hutchinson, *Bounty Lands*, 151–80; Gates, *Public Land Law*, 255–56.
77. Harrison, "Circular"; Harrison Land Act, ch. 55, 2 Stat. 73 (1800); 10 Annals of Cong. 625, 651–52, 681–84 (1800). Harrison noted one major source of contention behind closed doors—whether to sell the land in half (320 acres) or whole sections (640 acres). After some back-and-forth between House and Senate, Congress agreed to offer both.
78. Harrison, "Circular"; Harrison Land Act, ch. 55, 2 Stat. 73 (1800); Rohrbough, *Land Office Business*, 10, 22, 44.
79. Thomas Donaldson, *The Public Domain: Its History, with Statistics* (Washington: U.S. Government Printing Office, 1881), 175. On the intense antebellum politics concerning the public lands, *see* Rohrbough, *Land Office Business*; Daniel Feller, *The Public Lands in Jacksonian Politics* (Madison: University of Wisconsin Press, 1984); Frymer, *Building an American Empire*, 72–127; John Robert Van Atta, *Securing the West: Politics, Public Lands, and the Fate of the Old Republic, 1785–1850* (Baltimore: Johns Hopkins University Press, 2014).

Chapter 4

1. Act of Aug. 5, 1789, ch. 7, 1 Stat. 49. No recent academic biography of Knox exists. For background on his life, *see* Taylor, *Liberty Men and Great Proprietors*, 37–49; Mark Puls, *Henry Knox: Visionary General of the American Revolution* (New York: St. Martin's Press, 2008).
2. "Henry Knox's Notes on the State of the Frontier, Jan. 1790," Jan. 1790, in *GWP:PS*, 5:76–8; Report of the Secretary at War to Congress, July 10, 1787, in *TP: Vol. II*, 31–35.
3. On borderlands violence and its role in linking communities, *see* Hämäläinen and Truett, "On Borderlands," 351; Ned Blackhawk, *Violence over the Land: Indians and Empires in the Early American West* (Cambridge, Mass.: Harvard University Press, 2006); Brian DeLay, *War of a Thousand Deserts: Indian Raids and the U.S.-Mexican War* (New Haven, Conn.: Yale University Press, 2008); Silver, *Our Savage Neighbors*; Rob Harper, "Looking the Other Way: The Gnadenhutten Massacre and the Contextual Interpretation of Violence," *William and Mary Quarterly*, Third Series, 64, no. 3 (July 1, 2007): 621–44.
4. "Henry Knox's Notes on the State of the Frontier, Jan. 1790"; Report of the Secretary at War to Congress, July 10, 1787.
5. Act of July 22, 1790, ch. 33, 1 Stat. 137; Act of Mar. 1, 1793, ch. 19, 1 Stat. 329; Act of May 19, 1796, ch. 30, 1 Stat. 469; Act of Mar. 3, 1799, ch. 46, 1 Stat. 743; Act of Mar. 30, 1802, ch. 13, 2 Stat. 139. For a detailed study of the Trade and Intercourse Acts that relied almost entirely on territorial sources, especially the printed territorial papers, *see* Francis Paul Prucha, *American Indian Policy in the Formative Years: The Indian Trade and Intercourse Acts, 1780–1834* (Cambridge, Mass.: Harvard University Press, 1962). Significant Indian country also existed in New York and Georgia, particularly in Georgia's unceded western lands, although these would later become the Mississippi Territory.

6. "Report of Henry Knox on the Southwest Frontiers," Dec. 13, 1793, in *ASP:IA*, 363. For works emphasizing the rise of conceptions of Natives and whites as separate "races" in the late eighteenth century, *see* Joshua Piker, "Indians and Race in Early America: A Review Essay," *History Compass* 3, no. 1 (2005): 1–17; David J. Silverman, *Red Brethren: The Brothertown and Stockbridge Indians and the Problem of Race in Early America*, 1st ed. (Ithaca, N.Y.: Cornell University Press, 2010); Daniel K. Richter, *Facing East from Indian Country: A Native History of Early America* (Cambridge, Mass.: Harvard University Press, 2001), 190–236; Nancy Shoemaker, "How Indians Got to Be Red," *American Historical Review* 102, no. 3 (June 1997): 625–44. For works that emphasize the role of racial hostility in forestalling the punishment of crimes against Natives, *see* Patrick Griffin, *American Leviathan: Empire, Nation, and Revolutionary Frontier* (New York: Hill and Wang, 2007), 198–208; Silver, *Our Savage Neighbors*, 127–60.

   For works that stress the persistence of borderlands diplomacy in the late eighteenth century, *see* Ford, *Settler Sovereignty*; Kathleen DuVal, "Cross-Cultural Crime and Osage Justice in the Western Mississippi Valley, 1700–1826," *Ethnohistory* 54, no. 4 (Oct. 1, 2007): 697–722.
7. Henry Knox to George Washington, July 7, 1789, in *PGW:PS*, 3:134–40. On the diffusion of authority frustrating governmental aims, *see* Robert A. Kagan, *Adversarial Legalism: The American Way of Law* (Cambridge, Mass.: Harvard University Press, 2001).
8. George Thompson to James Madison, June 1, 1790, George Thompson Papers, Clements Library, University of Michigan.
9. "Report from H. Knox, Secretary of War, to the President of the United States, Relative to the Northwestern Indians," June 15, 1789, in *ASP:IA, 12–14*; Silver, *Our Savage Neighbors*, xviii–xxvi; "The Causes of the Existing Hostilities Between the United States, and Certain Tribes of Indians North-West of the Ohio, Stated and Explained From Official and Authentic Documents, and Published in Obedience to the Orders of the President of the United States," Jan. 26, 1792, in *TP: Vol. II*, 359–66; William Blount to Secretary of War, Nov. 10, 1794, in *TP: Vol. IV*, 364–70.
10. George Washington to Edmund Pendleton, Jan. 22, 1795, in *PGW:PS*, 17:424; John Gottlieb Ernestus Heckewelder, *A Narrative of the Mission of the United Brethren Among the Delaware and Mohegan Indians* (Philadelphia: Published by M'Carty & Davis, 1820), 395.
11. John Parrish, "Journal 1793 No. 2 Indian Treaty," John Parrish Journals, Clements Library, University of Michigan; Heckewelder, *History, Manners, and Customs of the Indian Nations*, 80–81. On Gnadenhuetten, *see* Harper, "Looking the Other Way"; on genocidal violence in early America, *see* Benjamin Madley, "Reexamining the American Genocide Debate: Meaning, Historiography, and New Methods," *American Historical Review* 120, no. 1 (Feb. 1, 2015): 98–139; Jeffrey Ostler, "'To Extirpate the Indians': An Indigenous Consciousness of Genocide in the Ohio Valley and Lower Great Lakes, 1750s–1810," *William and Mary Quarterly* 72, no. 4 (2015): 587–622.
12. William Blount and Andrew Pickens to Secretary of War, Aug. 6, 1793, in *TP: Vol. IV*, 296; Edward Telfair to Henry Knox, Dec. 5, 1792, Reel 2: The Territory Southwest of the River Ohio, Senate Territorial Papers (microfilm), M200, U.S. National Archives.

13. Henry Knox to Edward Telfair, Mar. 14, 1791, Northwest Territory Collection, Indiana Historical Society; William Blount to Secretary of War, Nov. 8, 1792, in *TP: Vol. IV*, 208–16; William Blount to Secretary of War, Aug. 6, 1793, in *id.*, 296. For fuller accounts depicting the intricacies of Indigenous legal practices, *see* John Phillip Reid, *A Law of Blood; the Primitive Law of the Cherokee Nation* (New York: New York University Press, 1970), 73–112; Strickland, *Fire and the Spirits*, 27–32; Nancy Gallman and Alan Taylor, "Covering Blood and Graves: Murder and Law on Imperial Margins," in Brian P. Owensby and Richard J. Ross eds., *Justice in a New World: Negotiating Legal Intelligibility in British, Iberian, and Indigenous America* (New York: NYU Press, 2018), 213–37.
14. "Message from the Secretary of War to the Hanging Maw, Sent by Governor Blount," Aug. 27, 1793, in *ASP:IA*, 431; Henry Burbeck, "Speeches to Indians," Aug. 1797, Ayer 121, Newberry Library.
15. William Cocke, "For the Gazette," *Knoxville Gazette*, Dec. 29, 1792; Blount to Secretary of War, Nov. 8, 1792. For additional discussion of this shared culture of retaliation, *see* Ford, *Settler Sovereignty*, 35–42, 85–97.
16. "Copy of a Letter from Colonel Arthur Campbell to Captain John Watts," *Knoxville Gazette*, Jan. 28, 1792; John Sevier to Benjamin Hawkins and Andrew Pickens, Apr. 19, 1797, in *Executive Journal of Governor Sevier*, 149–51.
17. "Knoxville, Saturday, June 1," *Knoxville Gazette*, June 1, 1793; "Genealogies: Col. Silas Dinsmoor" n.d., Dinsmoor Alumni File, Rauner Special Collections, Dartmouth College.
18. "Report of the Secretary at War to Congress," July 10, 1787, in *TP: Vol. II*, 31–35.
19. Benjamin Hawkins to James McHenry, Mar. 1, 1797, in C.L Grant ed., *Letters, Journals, and Writings of Benjamin Hawkins* (Savannah, Ga.: Beehive Press, 1980), 1:85–87. For discussions of the Cherokee and Creek repudiations of retaliation, *see* Silas Dinsmore to David Henley, July 8, 1795, Folder 3, Silas Dinsmore Papers, Ayer MS 241, Newberry Library; William Gerald McLoughlin, *Cherokee Renascence in the New Republic* (Princeton, N.J.: Princeton University Press, 1986), 43–46; Strickland, *Fire and the Spirits*, 57–72.
20. "Report of the Secretary at War to Congress," July 10, 1787. Knox's role in drafting the initial Trade and Intercourse Act is suggested in Henry Knox to George Washington, July 7, 1789, in *PGW:PS*, 3:134–40. The Trade and Intercourse Act was re-enacted, with expansions, in 1793, 1796, 1799, 1802, and then finally in 1834.
21. William Blount to James White, Dec. 14, 1795, in *TP: Vol. IV*, 411–14; 4 Annals of Cong. 775–76 (1794); George Washington to Secretary of State, July 1, 1796, in Worthington Chauncey Ford ed., *The Writings of George Washington* (New York; London: G.P. Putnam' Sons, 1889), 13:112.
22. Act of May 19, 1796, ch. 30, 1 Stat. 469, §§ 1–5, 19; Report of Secretary at War to Congress, July 10, 1787; Memorandum from Henry Knox and Andrew Pickens, July 24, 1793, in *PGW:PS*, 13:281–85.
23. Act of May 19, 1796, ch. 30, 1 Stat. 469, §§ 4, 14.
24. Act of July 22, 1790, ch. 33, 1 Stat. 137; Act of Mar. 1, 1793, ch. 19, 1 Stat. 329; Act of May 19, 1796, ch. 30, 1 Stat. 469; Act of Mar. 3, 1799, ch. 46, 1 Stat. 743. John Sevier to Andrew Jackson, William Claiborne, and Joseph Anderson, in *PAJ*, 1:171–72.

The Trade and Intercourse Act created one of only a handful of federal crimes in the early republic. The other major federal criminal statute was the Crimes Act, which created statutory provisions for the punishment of treason, for crimes committed within exclusive federal jurisdictions, and for crimes that obstructed the federal judiciary. Crimes Act, ch. 9, 1 Stat. 112 (1790). Part of the Crimes Act extended jurisdiction over the high seas, which, like Indian country, lay outside state jurisdiction. *Id.*, §§ 9–13. For the limited literature on early federal crimes, which omits discussion of the Trade and Intercourse Act entirely, *see* Kathryn Preyer, "Jurisdiction to Punish: Federal Authority, Federalism and the Common Law of Crimes in the Early Republic," *Law and History Review* 4, no. 2 (1986): 223–65; Adam H. Kurland, "First Principles of American Federalism and the Nature of Federal Criminal Jurisdiction," *Emory Law Journal* 45 (1996): 94.

25. Knox to Washington, July 7, 1789; Attorney General to Secretary of the Treasury, June 9, 1795, in *TP: Vol. II*, 520–21; Lord Grenville to George Hammond, June 8, 1792, in *The Correspondence of Lieut. Governor John Graves Simcoe, with Allied Documents Relating to His Administration of the Government of Upper Canada* (Toronto: Ontario Historical Society, 1923), 5:14. I discuss the legal status of Native nations during this period more fully in Gregory Ablavsky, "Beyond the Indian Commerce Clause," *Yale Law Journal* 124, no. 4 (2015): 1012–90.
26. Treaty of Fort Harmar, U.S.-Wyandots et al., Jan. 9, 1789, 7 Stat. 33; Treaty of Peace and Friendship, U.S.-Creeks, Aug. 7, 1790, 7 Stat. 35; Treaty of Holston, U.S.-Cherokees, July 2, 1791, 7 Stat. 39.
27. Henry Knox to George Washington, Feb. 22, 1791, in *PGW:PS*, 7:402–15.
28. George Washington to the Seneca Chiefs, Dec. 29, 1790, in *PGW:PS*, 7:146–50; Thomas Jefferson to George Washington, Mar. 13, 1793, in *PGW:PS*, 12:314–15; "Extract from 'an Act to Regulate Trade and Intercourse with the Indian Tribes, Passed by the Congress of the United States, March 1, 1793,' " *Knoxville Gazette*, Nov. 1, 1794; Rufus Putnam, "Charge to the Grand Jury" [N.D.], Box 2, Folder 6, Local Government Records, Marietta College Library.
29. Robert Buntin to Winthrop Sargent, June 21, 1793, Reel 2, *WSP*; "A True and Perfect Inventory . . . of the Deceased John Toulon called Gamuchon," Oct. 26, 1795, Box 2, Knox County Probate Records, Knox County Public Library, Vincennes, Ind.; "Journal Kept by George Hunter of a Tour from Philada. to Kentucky by the Illinois Country" 14-10.15 1796, American Philosophical Society, Philadelphia, Penn. For baptismal records in Vincennes in the 1780s and 1790s, *see St. Francis Xavier Catholic Church Records* (Bowie, Md.: Heritage Books, Inc., 1999). For account books, *see* Account of John Decker to Moses Henry, 1792, Box 1, Knox County Probate Records, Knox County Public Library; Account of Lewis Chatellereault, 1797, Box 1, Knox County Probate Records, Knox County Public Library. For a contrasting view of postwar Vincennes as a place where the preceding "face-to-face world" was in decline, *see* White, *The Middle Ground*, 421–33.
30. Winthrop Sargent to Secretary of State, Aug. 23, 1796, in *TP: Vol. III*, 451–56; Winthrop Sargent to Abner Prior, Oct. 25, 1792, in *TP: Vol. III*, 386–89; "Minutes of the Conference at Coyatee with the Chiefs and Warriors of the Cherokees, in May,

1792, with the Incidental Circumstances Relative Thereto," May 1792, in *ASP:IA*, 267; William Blount to Secretary of War, Apr. 9, 1793, *TP: Vol. IV*, 249–51; "Information by Governor Blount, Respecting the Cherokee Chiefs Whose Names Are Mentioned in the Narrative given by Richard Finnelson," Sept. 26, 1792, in *ASP:IA*, 288–91; John Sevier to Secretary of the Department of War, July 20, 1796, in *Executive Journal of Governor Sevier*, 111–14. In one suit from Detroit, a Detroit merchant sued Mrs. Rankin, described as an "Indian Woman" and "a sole Trader" (a woman authorized to transact business), for a substantial sum of money. Aiken v. Rankin, Sept. 12, 1797, No. 221, Box 2, Wayne County Court of Common Pleas Records, Michigan Supreme Court Records, Archives of Michigan, Lansing, Mich. On William Blount's "court," *see* J.G.M. Ramsey, *The Annals of Tennessee to the End of the Eighteenth Century* (Charleston: J. Russell, 1853), 645. On the significance of "cities"—broadly construed—as sites of encounter on the frontier, *see* Jay Gitlin, Barbara Berglund, and Adam Arenson eds., *Frontier Cities: Encounters at the Crossroads of Empire* (Philadelphia: University of Pennsylvania Press, 2012).

31. David Zeigler to Arthur St. Clair, June 1, 1791, Roll 3, *ASCP*; "For the Knoxville Gazette," *Knoxville Gazette*, May 19, 1792; "Knoxville Gazette, Monday, May 8, 1797," *Knoxville Gazette*, May 8, 1797. In Detroit, the employers of a French man named Lafond sued him for expropriating company property to maintain an Indian woman, reputedly the "best Clad in the Village." Leith, Shepherd & Duff v. Lafond, June 12, 1797, No. 194, Box 1, Wayne Cnty Court of Common Pleas Records, Michigan Supreme Court Records, Archives of Michigan.
32. Quotation in William H. Masterson, *William Blount*, Southern Biography Series (Baton Rouge: Louisiana State University Press, 1954), 91. For an exploration of the implications of sexual relationships between Natives and Europeans, *see* Richard Godbeer, *Sexual Revolution in Early America* (Baltimore: Johns Hopkins University Press, 2002), 154–89; Susan Sleeper-Smith, *Indian Women and French Men: Rethinking Cultural Encounter in the Western Great Lakes, Native Americans of the Northeast* (Amherst: University of Massachusetts Press, 2001). On the interrelationship between intimacy and power in U.S. history, *see* Ann Laura Stoler ed., *Haunted by Empire: Geographies of Intimacy in North American History* (Durham, N.C.: Duke University Press, 2006); and Ann Laura Stoler, "Tense and Tender Ties: The Politics of Comparison in North American History and (Post) Colonial Studies," *Journal of American History* 88, no. 3 (2001): 829–65.
33. William Blount to James White, Dec. 14, 1795, in *TP: Vol. IV*, 411–14.
34. Robert Buntin to Winthrop Sargent, June 21, 1793, Reel 3, *WSP*; Timothy Pickering, "Instructions to Edward Price," Nov. 25, 1795, Letter Book of the Creek Trade House, 1795–1816, M4, U.S. National Archives; Jean Francois Rivet to Bishop Carroll, Aug. 8, 1797, Correspondence—1796–1801 (typescript English translation of original French), Rivet Papers, RHC 102, Byron R. Lewis Historical Library, Vincennes University, Vincennes, Ind. Lt. Prior to Arthur St. Clair, Oct. 7, 1791, Reel 3, *ASCP*; John Francis Hamtramck to Secretary of War, Mar. 31, 1792, in *TP: Vol. II*, 380–83; Winthrop Sargent to the Courts of Common Pleas et al. of Knox County, July 22, 1793, in *TP: Vol. III*, 412–15.

35. "Testimony of Antoine Marchal" July 7, 1797, Box 1, Folder 10; "Testimony of Claude Coupin" July 7, 1797, Box 1, Folder 9; "Examination of Lambeir Burway" July 8, 1797, Box 1, Folder 8; "Recognizance Bond of Lambeir Burway" July 9, 1797, Box 1, Folder 8; "Recognizance Bond of Henry Rambout" Aug. 29, 1798, Box 1, Folder 11; all in General Court Records, Indiana State Archives. Burway's house had been the scene of another battery against a Potawatomi known as the brother of Grand Poo the year before, for which Leno Burway was indicted before the county court. United States v. Leno Burway, Apr. 21, 1796, Box 2, File 83, Knox County Court Records, Knox County Public Library, Vincennes, Ind.
36. "Jury Presentment," Aug. 4, 1800; "Examination of James Correy," Aug. 5, 1800; "Inquest for George Allen" Aug. 5, 1800; "Examination of William Prince," Aug. 6, 1800; "Testimony of H. Hurd" Aug. 6, 1800; "Presentment against Thomas Coulter," Sept. 1800; all in M98, William Hayden English Family Papers, Indianapolis, Ind.
37. William Blount to The Glass, Sept. 13, 1792, in "The Correspondence of Gen. James Robertson," *American Historical Magazine* 2, no. 1 (Jan. 1, 1897): 72–74.
38. A.M. Hoar to James Carey, July 28, 1802, Records of the Hiwasee and Tellico Trading House, RG 49, U.S. National Archives.
39. *Id.*
40. *Id.* The subsequent history of this incident is tangled and speaks to a period later than the subject of this study. But as related by the federal Indian agent, a Cherokee council accepted the conclusion that Samy's death was an accident and forbade his relatives from seeking retaliation, which they did nonetheless, killing Runion's son. The Council arrested the killer and turned him over the federal authorities pursuant to treaty; the federal government then turned the Cherokee over to the state of Tennessee, which tried and executed him. *See* McLoughlin, *Cherokee Renascence*, 50–51.
41. For some examples of criminal law in the Territory, *see* "William Goforth's Court Records," Box 12, Armstrong Papers, M6, Indiana Historical Society; "Minutes of Special General Court of Sessions of the Peace" Nov. 11, 1789, Box 1, Folder 2: 1789, Local Government Records, Marietta College Library; Government v. Alexander McMullin, Oct. 1793, Docket 4/7, Hamilton District Superior Court Records, Knox County Archives, Knoxville, Tenn. On the business of territorial county courts, including criminal law, *see* Michael Toomey, "'Doing Justice to Suitors': The Role of County Courts in the Southwest Territory," *Journal of East Tennessee History* 62 (1990): 33–53.
42. Henry Vanderburgh to Winthrop Sargent, Nov. 28, 1792, Reel 3, *WSP*; John Sevier to Andrew Jackson and William Claiborne, Nov. 19, 1797, in *PAJ*, 1:153–54.
43. William Cocke, "For the Gazette," *Knoxville Gazette*, Dec. 29, 1792; William Blount to Secretary of War, Nov. 8, 1792, in *TP: Vol. IV*, 208–16; "Cincinnati, April 5," *Centinel of the North-Western Territory*, Apr. 5, 1794; F. Johnston to John Armstrong, July 15, 1790, Box 2, Folder 7, Armstrong Papers, M6, Indiana Historical Society; Silver, *Our Savage Neighbors*. For the spread of anti-Indian rhetoric westward, especially to Kentucky, *see* Griffin, *American Leviathan*.

44. "For the Gazette," *Knoxville Gazette*, Oct. 20, 1792; William Blount, "For the Gazette," *Knoxville Gazette*, June 1, 1793; Timothy Pickering to David Campbell, Aug. 28, 1795, Folder 2, Timothy Pickering Letters, Ayers 926, Ayer Collection, Newberry Library. Peter Silver argues that the deployment of the "anti-Indian sublime" against political opponents was its "most crucial[]" function. Silver, *Our Savage Neighbors*, xviii–xxvi.
45. Samuel Mitchell to David Henley, Oct. 30, 1797, David Henley Papers, Rubenstein Rare Book and Manuscript Library, Duke University.
46. John Francis Hamtramck to Josiah Harmar, Feb. 18, 1791, in Thornbrough ed., *Outpost on the Wabash*, 277–79; Magistrates of Knox County to Arthur St. Clair, July 29, 1791, Roll 3, *ASCP*. Simpson's culpability, the magistrates noted, could not "be proved but by the Testimony of Indians." *Id.*
47. Magistrates of Knox County to St. Clair, July 29, 1791.
48. *Id.*; Arthur St. Clair to Lt. Prior, Aug. 15, 1791, Roll 3, *ASCP*; Arthur St. Clair to Henry Knox, Aug. 17, 1791, Arthur St. Clair Papers, Burton Historical Collection, Detroit Public Library; Henry Knox to George Washington, Aug. 28, 1792, in *PGW:PS*, 11:49–50.
49. Hoar to Carey, July 28, 1802. Rob Harper discovers a similar dynamic in the Ohio Valley in the 1770s and 1780s: "Violence," he notes, "often sprang from everyday interactions like tavern bickering or haggling over trade," but was often exacerbated by governmental intervention. Harper, *Unsettling the West*, 4–5.
50. Winthrop Sargent, "Speeches to Chippewas and Ottawas," Sept. 6, 1796, Ayer MS 790, Newberry Library.
51. On earlier efforts to assert criminal jurisdiction over Native peoples, *see* Yasuhide Kawashima, *Puritan Justice and the Indian: White Man's Law in Massachusetts, 1630–1763*, 1st ed. (Middletown, Conn.: Wesleyan University Press, 1986); Katherine A. Hermes, "The Law of Native Americans, to 1815," in *The Cambridge History of Law in America* (Cambridge, U.K.: Cambridge University Press, 2008), 32–62; on later efforts, *see* Ford, *Settler Sovereignty*, 129–98.
52. William Blount to John Gray Blount, July 29, 1794, in *JGBP*, 2:420–21; Willie Blount to John McKee, Aug. 5, 1794, Folder 2, John McKee Papers, Manuscript Division, Library of Congress. Two accounts of Abongphohigo's trial exist: a printed account in the *Knoxville Gazette* and a manuscript record in the territorial court records. "Knoxville, Monday, Aug. 4," *Knoxville Gazette*, Aug. 4, 1794; United States v. Abongphohigo, Aug. 1, 1794, Minutes of Oyer and Terminer Court, Hamilton District Superior Court (typescript copy, 1942), at 12–14, Tennessee State Library and Archives. Abongphohigo is spelled inconsistently in the historical record; I have adopted the spelling in the official caption of the case, although the court transcript and newspaper accounts also spelled his name as "Abongpohigo" and "Obongpohego." Ish left little trace in surviving archives, appearing in a single local court case over debts. George Bowerman v. John Ish, Sept. 9, 1793, Docket 77/97, Knox County Court of Common Please Records, Knox County Archives, Knoxville, Tenn.
53. Alexander Hamilton to George Mathews, Sept. 25, 1794, in *Papers of Alexander Hamilton*, 17:270–75; "Knoxville, Monday, Aug. 4," *Knoxville Gazette*; "A Charge Delivered by Judge Anderson, to the Grand Jury of the District of Hamilton, in

the Territory South of Ohio, at Oct. Term, 1794," *Knoxville Gazette*, Nov. 1, 1794. Abongphohigo's prosecution was hardly the first time Anglo-Americans had asserted criminal jurisdiction over Indians, which had a long history throughout the colonial period and afterward. *See, for instance*, Yasuhide Kawashima, *Igniting King Philip's War: The John Sassamon Murder Trial* (Lawrence, Kan.: University Press of Kansas, 2001). But those prosecutions had rested in the hands of the colonies and states; whereas Abongphohigo's trial in the territories was held under federal authority.

54. Both of these claims are, of course, subject to the limitations of the surviving court records. Most of the records of the Southwest Territory survive; Abongphohigo's prosecution is the only instance I have found where the territorial courts exercised criminal jurisdiction over Indians. The records in the Northwest Territory, especially of the General Court, are patchier. I have found only one other instance where territorial courts there exercised quasi-criminal jurisdiction over an Indian, when in 1798, Antoine Marchall, a Vincennes resident, filed suit against "John a Deleware Indian, with the advantage of only one Eye" for an assault and battery, seeking $700 in damages. But the case was dismissed after the parties failed to appear. "Antoine Marchall v. John (A Delaware Indian)" 1798; *Minutes of Common Pleas Court* (Indianapolis, Ind.: Indiana Historical Records Survey, 1940), 132; Warrant, May 14, 1798, Antoine Marchall v. John (A Delaware Indian), Knox County Court Records, Knox County Library, Vincennes, Ind.
55. "Knoxville, Monday, Aug. 4," *Knoxville Gazette*, Aug. 4, 1794; United States v. Abongphohigo, Minutes of Oyer and Terminer Court. The witness list included James Carey, the federal interpreter, and four other territorial citizens. Since Carey was the only witness who could converse with Abongphohigo, it was unclear what the other witnesses testified to. They may have been eyewitnesses, although accounts seemed to indicate that Ish was alone when he was killed.
56. "Knoxville, Monday, Aug. 4," *Knoxville Gazette*, Aug. 4, 1794; United States v. Abongphohigo, Minutes of Oyer and Terminer Court. Abongphohigo's view elided considerable debate among the Upper Creeks about the Treaty of New York: Alexander McGillivray, who negotiated the treaty, was himself an Upper Creek. Saunt, *A New Order of Things*, 67–89.
57. Vattel, *The Law of Nations*, Book II, §§ 101–03, at 312–13; Act of May 19, 1796, ch. 30, 1 Stat. 469, 472–74. Section 17 of the act, which allowed the arrest within U.S. territory of "any person" who had violated the statute, also plausibly warranted Indians' arrest and trial, as one state official would later argue. John Sevier to Benjamin Hawkins and Andrew Pickens, Apr. 19, 1797, in *Executive Journal of Governor Sevier*, 149–51.
58. Samuel R. David to John McKee, Aug. 1, 1794, Folder 5, John McKee Papers, Manuscript Division, Library of Congress; William Blount to John McKee, N.D., Folder 1, John McKee Papers, Manuscript Division, Library of Congress; Major King to William Blount, July 30, 1794, in "Knoxville, Monday, Aug. 4," *Knoxville Gazette*, Aug. 4, 1794.
59. King to Blount, July 30, 1794. On Native ideas of personal jurisdiction, *see* Katherine A. Hermes, "Jurisdiction in the Colonial Northeast: Algonquian, English and French Governance," *American Journal of Legal History* 43, no. 1 (Jan. 1999): 62–69.

60. United States v. Robert Slaughter, Sept. 1804, Box 1, Folder 17, General Court Records, Indiana State Archives; Zachariah John by Joseph Johnson v. Charles Raygan, Apr. 1794, Minutes of Oyer and Terminer Court, Hamilton District Superior Court, 28–30; John v. Raygan, Apr. 1794. Early American law generally disfavored extraterritorial application, even if the application of federal law to Indian country was not, strictly speaking, extraterritorial. *See* Kal Raustiala, *Does the Constitution Follow the Flag?: The Evolution of Territoriality in American Law* (New York: Oxford University Press, 2009), 31–58. Vattel, however, condoned punishing citizens for crimes committed against another sovereign, and suggested that the home country could punish citizens for such acts committed in a foreign jurisdiction. *See* Vattel, *The Law of Nations*, Book II, §§ 72–76, at 298–300. The idea that jurisdiction attached to people, rather than places, also had deep roots in imperial legal thought. *See* Lauren A. Benton, *A Search for Sovereignty: Law and Geography in European Empires, 1400–1900* (Cambridge [U.K.]: Cambridge University Press, 2010), 2–39.
61. King to Blount, July 30, 1794.
62. Blount to McKee, N.D.; "Conference at Tellico Blockhouse," Nov. 7, 1794, in "The Correspondence of Gen. James Robertson," *American Historical Magazine* 3, no. 4 (Oct. 1, 1898): 367–72; William Blount to Secretary of War, Nov. 10, 1794, in *TP: Vol. IV*, 364–70.
63. "Knoxville, Monday, Aug. 4," *Knoxville Gazette*, Aug. 4, 1794.
64. *Id.*; William Blount to James Robertson, Aug. 31, 1794, in "The Correspondence of Gen. James Robertson" (Oct. 1, 1898), 356.
65. "Presentment Against Delaware Indians" Sept. 1801, Box 30, Folder 4, M98, William Hayden English Papers, Indiana Historical Society; "Court of Oyer and Terminer," Nov. 10, 1801, Box 30, Folder 4, William Hayden English Papers. Wapikinomouk and Matayhikan are spelled inconsistently in the historical record; I have adopted the spellings from the court record. The examinations spelled the name "Wapihinomock," while the presentment recorded "Matashikan."
66. "Examination of Johny," Oct. 29, 1801, Box 30, Folder 4, William Hayden English Papers; "Examination of Wapihinomock," Oct. 29, 1801, Box 30, Folder 4, William Hayden English Papers; "[Second] Examination of Wapihinomock," Oct. 29, 1801, Box 30, Folder 4, William Hayden English Papers. A brief account of the trial can also be found in James Joseph Buss, *Winning the West with Words: Language and Conquest in the Lower Great Lakes* (Norman: University of Oklahoma Press, 2013).
67. "Examination of Johny," Oct. 29, 1801; "Examination of Wapihinomock," Oct. 29, 1801; "[Second] Examination of Wapihinomock," Oct. 29, 1801. The only meaningful discrepancy between the testimony of Johny and Wapihinomock was that Johny testified that Harrison asked to accompany them toward Kaskaskia, while Wapihinomock testified that he planned to accompany them toward the Spanish lands.
68. Examination of Johny," Oct. 29, 1801; "Examination of Wapihinomock," Oct. 29, 1801; "[Second] Examination of Wapihinomock," Oct. 29, 1801.
69. Examination of Johny," Oct. 29, 1801; "Examination of Wapihinomock," Oct. 29, 1801; "[Second] Examination of Wapihinomock," Oct. 29, 1801; "Court of Oyer and Terminer," Nov. 10, 1801. The treaty basis for Wapikinomouk's extradition is unclear

and was never discussed. In the Treaty of San Lorenzo, the Spanish pledged to restrain "her Indians" from attacking U.S. citizens. Treaty of Friendship, Limits, and Navigation, Art. V, U.S.-Spain, Oct. 27, 1795, 8 Stat. 138. Similarly, in the Treaty of Fort Harmar, the Delawares had promised to "deliver up" any member who had committed a murder "on any of the citizens of the United States," although this provision's continued force after the Treaty of Greenville was unclear. Treaty of Fort Harmar, Art. V, U.S.-Wyandots et al., Jan. 9, 1789, 7 Stat. 28.

70. For works exploring prior efforts to prosecute whites for crimes against Indians, *see* Jenny Hale Pulsipher, *Subjects unto the Same King: Indians, English, and the Contest for Authority in Colonial New England* (Philadelphia: University of Pennsylvania Press, 2005), 136–58; Gregory Evans Dowd, *War Under Heaven: Pontiac, the Indian Nations & the British Empire* (Baltimore: Johns Hopkins University Press, 2002), 174–211.
71. "Address of Governor St. Clair to the Territorial Legislature, at the Opening of the Second Session, at Chillicothe" Nov. 5, 1800, in *SCP*, 2:501–10; Silas Dinsmore to John Sevier, Mar. 8, 1797, Box 2, Folder 2, John Sevier Papers, 1796–1801, First Administration, Governor's Papers, Tennessee State Library and Archive.
72. Josiah Harmar to Henry Knox, Mar. 18, 1787, Vol. 28, Letterbook B, at 55–59, *JHP*; Henry Knox to George Washington, Dec. 27, 1790, in *PGW:PS*, 7:121–27; Washington to Pendleton, Jan. 22, 1795.
73. Northwest Ordinance, ch. 8, 1 Stat. 50 (1789). I explore this aspect of territorial governance more fully elsewhere. Gregory Ablavsky, "Administrative Constitutionalism and the Northwest Ordinance," *University of Pennsylvania Law Review* 167 (2019): 1631–67.
74. David Campbell to President Washington, Nov. 9, 1791, in *PGW:PS*, 9:157–58. On the absence of federal appeal, *see* Arthur St. Clair to Secretary of State, in *TP: Vol. II*, 499–500; Clarke v. Bazadone, 5 U.S. (1 Cranch) 212 (U.S. 1803). In the Northwest Territory, there was a single appellate court known as the "General" or "Supreme" Court, while the Southwest Territory maintained North Carolinian practice and organized three regional "Superior Courts." Literature on these territorial courts is relatively sparse. Exceptions include Andrew Cayton, "Law and Authority in the Northwest Territory," in Michael Les Benedict and John F. Winkler eds., *The History of Ohio Law* (Athens: Ohio University Press, 2004), 13–39; Toomey, "'Doing Justice to Suitors.'" William Blume published a series of law review articles focused specifically on territorial courts in Michigan. *See* William Wirt Blume, "Civil Procedure on the American Frontier a Study of the Records of a Court of Common Pleas of the Northwest and Indiana Territories (1796–1805)," *Michigan Law Review* 56 (1958): 161; William Wirt Blume, "Legislation on the American Frontier: Adoption of Laws by Governor and Judges: Northwest Territory 1788–1798; Indiana Territory 1800–1804; Michigan Territory 1805–1823," *Michigan Law Review* 60, no. 3 (1962): 317–72; William Wirt Blume and Elizabeth Gaspar Brown, "Territorial Courts and Law: Unifying Factors in the Development of American Legal Institutions: Part I. Establishment of a Standardized Judicial System," *Michigan Law Review* 61, no. 1 (1962): 39–106; William Wirt Blume and Elizabeth Gaspar Brown,

"Territorial Courts and Law: Unifying Factors in the Development of American Legal Institutions: Part II. Influences Tending to Unify Territorial Law," *Michigan Law Review* 61, no. 3 (1963): 467–538.

75. Gov. Arthur St. Clair to Secretary of War, Apr. 19, 1791, in *SCP*, 203–05; Act of July 22, 1790, § 5; Act of Mar. 1, 1793, § 10.
76. "Charge to Grand Jury, General Court," Box 1, Folder 1, Local Government Records, Marietta College Library (this document is dated July 1788 in the archival collection, but internal evidence suggests that a date of 1794 or 1795, as Putnam references the 1793 version of the Trade and Intercourse Act [replaced in 1796] as well as the 1794 Whiskey Rebellion); David Campbell to Secretary of State, Feb. 25, 1792, in *TP: Vol. IV*, 121–28; David Campbell to President, Nov. 9, 1791, *TP: Vol. IV*, 101–02; Josiah Harmar to Henry Knox, Mar. 18, 1787, Vol. 28, Letterbook A, at 55–59, *JHP*.
77. "Report of Henry Knox to President Washington," Dec. 29, 1794, Reel 2: Territory SW of the Ohio River, M200, Senate Territorial Papers, U.S. National Archives; "Charge to Grand Jury, General Court"; Secretary of War to William Blount, Apr. 22, 1792, in *TP: Vol. IV*, 137–42; Gov. Arthur St. Clair to Henry Knox, Jan. 27, 1788, in *SCP*, 2:40–42; On federal officials' embrace of civility in their treatment of Natives, *see* David Andrew Nichols, *Red Gentlemen & White Savages: Indians, Federalists, and the Search for Order on the American Frontier* (Charlottesville: University of Virginia Press, 2008).
78. Arthur St. Clair to Governor Shelby, June 20, 1795, Reel 1: Territory Northwest of the River Ohio, M200, Senate Territorial Papers (microfilm), U.S. National Archives; Winthrop Sargent to Governor of Kentucky, Jan. 3, 1798, in *TP: Vol. III*, 495–96; Winthrop Sargent to Harry Toulman, Secretary of Kentucky, Apr. 20, 1798, in *TP: Vol. III*, 505; U.S. CONST. art. IV, § 2. A similar riot occurred in Kentucky in 1802, in which an extradition request from Governor Harrison of the Indiana Territory for an alleged murderer of an Indian prompted a constitutional debate over the scope and nature of federal criminal jurisdiction. *See* Thomas Jefferson, "Observations on the Common Law and Hardin's Case," Nov. 11, 1802, in *PTJ:MS*, 38:668–71; "Albert Gallatin's Opinion on the Common Law and Hardin's Case," c. Nov. 11, 1802, in *PTJ:MS*, 38:672–74.
79. Rufus Putnam, "Draft Notices to the Inhabitants of Vincennes," Sept. 16, 1792, Box 2, Folder 4, Rufus Putnam Papers, Marietta College Library; Judges Parsons and Varnum to Arthur St. Clair, July 31, 1788, in *SCP*, 2:69–72; G. Turner to Arthur St. Clair, Oct. 25, 1790, Reel 3, *ASCP*. The Cherokee Richard Finnelson, for instance, was allowed to swear a deposition once he "declar[ed] that he believed in the doctrines contained in the New Testament, and its divine authority." "Information by Richard Finnelson," Nov. 1, 1792, in *ASP:IA*, 288–91. In Wapikinomouk's trial recounted earlier, "Johny the Delaware" was "Sworn with an uplifted hand after the Custom and manner of the Indians." "Court of Oyer and Terminer," Nov. 10, 1801. On debates over non-Christian testimony during this period, *see* Jud Campbell, "Testimonial Exclusions and Religious Freedom in Early America," *Law & History Review* 37, no. 2 (2019): 431–92; Ronald P. Formisano and Stephen Pickering, "The Christian Nation Debate and Witness Competency," *Journal of the Early Republic* 29, no.

2 (2009): 219–48. For a discussion of restrictions on Native testimony focused on Indiana, where the territorial legislature later adopted an affirmative bar on Indian testimony, *see* Ryan T. Schwier, "'According to the Custom of the Country': Indian Marriage, Property Rights, and Legal Testimony in the Jurisdictional Formation of Indiana Settler Society, 1717–1897" (MA thesis, Indiana University, 2011), 227–59.

80. Northwest Ordinance, *JCC*, 33:340; Blount and Pickens to Secretary of War, Aug. 6, 1793; 4 Annals of Cong. 1254 (1795).
81. Henry Vanderburgh to Winthrop Sargent, Apr. 3, 1795, Reel 4, *WSP*; St. Clair, "Report of Official Proceedings in the Illinois Country," 1796.
82. James McHenry to Arthur St. Clair, Mar. 29, 1799, Roll 4, ASC Papers; Gov. Arthur St. Clair to Secretary of State, Jan. 1796, in *TP: Vol. II*, 542. For another instance when St. Clair bemoaned a jury acquittal, *see* "Address of Governor St. Clair to the Territorial Legislature, at the Opening of the Second Session, at Chillicothe," Nov. 5, 1800, in *SCP*, 2:501–10.
83. Davidson County Court Minutes (microfilm), Vol. A, at 38, Roll 1597, Tennessee State Library and Archives; Davidson County Court Minutes (microfilm), at 41, Roll 1602, Tennessee State Library and Archives; "Cincinnati, March 26," *Centinel of the North-Western Territory*, Mar. 26, 1796. On the Vincennes indictments, *see* material in *supra* notes 35–36.
84. Jessica Lowe has described this conception of the judicial role as casting judges as "guardians of republican liberty." Jessica K. Lowe, *Murder in the Shenandoah: Making Law Sovereign in Revolutionary Virginia* (New York: Cambridge University Press, 2019), 122–41. On this view of both judges and juries, *see* John Phillip Reid, *Constitutional History of the American Revolution*, abridged ed. (Madison: University of Wisconsin Press, 1995).
85. Blount and Pickens to Secretary of War, Aug. 6, 1793.
86. Winthrop Sargent to Arthur St. Clair, Feb. 7, 1793, *TP: Vol. II*, 432–33; Winthrop Sargent to Arthur St. Clair, Jan. 20, 1793, Roll 4, *ASCP*. As territorial secretary, Sargent acted as governor during St. Clair's frequent absences. Sargent had been filling this role when, unbeknownst to him, St. Clair returned to another part of the territory. A grand jury indicted Sargent for unconstitutionally exercising St. Clair's duties. *See* Winthrop Sargent to Secretary of State, Sept. 30, 1796, in *TP: Vol. III*, 456–68.
87. "To the Inhabitants of Western America," *Centinel of the North-Western Territory*, Feb. 8, 1794; Winthrop Sargent to Justices of the Peace, Nov. 5, 1794, Reel 1, M200: Senate Territorial Papers, Microfilm, U.S. National Archives; J Lameille to Winthrop Sargent, Nov. 15, 1794, *WSP*. On the Whiskey Rebellion, *see* Thomas P. Slaughter, *The Whiskey Rebellion: Frontier Epilogue to the American Revolution* (New York: Oxford University Press, 1986).
88. Freeman Atty for County, "A True Abstract of the Testimony Offerd to the Grand Jury at a Special Court, as Taken down by the Clk," Sept. 18, 1794, Reel 7, *ASCP*; N.R. Hopkins, "Deposition," Sept. 19, 1794, Reel 7, *ASCP*. Accounts of the riot can also be found in Cayton, *The Frontier Republic*, 66–67; Cayton, "Law and Authority," 28–29.

89. Winthrop Sargent to Secretary of State, Sept. 13, 1794, in *TP: Vol. III*, 423–25; "Enclosure in Winthrop Sargent to Rufus Putnam," Oct. 6, 1794, Reel 4, *ASCP*; "A True Abstract of Testimony," Sept. 18, 1794; Hopkins, "Deposition," Sept. 19, 1794; "Testimony of James Leonard" Sept. 19, 1794, Reel 7, *ASCP*.
90. Winthrop Sargent, "Proclamation" Sept. 10, 1794, Reel 1: Territory NW of the Ohio River, M200, Senate Territorial Papers, U.S. National Archives; Winthrop Sargent to Secretary of State Randolph, Nov. 1, 1794, in *TP: Vol. III*, 426–31.
91. "[Inquiries of Winthrop Sargent]," Oct. 8, 1794, Reel 7, *ASCP*; G. Turner to Arthur St. Clair, Oct. 25, 1790, Roll 3, *ASCP*.
92. William Blount to James Robertson, Jan. 2, 1792, in *TP: Vol. IV*, 108–09; Andrew Jackson to John McKee, Jan. 30, 1793, in *PAJ*, 1:40–41. On the dispute between Sargent and the Cincinnati judges over their tenure, *see* William Gosforth et al. to Winthrop Sargent, Feb. 5, 1793, *WSP*; Winthrop Sargent to William Gosforth et al., Feb. 9, 1793, *WSP*.
93. Benjamin Hawkins to Thomas Butler, Nov. 9, 1797, in C.L Grant ed., *Letters, Journals, and Writings of Benjamin Hawkins* (Savannah, Ga.: Beehive Press, 1980), 148–49; John Cleves Symmes to Winthrop Sargent, Jan. 7, 1793, Reel 3, *WSP*; Winthrop Sargent to Arthur St. Clair, Jan. 20, 1793, Roll 4, *ASCP*; Judge Symmes to Thomas Jefferson, Jan. 23, 1802, in *TP: Vol. III*, 205–07.
94. Henry Vanderburgh to Winthrop Sargent, Apr. 3, 1795, Reel 4, *WSP*; Gov. Arthur St. Clair to Judge Turner, May 25, 1795, in *SCP*, 351; "Deposition of Christopher Wyant Esq. Sheriff of Knox County," May 9, 1795, Box 30, Folder 2, William Hayden English Family Papers, Indiana Historical Society; "Depositions of Christopher Wyant & Paul Pierre" Sept. 7, 1795, Box 1, Folder 6-6A; General Court Records, Indiana State Archives; "Recognizance Bond" Sept. 10, 1795, Box 1, Folder 4, General Court Records, Indiana State Archives. On the friendship between Symmes and Turner, *see* John Cleves Symmes to Robert Morris, June 22, 1790, in *CJCS*, 287.
95. Gov. Arthur St. Clair to Winthrop Sargent, Apr. 28, 1795, in *SCP*, 2:340–43; *Letter from the Attorney General, Accompanying His Report on the Petition of Sundry Inhabitants of the County of St. Clair* (Philadelphia: n.p., 1796); "Circuit Court, Oct. Term, 1795," Northwest Territory Archives, Burton Historical Collection, Detroit Public Library; President to Secretary of State, Apr. 5, 1793, in *TP: Vol. II*, 450.
96. Knox to President, July 7, 1789; Vitrivius, "Cincinnati, Sept. 27," *Centinel of the North-Western Territory*, Sept. 27, 1794.
97. Act of May 19, 1796, ch. 30, 1 Stat. 469, § 5; 3 Annals of Cong. 750–52 (1792). The most controversial addition to the Trade and Intercourse Acts, concerning the forfeiture of land, is discussed in Chapter Seven.
98. Nicholas Guyatt, *Bind Us Apart: How Enlightened Americans Invented Racial Segregation* (New York: Basic Books, 2016), 4–13. On the federal government's role in Removal, *see* Ethan Davis, "An Administrative Trail of Tears: Indian Removal," *American Journal of Legal History* 50, no. 1 (2008): 49–100; Rockwell, *Indian Affairs and the Administrative State*, 159–216.
99. Ford, *Settler Sovereignty*, 183–98.

Chapter 5

1. Piomingo to General Robertson, June 17, 1793, in *ASP:IA*, 466; "A Talk Delivered [to] Genl Joseph Martin by Piamingo [*sic*] Chief Warrior of the Chickasaw Nation," Sept. 28, 1789, Ayer MS 722, Newberry Library; "Extract of a Letter from General James Robertson, of Mero District, to General Smith, Dated Nashville," July 20, 1793, in *ASP:IA*, 465. Anglo-Americans sometimes referred to Piomingo as the Mountain Leader. For background on Piomingo, *see* Atkinson, *Splendid Land, Splendid People*, 11–70; Duval, *Independence Lost*, 304–09. On the Chickasaw alliance with the United States, *see* Wendy St. Jean, "How the Chickasaws Saved the Cumberland Settlement in the 1790s," *Tennessee Historical Quarterly* 68, no. 1 (Apr. 1, 2009): 2–19.
2. Piomingo to Robertson, June 17, 1793; Piomingo to Agent, Apr. 29, 1793, 5XX27, Draper Manuscripts, Reel 117, Wisconsin Historical Society, Madison, Wis.
3. Piomingo to Robertson, June 17, 1793.
4. On cultures of violence in the early American borderlands, *see* Ned Blackhawk, *Violence over the Land: Indians and Empires in the Early American West* (Cambridge, Mass.: Harvard University Press, 2006); Silver, *Our Savage Neighbors*; Karl Jacoby, *Shadows at Dawn: A Borderlands Massacre and the Violence of History* (New York: Penguin Press, 2008); James Brooks, *Captives & Cousins: Slavery, Kinship, and Community in the Southwest Borderlands* (Chapel Hill: University of North Carolina Press, 2002); Ann M. Little, *Abraham in Arms: War and Gender in Colonial New England* (Philadelphia: University of Pennsylvania Press, 2007); Jill Lepore, *The Name of War: King Philip's War and the Origins of American Identity* (New York: Knopf, 1998).
5. Thomas Sheridan, *A Complete Dictionary of the English Language, Both with Regard to Sound and Meaning*, 5th ed. (Philadelphia: Printed by William Young, 1789), entry for "war"; Samuel Johnson, *Dictionary of the English Language: In Which the Words Are Deduced from Their Originals, and Illustrated in Their Different Significations by Examples from the Best Writers*, 6th ed. (London: Printed by J.F. and C. Rivington et al., 1785), 2:[mxx]; Vattel, *Law of Nations*, 469.
6. U.S. CONST. art. 1, §§ 8, 10. Legal scholars have hotly debated the division of the war power between the president and Congress; the issue of *state* and local authority to engage in conflicts has received much less attention. For representative works, *see* William Michael Treanor, "Fame the Founding and the Power to Declare War," *Cornell Law Review* 82 (1997): 695; John C. Yoo, "The Continuation of Politics by Other Means: The Original Understanding of War Powers," *California Law Review* 84, no. 2 (1996): 167–305; John Hart Ely, *War and Responsibility: Constitutional Lessons of Vietnam and Its Aftermath* (Princeton, N.J.: Princeton University Press, 1993); Adam Mendel, "The First AUMF: The Northwest Indian War, 1790–1795, and the War on Terror," *University of Pennsylvania Journal of Constitutional Law* 17 (2016).
7. A growing literature has explored the laws of war, including as applied to Natives, and the unsettled questions of legitimate violence into the nineteenth century. *See* John Fabian Witt, *Lincoln's Code: The Laws of War in American History* (New York: Free Press, 2012); Deborah A. Rosen, *Border Law: The First Seminole War and American Nationhood* (Cambridge, Mass.: Harvard University Press, 2015), 40–70.

8. Secretary of War to Gov. Arthur St. Clair, Dec. 19, 1789, in *TP: Vol. II*, 224–26.
9. On mobs in early America, *see* Pauline Maier, "Popular Uprisings and Civil Authority in Eighteenth-Century America," *William and Mary Quarterly*, Third Series, 27, no. 1 (Jan. 1970): 4–35; Paul A. Gilje, *Rioting in America* (Bloomington, Ind.: Indiana University Press, 1999), 12–84.
10. On the Revolution in Shawnee and Cherokee territory, *see* Colin G. Calloway, *The American Revolution in Indian Country: Crisis and Diversity in Native American Communities* (Cambridge, [U.K.]: Cambridge University Press, 1995), 158–212; Richard Gildrie, "Tennessee in the American Revolution: A Reconsideration," in Kristofer Ray ed., *Before the Volunteer State*, 110–22; Patrick Griffin, *American Leviathan: Empire, Nation, and Revolutionary Frontier* (New York: Hill and Wang, 2007), 125–50; Patrick Griffin, *America's Revolution* (New York: Oxford University Press, 2012), 157–190; Tom Hatley, *The Dividing Paths: Cherokees and South Carolinians Through the Revolutionary Era* (New York: Oxford University Press, 1995), 192–228.
11. Capt. W. Finney to Josiah Harmar, Oct. 31, 1786, Vol. 4, *JHP*; Josiah Harmar to John Francis Hamtramck, Nov. 14, 1786, Vol. 28, Letterbook B, at 5, *JHP*; "Information from Mr. Lewis Westell," Nov. 14, 1786, Vol. 4, *JHP*; Josiah Harmar to Henry Knox, Nov. 15, 1786, in *Papers of Arthur St. Clair*, 2:18–19; Josiah Harmar to Thomas Hutchins, Dec. 5, 1786, Vol. 28, Letterbook B, at 11–12, *JHP*; Arthur Campbell to Edmund Randolph, Mar. 9, 1787, Cherokee Collection (microfilm), Tennessee State Library and Archives. The precise numbers in the accounts varied, positing somewhere between twenty-seven and thirty-six prisoners, seven to eleven Shawnees killed, and the militia suffering one to three casualties of their own.
12. "Depositions from Greene Co. in Defense of John Sevier, Concerning the Murder of Certain Indians," Oct. 25, 1788, Petitions Rejected or Nor Acted Upon Folder, GASR Nov.–Dec. 1788, Box 1, North Carolina State Archives. Additional accounts of the attack appear in Richard Winn to Henry Knox, Aug. 5, 1788, in *ASP:IA*, 28; "Deposition Apparently Enclosed with Letter from Alex. Drumgoole to Governor Johnston, April 4, 1789 (enclosure Only)," Nov. 5, 1789, Joint Standing Comm., Committee on Indian Affairs, GASR Nov.–Dec. 1789, Box 1, North Carolina State Archives; Joseph Martin to Henry Knox, Jan. 15, 1789, in *ASP:IA*, 46.
13. Edmund Randolph to Henry Innes, May 1, 1787, Folder 1, Harry Innes Papers, Manuscript Division, Library of Congress; "Proclamation of the Governor," July 29, 1788, Committee on Ind Affairs Folder, GASR Nov.–Dec. 1788, Box 1, North Carolina State Archives; *JCC*, 34:368–71; Knox to President of the United States, July 7, 1789.
14. Adair, *History of the American Indians*, "Mr. McKee's Report to Governor Blount," Mar. 28, 1793, in *ASP:IA*, 444–46; Henry Knox to President Washington, in *PGW:PS*, 5:140–47; Patrick Henry to Virginia Delegates, July 5, 1786, in *Papers of James Monroe*, 2:315–18.
15. John Watts to John Sevier, Mar. 4, 1797, Box 2, Folder 2, John Sevier Papers, 1796–1801, First Administration, Governor's Papers, Tennessee State Library and Archive; John Sevier to James McHenry, June 6, 1797, in "Executive Journal of Governor Sevier," 2:136; George Washington to Tobias Lear, Apr. 3, 1791, in *PGW:PS*, 8:49–50.

16. "Report of Antoine Gamelin," May 17, 1790, in *SCP*, 2:155–60.
17. William Blount to Secretary of War, Mar. 20, 1793, in *TP: Vol. IV*, 244–47; William Blount to Secretary of War, Nov. 8, 1792, in *TP: Vol. IV*, 208–16; James Seagrove to Secretary of War, Sept. 17, 1793, in *ASP:IA*, 409–10; William Blount to Secretary of War, May 28, 1793, in *TP: Vol. IV*, 262–64. On the role of rumor in Native relations during this period, *see* Gregory Evans Dowd, *Groundless: Rumors, Legends, and Hoaxes on the Early American Frontier* (Baltimore: Johns Hopkins University Press, 2015).
18. Reid, *A Law of Blood*, 201–28; Calloway, *Pen and Ink Witchcraft*, 13–48, 97–118; Heckewelder, *History, Manners, and Customs*, 185–86, 335.
19. "Treaty of Holston—June & July, 1791. Between Gov. Wm. Blount & the Cherokees" (n.d.), 15U1-59, Draper Manuscripts, Reel 58, Wisconsin Historical Society, Madison, Wis.; Andrew Jackson to John McKee, May 16, 1794, in *PAJ*, 1:48–49.
20. Bold Hunter and Others to Secretary Smith, June 18, 1793, in *ASP:IA*, 1:462; John McKee to Glass and Other Chiefs of the Lower Towns of the Cherokees, July 14, 1794, in *CJR*, 352. On the parallel challenges for Native and federal leaders to control their "unruly young men," *see* David Andrew Nichols, *Red Gentlemen & White Savages: Indians, Federalists, and the Search for Order on the American Frontier* (Charlottesville: University of Virginia Press, 2008), 57–75.
21. William Blount to Alexander Kelley and Littlepage Sims, Dec. 1, 1795, in *TP: Vol. IV*, 408–10; William Blount to Secretary of War, May 16, 1792, in *ASP:IA*, 1:267. A similar description of "the policy of half war, half peace" appears in P.Q., "For the Gazette," *Knoxville Gazette*, July 13, 1793.
22. Secretary of War to William Blount, Apr. 22, 1792, in *TP: Vol. IV*, 137–42; Henry Knox to President Washington, Jan. 22, 1791, in *PGW:PS*, 262–71.
23. Secretary of War to Blount, Apr. 22, 1792; Secretary of War to President, Oct. 9, 1792, in *TP: Vol. IV*, 194.
24. U.S. CONST. art. 1 § 10; Thomas Jefferson, "Opinion on Certain Georgia Land Grants," May 3, 1790, in *PTJ:MS*, 16:406–07; Charles Pinckney to President Washington, Sept. 30, 1792, in *PGW:PS*, 11:175–80. On federal fiscal-military authority, *see* Edling, *A Revolution in Favor of Government*; on the small federal army at the time of the Constitution's adoption, *see* Richard H. Kohn, *Eagle and Sword: The Federalists and the Creation of the Military Establishment in America, 1783–1802* (New York: Free Press, 1975).
25. Vattel, *Law of Nations*, 500–01. On the significance of the law of nations in early American governance, *see* Golove and Hulsebosch, "A Civilized Nation"; Gould, *Among the Powers of the Earth*; Max M. Edling, "Peace Pact and Nation: An International Interpretation of the Constitution of the United States," *Past & Present* 240, no. 1 (Aug. 1, 2018): 267–303. On the Washington administration's views of Native nations under the law of nations, *see* Gregory Ablavsky, "Species of Sovereignty: Native Nationhood, the United States, and International Law, 1783–1795," *Journal of American History* 106, no. 3 (2019): 591–613.
26. Northwest Ordinance, *JCC*, 34:340. Jeffrey Ostler has stressed how this language also *empowered* the United States. Jeffrey Ostler, "'Just and Lawful War' as Genocidal War

in the (United States) Northwest Ordinance and Northwest Territory, 1787–1832," *Journal of Genocide Research* 18, no. 1 (Jan. 2, 2016): 1–20.

27. John Francis Hamtramck to Josiah Harmar, Aug. 31, 1788, in Gayle Thornbrough ed., *Outpost on the Wabash, 1787-1791; Letters of Brigadier General Josiah Harmar and Major John Francis Hamtramck, and Other Letters and Documents Selected from the Harmar Papers in the William L. Clements Library* (Indianapolis: Indiana Historical Society, 1957), 114–20.
28. Secretary of War to St. Clair, Dec. 19, 1789; Secretary of War to William Blount, Oct. 9, 1792, in *TP: Vol. IV*, 194–95.
29. Henry Knox to Gov. Arthur St. Clair, Sept. 14, 1790, in *SCP*, 2:181–83; Henry Knox to Gov. Arthur St. Clair, June 7, 1790, in *SCP*, 2:147–48; "To the United States Senate and House of Representatives," Dec. 8, 1790, in *PGW:PS*, 7:45–49.
30. "Summary Statement of the Situation of the Frontiers by the Secretary of War," May 27, 1790, in *SCP*, II:146–47; Henry Knox to President Washington, Feb. 22, 1791, in *PGW:PS*, 7:402–15; Act of Sept. 29, 1789, ch. 25, § 5, 1 Stat. 95, 96. On this authorization, *see* Mendel, "The First AUMF," 1318–46.
31. "Report of a Special Committee of the House of Representatives on the Failure of the Expedition Against the Indians," Mar. 27, 1792, *SCP*, 2:286–99. For further discussion of the role of the militia in U.S. military defeats, *see* Ebenezer Denny, "Copy of Lieut. Denny's Report to the Secretary at War" Jan. 1, 1791, Reel 3, ASCP.
32. Henry Knox, "A View of the Present State of the Military Force of the United States," Mar. 19, 1791, Northwest Territory Collection, 1721–1825, Indiana Historical Society. On St. Clair's defeat, *see* Calloway, *The Victory With No Name*; Kohn, *Eagle and Sword*.
33. Tobias Lear to George Washington, July 21, 1792, in *PGW:PS*, 10:556–59; "The Causes of the Existing Hostilities Between the United States, and Certain Tribes of Indians North-West of the Ohio, Stated and Explained from Official and Authentic Documents, and Published in Obedience to the Orders of the President of the United States," Jan. 26, 1792, in *TP: Vol. II*, 359–66. A number of works have suggested that the Northwest Indian War cost $5 million, which they suggested was at least 80% of the federal budget: *see, e.g.*, Stephen Aron, "Lessons in Conquest: Towards a Greater Western History," *Pacific Historical Review* 63, no. 2 (1994): 139. This claim seems to stem from John Chester Miller, *The Federalist Era 1789–1801* (New York: Harper, 1960), 183. Miller's estimate of a cost of $5 million is perhaps even conservative: writing in 1796, Albert Gallatin put the war's cost in the years 1792, 1794, and 1795 alone at $4.5 million. Albert Gallatin, *A Sketch of the Finances of the United States* (New York: Printed by William A. Davis, 1796), 58. However, this amount does not seem to have been as high a proportion of the federal budget as Miller suggests. If we mean "budget" as a synonym for nondebt expenditures, those totaled nearly $10 million annually during the three years that Gallatin tracks. Based on this data, the precise ratio of the war's cost to overall nondebt expenditures is 46%. Susan B. Carter et al., "Table Ea636–643: Federal Government Expenditure, by Major Function: 1789–1970," in *Historical Statistics of the United States Millennial Edition Online* (New York: Cambridge University Press, 2006). Expenditures on the war

totaled a lower but still impressive proportion of federal *revenue* during those same three years: 29.6%. Table Ea584–587: Federal Government Finances—Revenue, Expenditure, and Debt: 1789–1939, in *Historical Statistics*.

34. U.S.-Wyandot Nation et al., Aug. 3, 1795, 7 Stat. 49. On the negotiation of the Treaty of Greenville, *see* Daniel F. Harrison, "Change Amid Continuity, Innovation within Tradition: Wampum Diplomacy at the Treaty of Greenville, 1795," *Ethnohistory* 64, no. 2 (Apr. 1, 2017): 191–215; Andrew Cayton, "'Noble Actors' upon 'the Theatre of Honour': Power and Civility in the Treaty of Greenville," in Andrew R.L Cayton and Fredrika J. Teute eds., *Contact Points: American Frontiers from the Mohawk Valley to the Mississippi, 1750–1830* (Chapel Hill: University of North Carolina Press, 1998), 235–69.
35. "Copy of a Letter from John McKee to His Excellency Governor Blount," *Knoxville Gazette*, June 19, 1794. One study of the *Knoxville Gazette* counted 190 notices of deaths at Cherokee and Creek hands between Nov. 1791 and Sept. 1795. *See* George F. Bentley, "Printers and Printing in the Southwest Territory, 1790–1796," *Tennessee Historical Quarterly* 8, no. 4 (Dec. 1, 1949): 332, 336.
36. Secretary of War to William Blount, Aug. 15, 1792, in *TP: Vol. IV*, 162–64; Secretary of War to William Blount, Nov. 26, 1792, in *TP: Vol. IV*, 220–26.
37. Secretary of War to Governor of Georgia, July 11, 1792, in *ASP:IA*, 256; Henry Knox to George Washington, Feb. 22, 1791, in *PGW:PS*, 7:402–15.
38. "Mr. Roulstone," *Knoxville Gazette*, Aug. 13, 1793; "Memorial to Congress," Sept. 18, 1794, in *TP: Vol. IV*, 354–55 n.21; *Journal of the Proceedings of the Legislative Council, of the Territory of the United States of America, South of the River Ohio. Begun and Held at Knoxville the 25th Day of Aug., 1794* (Knoxville: Printed by George Roulstone, printer to the Territory, 1794).
39. Secretary Smith to Secretary of War, Oct. 27, 1792, in *TP: Vol. IV*, 198–99; William Blount to John Steele, Nov. 8, 1792, Vol. 1, John Steele Papers, North Carolina State Archives.
40. James White to William Blount, Mar. 19, 1795, in *TP: Vol. IV*, 385–86. Secretary of War to President, Oct. 9, 1792, in *TP: Vol. IV*, 194.
41. William Blount to James Robertson, 1795, in *CJR*, 93; William Blount to John Gray Blount, Sept. 19, 1793, in *JGBP*, 2:314–15.
42. Robert Anderson to Governor of South Carolina, Sept. 20, 1792, in *ASP:IA*, 317–18; William Blount, "Order to Lieutenant Colonel Kelly," Jan. 23, 1793, in *ASP:IA*, 435; "Proclamation of Governor Blount," Jan. 28, 1793, in *TP: Vol. IV*, 235–36; William Blount to Secretary of War, Nov. 8, 1792, in *TP: Vol. IV*, 208–16; Lieutenant Colonel White to William Blount, Jan. 30, 1793, in *ASP:IA*, 435; William Blount to Secretary of War, Mar. 20, 1793, in *TP: Vol. IV*, 244–47.
43. *Letter from the Secretary at War, Inclosing His Report on the Petition of Hugh Lawson White. 26th Dec., 1796* (Philadelphia: William Ross, 1797).
44. *Letter from the Secretary at War*; "Knoxville, Saturday, June 15," *Knoxville Gazette*, June 15, 1793; "Major King and Daniel Carmichael's Report to Secretary Smith, Referred to in the Foregoing Letter," June 12, 1793, in *ASP:IA*, 459; James Davis and The War Club to John McKee, Jan. 10, 1794, Folder 5, John McKee Papers,

Manuscript Division, Library of Congress; J McDonald to William Panton, June 22, 1793, in Roberta Corbitt and D.C. Corbitt, "Papers from the Spanish Archives Relating to Tennessee and the Old Southwest, 1783–1800," *East Tennessee Historical Society's Publications* 33 (1961): 61, 77. Initial reports also erroneously indicated that Scolocutta's wife Betty was killed in the attack.

45. "General Robertson's Order to Major Ore," Sept. 6, 1794, in *ASP:IA*, 530; James Robertson to William Blount, Oct. 1, 1794, in "The Correspondence of Gen. James Robertson" (Oct. 1, 1898), 360–62; James Robertson to William Blount, Oct. 8, 1794, in *TP: Vol. IV*, 358–59.
46. James Robertson to William Blount, Oct. 1, 1794, in "The Correspondence of Gen. James Robertson" (Oct. 1, 1898), 360–62; James Ore to Governor Blount, Sept. 24, 1794, in *Letter from the Secretary of War, Inclosing His Report on the Petition of Stephen Cantrill* (Philadelphia: Printed by Joseph Gales, 1798), 7–8; "Nickajack Expedition, Sept. 1794," n.d., 6XX72a, Draper Manuscripts, Reel 117, Wisconsin Historical Society, Madison, Wis.; Henry Knox to Governor Blount, Dec. 29, 1794, in *Letter from the Secretary of War*, 19–23.
47. Doublehead to Secretary Smith, June 15, 1793, in *ASP:IA*, 460, Secretary of War to William Blount, Aug. 26, 1793, in *TP: Vol. IV*, 299–300.
48. A Fellow Sufferer, "For the Gazette," *Knoxville Gazette*, June 15, 1793; Abishai Thomas to John Gray Blount, Oct. 26, 1794, in *JGBP*, 2:447–48.
49. William Blount to Alexander Kelley and Littlepage Sims, Dec. 1, 1795, in *TP: Vol. IV*, 408–10; Anonymous to James Robertson, July 10, 1792, in "The Correspondence of Gen. James Robertson" (Jan. 1, 1897), 68–69; Acting Governor Smith to Secretary of War, July 19, 1793, in *TP: Vol. IV*, 280–83; P.Q., "For the Gazette," *Knoxville Gazette*, July 13, 1793.
50. Secretary of War to Blount, Aug. 26, 1793; Acting Governor Smith to Secretary of War, June 13, 1793, in *TP: Vol. IV*, 271–72; Acting Governor Smith to Secretary of War, June 22, 1793, in *TP: Vol. IV*, 276–77; "Report of Henry Knox on the Southwest Frontiers," Dec. 13, 1793, in *ASP:IA*, 363; Doublehead to Smith, June 15, 1793; Hanging Maw to Secretary Smith, June 15, 1793, in *ASP:IA*, 460.
51. William Blount to John Gray Blount, Sept. 19, 1793, in *JGBP*, 2:314–15; William Blount to John Gray Blount, Oct. 22, 1793, in *JGBP*, 2:323–26; William Blount to John Sevier, June 16, 1793, 4XX32, Draper Manuscripts, Reel 116, Wisconsin Historical Society, Madison, Wis.; Thomas to John Gray Blount, Oct. 26, 1794.
52. William Blount to James Robertson, Sept. 9, 1794, in "The Correspondence of Gen. James Robertson" (Oct. 1, 1898), 357.
53. A Fellow Sufferer, "For the Gazette," *Knoxville Gazette*, June 15, 1793; "To the Honorable Judge of the Territory of the United States of America South of the River Ohio," *Knoxville Gazette*, Nov. 1, 1794; "A Charge Delivered by Judge Anderson," *Knoxville Gazette*, Nov. 1, 1794.
54. Blount to Robertson, Sept. 9, 1794; William Blount to Judge Campbell, Judge McNairy, and Judge Anderson, Aug. 28, 1793, *TP: Vol. IV*, 301–03; A Fellow Sufferer, *Knoxville Gazette*, June 15, 1793; "A Charge Delivered by Judge Anderson," *Knoxville Gazette*, Nov. 1, 1794.

55. X, "For the Knoxville Gazette," *Knoxville Gazette*, Apr. 20, 1793; P.Q., *Knoxville Gazette*, July 13, 1793.
56. Swan, "Report from Caleb Swan to Henry Knox," May 2, 1791.
57. "Extract of a Letter from General James Robertson, of Mero District, to General Smith, Dated Nashville," July 20, 1793, in *ASP:IA*, 465; "Minutes of Information given Governor Blount by James Carey, One of the Interpreter of the United States, in the Nation.," Nov. 3, 1792, in *ASP:IA*, 327–29. On perceived rarity of Native rapes on the frontier, *see* Joyce E. Chaplin, *Subject Matter: Technology, the Body, and Science on the Anglo-American Frontier, 1500–1676* (Cambridge, Mass.: Harvard University Press, 2001), 262; Sharon Block, *Rape and Sexual Power in Early America* (Chapel Hill: University of North Carolina Press, 2006), 221–30. One exception is the somewhat ambiguous rape accusation against a Creek presented in Ford, *Settler Sovereignty*, 108–16.
58. James Wilkinson to Winthrop Sargent, Nov. 17, 1797, Reel 4, WSP; "Mr. McKee's Report to Governor Blount," Mar. 28, 1793, in *ASP:IA*, 444–46; "The Information of Samuel Fulton, Native of Fayettville, North Carolina," June 21, 1793, in *ASP:IA*, 463.
59. "Talk from the Heads of the Upper and Lower Creeks, by Order of the Mad Dog . . . to Be Forwarded to His Excellency General Washington," July 21, 1793, *ASP:IA*, 408; "Conference at Tellico Blockhouse," Dec. 28, 1794, *CJR*, 82–94.
60. "Mr. McKee's Report to Governor Blount," Mar. 28, 1793; William Blount to Bloody Fellow, Sept. 13, 1792, in H. Dearborn et al., *CJR*, 74–76; "Conference at Tellico Blockhouse," Dec. 28, 1794.
61. "Anecdote," *Knoxville Gazette*, June 19, 1794; "Knoxville, Saturday, June 15," *Knoxville Gazette*, June 15, 1793; "Knoxville, June 2," *Knoxville Gazette*, June 2, 1792. On the association between women and novel reading in the early republic, *see* Cathy N. Davidson, *Revolution and the Word: The Rise of the Novel in America* (Oxford: Oxford University Press, 2004).
62. James Robertson to William Blount, Mar. 12, 1793, in *ASP:IA*, 441–42.
63. James Ore to Governor Blount, Sept. 24, 1794, in *Letter from the Secretary of War*, 7–8; Smith to Pickering, Oct. 1, 1795.
64. "Mr. Roulstone," *Knoxville Gazette*, Aug. 13, 1793; Andrew Jackson to John McKee, May 16, 1794, in *PAJ*, 1:48–49; Similarly, James Robertson argued that Ore's expedition was justified "by the usage of Nations in such cases." James Robertson to William Blount, Oct. 8, 1794, in *TP: Vol. IV*, 358–59.
65. U.S. CONST. art. I, § 10; A Fellow Citizen, "For the Knoxville Gazette," *Knoxville Gazette*, Apr. 6, 1793; "To the Congress of the United States in Session at Philadelphia," *Knoxville Gazette*, Mar. 27, 1794; "Mr. Roulstone," *Knoxville Gazette*, Aug. 13, 1793; William Cocke, "For the Gazette," *Knoxville Gazette*, Dec. 29, 1792; Daniel Smith to Timothy Pickering, Oct. 1, 1795, in *Letter from the Secretary at War, Inclosing His Report on the Petition of Hugh Lawson White* (Philadelphia: William Ross, 1797).
66. William Barry Grove and Alex D. Orr to John Steele, Dec. 12, 1794, in John Steele, *The Papers of John Steele*, ed. Henry McGilbert Wagstaff (Raleigh, N.C.: Edwards & Broughton, 1924), 1:127–31.

67. "Congress of the United States, House of Representatives, Friday, June 6," *Knoxville Gazette*, Sept. 6, 1794; 4 Annals of Cong. 123–26, 696–97, 774–79, 1253–70 (1794–95).
68. Henry Knox to President of the United States, July 7, 1789, in *ASP:IA*, 53; George Washington to the United States Senate and House of Representatives, Jan. 30, 1794, in *PGW:PS*, 15:157–58.
69. 4 Annals of Cong. 1253–70 (1795). On prerevolutionary plans to deploy courts material, *see* Hulsebosch, *Constituting Empire*, 109–22; on martial law's global history, *see* Lauren A. Benton, *A Search for Sovereignty: Law and Geography in European Empires, 1400–1900* (Cambridge, [U.K.]: Cambridge University Press, 2010), 163–221. On martial law as practiced in the early United States, *see* Bradley J. Nicholson, "Courts-Martial in the Legion Army: American Military Law in the Early Republic, 1792–1796," *Military Law Review* 144 (1994): 77–109.
70. Hulsebosch, *Constituting Empire*, 157–68; Lawrence B.A. Hatter, *Citizens of Convenience: The Imperial Origins of American Nationhood on the U.S.-Canadian Border* (Charlottesville: University of Virginia Press, 2016), 78–103; Gregory Ablavsky, "Administrative Constitutionalism and the Northwest Ordinance," *University of Pennsylvania Law Review* 167 (2019): 1631–67.
71. 4 Annals of Cong. 1253–70 (1795).
72. *Id.*; "Congress of the United States, House of Representatives, Wednesday, Feb. 25," *Knoxville Gazette*, Apr. 10, 1795.
73. Act of May 19, 1796, ch. 30, 1 Stat. 469.
74. On mediation, *see* Vattel, *The Law of Nations*, Book II, 450–51.
75. On violence and kinship among these nations, *see* Perdue, *Cherokee Women*, 86–108; Theda Perdue, *"Mixed Blood" Indians: Racial Construction in the Early South* (Athens: University of Georgia Press, 2003), 1–32; Reid, *A Law of Blood*, 186–227; Smithers, *Native Southerners*, 55–106.
76. "Washington's Memoranda on Indian Affairs, 1789," in *PGW:PS*, 4:468–93; "Knoxville, Friday, April 10, 1795," *Knoxville Gazette*, Apr. 10, 1795; Greg O'Brien, "Quieting the Ghosts: How the Choctaws and Chickasaws Stopped Fighting," in Tim Alan Garrison and Greg O'Brien eds., *The Native South: New Histories and Enduring Legacies* (Lincoln: University of Nebraska Press, 2017). On the Chickasaws in this period, *see* Atkinson, *Splendid Land, Splendid People*; Wendy St. Jean, "Trading Paths: Chickasaw Diplomacy in the Greater Southeast, 1690s–1790s" (Ph.D. dissertation, University of Connecticut, 2004); Charles A. Weeks, "Of Rattlesnakes, Wolves, and Tigers: A Harangue at the Chickasaw Bluffs, 1796," *William and Mary Quarterly* 67, no. 3 (2010): 487–518.
77. Piomingo, "A Talk Delivered [to] Genl Joseph Martin by Piamingo [*sic*] Chief Warrior of the Chickasaw Nation . . . for His Excellency Samuel Johnson [i.e., Johnston] . . . Governor of the State of North Carolina Long Island of the Holston," Sept. 28, 1789, Ayer MS 722, Newberry Library, Chicago. On divides within the Chickasaw Nation, *see* Calloway, *Revolution in Indian Country*, 213–42; Weeks, "Of Rattlesnakes, Wolves, and Tigers."

78. Bloody Fellow to Baron de Carondelet, Feb. 1793, in Roberta Corbitt and D.C. Corbitt, "Papers from the Spanish Archives Relating to Tennessee and the Old Southwest, 1783–1800," *East Tennessee Historical Society's Publications* 29 (1957): 141, 155–56; Little Turkey to James Robertson, Apr. 10, 1795, in *CJR*, 191–92.
79. Anthony Forster to William Blount, July 29, 1792, in *ASP:IA*, 283–84; Piomingo, "A Talk Delivered [to] Genl Joseph Martin by Piamingo"; Joseph Asheton to Josiah Harmar, Mar. 26, 1790, *JHP*, Vol. 12.
80. William Blount to Secretary of War, Mar. 23, 1793, in *TP: Vol. IV*, 247–48; The Chickasaw Chiefs to James Robertson, Feb. 13, 1793, in *ASP:IA*, 442.
81. Piomingo to James Seagrove, Sept. 1, 1793, in Roberta Corbitt and D.C. Corbitt, "Papers from the Spanish Archives Relating to Tennessee and the Old Southwest, 1783–1800," *East Tennessee Historical Society's Publications* 35 (1963): 85–95; Piomingo to Agent, Apr. 29, 1793; Chickasaw Chiefs to Robertson, Feb. 13, 1793.
82. Piomingo to Agent, April 29, 1793; Chickasaw Chiefs to Robertson, Feb. 13, 1793.
83. Governor Blount to James Robertson, Mar. 28, 1793, in *ASP:IA*, 1:452; William Blount and Andrew Pickens to Secretary of War, Aug. 1, 1793, in *TP: Vol. IV*, 291–93.
84. "Talk from the Heads of the Upper and Lower Creeks, by Order of the Mad Dog . . . to Be Forwarded to His Excellency General Washington," July 21, 1793, in *ASP:IA*, 1:408.
85. "Cabinet Opinion on Sending an Agent to the Choctaws, 1–5 June 1793," June 1, 1793, in *PGW:PS*, 13:3–4. On the struggles over neutrality in the Washington administration, *see* Christopher J. Young, "Connecting the President and the People: Washington's Neutrality, Genet's Challenge, and Hamilton's Fight for Public Support," *Journal of the Early Republic* 31, no. 3 (2011): 435–66.
86. William Blount to Secretary of War, Mar. 23, 1793; "Talk of the Choctaw Nation Assembled to Their Older Brothers . . . the Creeks in General, Both Upper and Lower Towns," June 10, 1795, in *CJR*, 269–70; "Extract of a Letter from General James Robertson," July 20, 1793.
87. William Blount to James Robertson, Aug. 6, 1794, in *CJR*, 355–56; James Robertson to Governor Blount, Jan. 13, 1795, in *ASP:IA*, 1:556–57; James Robertson to William Blount, Apr. 20, 1795, in *CJR*, 250–52; Atkinson, *Splendid Land*, 174–76.
88. "Talk of the President to Chickasaws," Aug. 22, 1795, in *CJR*, 393–94.
89. Timothy Pickering to David Henley, Aug. 26, 1795, Folder 16, Timothy Pickering Letters, Ayers 926; Secretary of War to William Blount, Mar. 23, 1795, in *TP: Vol. IV*, 386–93; Timothy Pickering to David Campbell, Aug. 28, 1795, Folder 2, Timothy Pickering Letters, Ayers 926.
90. John Chisholm, James Colbert, and James Kemp to William Blount, Aug. 2, 1795, Folder 7: 1795, WBP:LC.
91. Alexander Cornell to William Blount, July 27, 1795, in *CJR*, 379–80; Willie Blount to John Haywood, Sept. 15, 1795, Box 2, Folder 13, Ernest Haywood Collection of Haywood Family Papers, Southern Historical Collection, University of North Carolina Special Collections.
92. William Blount to James Robertson, Aug. 11, 1795, in *CJR*, 387–89.

93. Atkinson, *Splendid Land*, 174–76; Piomingo to James Robertson, Sept. 29, 1795, Box 1, Folder 11, David Henley Papers, Tennessee State Library and Archives; William Blount to Isaac Shelby, Dec. 21, 1795, 4XX58, Draper Manuscripts, Reel 116, Wisconsin Historical Society, Madison, Wis.; William Blount to James Robertson, Mar. 29, 1796, in *CJR*, 278–79.
94. Benjamin Hawkins, "[Speech to Creeks]," Oct. 27, 1797, in *The Collected Works of Benjamin Hawkins*, 212; Benjamin Hawkins to James Robertson, Apr. 12, 1797, in *CJR*, 341; Richard Thomas to Benjamin Hawkins, Aug. 6, 1798, in *The Collected Works of Benjamin Hawkins*, 489.
95. James McHenry, "Memo Re: Military Affairs," Mar. 12, 1796, Box 1, James McHenry Papers, Clements Library, University of Michigan; Gov. Arthur St. Clair to Secretary of War, Apr. 8, 1801, in *TP: Vol. III*, 129.
96. For recent works emphasizing the continued importance over relations *among* Native nations, *see* Michael J. Witgen, *An Infinity of Nations: How the Native New World Shaped Early North America*, Early American Studies (Philadelphia: University of Pennsylvania Press, 2012); Pekka Hamalainen, *Lakota America: A New History of Indigenous Power* (New Haven, Conn.: Yale University Press, 2019).
97. Thomas to Hawkins, Aug. 6, 1798.
98. William Blount to Reverand Joseph Dorris, Oct. 11, 1795, in *CJR*, 363.
99. William Blount to John Sevier, Aug. 28, 1793, in *TP: Vol. IV*, 303–04.
100. On the significance of the Jay and Pinckney Treaties, *see* Gould, *Among the Powers of the Earth*, 131–40; Leonard J. Sadosky, *Revolutionary Negotiations: Indians, Empires, and Diplomats in the Founding of America* (Charlottesville: University of Virginia Press, 2009), 149–75. On the transformation of the Creek Nation, *see* Kevin Kokomoor, *Of One Mind and of One Government: The Rise and Fall of the Creek Nation in the Early Republic* (Lincoln: University of Nebraska Press, 2019); Saunt, *A New Order of Things*, 90–110.
101. "No. 83: Supplies Furnished An Expedition Against the Creeks," Feb. 3, 1797, in Walter Lowrie and Walter S. Franklin eds., *American State Papers: Claims* (Washington: Gales and Seaton, 1834), 1:196; James McHenry to Dwight Foster, Jan. 16, 1797, Chamberlain Collection, Boston Public Library, Boston, Mass.

Chapter 6

1. "Widow of a Cherokee Chief," Jan. 17, 1797, in *ASP:IA*, 621; John Adams to Abigail Adams, Dec. 4, 1796, in Margaret A. Hogan et al. eds., *The Adams Papers: Adams Family Correspondence* (Cambridge, Mass.: Harvard University Press, 2013), 430–432. On Scolocutta's death, *see Claypoole's American Daily Advertiser*, Philadelphia, Pa., May 11, 1796.
2. "Widow of a Cherokee Chief," Jan. 17, 1797.
3. *Id.*

4. "Report of the Committee To Whom Were Re-Committed the Petition of Hugh Lawson White," Jan. 17, 1797, in *ASP:IA*, 621–23. For additional background, *see* 6 Annals of Cong. 1737–38, 2155–56 (1796–97).
5. For payment of the militia, *see* Act of Mar. 3, 1797, 1 Stat. 508. The committee ultimately recommended that, instead of a congressional pension, Betty receive payment from "contingent expenses" fund in the Indian Department, "Widow of a Cherokee Chief," a recommendation Congress adopted, 6 Annals of Cong. 2333–35 (1797). Testimony taken during Blount's Conspiracy suggests that Blount was likely the conduit for the money paid to Betty. "Deposition of James Carey," Sept. 29, 1797, in *Report of the Committee of the House of Representatives of the United States, Appointed to Prepare and Report Articles of Impeachment against William Blount, a Senator of the United States* (Philadelphia: Printed by John Fenno, 1797), cxiv–cxxi.
6. Richard Platt to Winthrop Sargent, Nov. 15, 1789, Reel 3, *WSP*; "Report of the Secretary of War to the President," Dec. 10, 1790, in *TP: Vol. II*, 313–14; "Report from H. Knox, Secretary of War, to the President of the United States, Relative to the Northwestern Indians," June 15, 1789, in *ASP:IA*, 12–14. On the government's "most pervasive role" of "distributing resources and privileges to individuals and groups" over the long nineteenth century, *see* McCormick, *The Party Period and Public Policy*, 197–225; on the financial resources of the early federal government, *see* Max M. Edling, *A Hercules in the Cradle: War, Money, and the American State, 1783–1867* (Chicago: University of Chicago Press, 2014); on the role of patronage in earlier imperial governance, *see* Bernard Bailyn, *The Origins of American Politics* (New York: Knopf, 1968); Richard L. Bushman, *King and People in Provincial Massachusetts* (Chapel Hill: University of North Carolina Press, 1985), 55–87.
7. On the early Indian Department, *see* Prucha, *American Indian Policy in the Formative Years*, 51–63; on the War Department, *see* White, *Federalists*, 145–54.
8. For the history of dependence in American history, *see* Nancy Fraser and Linda Gordon, "A Genealogy of Dependency: Tracing a Keyword of the U.S. Welfare State," *Signs* 19, no. 2 (1994): 309–36.
9. Treaty of Holston, U.S.-Cherokees, July 2, 1791, 7 Stat. 39. Identical language also appeared in the Treaty of New York, U.S.-Creeks, Aug. 7, 1790, 7 Stat. 35.
10. On compensation and "covering the grave," *see* Nancy Gallman and Alan Taylor, "Covering Blood and Graves: Murder and Law on Imperial Margins," in Brian P. Owensby and Richard J. Ross eds., *Justice in a New World: Negotiating Legal Intelligibility in British, Iberian, and Indigenous America* (New York: NYU Press, 2018), 213–37; Reid, *A Law of Blood*, 93–112; Alan Taylor, *The Divided Ground: Indians, Settlers and the Northern Borderland of the American Revolution* (New York: Alfred A. Knopf, 2006), 28–30, 239–44; Katherine A. Hermes, "The Law of Native Americans, to 1815," in Chris Tomlins et al., *The Cambridge History of Law in America* (Cambridge, U.K.: Cambridge University Press, 2008), 1:32.
11. Vattel, *Law of Nations*, Bk. II, ch. 6, § 77. On suits for private wrongs, *see* Blackstone, *Commentaries*, XX; on petitioning, *see* Maggie McKinley, "Petitioning and the Making of the Administrative State," *Yale Law Journal* 127 (2018): 1538–1637; on compensation for disasters, *see* Michele Landis Dauber, *The Sympathetic State: Disaster Relief and the Origins of the American Welfare State* (Chicago: University of Chicago Press,

2013); on subsequent use of payments during war, *see* Craig B. Hollander, "'The Citizen Complains': Federal Compensation for Property Lost in the War of 1812," *Law and History Review*, Oct. 2019, 1–40.

12. Secretary of War to Alexander McGillivray, July 13, 1791, *ASP:IA*, 1:127–28.
13. William Blount and Andrew Pickens to Secretary of War, Aug. 6, 1793, *TP: Vol. IV*, 296; "Message from the Secretary of War to the Hanging Maw, Sent by Governor Blount," Aug. 27, 1793, *ASP:IA*, 431; Secretary of War to William Blount, Aug. 26, 1793, *TP: Vol. IV*, 299–300.
14. Secretary of War to Arthur St. Clair, Mar. 28, 1791, in *ASP:IA*, 174; William Blount to Secretary of War, May 24, 1793, in *TP: Vol. IV*, 261–62; William Blount to Secretary of War, May 28, 1793, in *TP: Vol. IV*, 262–64. For a newspaper account of Morris's funeral, *see* "Knoxville, Saturday, June 1," *Knoxville Gazette*, June 1, 1793.
15. Benjamin Hawkins to David Henley, Nov. 9, 1797, David Henley Papers, Rubenstein Rare Book and Manuscript Library, Duke University. Despite its frequency in the sources, historiographic discussion of horse theft between Natives and American settlers has been sporadic. A comprehensive consideration appears in Prucha, *American Indian Policy in the Formative Years*, 203–10; other brief discussions appear in Robbie Franklyn Ethridge, *Creek Country: The Creek Indians and Their World* (Chapel Hill: University of North Carolina Press, 2003), 177–88; McLoughlin, *Cherokee Renascence*, 44–47.
16. Numbers derive from "To the Congress of the United States in Session at Philadelphia," *Knoxville Gazette*, Mar. 27, 1794. Discussions of the networks for stolen horses appear in William Blount to Secretary of War, May 5, 1792, in *TP: Vol. IV*, 148–49; William St. Clair to Arthur St. Clair, Oct. 25, 1796, Roll 4, *ASCP*. For accounts of having horses stolen, *see* "Journal Kept by George Hunter of a Tour from Philada. to Kentucky by the Illinois Country," July 14–Oct. 15, 1796, American Philosophical Society, Philadelphia, Penn; "Deposition," Jan. 30, 1796, typescript translation from French, Doc. 340a, Lasselle Family Papers, L127, Indiana State Library, Manuscripts & Rare Books Division, Indianapolis, Ind. On the trade in illegal horses, *see* Benjamin Hawkins to David Henley, June 5, 1798, Benjamin Hawkins Letters, Ayer MS 368, Newberry Library, Chicago, Ill.; William Blount to Secretary of War, Nov. 10, 1794, in *TP: Vol. IV*, 364–70; Silas Dinsmore to David Henley, July 8, 1795, Folder 3, Silas Dinsmore Papers, Ayer MS 241, Newberry Library, Chicago, Ill.
17. William Blount to Secretary of War, May 5, 1792, in *TP: Vol. IV*, 148–49.; William Blount to Secretary of War, Nov. 8, 1792, in *TP: Vol. IV*, 208–16; Gov. Arthur St. Clair to John Marshall, Aug. 5, 1800, in *SCP*, 497.
18. 9; Wyandot Chiefs to Simon Kenton and William Ward, Aug. 25, 1799, Ayer MS 1019, Newberry Library, Chicago, Ill.
19. Act of Mar. 1, 1793, § 6, ch. 19, 1 Stat. 329, 330; Writ of Replevin in Henry Pea v. the Grand Blue, an Indian, Aug. 4, 1797, Box 2, File 128, Knox County Court File, Knox County Public Library, Vincennes, Ind.; *Common Pleas Court Minutes 1796–1799 Pt. 1* (Indianapolis: Indiana Historical Records Survey, 1941),186; Sam'l Moore Adm. of John More Deceased v. James Robertson (Sup. Ct. of L. & Eq., Mero Dist., 1797), in Mrs. Josie Smith ed., *Minutes of the Superior Court of the Mero District, 1788–1803; Part I, 1788–1798* (Nashville: Tennessee Historical Records Survey, Works Progress

Administration, 1938), 234–35. For instances when U.S. citizens were indicted for stealing Native horses, *see* John Rice Jones to Winthrop Sargent, Oct. 17, 1797, Reel 4, *WSP*; William St. Clair to Arthur St. Clair, Oct. 25, 1796, Roll 4, Arthur St. Clair Papers; Government v. James Hawthorn & James Blackbourne (Sup. Ct., Hamilton Dist. 1795), Knox County (Tenn.) Archives, Knoxville, Tenn.

20. "Journal of the Grand Cherokee National Council," June 26, 1792, in *ASP:IA*, 271–74; William Blount to Secretary of War, May 28, 1793, in *TP: Vol. IV*, 262–64.
21. Testimony of Benjamin Springer, Mar. 27, 1797, William Hayden English Papers, M98, Indiana Historical Society; William Dever to John Sevier, Dec. 20, 1796, Box 2, Folder 1, John Sevier Papers, 1796–1801, First Administration, Governor's Papers, Tennessee State Library and Archive.
22. "Journal Kept by George Hunter." Other instances of whites hiring Natives to recover lost horses can be found in Account of Lewis Chatellereault, 1797, Knox County (Ind.) Probate Records, Box 1, Knox County Public Library; John Duley v. Jonathan Purcell, Nov. 4, 1798, Knox County (Ind.) Court File, Box 4, File 291, Knox County Public Library.
23. Gen'l Wilkinson to Jonathan Cass, Mar. 19, 1796, William Hayden English Family Papers, M98, Indiana Historical Society; William Blount to James Robertson, Aug. 24, 1795, in *CJR*, 67–68.
24. "Conference at Tellico Blockhouse," Dec. 28, 1794, in *CJR*, 82–94.
25. On slavery in the Tennessee Country, *see* Cynthia Cumfer, *Separate Peoples, One Land: The Minds of Cherokees, Blacks, and Whites on the Tennessee Frontier* (Chapel Hill: University of North Carolina Press, 2007), 125–53; Carroll Van West ed., *Trial and Triumph: Essays In Tennessee's African American History* (Knoxville: University of Tennessee Press, 2002). On African slavery in the Northwest Territory, *see* M. Scott Heerman, *The Alchemy of Slavery: Human Bondage and Emancipation in the Illinois Country, 1730–1865* (Philadelphia: University of Pennsylvania Press, 2018); Matthew Salafia, *Slavery's Borderland: Freedom and Bondage Along the Ohio River* (Philadelphia: University of Pennsylvania Press, 2013); Patrick Bottiger, "Stabbed in the Back: Vincennes, Slavery, and the Indian 'Threat,'" *Indiana Magazine of History* 107, no. 2 (2011): 89–122. On Native captivity practices in the Southeast, *see* Christina Snyder, *Slavery in Indian Country: The Changing Face of Captivity in Early America* (Cambridge, Mass.: Harvard University Press, 2010); on Indigenous slaves north of the Ohio, *see* Brett Rushforth, *Bonds of Alliance: Indigenous and Atlantic Slaveries in New France* (Chapel Hill: University of North Carolina Press, 2012); Carl J. Ekberg, *Stealing Indian Women: Native Slavery in the Illinois Country* (Urbana: University of Illinois Press, 2007).
26. "Information of Joseph Baird," June 13, 1794, Box 2, Folder 7, William H. English Collection, Special Collection Research Center, University of Chicago Library; James Robertson, "Deposition," [after 1799], Box 2, Stanley F. Horn Collection, Special Collections, Jean and Alexander Heard Library, Vanderbilt University; John Jones, "Deposition," June 2, 1800, Box 2, Stanley F. Horn Collection, Special Collections, Jean and Alexander Heard Library, Vanderbilt University.
27. On captives within Native societies, *see* Perdue, *Cherokee Women*, 41–85; Snyder, *Slavery in Indian Country*.

28. For an introduction to the large literature on this topic, *see* Tiya Miles, *Ties That Bind: The Story of an Afro-Cherokee Family in Slavery and Freedom* (Berkeley: University of California Press, 2005); Barbara Krauthamer, *Black Slaves, Indian Masters: Slavery, Emancipation, and Citizenship in the Native American South* (Chapel Hill: University of North Carolina Press, 2015); Saunt, *A New Order of Things*, 111–32.
29. "Conference at Tellico Blockhouse," Dec. 28, 1794; John Sevier to The Little Turkey, Aug. 25, 1796, in *Executive Journal of Governor Sevier*, 119.
30. For cases involving alleged slave theft, *see* The State v. John Chisholm (Superior Court, Hamilton District 1794), Docket 657/580, Knox County (Tenn.) Archives; George Mitchell v. William Blount (Superior Court, Hamilton District 1795); The Territory v. Page Billow, Minutes of the Superior Court of Law & Equity of the Mero District (1792), 82–83.
31. "Arthur St. Clair's Commentary on the Trade and Intercourse Act," 1794, Reel 7, *ASCP*. John Francis Hamtramck to Maj. Wyllys, May 27, 1789, Vol. 10, JAH.
32. Conference at Tellico Blockhouse," Dec. 28, 1794; James Seagrove to Secretary of War, Dec. 31, 1794, *ASP:IA*, 546.
33. Little Turkey to William Blount, Apr. 10, 1795, in *CJR*, 247–49; William Blount to James Robertson, Nov. 30, 1795, in *CJR*, 80–81; John Sevier to The Little Turkey, Aug. 25, 1796, in *Executive Journal of Governor Sevier*, 119.
34. Benjamin Hawkins to Chiefs, Head Men, and Warriors of the Chickasaw Nation, May 21, 1797, in C.L Grant ed., *Letters, Journals, and Writings of Benjamin Hawkins* (Savannah, Ga.: Beehive Press, 1980), 1:112–13; Benjamin Hawkins to James McHenry, July 5, 1797, in Thomas Foster ed., *The Collected Works of Benjamin Hawkins, 1796–1810* (Tuscaloosa: University of Alabama Press, 2003), 181–82; Letters of Benjamin Hawkins, June 24, 1797, in *Collected Works of Benjamin Hawkins*, 179.
35. Act of May 19, 1796, ch. 30, 1 Stat. 469. Winthrop Sargent to Secretary of State, May 23, 1797, in *TP: Vol. III*, 468–71; Arthur St. Clair to Samuel Dexter, Sec'y of War, Nov. 29, 1800, Box 30, Folder 3, William Hayden English Papers, Indiana Historical Society. For instances when federal officials paid Native claims they thought dubious, *see* William Blount to Bloody Fellow, Sept. 13, 1792, in "The Correspondence of Gen. James Robertson," *American Historical Magazine* 2, no.1 (Jan. 1, 1897): 74–76; James McHenry to Arthur St. Clair, Aug. 15, 1799, Folder 2, James McHenry Letters, Ayers MS 931, Newberry Library; J. Winchester to David Henley, Apr. 21, 1800, Box 2, Stanley F. Horn Collection, Special Collections, Jean and Alexander Heard Library, Vanderbilt University.
36. St. Clair to Dexter, Nov. 29, 1800; Sargent to Secretary of State, May 23, 1797.
37. For the subsequent history of claims under the Trade and Intercourse Acts, *see* the exploration in Larry C. Skogen, *Indian Depredation Claims, 1796–1920* (Norman: University of Oklahoma Press, 1996). For a sampling of some of the claims presented to Congress, including the claim of Daniel Smith, *see* Walter Lowrie and Walter S. Franklin eds., *American State Papers: Claims* (Washington: Gales and Seaton, 1834), 1:193, 222, 309, 379, 445.

38. Arthur St. Clair to Henry Dearborn, Sec'y of War, Oct. 2, 1802, Roll 5, *ASCP*.
39. John Francis Hamtramck to Winthrop Sargent, July 21, 1790, Reel 3, *WSP*; "Report of Antoine Gamelin" May 17, 1790, in *SCP*, 2:155–60; "Speech of Chief of the Chippewas," 1791, Reel 47, Henry Knox Papers; John Francis Hamtramck to Winthrop Sargent, Aug. 9, 1792, Reel 3, *WSP*. On earlier French and British gift-giving practices in the region, *see* White, *The Middle Ground*, 112–19, 403–04.
40. "Winthrop Sargent Diary," Sept. 1, 1789, *WSP*, Massachusetts Historical Society; Erskurius Beatty to John Armstrong, June 14, 1786, Box 1, Folder 18, Armstrong Papers, M6, Indiana Historical Society. For other examples of officials calling Natives beggars, *see* Hopewell Commissioners to John Hancock, Jan. 4, 1786, No. 138, Reel 47, Henry Knox Papers; Gov. Arthur St. Clair to Secretary of War, May 1, 1790, in *SCP*, 2:136–40.
41. "A Talk Delivered [to] Genl Joseph Martin Piamingo." For an overview of the large literature on gifts and trade goods in Native culture, focusing particularly on the Native Southeast, *see* Joseph M. Hall, *Zamumo's Gifts: Indian-European Exchange in the Colonial Southeast* (Philadelphia: University of Pennsylvania Press, 2009); Kathryn E. Holland Braund, *Deerskins & Duffels: The Creek Indian Trade with Anglo-America, 1685–1815* (Lincoln: University of Nebraska Press, 1993); Daniel K. Richter, *Trade, Land, Power: The Struggle for Eastern North America* (Philadelphia: University of Pennsylvania Press, 2013), 53–68.
42. Little Turkey to Governor Blount, June 5, 1793, in *ASP:IA*, 1:461. On beads, *see* John McKee to Glass and Other Chiefs of the Lower Towns of the Cherokees, July 14, 1794, *CJR*, 352. Silas Dinsmore to David Henley, July 8, 1795, Folder 3, Silas Dinsmore Papers, Ayer MS 241, Newberry Library, Chicago, Ill.
43. Henry Burbeck, "Speeches to Indians," Oct. 1799, Ayer 121, Newberry Library; James Wilkinson, "Talk to the Warring Nations," Apr. 3, 1792, James Wilkinson Letters, Ayer MS 982, Newberry Library. For a discussion of the devastation wrought in Native communities, *see* Colin G. Calloway, *The American Revolution in Indian Country: Crisis and Diversity in Native American Communities* (Cambridge, [U.K.]: Cambridge University Press, 1995), 108–57.
44. White, *Middle Ground*; "A Journal of the Proceedings at a Council Held with the Indians of the Wabash and Illinois at Post Vincents, by Brigadier General Putnam," Oct. 1792, in *Memoirs of Rufus Putnam*, 335; Speeches of the Wabash and Illinois Indians, Feb. 1–4, 1793, in *PGW:PS*, 12:82–89; "Speech of the Commissioners of the United States to the Deputies of the Confederated Indian Nations at the Rapids of the Miami River," July 31, 1793, in *ASP:IA*, 352–54; John Francis Hamtramck to Gen. James Wilkinson, Jan. 24, 1796, Northwest Territory Collection, Indiana Historical Society. On gendered understandings of dependency during this period, *see* Christine Stansell, *City of Women: Sex and Class in New York, 1789–1860*, 1st ed. (New York: Knopf, 1986), 3–38; Daniel Scott Smith, "Female Householding in Late Eighteenth-Century America and the Problem of Poverty," *Journal of Social History* 28, no. 1 (1994): 83–107. Explorations of gender in Native societies appear in Perdue, *Cherokee Women*; Nancy Shoemaker, "An Alliance between Men: Gender Metaphors in Eighteenth-Century American Indian Diplomacy East of the Mississippi,"

Ethnohistory 46, no. 2 (1999): 239–63; Juliana Barr, *Peace Came in the Form of a Woman: Indians and Spaniards in the Texas Borderlands* (Chapel Hill: University of North Carolina Press, 2007); Ann M. Little, *Abraham in Arms: War and Gender in Colonial New England*, Early American Studies (Philadelphia: University of Pennsylvania Press, 2007); Gregory Evans Dowd, "The Spinning Wheel Revolution," in James P.P. Horn, Jan Lewis, and Peter S. Onuf eds., *The Revolution of 1800: Democracy, Race, and the New Republic* (Charlottesville: University of Virginia Press, 2002), 267–83.

45. "A Journal of the Proceedings at a Council Held with the Indians of the Wabash and Illinois at Post Vincents, by Brigadier General Putnam," Oct. 1792; "Journal of the Grand Cherokee National Council," June 26, 1792, in *ASP:IA*, 1:271–74; "Treaty of Holston—June & July, 1791. Between Gov. Wm. Blount & the Cherokees," June 26–July 3, 1791, 15U1-59, Draper Manuscripts, Reel 58, Wisconsin Historical Society, Madison, Wis. On paternalistic metaphors, *see* Cumfer, *Separate Peoples, One Land*, 78–97; Bethel Saler, *The Settlers' Empire: Colonialism and State Formation in America's Old Northwest* (Philadelphia: University of Pennsylvania Press, 2014), 71–72; Richard White, *The Middle Ground: Indians, Empires, and Republics in the Great Lakes Region, 1650–1815* (Cambridge, U.K.: Cambridge University Press, 1991), 84–90; Shoemaker, "An Alliance Between Men."
46. Henry Knox to Joseph Martin, June 23, 1788, 2XX20, Draper Manuscripts, Reel 116, Wisconsin Historical Society; "Draft of Proposal for a Person to Examine Public Property," May 23, 1800, Box 5, James McHenry Papers, Clements Library; Sargent to Hamtramck, July 16, 1790; Magistrates of Knox County to Arthur St. Clair, July 29, 1791, Reel 3, *ASCP*. For other instances where "oeconomy" was urged, *see* William Blount to James Robertson, Apr. 15, 1794, in *TP: Vol. IV*, 340–41; William Blount to John McKee, N.D., Folder 8, John McKee Papers, Manuscript Division, Library of Congress.
47. Henry Knox to George Washington, June 15, 1789, in *PGW:PS*, 2:490; Thomas Jefferson to Charles Carroll, Apr. 15, 1791, in *PTJ:MS*, 20:214.
48. John Francis Hamtramck to Secretary of War, Mar. 31, 1792, *TP: Vol. II*, 380–83; Arthur St. Clair to Henry Knox, Jan. 27, 1788, *TP: Vol. II*, 89–91; "Minutes of Information given Governor Blount by James Carey, One of the Interpreters of the United States, in the Nation," Nov. 3, 1792, in *ASP:IA*, 1:327–29; "The Following Information Delivered on Oath, by James Leonard, a Citizen of the United States, to James Seagrove, Agent of Indian Affairs, Southern Department Rock Landing, on the Oconee. in Georgia," July 24, 1792, in *ASP:IA*, 307–08.
49. James Robertson to William Blount, Oct. 12, 1792, in *TP: Vol. IV*, 197–98; "Talk of the Chickasaw Chiefs at the Bluffs, Represented by Wolf's Friend Ugalayacabe, to Cammandt. Balshase," 1797, in Box 2, James McHenry Papers, Clements Library.
50. "Memorial to Congress," Sept. 18, 1794, in *TP: Vol. IV*, 354–55. For an instance when federal officials emphasized national wealth in distributing goods, *see* Henry Knox, "Message from the Sec'y of War to Frenclehemastubre the Great Leading King of All the Choctaw Nation of Indians" June 27, 1787, vol. 6, JHP.

51. Sargent to Hamtramck, July 16, 1790; Andrew Jackson to John Sevier, Feb. 24, 1797, in *PAJ*, I:126–27; Timothy Pickering to David Henley, Aug. 26, 1795, Folder 16, Timothy Pickering Letters, Ayers 926, Newberry Library.
52. Benjamin Hawkins to David Henley, June 5, 1798, Benjamin Hawkins Letters, Ayer 368, Newberry Library.
53. Acting Governor Smith to Secretary of War, June 22, 1793, in *TP: Vol. IV*, 276–77; William Blount, "Report to Henry Knox Regarding Preparations for War by Cherokee Indians: Knoxville, Southwest Territory" Oct. 7, 1792, Beinecke Library, Yale University, New Haven, Conn.; "Information by Richard Finnelson," Nov. 1, 1792, in *ASP:IA*, 1:288–91.
54. On criticism during this period of the poor as idlers, *see* Gary B. Nash, "Poverty and Poor Relief in Pre-Revolutionary Philadelphia," *William and Mary Quarterly* 33, no. 1 (1976): 3.
55. "Report of the Secretary of War to the President," Dec. 10, 1790, in *TP: Vol. II*, 313–14. Calculating the acreage purchased by the United States during this period is difficult. One figure, of nearly twelve million comes from Susan B. Carter et al., "Table Ag542–543: Lands Purchased by the United States from American Indian Tribes: 1795–1838," in *Historical Statistics of the United States Millennial Edition Online* (New York: Cambridge University Press, 2006), which relies on an 1839 report. But this calculation is almost certainly too low, since it seems to only include land obtained at the Treaty of Greenville. Another estimate puts the amount at over eighteen million, based on map measurements, but this estimate, too, seems to include principally the Treaty of Greenville, ignoring the other land cession treaties the federal government entered during the decade. Stanley Lebergott, "The Demand for Land: The United States, 1820–1860," *Journal of Economic History* 45, no. 2 (1985): 181, 211, app'x B. On work that suggests that Natives were substantially undercompensated for their lands, *see* Eric Kades, "Dark Side of Efficiency: Johnson v. M'Intosh and the Expropriation of American Indian Lands," *University of Pennsylvania Law Review* 148 (2000): 1065; Banner, *How the Indians Lost Their Land*, 74–82.
56. The federal government received $101,000 in land revenue between 1789 and 1800, though revenue quickly increased afterward. Susan B. Carter et al., "Table Ea588–593: Federal Government Revenue, by Source: 1789–1939," in *Historical Statistics of the United States Millennial Edition Online* (New York: Cambridge University Press, 2006).
57. On treaties as a grand affairs—and U.S. efforts to convert them into a simple land transaction—*see* Colin G. Calloway, *Pen and Ink Witchcraft: Treaties and Treaty Making in American Indian History* (New York: Oxford University Press, 2013), 13–118; Dorothy V. Jones, *License for Empire: Colonialism by Treaty in Early America* (Chicago: University of Chicago Press, 1982).
58. Richard Wynne to John Steele, Feb. 19, 1789, Box 1, Folder 4, John Steele Papers, Southern Historical Collection; William Blount to Secretary of War, Sept. 20, 1792, in *ASP:IA*, in 1:282–83; John Steele to Cairy [Carey], Linguist, June 8, 1789, Box 1, Folder 4, John Steele Papers, Southern Historical Collection. For more discussion of complaints about expenses, *see* Calloway, *Pen and Ink Witchcraft*, 20–48.

59. "Schedule of Goods Delivered by Joseph Baird at the Indian Treaty," Sept. 1792, Folder 4, RPP; "Invoice of Items Purchased by Tench Francis for Proposed Conference with the Cherokee Indians," Aug. 1793, Folder 1, Silas Dinsmore Papers, Ayer MS 241, Newberry Library.
60. David Allison, "Estimate of the Supposed Expense of the Chickasaw and Choctaw Indian Conference to Be Held at NashVille 1st. June Next." 1792, Folder 4: 1792, *WBP:LC*; Arthur St. Clair to Congress, May 16, 1789, Roll 2, *ASCP*; 4 Annals of Cong. 774–79 (1794); "Cumberland District Ct. Records," R6, 1783–87, Roll 224, Tennessee State Library and Archives. R6.
61. William Blount and Andrew Pickens to Secretary of War, Aug. 1, 1793, in *TP: Vol. IV*, 291–93; Timothy Pickering to David Henley, May 11, 1795, Folder 6, Timothy Pickering Letters, Ayers 926, Newberry Library; "Supply for the Chickasaws," April 27, 1793, in "The Correspondence of Gen. James Robertson," *American Historical Magazine* 2, no. 4 (Oct. 1, 1897): 363.
62. Henry Knox to Arthur St. Clair, Feb. 25, 1793, Reel 4, ASC Papers; James Wilkinson to Winthrop Sargent, Nov. 17, 1797, Reel 4, *WSP*; "Abstract of Provisions Issued at Ft. Defiance" Apr. 1798, Box 8, Solomon Sibley Papers, Burton Historical Collection, Detroit, Mich.; "Abstract of Provisions Issued at Ft. Washington to the Indians" Oct. 31, 1801, Roll 7, *ASCP*; "The Secretary of War to Governor St. Clair," Apr. 25, 1800, in *TP: Vol. III*, 82–83; William Blount to James Robertson, Oct. 11, 1793, in "The Correspondence of Gen. James Robertson," *American Historical Magazine* 2, no. 4 (Oct. 1, 1897): 373.
63. John Adams to Abigail Adams, Dec. 4, 1796; John Steele to William Blount, Apr. 1, 1792, Folder 4: 1792, *WBP:LC*. For other instances of Native visits to Philadelphia, *see* "General Robertson's Acct," Mar. 28, 1792, Box 1, Folder 3, James Robertson Papers, Special Collections, Vanderbilt University Library; James Wilkinson to Harry Innes, May 10, 1792, Box 1, Folder 6, Harry Innes Papers, Manuscript Division, Library of Congress; William Blount to Daniel Smith, Mar. 12, 1793, Box 1, Folder 1, Daniel Smith Papers, Tennessee State Library and Archives; David Henley to John Chisholm, Oct. 29, 1796, Box 1, Folder 29, David Henley Papers, Tennessee State Library and Archives.
64. David Allison to Benjamin Hawkins, Apr. 21, 1792, Folder 4: 1792, *WBP:LC*. For federal officials who saw advantage in Indian visits, *see* Henry Knox, "Instructions to Captain Alexander Trueman, of the First United States' Regiment," Apr. 3, 1792, *ASP:IA*, 230; Rufus Putnam to Henry Knox, July 5, 1792, in *The Memoirs of Rufus Putnam*, 273. For an instance when Natives spontaneously organized a trip to Philadelphia, *see* William Blount to Hugh Williamson, Apr. 14, 1792, in *JGBP*, 2:194–96. Blount reported that three Chickasaws appeared en route to Philadelphia with a letter to Washington from Piomingo; Blount reported that he would endeavor to "turn them back," but doubted whether he would succeed. *Id.*
65. William Blount to John McKee, N.D., Folder 8, John McKee Papers, Manuscript Division, Library of Congress; Secretary of War to William Blount, Feb. 8, 1793, in *TP: Vol. IV*, 237–38; Blount to Robertson, Oct. 11, 1793; William Blount to Secretary Smith, Apr. 27, 1792, in *TP: Vol. IV*, 143–45.

66. "Expenditures for the Indian Department Since the Declaration of Independence," Dec. 7, 1820, in *ASP:IA*, 2:209–12. This calculation includes expenditures on treaties (tbl. 2), expenditures on the Indian Department under military appropriations (tbl. 3), and expenditures on Indian trading posts (tbl. 4). Federal government nondebt expenditures derived from Susan B. Carter et al., "Table Ea636–643: Federal Government Expenditure, by Major Function: 1789–1970," in *Historical Statistics of the United States Millennial Edition Online* (New York: Cambridge University Press, 2006). The evidence that this amount undercounts actual expenditures comes from several sources. Some historical sources indicate that many expenditures on Indian affairs did not receive the "Indian Department" label. Arthur St. Clair to Congress, May 16, 1789, Roll 2, *ASCP*. Other federal records provide numbers that contradict those presented in the report. For in instance, while the 1820 report records only $28,8288.37 in Indian-related expenditures that year, another source indicates $41,000. "Estimates for the Year 1789," July 9, 1789, Walter Lowrie and Matthew St. Clair Clarke eds., *American State Papers: Finance* (Washington: Gales and Seaton, 1832), 1:11–13. Some of this disparity is likely due to the destruction of records in a War Office fire in 1800. For an additional discussion of Indian Department finance, *see* Rockwell, *Indian Affairs*, 49–50.
67. For estimates of these amounts, *see* Henry Knox to George Washington, June 15, 1789, in *PGW:PS*, 2:490 ($15,000); Rufus Putnam to Fisher Ames, Jan. 9, 1790, Mss. Misc. Boxes P, American Antiquarian Society ($20,000). In 1791, Jefferson similarly argued, "The expedition of this year [against the Northwest Indian Confederacy] would have served for presents on the most liberal scale for 100. years." Jefferson to Carroll, Apr. 15, 1791. Tax revenue from Ohio and Tennessee comes from "No. 145: Internal Revenues," Feb. 5, 1800, *American State Papers: Finance*, 1:616–21. Military expenditures and expenditures on veterans derived from Susan B. Carter et al., "Table Ea636–643: Federal Government Expenditure, by Major Function: 1789–1970," in *Historical Statistics of the United States Millennial Edition Online*. Other categories of federal expenditure from the period from Albert Gallatin, *A Sketch of the Finances of the United States* (New York: Printed by Willliam A. Davis, 1796), tbl. X, 180–94.
68. William Cocke, "For the Gazette," *Knoxville Gazette*, Dec. 29, 1792; James Mulryne to President Washington, Nov. 22, 1792, in *PGW:PS*, 11:420–23; John Sevier to Andrew Jackson, Jan. 29, 1797, in *PAJ*, 1:120–21.
69. Magistrates of Knox County to Arthur St. Clair, July 29, 1791, Roll 3, *ASCP*; "Testimony of James Leonard," Sept. 19, 1794, Roll 7, *ASCP*.
70. William Blount to John Gray Blount, July 29, 1794, in *JGBP*, 2:420–21; John Sevier to William Cocke, July 6, 1797, in *Executive Journal of Governor Sevier*, 2:139; "Mr. Roulstone," *Knoxville Gazette*, Aug. 13, 1793.
71. Judge Turner to Gov. Arthur St. Clair, June 14, 1794, in *SCP*, 2:325; Winthrop Sargent to Secretary of War, July 6, 1792, *TP: Vol. II*, 404–05; Oliver Wolcott to David Henley, May 30, 1795, Box 16, Folder 9, Oliver Wolcott Papers, Connecticut Historical Society; "Deposition of Samson Williams," July 7, 1795, Documents, Box 1, Folder 3, David Henley Papers, Tennessee State Library and Archives; Timothy

Pickering to David Henley, July 22, 1795, Folder 12, Timothy Pickering Letters, Ayers 926, Newberry Library. For examples of local financial connections to the Indian Department, *see* "Articles of Agreement Between John Chisholm and David Moore," Sept. 21, 1795, William Blount Papers, McClung Historical Collection, Knoxville Public Library, Knoxville, Tenn.; William Blount to David Henley, July 23, 1795, William Blount Papers, McClung Historical Collection; Hamtramck to Sargent, Aug. 9, 1792.

72. Gov. Arthur St. Clair to Oliver Wolcott, Dec. 5, 1795, in *SCP*, 2:378–83. I explore the issue of territories' constitutional status more fully in Ablavsky, "Administrative Constitutionalism and the Northwest Ordinance." On Native nations' ambiguous autonomous legal status in this period, *see* Ablavsky, "Species of Sovereignty."
73. Gov. Arthur St. Clair to Secretary of Treasury, Aug. 9, 1793, in *TP: Vol. II*, 458–59; William Blount to John Sevier, May 31, 1793, in *TP: Vol. IV*, 264–66.
74. David Campbell to Secretary of State, Feb. 25, 1792, in *TP: Vol. IV*, 121–28.
75. "Petition to Congress of the Inhabitants of the Territory Northwest of the Ohio" Dec. 24, 1801, Roll 5, *ASCP*; "Reply of Council to the Governor," Sept. 28, 1799, in *SCP*, 2:457–58.
76. Acting Governor Smith to Secretary of War, Sept. 27, 1793, in *TP: Vol. IV*, 305–07. On the displacement of suffering at Native hands onto women and children, *see* Carroll Smith-Rosenberg, *This Violent Empire: The Birth of an American National Identity* (Chapel Hill: University of North Carolina Press, 2010), 229–40.
77. Patrick Henry to Virginia Delegates, May 16, 1786, in Daniel Preston and Marlena C. DeLong eds., *The Papers of James Monroe* (Westport, Conn.: Greenwood Press, 2003), 301–03; Patrick Henry to Virginia Delegates, July 5, 1786, in *Papers of James Monroe*, 2:315–18; A Fellow Citizen, "For the Knoxville Gazette," *Knoxville Gazette*, Apr. 6, 1793. Patrick Griffin has argued that protection was the "organizing principle for [the] West." Patrick Griffin, *American Leviathan: Empire, Nation, and Revolutionary Frontier* (New York: Hill and Wang, 2007). On protection in the law of nations during this period, *see* Lauren A. Benton and Lisa Ford, *Rage for Order: The British Empire and the Origins of International Law, 1800–1850* (Cambridge: Harvard University Press, 2016), 85–117; Ablavsky, "Species of Sovereignty," 601–06.
78. White to Monroe, Aug. 9, 1792; "Address of the Grand Inquest of the District of Hamilton," *Knoxville Gazette*, Nov. 23, 1793; "To the Congress of the United States in Session at Philadelphia," *Knoxville Gazette*, Mar. 27, 1794; "Knoxville, Saturday, Jan. 12," *Knoxville Gazette*, Jan. 12, 1793.
79. "Letter from Rufus Putnam to Fisher Ames," Jan. 9, 1790, Mss. Misc. Boxes P, American Antiquarian Society. For a recent overview of these widespread flirtations with secession, *see* David E. Narrett, "Geopolitics and Intrigue: James Wilkinson, the Spanish Borderlands, and Mexican Independence," *William and Mary Quarterly* 69, no. 1 (2012): 101–46; Gene Allen Smith and Sylvia L. Hilton eds., *Nexus of Empire:* Furstenberg, "The Significance of the Trans-Appalachian Frontier in Atlantic History." An older but valuable overview appears in Whitaker, *The Spanish-American Frontier: 1783–1795.*

80. For discussions of alleged foreign agents in the territories, *see* Arthur St. Clair to Isaac Dunn, Dec. 9, 1788, Beinecke Library, Yale University; Henry Knox to Josiah Harmar, Nov. 14, 1787, Vol. 6, JAH; James McHenry to Arthur St. Clair, May 24, 1796, Box 1, James McHenry Papers, Clements Library, University of Michigan; James Wilkinson to Winthrop Sargent, May 28, 1797, Reel 4, *WSP*.
81. George Thompson to James Madison, June 1, 1790, George Thompson Papers, Clements Library, University of Michigan; Henry Knox, "A View of the Present State of the Military Force of the United States," Mar. 19, 1791, Northwest Territory Collection, Indiana Historical Society; Fisher Ames to Rufus Putnam, Feb. 22, 1791, in *Memoirs of Rufus Putnam*, 250.
82. "The CAUSES of the Existing HOSTILITIES between the UNITED STATES, and Certain Tribes of INDIANS North-West of the OHIO . . . Jan. 26, 1792, in *TP: Vol. II*, 359–66; Henry Knox to Arthur St. Clair, Mar. 19, 1791, Northwest Territory Collection, Indiana Historical Society; "At a Meeting of a Number of the Inhabitants of Columbia at the House of Mr. William Stanley, on Monday the 25th of January 1796, Pursuant to Public Notice," *Centinel of the North-Western Territory*, Feb. 20, 1796.
83. John Cleves Symmes to Jonathan Dayton, Nov. 4, 1790, in *CJCS*, 132–38; Journal of Ichabod Nye (typescript), at 39–40, Folder 2, Box 3, Marietta, Ohio Collection, Ohio Historical Society. On the role of federal military spending in encouraging the development of the Northwest Territory, *see also* William H. Bergmann, *The American National State and the Early West* (Cambridge; New York: Cambridge University Press, 2012), 53–93.
84. William St. Clair to Arthur St. Clair, Sept. 13, 1798, Roll 4, *ASCP*; James McHenry to Arthur St. Clair, Aug. 15, 1799, Folder 2, James McHenry Letters, Ayers MS 931, Newberry Library; John Francis Hamtramck to Josiah Harmar, Jan. 19, 1789, in *Outpost on the Wabash*, 145–47; Masterson, *William Blount*, 254.
85. Cayton, "'Separate Interests' and the Nation-State." For a broader discussion, *see* the sources cited in the Introduction, n. 33.
86. Act of Sept. 29, 1789, ch. 25, 1 Stat. 95; Act of Apr. 30, 1790, ch. 10, 1 Stat. 119; Act of May 2, 1792, ch. 28, 1 Stat. 268. On the early federal military, *see* Richard H. Kohn, *Eagle and Sword: The Federalists and the Creation of the Military Establishment in America, 1783–1802* (New York: Free Press, 1975); Francis Paul Prucha, *The Sword of the Republic, the United States Army on the Frontier, 1783–1846* (New York: Macmillan, 1968). On early militias and debates over their role in federalism, *see* Saul Cornell, *A Well-Regulated Militia: The Founding Fathers and the Origins of Gun Control in America* (Oxford: Oxford University Press, 2006), 41–71; Lawrence Delbert Cress, *Citizens in Arms: The Army and the Militia in American Society to the War of 1812* (Chapel Hill: University of North Carolina Press, 1982); Don Higginbotham, "The Federalized Militia Debate: A Neglected Aspect of Second Amendment Scholarship," *William and Mary Quarterly* 55, no. 1 (1998): 39–58.
87. William Irvine to James White, July 22, 1787, Vol. 6, 35, JHP; Gov. Arthur St. Clair to Hon. John Brown, July 18, 1791, in *SCP*, 2:225–26.
88. Henry Knox to Josiah Harmar, Apr. 25, 1788, Vol. 7, 67, JHP; Henry Knox to Josiah Harmar, Dec. 22, 1788, Vol. 9, 53, JHP; Henry Knox, "Circular to the County

Lieutantants," July 29, 1790, Folder 4, Harry Innes Papers, Manuscript Division, Library of Congress; Henry Knox to Harry Innes, Apr. 13, 1790, Folder 4, Harry Innes Papers.

89. "Report from H. Knox, Secretary of War, to the President of the United States, Relative to the Northwestern Indians," Jan. 5, 1791, *ASP:IA*, 2:108–09; Hugh Williamson to John Gray Blount, Dec. 12, 1792, in *JGBP*, 2:221–22; "David Henley In Account with David Allison," Oct. 21–Nov. 6, 1793, Folder 3, *WBP:LC*; William Blount to James Robertson, Apr. 15, 1794, in *TP: Vol. VI*, 340–31; David Henley to Gabriel Duvoll, Mar. 3, 1808, Box 1, Folder 41, David Henley Papers, Tennessee State Library and Archives.
90. L.M., "For the Gazette," *Knoxville Gazette*, Feb. 27, 1794.
91. Timothy Pickering to David Henley, May 29, 1795, Folder 9, Timothy Pickering Letters, Ayers 926, Newberry Library; James McHenry to David Henley, May 18, 1797, Box 2, James McHenry Papers, Clements Library; William Clairborn to David Henley, Jan. 31, 1796, Box 1, Folder 21, David Henley Papers, Tennessee State Library and Archives. On the use of militia vouchers for payment to merchants, *see* Durham, *Before Tennessee*, 227.
92. Timothy Pickering and Oliver Wolcott to John McNairy, May 30, 1795, Folder 23, Timothy Pickering Letters, Ayers 926, Newberry Library.
93. A Fellow Citizen, "For the Knoxville Gazette," *Knoxville Gazette*, Apr. 6, 1793; William Blount to James Robertson, Sept. 9, 1794, in "The Correspondence of Gen. James Robertson," *American Historical Magazine* 3, no. 4 (Oct. 1, 1898): 357.
94. William Blount to John Gray Blount, Oct. 26, 1794, in *JGBP*, Vol. 2, 448–50; Robert Hays to William Blount, Apr. 1, 1794, Folder 6: 1794, *WBP:LC*; William Clairborn to David Henley, Jan. 31, 1796, Box 1, Folder 21, David Henley Papers, Tennessee State Library and Archives; "Hamilton District, Superior Court of Law, April Term, 1795," *Knoxville Gazette*, Apr. 24, 1795.
95. "Hamilton District, Superior Court of Law, April Term, 1795"; X, "For the Knoxville Gazette," *Knoxville Gazette*, Apr. 20, 1793.; "Mr. Roulstone," *Knoxville Gazette*, Aug. 13, 1793; Blount to Robertson, Sept. 9, 1794.
96. Northwest Ordinance, *JCC*, 342; "Knoxville, Monday, Aug. 25," *Knoxville Gazette*, Aug. 25, 1794; William Blount to John Sevier, Mar. 20, 1795, 4XX40, Draper Manuscripts, Reel 116, Wisconsin Historical Society, Madison, Wis.
97. *Letter from the Secretary at War, Inclosing His Report on the Petition of Hugh Lawson White* . . . (Philadelphia: William Ross, 1797); *Letter from the Secretary of War, Inclosing His Report on the Petition of Stephen Cantrill*, . . . (Philadelphia: Joseph Gale, 1798); Annals of Cong., 4 Cong., 2nd Sess., 1737–38; "Speech before the U.S. House of Representatives," Dec. 29, 1796, in *PAJ*, 1:106–07; William C.C. Claiborne to Andrew Jackson, July 20, 1797, in *PAJ*, 1:146–48; Act of Mar. 3, 1797, 1 Stat. 508; Act of May 8, 1798, ch. 41, 1 Stat. 556; 8 Annals of Cong. 1521–22 (1798).
98. "Report of the Secretary of War to the President," Dec. 10, 1790, *TP: Vol. II*, 313–14; Arthur St. Clair to Unknown, Jan. 24, 1790, Reel 2, *ASCP*.
99. Griffin Greene to Winthrop Sargent, Nov. 25, 1792, Reel 3, *WSP*.
100. Adelaide Lisetta Fries ed., "Report of the Brethren Abraham Steiner and Friedrich Christian Von Schweinitz of Their Journey to the Cherokee Nation and in the

Cumberland Settlements in the State of Tennessee from 28th October to 28th December, 1799," *North Carolina Historical Review* 21, no. 4 (1944): 330–75. For the history of the Moravians' subsequent mission in the Cherokee Nation, *see* Anna Rosina Gambold, *The Moravian Springplace Mission to the Cherokees*, ed. Rowena McClinton, 2 vols. (Lincoln: University of Nebraska Press, 2007).

101. Ford, "Report of the Brethren."
102. *Id.*
103. *Id.*
104. *Id.*; Cherokee Nation v. Georgia, 30 U.S. (5 Peter) 1 (1831). Later, the Supreme Court would employ Marshall's language to justify expansive federal power over Indians, describing their "weakness," "helplessness," and "dependen[ce] on the United States . . . for their daily food." United States v. Kagama, 118 U.S. 375 (1886). For further exploration of the legal significance of the concept of dependence for Natives, *see* Gregory Evans Dowd, *War Under Heaven: Pontiac, the Indian Nations & the British Empire* (Baltimore: Johns Hopkins University Press, 2002). 174–211; Ablavsky, "Beyond the Indian Commerce Clause." On the subsequent history of Native economic dependence, *see* Richard White, *The Roots of Dependency: Subsistence, Environment, and Social Change Among the Choctaws, Pawnees, and Navajos* (Lincoln: University of Nebraska Press, 1983).
105. Nancy N. Scott, *A Memoir of Hugh Lawson White* (Philadelphia: J.B. Lippincott & Co., 1856); L. Paul Gresham, "The Public Career of Hugh Lawson White," *Tennessee Historical Quarterly* 3, no. 4 (1944): 291–318.

    The contrast between "needs" and "rights," and its consequences for the American state and its social policies, is a central theme of the work of Linda Gordon. *See* Linda Gordon ed., *Women, the State, and Welfare* (Madison, Wis.: University of Wisconsin Press, 1990); Linda Gordon, *Pitied but Not Entitled: Single Mothers and the History of Welfare, 1890–1935* (Cambridge, Mass.: Harvard University Press, 1995).
106. Scott, *A Memoir of Hugh Lawson White*, 157–58; Act of May 23, 1830, ch. 148, 4 Stat. 411. On the debate over the Removal Act and its subsequent cost, *see* Claudio Saunt, *Unworthy Republic: The Dispossession of Native Americans and the Road to Indian Territory* (New York: W.W. Norton & Company, 2020), 54–81, 306; on the destruction of Native wealth, *see* Saunt, 256–78; Alexandra Harmon, *Rich Indians: Native People and the Problem of Wealth in American History* (Chapel Hill: University of North Carolina Press, 2013), 92–132.

Chapter 7

1. Northwest Ordinance, *JCC*, 33:342; 5 Annals of Cong. 1303–04 (1796).
2. Northwest Ordinance, *JCC*, 33:342. For studies of early federalism, *see* Alison L. LaCroix, *The Ideological Origins of American Federalism* (Cambridge, Mass.: Harvard University Press, 2010); Forrest McDonald, *States' Rights and the Union: Imperium in Imperio, 1776–1876* (Lawrence: University Press of Kansas,

2000); Jack N. Rakove, *Original Meanings: Politics and Ideas in the Making of the Constitution* (New York: A.A. Knopf, 1996), 162–201. On Tennessee's admission to statehood, *see* Jo Tice Bloom, "Establishing Precedents: Dr. James White and the Southwest Territory," *Tennessee Historical Quarterly* 54, no. 4 (Dec. 1, 1995): 324–35; Samuel C. Williams, "The Admission of Tennessee into the Union," *Tennessee Historical Quarterly* 4, no. 4 (Dec. 1, 1945): 291–319.

3. "Enumeration of Inhabitants of the Southwest Territory," Nov. 28, 1795, Reel 2: Territory Southwest of the River Ohio, Senate Territorial Papers, M200, U.S. National Archives. On the absence of discussion of slavery in Tennessee's admission, *see* George Van Cleve, *A Slaveholders' Union: Slavery, Politics, and the Constitution in the Early American Republic* (Chicago: University of Chicago Press, 2010), 213.
4. Judicial review in the early republic is the subject of a vast literature. For an overview, *see* Larry Kramer, *The People Themselves: Popular Constitutionalism and Judicial Review* (Oxford: Oxford University Press, 2004); William Michael Treanor, "Judicial Review before Marbury," *Stanford Law Review* 58 (2005): 455–562. As Alison LaCroix has stressed, "in the early nineteenth century, the project of fleshing out precisely what federalism ought to took like in practice took place primarily in the political branches." Alison L. LaCroix, "The Interbellum Constitution: Federalism in the Long Founding Moment," *Stanford Law Review* 67 (2015): 397, 442.
5. William Blount to James Robertson, Feb. 2, 1795, in "The Correspondence of Gen. James Robertson," *American Historical Magazine* 4, no. 2 (Apr. 1, 1899): 171–72; "Enumeration of Inhabitants of the Southwest Territory"; William Blount to John Gray Blount, Mar. 28, 1795, in *JGBP*, 2:520–23; "Proclamation by Governor Blount," Nov. 28, 1795, in *TP: Vol. IV*, 407–08.
6. *Journal of the Proceedings of a Convention, Began and Held at Knoxville, Jan. 11, 1796* (Knoxville: Printed by George Roulstone, 1796), 9–10; Tenn. Const. of 1796 (superseded 1835), art. 11, §§ 31, 32. For more background on the convention, *see* Edward Terry Sanford, *The Constitutional Convention of Tennessee of 1796* (Nashville: Marshall & Bruce, 1896). On Tănăsĭ', see James Mooney, *Myths of the Cherokee* (Washington, D.C.: Government Printing Office, 1902), 534.
7. *Journal of the Proceedings of a Convention, Began and Held at Knoxville, Jan. 11, 1796* (Knoxville: Printed by George Roulstone, 1796), 9–10. I derived the proportion of Tennessee land that was Indian country from McLoughlin, *Cherokee Renascence*, 26 tbl. 3.
8. 5 Annals of Cong. 1300–30 (1796). For contemporaneous comments on the process of statehood, *see* William Blount to John Sevier, June 2, 1796, William Blount Papers, McClung Historical Collection, Knoxville, Tenn.; James Winchester to John Sevier, July 19, 1796, Box 2, Folder 1, James Winchester Papers, Tennessee State Library and Archives; John McNairy to John Sevier, July 24, 1796, Box 2, Folder 1, John Sevier Papers, 1796–1801, First Administration, Governor's Papers, Tennessee State Library and Archive. On the congressional debates over Tennessee's admission, *see* David P. Currie, *The Constitution in Congress: The Federalist Period 1789–1801* (Chicago: University of Chicago Press, 1997), 217–22.

9. 5 Annals of Cong. 1300–30 (1796); Act of June 1, 1796, Ch. 47, 1 Stat. 491.
10. 5 Annals of Cong. 1300–30 (1796); "Address and Remonstrance of the General Assembly of the State of Tennessee," [Aug. 9, 1796], in *ASP:IA*, 625–26. The document's date derives from Ramsey, *Annals of Tennessee*, 675–76.
11. George Washington to Timothy Pickering, Dorothy Twohig ed., *The Papers of George Washington: Retirement Series* (Charlottesville: 4 vols., University Press of Virginia, 1998–1999), 2:598; John Sevier to Andrew Jackson, Dec. 12, 1796, in *PAJ*, 1:102; Andrew Jackson to John Sevier, Jan. 18, 1797, in *PAJ*, 1:116–18; Andrew Jackson to John Overton, Jan. 22, 1798, in *PAJ*, 1:168–71.
12. Andrew Jackson to John Sevier, Feb. 24, 1797, in *PAJ*, 1:126–27.
13. John Sevier to Secretary of the Department of War, July 20, 1796, in *Executive Journal of Governor Sevier*, 111–14. For Indian country passports issued by Sevier, *see* Folder 4, Box 5, John Sevier Papers, 1796–1801, First Administration, Governor's Papers, Tennessee State Library and Archive. Examples of Sevier's negotiations with Natives are myriad; a sample include "A Talk from Dog Warrrior & Mad Blew and All the Principle Chiefs of the Creek Nation" Oct. 1796, Box 2, Folder 1, John Sevier Papers, 1796–1801; John Sevier to John Watts and other Chiefs of the Cherokee Nation, Mar. 5, 1797, in *Executive Journal of Governor Sevier*, 136–37; John Sevier to James Ore, May 12, 1798, in *Executive Journal of Governor Sevier*, 4:151–53. Cynthia Cumfer convincingly describes Sevier's actions as part of a broader Tennessean approach of what she terms "limited federalism"—that is, arrogating seemingly federal power over Indian affairs to the state. Cynthia Cumfer, "Local Origins of National Indian Policy: Cherokee and Tennessean Ideas about Sovereignty and Nationhood, 1790–1811," *Journal of the Early Republic* 23, no. 1 (Apr. 1, 2003): 21–46.
14. "Memorial of David Campbell," 1797, in Robert H. White ed., *Messages of the Governors of Tennessee* (Nashville: Tennessee Historical Commission, 1952), 29; John Sevier, "Second Inaugural Address," Sept. 22, 1797, in *Messages of the Governors*, 24–26; Andrew Jackson to David Campbell, Jan. 11, 1798, in *PAJ*, 1:164.
15. 5 Annals of Cong 891–906, 1299–1329 (1796). For an account of this debate focused on the question of Native title, *see* Banner, *How the Indians Lost Their Land*, 166–69.
16. Act of May 19, 1796, 1 Stat. 469.
17. "Address and Remonstrance of the General Assembly of the State of Tennessee," [Aug. 9, 1796].
18. Hawkins was distinctive among politicians in the early republic in using the formulation "Indian rights" or "rights of the Indians." For instances, *see* Hawkins to Blount, Mar. 10, 1791; Benjamin Hawkins to George Washington, Feb. 10, 1792, in *PGW:PS*, 9:554–57. On Hawkins's political views, *see* C.L. Grant, "Senator Benjamin Hawkins: Federalist or Republican?," *Journal of the Early Republic* 1, no. 3 (1981): 233–47.
19. James Robertson to David Henley, June 19, 1797, David Henley Papers, Rubenstein Rare Book and Manuscript Library, Duke University; Benjamin Hawkins to Keanetoh the Turkey and Ocunna the Badger, June 10, 1797, in *The Collected Works of Benjamin Hawkins*, 183. On Hawkins's biography and role in the civilization policy, *see* Ethridge, *Creek Country*; Ford, *Settler Sovereignty*, 30–107; Hudson, *Creek Roads and Federal Paths*.

20. Benjamin Hawkins, "Reports to the Secretary of War about the Indian Boundary," June 9, 1797, Hawkins Family Papers, Southern Historical Collection, University of North Carolina, Chapel Hill, N.C.; "Intelligence Re a Mr. Cox of Savannah," June 12, 1796, Box 1, James McHenry Papers; "The Philadelphia Gazette, and Universal Daily Advertiser. Friday, 11th Aug., 1797," *Philadelphia Gazette*, Aug. 11, 1797; John Sevier to Andrew Jackson, William Claiborne, and Joseph Anderson, Jan. 22, 1798, in *PAJ*, 1:171–72; Benjamin Hawkins to James McHenry, Aug. 6, 1797, Thomas Foster ed., *The Collected Works of Benjamin Hawkins, 1796–1810* (Tuscaloosa: University of Alabama Press, 2003), 190; Zachariah Cox to John Sevier, Aug. 31, 1797, in McGrane ed., *Documents Relating to Zachariah Cox*, 97–98.
21. James Robertson to John Sevier, Apr. 15, 1797, Box 2, Folder 2, John Sevier Papers, 1796–1801, First Administration, Governor's Papers, Tennessee State Library and Archives; "A Talk of the Chiefs and Warriors of All the Cherokees to the President of the United States," Apr. 28, 1797, in *The Collected Works of Benjamin Hawkins, 1796–1810*, 163–64; Benjamin Hawkins to James McHenry, July 5, 1797, in *The Collected Works of Benjamin Hawkins, 1796–1810*, 181–82.
22. Benjamin Hawkins to Zachariah Cox, Aug. 6, 1797, in *The Collected Works of Benjamin Hawkins, 1796–1810*, 189–90; Benjamin Hawkins to James McHenry, Aug. 6, 1797, in *The Collected Works of Benjamin Hawkins, 1796–1810*, 190; James McHenry to Oliver Wolcott, Sept. 22, 1797, Box 2, James McHenry Papers, Clements Library, University of Michigan.
23. Zachariah Cox to Andrew Jackson, Apr. 27, 1797, in *PAJ*, 1:131–32; John Sevier to Andrew Jackson, William Claiborne, and Joseph Anderson, Nov. 26, 1797, in *PAJ*, 1:154–56; William Polk to John Steele, Aug. 27, 1797, John Steele Papers, Rubenstein Rare Book and Manuscript Library, Duke University.
24. Zachariah Cox, *An Estimate of Commercial Advantages by Way of the Mississippi and Mobile Rivers, to the Western Country* (Nashville: J. M'Laughlin, 1799), 18; Arthur St. Clair to Gen'l Wilkinson, July 16, 1798, in *SCP*, 2:427–28; "Deposition of Martin H. Wickliff," Aug. 9, 1798, in *Documents Relating to Zachariah Cox*, 106–11.
25. "166: Arrest of Zachariah Cox by the Governor of the Mississippi Territory," Nov. 24, 1803, in *American State Papers: Miscellaneous*, 1:358–61; "Deposition of Robert Prior," Jan. 12, 1799, in *Documents Relating to Zachariah Cox*, 103–06; Cox, *Estimate of Commercial Advantages*, 22, 20, 25, 31, 62–63.
26. Cox, *Estimate of Commercial Advantages*, 36–42, 49–51, 62–70; Zachariah Cox to Winthrop Sargent, Sept. 3, 1798, Reel 4, *WSP*; Zachariah Cox to Winthrop Sargent, Sept. 20, 1798, Reel 4, *WSP*.
27. Charles Lee to Timothy Pickering, Sept. 11, 1798, Reel 4, *WSP*; "Zachariah Cox," *Philadelphia Gazette*, Jan. 11, 1799.
28. "167: Arrest of Zachariah Cox by the Governor of the Mississippi Territory," Nov. 28, 1803, in *American State Papers: Miscellaneous*, 361–62.
29. Stockly Donelson v. Etheldred Williams (Hamilton District Court of Equity 1801), in Historical Records Survey, Works Progress Administration, *Records of Knox County, Superior Court Record Book "B", 1797–1804* (Nashville: Historical Records Survey, 1939), 202–11; Hobson, *The Great Yazoo Lands Sale*, 56–81.

30. "Articles of Agreement and Cession Regarding Georgia's Western Lands," Apr. 24, 1802, Governor's Subject Files, Executive Dept., Governor, RG 1-1-5, Georgia Archives, *available at* https://vault.georgiaarchives.org/digital/collection/adhoc/id/420; Hobson, *Great Yazoo Land Sale*, 71–81.
31. Fletcher v. Peck, 10 U.S. 87 (1810); William Wirt, "The Yazoo Claims," June 24, 1826, in *Official Opinions of the Attorneys General of the United States*, 2:35–38; Hobson, *The Great Yazoo Lands Sale*, 143–76.
32. "Deposition of Doctor Nicholas Romayne," July 15–20, 1797, in *Report of the Committee of the House of Representatives of the United States*, [*see* Introduction, n. 22], lviii–lxxii. For Blount's disagreements with Pickering, *see* Secretary of War to William Blount, Mar. 23, 1795, *TP: Vol. IV*, 386–93; Timothy Pickering to David Campbell, Aug. 28, 1795, Folder 2, Timothy Pickering Letters, Ayers 926, Ayers Collection, Newberry Library; Timothy Pickering to David Henley, July 22, 1795, Folder 12, Timothy Pickering Letters, Ayers 926. Blount's biographer suggests that it was Blount's dislike for Pickering that prompted his rupture with the Federalists. Masterson, *William Blount*, 271–75.
33. "Deposition of James Carey" Sept. 29, 1797, in *Report of the Committee of the House of Representatives*, cxiv–cxxi; "Examination of James Carey" July 8, 1797, in *Report of the Committee of the House of Representatives*, cvi–cxii; "Deposition of Doctor Nicholas Romayne," July 15–20, 1797. The principal interpretation of Blount's conspiracy appears in Andrew R.L Cayton, "'When Shall We Cease to Have Judases?' The Blount Conspiracy and the Limits of the 'Extended Republic,'" in Ronald Hoffman and Peter J. Albert eds., *Launching the "Extended Republic": The Federalist Era* (Charlottesville: University Press of Virginia, 1996), 157–89. Consistent with his broader interpretation of the Southwest Territory, Cayton argues that Blount's Conspiracy stemmed from an effort to fill the "vacuum" that purported federal inaction had produced in the Southwest. Other discussions and materials appear in Frederick J. Turner, "Documents on the Blount Conspiracy, 1795–1797," *American Historical Review* 10, no. 3 (Apr. 1, 1905): 574–606; Alfred Byron Sears, *The Blount Conspiracy* (Madison: University of Wisconsin Press, 1928). A contemporaneous account of the conspiracy, possibly written by Blount himself, appears in "A Short Account of the Origin and Progress of a Speculation That Terminated in a Project That Was Called Blounts Conspiracy," n.d., Undated Material, *WBP:LC*.
34. "Deposition of Doctor Nicholas Romayne," July 15–20, 1797; William Blount to James Carey, Apr. 21, 1797, in *Report of the Committee of the House of Representatives*, xlvi–xlviii.
35. James Grant to William Blount, May 24, 1797, in *Report of the Committee of the House of Representatives*, liii–liv; "Examination of James Carey" Aug. 3, 1797, *Report of the Committee of the House of Representatives*, ci–cv; Blount to Carey, Apr. 21, 1797.
36. Benjamin Hawkins to Elizabeth House Trist, Nov. 25, 1797, in C.L Grant ed., *Letters, Journals, and Writings of Benjamin Hawkins* (Savannah, Ga.: Beehive Press, 1980), 162–64; Blount to Carey, Apr. 21, 1797.
37. On Carey's actions, *see* "Deposition of James Carey," Sept. 29, 1797; on Hawkins's response, *see* Benjamin Hawkins to James McHenry, June 4, 1797, in Thomas Foster

ed., *The Collected Works of Benjamin Hawkins, 1796–1810* (Tuscaloosa: University of Alabama Press, 2003), 177–78. For a thorough analysis of Blount's impeachment and subsequent trial focused on the constitutional interpretation, *see* Buckner F. Melton, *The First Impeachment: The Constitution's Framers and the Case of Senator William Blount* (Macon, Ga.: Mercer University Press, 1998).

38. George Washington to David Henley, July 3, 1797, in Dorothy Twohig ed., *The Papers of George Washington: Retirement Series* (Charlottesville: University Press of Virginia, 1998), 1:229; William Blount to John Gray Blount, Nov. 7, 1797, in *JGBP*, 3:174–86. Washington was particularly incensed by Blount's efforts to undercut Hawkins's influence among the Indians, which Washington described as "a crime of so deep a dye as no epithet can convey an adequate idea of to my mind." George Washington to Secretary of War [James McHenry], July 7, 1797, George Washington Collection, MS-1033, Rauner Special Collection, Dartmouth College. On Burr, *see* Nancy Isenberg, *Fallen Founder: The Life of Aaron Burr* (New York: Penguin Books, 2008).
39. John Sevier to John Overton, Aug. 17, 1797, Box 2, Folder 12, Murdock Collection of Overton Papers, Tennessee State Library and Archives; William Blount to John Gray Blount, Nov. 7, 1797, in *JGBP*, 3:174–86; Polk to Steele, Aug. 27, 1797.
40. Polk to Steele, Aug. 27, 1797.
41. *Id.*; William Blount to John Gray Blount, Nov. 7, 1797.
42. *Letter from the Secretary at War, Accompanying His Report Relative to the Running of a Line of Experiment from Clinch River to Chilhowee Mountain* (Philadelphia: Joseph Gales, 1798); "Letters of Benjamin Hawkins," Apr. 6, 1797, in *The Collected Works of Benjamin Hawkins*, 116–17.
43. Benjamin Hawkins, "Journal of the Proceedings of the Commissioners Appointed to Ascertain and Mark the Boundary Lines Agreeably to Treaties Between the Indian Nations and the United States," Feb. 28–May 4, 1797, in *The Collected Works of Benjamin Hawkins*, 160–61; James Winchester, "Surveying Notebook," 1797–1800, Box 4, Folder 16, James Winchester Paper, Tennessee State Library and Archives.
44. "A Talk of the Chiefs and Warriors of All the Cherokees to the President of the United States," Apr. 28, 1797, in *The Collected Works of Benjamin Hawkins, 1796–1810*, 163–64; William Blount to David Henley, Dec. 17, 1795, 1/6, William Blount Papers, Ayer MS 74, Newberry Library, Chicago, Ill.
45. Hawkins, "Journal of the Proceedings."
46. *Id.*; Silas Dinsmoor [sic], "Conference Between Commissioners of the United States and Settlers North of the Clinch River," July 24, 1797, David Henley Papers, Rubenstein Rare Book and Manuscript Library, Duke University. On death threats against Hawkins, *see* Benjamin Hawkins to David Henley, July 28, 1797, David Henley Papers, Rubenstein Rare Book and Manuscript Library, Duke University.
47. Dinsmoor, "Conference Between Commissioners and Settlers."
48. John Sevier to Benjamin Hawkins and Andrew Pickens, Apr. 13, 1797, in *The Collected Works of Benjamin Hawkins*, 1156–57.
49. *Id.*; John Sevier to William Cocke, July 6, 1797, in "Executive Journal of Governor Sevier," 139; Hawkins, "Journal of the Proceedings," 152–55; Benjamin Hawkins to

James McHenry, June 4, 1797, in *The Collected Works of Benjamin Hawkins*, 177–78; Hawkins to Trist, Nov. 25, 1797.

50. Winchester, "Surveying Notebook."
51. *Id.*
52. *Id.*; Benjamin Hawkins to Silas Dinsmoor [sic], Sept. 20, 1797, in *The Collected Works of Benjamin Hawkins, 1796–1810*, 196–97.
53. *To the Settlers Within the Cherokee Boundary, as Established by the Treaty of Holston, on the Second Day of July, One Thousand Seven Hundred and Ninety-One* (Knoxville, Tenn.: Printed by George Roulstone, 1797). The estimate of the number of residents within the Indian lands—potentially inflated—comes from *The Remonstrance and Petition of the Legislature of the State of Tennessee*, 4.
54. Campbell, "To the Citizens of the State of Tennessee, Who Are about to Be Alienated and Dismembered by the Acts and Proceedings of the Federal Government," *Knoxville Gazette*, Mar. 13, 1797.
55. Ware v. Hylton, 3 U.S. (3 Dall.) 199 (1796); *The Remonstrance and Petition of the Legislature of the State of Tennessee, to the Senate of the United States* (Philadelphia: John Fenno, 1797).
56. "Report of the Commissioners Appointed to Trace the Line Lately Designated by the Commissioners of the United States," 1797, Box 193.28, Business/Legal/Land/Miscellaneous Records, John Gray Blount Papers, North Carolina State Archives, Raleigh, N.C.
57. *Remonstrance and Petition*, 192; "To Captains Richard Sparks and John Wade," *Knoxville Gazette*, Feb. 27, 1797; Andrew Rights, "For the Knoxville Gazette," *Knoxville Gazette*, Mar. 6, 1797; The Frontier People of Tennessee, "To the People of America," *Knoxville Gazette*, Mar. 6, 1797.
58. Campbell, "To the Citizens of the State of Tennessee"; Campbell, "For the Knoxville Gazette," *Knoxville Gazette*, Apr. 3, 1797; Campbell, "For the Knoxville Gazette," *Knoxville Gazette*, May 22, 1797; Campbell, "For the Knoxville Gazette," *Knoxville Gazette*, June 12, 1797."
59. Benjamin Hawkins to Thomas Butler, Nov. 9, 1797, in *Letters, Journals, and Writings of Benjamin Hawkins*, 148–49. On David Campbell's authorship of the newspaper pieces, *see* John Sevier to John Adams, Esq., President of the United States, Apr. 1798, in *Executive Journal of Governor Sevier*, 4:140–41.
60. Benjamin Hawkins to David Henley, July 25, 1797, David Henley Papers, Rubenstein Rare Book and Manuscript Library, Duke University; *Remonstrance and Petition of the Legislature of the State of Tennessee. 4th Dec., 1797* (Philadelphia: William Ross, 1797); John Sevier to Andrew Jackson, William Claiborne, and Joseph Anderson, Apr. 5, 1798, in *PAJ*, 1:191; John Sevier to Andrew Jackson, William Claiborne, and Joseph Anderson, Feb. 5, 1798, in *PAJ*, 1:176.
61. "Copy of a Letter from Judge Campbell to the Members of Congress from the State of Tennessee, Dated Jan. 16, 1798," *Knoxville Gazette*, Feb. 2, 1798. The exact date of Campbell's arrest is a bit unclear: Sevier reports it as Feb. 3, but Campbell's letter to the *Knoxville Gazette* predates that. It seems most likely that Campbell's letter described his initial *expulsion* rather than arrest.

62. *Id.*
63. Andrew Jackson to John Adams, Mar. 5, 1798, in *PAJ*, 1:185–86; John Sevier to President John Adams, Feb. 6, 1798, in *Executive Journal of Governor Sevier*, 3:170; Sevier to Jackson, Apr. 5, 1798.
64. James McHenry to Alfred Moore, John Steel, and George Walton, Mar. 30, 1798, in *ASP:IA*, 1:639–40;
65. John Sevier to Robert Searcy, Apr. 24, 1798, in "Executive Journal of Governor Sevier," No. 4, 144–45; Colonel Ore to John Sevier, May 31, 1798, in *Messages of the Governors*, 60–62.
66. Ramsay, *Annals of Tennessee*, 695. No copy of this paper appears to survive.
67. John Sevier to Joseph Anderson and William Claiborne, July 15, 1798, in *Messages of the Governors*, 65; John Sevier to James Robertson, Lachlan McIntosh, and James Stewart, July 4, 1798, in *id.*; State Treaty Agents to Federal Treaty Commissioners, July 19, 1798, in *CJR*, 357–65.
68. James Robertson to Knoxville Printers, Aug. 20, 1798, in *CJR*, 365–68; Campbell, "Messrs. Roulstone and Parrington," *Knoxville Register: The Genius of Liberty*, Aug. 14, 1798; William Blount to James Robertson, Aug. 5, 1798, in *CJR*, 355–57.
69. John Sevier, "Talk to the Indians at Tellico," Sept. 1798, in Cora Bales Sevier and Nancy Sawyer Sevier Madden eds., *Sevier Family History, with Collected Letters of Gen. John Sevier, First Governor of Tennessee* (Washington: N.S. Madden, 1961), 144–45; Treaty of Tellico Blockhouse, Cherokees-U.S., 7 Stat. 62 (Oct. 2, 1798).
70. "Talk to the President of the United States to His Beloved Chiefs, Warriors, and Children, of the Cherokee Nation," Aug. 27, 1798, in *ASP:IA*, 640–41.
71. For celebration of the treaty, *see* William Blount to James Robertson, Oct. 1, 1798, in *CJR*, 370; "Knoxville, Tuesday, Oct., 9," *Knoxville Register: The Genius of Liberty*, Oct. 9, 1798.
72. United States v. Lackey & Trimble, Jan.–Oct. 1798, Minute Book of the Nashville Division (microfilm), U.S. District Court of Tennessee, 4–9, M1213, U.S. National Archives.
73. Campbell, "Copy of the Letter"; William Blount to James Robertson, Mar. 14, 1798, in *CJR*, 351–53.
74. United States v. Lackey & Trimble; Blount to Robertson, Mar. 14, 1798; Lachlan McIntosh to Andrew Jackson, Nov. 6, 1798, in *PAJ*, 1:211–14; John Sevier, "Legislative Message," Dec. 18, 1798, in White, *Messages of the Governors*, 88–90.
75. White, *Messages of the Governors*, 74–88; McIntosh to Jackson, Nov. 6, 1798.
76. White, *Messages of the Governors*, 74–88. For additional background on Campbell's impeachment, *see* Carroll Van West, "Judge David Campbell," *The Tennessee Encyclopedia of History and Culture, Version 2.0* (2009), http://tennesseeencyclopedia.net/entry.php?rec=186.
77. John Summerville to Thomas Blount, Mar. 27, 1800, in *JGBP*, 3:352–53; Willie Blount, "Sketch of William Blount," n.d., 4XX42, Draper Manuscripts, Reel 116, Wisconsin Historical Society, Madison, Wis.
78. John Sevier, "Legislative Message," Dec. 18, 1798, in *Messages of the Governors*, 88–90; "Act for Establishing Offices for Receiving Entries and Claims for All Vacant Lands

within the Several Counties in This State, and Ascertaining the Method of Obtaining Titles to the Same," ch. 24, *Tennessee Statutes*, 2nd General Assembly, 2nd Session (Jan. 5, 1799): 174.

79. 10 Annals of Cong. 53–54, 66, 531–32 (1800); "No. 57: Sales of Lands Acquired by the Cession of North Carolina," May 9, 1800, in *ASP:PL*, 97–99. The committee ignored an additional argument in favor of federal title: the sole federal right to purchase Native lands. The secretary of war had specifically stated that unoccupied lands purchased at Tellico would remain under federal control until "sold by, and under the authority of, the United States." McHenry to Moore, Steel, and Walton, Mar. 30, 1798.
80. "No. 57: Sales of Lands Acquired by the Cession of North Carolina."
81. 11 Annals of Cong. 255–56, 259–64, 425–26 (1802); 14 Annals of Cong 27–32 (1805); *ASP:PL*, 148, 164–66, 193–96; Thomas Jefferson to Levi Lincoln, Apr. 17, 1802, in *PTJ:MS*, 37:251.
82. Citizens of Mero to John Sevier, Oct. 14, 1800, Box 2, Folder 5, John Sevier Papers, 1796–1801, First Administration, Governor's Papers, Tennessee State Library and Archive.
83. John Sevier to Joseph Anderson, William Cocke, and William Clairborn, Mar. 20, 1800, in *Executive Journal of Governor Sevier*, 110–11.
84. 4 Annals of Cong. 1147–59 (1795); Henry D. Whitney ed., *The Land Laws of Tennessee: Being a Compilation of the Various Statutes of North Carolina, the United States and Tennessee, Relative to Titles to Lands Within the State of Tennessee, from the Second Royal Charter to the Present Time* (J.M. Deardoff & Sons, printers, 1891), 118.
85. 4 Annals of Cong. 1147–59 (1795).
86. John Sevier, "Legislative Message," Sept. 22, 1801, in White, *Messages of the Governor*, 97; Governor Ashe to the General Assembly, 1798, in *JGBP*, 3:591–94; "An Act ratifying and confirming an act of the General Assembly of the State of North Carolina," 1804, ch. 14, in *The Land Laws of Tennessee*, 55–56; U.S. CONST., art. I, § 10. In seizing North Carolina's records, Tennesseans were also seeking to avoid implication in North Carolina's investigation into earlier land frauds. Russell S. Koonts, "'An Angel Has Fallen!': The Glasgow Land Frauds and the Emergence of the North Carolina Supreme Court," *North Carolina Historical Review* 72, no. 3 (July 1, 1995): 301–28; Masterson, *William Blount*, 324–47.
87. Act of Apr. 18, 1806, ch. 31, 2 Stat. 381. For more discussion of the tripartite negotiation between Tennessee, North Carolina, and the federal government, *see* Thomas B. Jones, "The Public Lands of Tennessee," *Tennessee Historical Quarterly* 27, no. 1 (Apr. 1, 1968): 19–24.
88. "No. 141: Claim of the United States to Lands in Tennessee," Feb. 17, 1807, in *ASP: PL*, 1:534.
89. Burton's Lessee v. Williams, 16 U.S. (3 Wheat) 529 (1818).
90. Accounts of Ohio's statehood that focus on its partisan context appear in Andrew R.L. Cayton, *The Frontier Republic: Ideology and Politics in the Ohio Country, 1780–1825* (Kent, Ohio: Kent State University Press, 1986), 68–80; Onuf, *Statehood and Union*, 67–87; Donald J. Ratcliffe, *Party Spirit in a Frontier Republic: Democratic Politics in Ohio, 1793–1821* (Columbus: Ohio State University Press, 1998).

91. Arthur St. Clair to Paul Fearing, Dec. 25, 1801, in *SCP*, 2:549–51; Arthur St. Clair to James Ross, Dec. 1799, in *SCP*, 2:48–84. Thomas Worthington complained that St. Clair had "near 700" offices and officers "under his controul." Thomas Worthington to Secretary of the Treasury, May 17, 1802, in *TP: Vol. III*, 224–27. For a biography of Worthington, *see* Alfred Byron Sears, *Thomas Worthington, Father of Ohio Statehood* (Columbus: Ohio State University Press, 1958).
92. Harrison Land Act, ch. 55, 2 Stat. 73 (1800). On continuity in the Jefferson Administration, *see* Jerry L. Mashaw, "Reluctant Nationalists: Federal Administration and Administrative Law in the Republican Era, 1801–1829," *Yale Law Journal* 116 (2007): 1636; Leonard D. White, *The Jeffersonians A Story In Administrative History 1801–1829* (New York: The Macmillan Company, 1951); Bethel Saler, "An Empire for Liberty, A State for Empire: The U.S. National State Before and After the Revolution of 1800," in James P.P. Horn, Jan Lewis, and Peter S. Onuf eds., *The Revolution of 1800: Democracy, Race, and the New Republic* (Charlottesville: University of Virginia Press, 2002), 360–82.
93. Thomas Worthington to Secretary of the Treasury, May 11, 1801, in *TP: Vol. III*, 133–36; Attorney General to Secretary of the Treasury, July 29, 1801, in *id.*, 156–68; Thomas Worthington to Secretary of the Treasury, Aug. 21, 1801, in *id.*, 168–70; Gov. Arthur St. Clair to Secretary of the Treasury, Oct. 11, 1802, in *id.* 248–51. On the role of the federal government in furthering Worthington's political career, *see* Marion Nelson Winship, "Enterprise in Motion in the Early American Republic: The Federal Government and the Making of Thomas Worthington," *Business and Economic History* 23, no. 1 (1994): 81–91. For more on Worthington's role as land registrar, *see* Gautham Rao, "Thomas Worthington and the Great Transformation: Land Markets and Federal Power in the Ohio Valley, 1790–1805," *Ohio Valley History* 3, no. 4 (2003): 15.
94. Northwest Ordinance, ch. 8, 1 Stat 50, 53. On the division of the territory, *see* Act of May 2, 1800, ch. 41, 2 Stat. 60. On the effort to remove St. Clair, *see* "Thomas Worthington's Memorandum to the President," Feb. 20, 1802, in *TP: Vol. II*, 212–15.
95. 11 Annals of Cong. 1097–1100 (1802).
96. *Id.* 1119–26 (1802); Onuf, *Statehood and Union*, 76–85; Sears, *Thomas Worthington*, 83.
97. 11 Annals of Cong. 1097–1126 (1802); Albert Gallatin to William B. Giles, Feb. 13, 1802, in Henry Adams ed., *The Writings of Albert Gallatin* (Philadelphia: J.B. Lippincott & Co., 1879), 1:76–79; Act of Apr. 30, 1802, ch. 40, 2 Stat. 173. The bill also promised the new state rights to several salt springs, as well as reserving the proceeds of the sixteenth township sold by the United States to support education; this latter provision, however, merely duplicated the stipulations of the Ordinance of 1785. *Id.*
98. 11 Annals of Cong. 1097–1126 (1802).
99. Arthur St. Clair, "Remarks of Governor St. Clair Before the Constitutional Convention," Nov. 3, 1802, in *SCP*, 2:592–97.
100. *Journal of the Convention, of the Territory of the United States North-West of the Ohio, Begun and Held at Chillicothe* . . . (Chillicothe: Printed by N. Willis, 1802); Thomas Worthington to William B. Giles, Nov. 17, 1802, in *TP: Vol. III*, 257–58; Secretary of

State to Gov. Arthur St. Clair, Nov. 22, 1802, in *TP: Vol. III*, 260–63; Arthur St. Clair to James Madison, Dec. 21, 1802, in *SCP*, 2:599–601; Albert Gallatin to Thomas Jefferson, Nov. 20, 1802, in PTJ:MS, 39:47.

101. 11 Annals of Cong. 1097–1126 (1802); Onuf, *Statehood and Union*, 85.
102. Act of Feb. 19, 1803, ch. 7, 2 Stat. 201; Arthur St. Clair to M. de Luziere, Mar. 4, 1800, in *SCP*, 2:491–94.
103. United States v. Cisna, 25 F. Cas. 422, 423 (C.C.D. Ohio 1835).
104. On the amount of Indian country in the two states, *see* n. 16 in the Epilogue.
105. On the westward movement of these nations after the Treaty of Greenville, *see* Stephen Warren, *The Shawnees and Their Neighbors, 1795–1870* (Urbana: University of Illinois Press, 2005); Amy C. Schutt, *Peoples of the River Valleys: The Odyssey of the Delaware Indians* (Philadelphia: University of Pennsylvania Press, 2007).
106. On Harrison and his role in the Indiana Territory, *see* Cayton, *Frontier Indiana*, 167–226; Adam Jortner, *The Gods of Prophetstown: The Battle of Tippecanoe and the Holy War for the American Frontier* (New York: Oxford University Press, 2011); Robert M. Owens, *Mr. Jefferson's Hammer: William Henry Harrison and the Origins of American Indian Policy* (Norman: University of Oklahoma Press, 2007).
107. Quotation in Bowes, *Land Too Good for Indians*, 123. On Natives within Ohio after the Treaty of Greenville, *see* Hurt, *The Ohio Frontier*, 362–68; Shannon Bontrager, "'From a Nation of Drunkards, We Have Become a Sober People': The Wyandot Experience in the Ohio Valley during the Early Republic," *Journal of the Early Republic* 32, no. 4 (2012): 603–32; Karim M. Tiro, "The View from Piqua Agency," *Journal of the Early Republic* 35, no. 1 (Spring 2015): 24–54; Lori J. Daggar, "The Mission Complex: Economic Development, 'Civilization,' and Empire in the Early Republic," *Journal of the Early Republic* 36, no. 3 (2016): 467–91.
108. Governor Meigs, Jeremiah Morrow, and Thomas Worthington—now a U.S. Senator—all served as treaty commissioners at the 1812 Piqua conference. Tiro, "The View from Piqua Agency," 33.
109. On the continued presence of the federal state in the West, *see* Richard White, *"It's Your Misfortune and None of My Own": A History of the American West* (Norman: University of Oklahoma Press, 1991); Heather Cox Richardson, *West from Appomattox: The Reconstruction of America after the Civil War* (New Haven, Conn.: Yale University Press, 2007); Brian Balogh, *A Government Out of Sight: The Mystery of National Authority in Nineteenth-Century America* (Cambridge; New York: Cambridge University Press, 2009), 151–218.

Epilogue

1. Act of Apr. 7, 1798, ch. 28, 1 Stat. 549; Winthrop Sargent, *Political Intolerance, or, the Violence of Party Spirit* (Boston: printed by Benjamin Russell, 1801), 23 (emphasis in original). On the controversy over Sargent, *see Report of the Committee, Appointed to Enquire into the Official Conduct of Winthrop Sargent, Governor of the Mississippi*

Territory (Washington, D.C.: 1801); *Papers in Relation to the Official Conduct of Winthrop Sargent* (Washington, D.C.: 1801); John R. Wunder, "American Law and Order Comes to Mississippi Territory. The Making of Sargent's Code 1798–1800," *Journal of Mississippi History* 38, no. 2 (1976): 131–55.

2. On Claiborne, *see* Joseph Hatfield, *William Claiborne: Jeffersonian Centurion in the American Southwest* (Baton Rouge: University of Louisiana, 2016). On the Louisiana Purchase, *see* Peter J. Kastor, *The Nation's Crucible: The Louisiana Purchase and the Creation of America* (New Haven, Conn.: Yale University Press, 2004); Sanford Levinson and Bartholomew Sparrow eds., *The Louisiana Purchase and American Expansion, 1803–1898* (Oxford, U.K.: Rowman & Littlefield Publishers, 2005).
3. Thomas Sheridan, *A Complete Dictionary of the English Language*, ed. John Andrews, 6th ed. (Philadelphia: Printed for W. Young, Mills & Son, 1796).
4. *Report of the Committee on Public Lands, to Whom Were Referred, on the 18th and 24th of Dec. Last, Two Petitions of Edwin Lewis* (Washington: A. & G. Way, 1806), 4. On the durability of the principles of the Harrison Land Act, *see* Dick, *Lure of the Land*, 9–50; Rohrbough, *Land Office Business*; Gates, *History of Public Land Law Development*, 121–218.
5. Act of Mar. 3, 1803, ch. 27, Stat. 229, 230–31 (1803).
6. Gates, *History of Public Land Law Development*, 87–120. For additional background on the process of resolving private claims, *see* Rohrbough, *Land Office Business*, 38–44; Jerry L. Mashaw, *Creating the Administrative Constitution: The Lost One Hundred Years of American Administrative Law* (New Haven, Conn.: Yale University Press, 2012), 119–46; Treat, *National Land System*, 198–228; Dick, *Land Office Business*, 72–84. For a case study of one controversial private land claim, *see* María E. Montoya, *Translating Property: The Maxwell Land Grant and the Conflict over Land in the American West, 1840–1900* (Berkeley: University of California Press, 2002).
7. On Native property rights over the nineteenth century, *see* Banner, *How the Indians Lost Their Lands*, 191–292. On the origins and history of the Indian Claims Commission, *see* Christian W. McMillen, *Making Indian Law: The Hualapai Land Case and the Birth of Ethnohistory* (New Haven, Conn.: Yale University Press, 2007); Wilkins, *Hollow Justice*.
8. James McHenry, "Draft of Proposal for a Person to Examine Public Property" (May 23, 1800), Box 5, James McHenry Papers. On the creation, history, and purpose of the trading factories, *see* David Andrew Nichols, *Engines of Diplomacy: Indian Trading Factories and the Negotiation of American Empire* (Chapel Hill: The University of North Carolina Press, 2016); Prucha, *The Great Father*, 69–98. On fiduciary colonialism, *see* Emilie Connolly, "Indian Trust Funds and the Routes of American Capitalism, 1795–1865" (Ph.D. dissertation, New York University, 2019). And on the expansion of federal criminal jurisdiction, *see* Act of Mar. 3, 1817, ch. 92, 3 Stat. 383; Witgen, "Seeing Red," 604–05.
9. Budget figures from "Report of the Secretary of the Treasury of the State of the Finances for the Year 1866" (U.S. Government Printing Office, 1866), 39th Cong., 2d session, H.R. Ex. Doc. 4, tbl. 8. On Native peoples' enrichment from federal

largesse, *see* Daggar, "The Mission Complex," 467–91; Alexandra Harmon, *Rich Indians: Native People and the Problem of Wealth in American History* (Chapel Hill: University of North Carolina Press, 2013), 55–132. On the Office of Indian Affairs and the nineteenth-century Indian affairs bureaucracy more generally, *see* Stephen J. Rockwell, *Indian Affairs and the Administrative State in the Nineteenth Century* (Cambridge: Cambridge University Press, 2010); Prucha, *American Indian Policy in the Formative Years*, 51–63; Ronald N. Satz, *American Indian Policy in the Jacksonian Era* (Lincoln: University of Nebraska Press, 1974).

10. On the history of Indian Depredations Claims, *see* Larry C. Skogen, *Indian Depredation Claims, 1796–1920* (Norman: University of Oklahoma Press, 1996); K-Sue Park, "Insuring Conquest: U.S. Expansion and the Indian Depredation Claims System, 1796–1920," *History of the Present* 8, no. 1 (2018): 57–87.
11. Park, "Insuring Conquest"; J.M. Opal, *Avenging the People: Andrew Jackson, the Rule of Law, and the American Nation* (New York: Oxford University Press, 2017), 137–71; Benjamin Madley, *An American Genocide: The United States and the California Indian Catastrophe, 1846–1873* (New Haven, Conn.: Yale University Press, 2016), 174–230.
12. 1 Annals of Cong. 1319 (1796); *History of the Last Session of Congress, Which Commenced on the Seventh of Dec., 1801: Taken from the National Intelligencer* (Washington: Printed by Samuel H. Smith, 1802), 112. On the later history of territorial governance, *see* Eblen, *The First and Second United States Empires*; Howard R. Lamar, *The Far Southwest, 1846–1912: A Territorial History* (New York: W.W. Norton & Company, 1970), 1–19; Bloom ed., *The American Territorial System*; Heumann, "The Tutelary Empire."
13. On the subsequent history of conditional admission, *see* Eric Biber, "The Price of Admission: Causes, Effects, and Patterns of Conditions Imposed on States Entering the Union," *American Journal of Legal History* 46 (2004): 119–208; Peter S. Onuf, "New State Equality: The Ambiguous History of a Constitutional Principle," *Publius* 18, no. 4 (1988): 53–69.
14. Patricia Nelson Limerick, *The Legacy of Conquest: The Unbroken Past of the American West* (New York: W.W. Norton, 1987), 17–32. Pekka Hämäläinen and Samuel Truett described this view as the "centrist narrative" of U.S. history that presents frontiers as "spaces of narrative closure." Hämäläinen and Truett, "On Borderlands."
15. On these aspirations, *see* Michael Witgen, "A Nation of Settlers: The Early American Republic and the Colonization of the Northwest Territory," *William and Mary Quarterly* 76, no. 3 (2019): 391–98.
16. John Sevier, "Legislative Message," July 23, 1804, in Robert H. White ed., *Messages of the Governors of Tennessee* (Nashville: Tennessee Historical Commission, 1952), 182–84. Rough calculations of amount of Indian country in Ohio based on treaty maps and descriptions in J.W. Powell, *Eighteenth Annual Report of the Bureau of American Ethnology*, 2 vols. (Washington: Government Printing Office, 1899), and in Tennessee, based on square mileage in McLoughlin, *Cherokee Renascence*, 26 tbl. 3. Although McLoughlin only presents Cherokee cessions, no other Native

nation had sold the United States land within borders of Tennessee at the time of statehood.

17. On the shortcomings of "enlightened" Anglo-Americans in protecting Native interests, *see* Guyatt, *Bind Us Apart*; Silver, *Our Savage Neighbors*, 294–301.
18. Act of May 29, 1830, ch. 208, 4 Stat. 420; Act of Sept. 4, 1841, ch. 16, 5 Stat. 453. On these developments, *see* Gates, *History of Public Land Law*, 219–40, 285–386; Daniel Feller, *The Public Lands in Jacksonian Politics* (Madison: University of Wisconsin Press, 1984); John Robert Van Atta, *Securing the West: Politics, Public Lands, and the Fate of the Old Republic, 1785–1850* (Baltimore: Johns Hopkins University Press, 2014).
19. For an overview of the large scholarly literature on Removal, *see* Saunt, *Unworthy Republic*; Grant Foreman, *Indian Removal: The Emigration of the Five Civilized Tribes of Indians* (Norman: University of Oklahoma Press, 1953); John P. Bowes, *Land Too Good for Indians: Northern Indian Removal* (Norman: University of Oklahoma Press, 2017); Jill Norgren, *The Cherokee Cases: The Confrontation of Law and Politics* (New York: McGraw-Hill, 1996); Ford, *Settler Sovereignty*. As K-Sue Park rightly notes, what has become known as the Removal Era perpetuated earlier policies of dispossession and displacement, even if Anglo-Americans believed "removal" a new, and controversial, federal policy. K-Sue Park, "Self-Deportation Nation," *Harvard Law Review* 132 (2019): 1878, 1898 n.83.
20. Tennessee v. Forman, 16 Tenn. 256, 288, 315 (1835). For background on the additional state cases advancing this claim, *see* Tim Alan Garrison, *The Legal Ideology of Removal: The Southern Judiciary and the Sovereignty of Native American Nations* (Athens, Ga.: University of Georgia Press, 2002); Deborah A Rosen, *American Indians and State Law: Sovereignty, Race, and Citizenship, 1790–1880* (Lincoln: University of Nebraska Press, 2007), 19–78.
21. On Native resistance to Removal, particularly among the Cherokees, *see* Saunt, *Unworthy Republic*, 85–109; Theda Perdue and Michael D. Green, *The Cherokee Nation and the Trail of Tears* (New York: Viking, 2007); McLoughlin, *Cherokee Renascence*, 411–51.
22. Thomas Loraine McKenney, *Sketches of Travels Among the Northern and Southern Indians* (New York: Daniel Burgess & Company, 1854), 258–59. On federal officials as proponents of Removal, *see* Michael Morris, "Georgia and the Conversation over Indian Removal," *Georgia Historical Quarterly* 91, no. 4 (2007): 403, 406–07.
23. On the duration of territorial status, *see* Eblen, *First and Second U.S. Empires*, 140.
24. Political scientists have been particularly prone to see early federal history as the consequence of self-conscious efforts at state-building. Paul Frymer speaks of the early federal government as "regulat[ing] the task of settlement by controlling its direction, pay, and scale" through land laws. Paul Frymer, *Building an American Empire: The Era of Territorial and Political Expansion* (Princeton, N.J.: Princeton University Press, 2017), 7. Similarly, Stephen Rockwell argues that "[e]xpansion and Indian affairs arose from the careful, planned, and effective actions" of a "vibrant, complex federal bureaucracy." Rockwell, *Indian Affairs and the Administrative State*, 1–8. Both arguments accurately capture the central federal role in expansion, but,

because the authors confessedly focus on federal policymakers, they often posit a misleadingly straightforward cause-and-effect relationship between federal aims and outcomes.

25. As Michael Witgen observes, "Power and money flowed to territorial officials and businessmen in Michigan and Wisconsin from the presence of Native peoples who remained on the land," in what he describes as a "political economy of plunder." Witgen, "Seeing Red." Bethel Saler has similarly stressed the significance of what she terms the "treaty polity" in Wisconsin, where she notes the "long gap" between territorial rule and Anglo-American settlement. Saler, *Settlers' Empire*, 84.
26. As Howard Lamar observes, "[M]ost historians have assumed that the Old Northwest served as a normal prototype for the history of all subsequent territories." Lamar, *The Far Southwest*, 9. On the abandonment of statehood as the culmination of the territorial system, *see* Sam Erman, *Almost Citizens: Puerto Rico, the U.S. Constitution, and Empire* (New York: Cambridge University Press, 2019); Christina Duffy Burnett, "*Untied* States: American Expansion and Territorial Deannexation," *University of Chicago Law Review* 72 (2005): 797–879.
27. Richard White observes, "More than any other region, the West has been historically a dependency of the federal government," but westerners envisioned themselves as a "people who carved out their own destiny." Richard White, *"It's Your Misfortune and None of My Own": A History of the American West* (Norman: University of Oklahoma Press, 1991), 57–59; Limerick, *The Legacy of Conquest*, 78–94.
28. Richard White, *The Republic for Which It Stands: The United States During Reconstruction and the Gilded Age, 1865–1896* (New York: Oxford University Press, 2017), 591.
29. For histories stressing the transformation of federal governance in the late nineteenth century, *see* Nicholas R. Parrillo, *Against the Profit Motive: The Salary Revolution in American Government, 1780–1940* (New Haven, Conn.: Yale University Press, 2013); Stephen Skowronek, *Building a New American State: The Expansion of National Administrative Capacities, 1877–1920* (Cambridge, U.K.: Cambridge University Press, 1982); Richard Franklin Bensel, *Yankee Leviathan: The Origins of Central State Authority in America, 1859–1877* (New York: Cambridge University Press, 1990); Daniel P. Carpenter, *The Forging of Bureaucratic Autonomy: Reputations, Networks, and Policy Innovation in Executive Agencies, 1862–1928* (Princeton, N.J.: Princeton University Press, 2001).
30. On pensions, *see* Theda Skocpol, *Protecting Soldiers and Mothers: The Political Origins of Social Policy in the United States* (Cambridge, Mass.: Belknap Press of Harvard University Press, 1992); on petitions, *see* Maggie McKinley, "Petitioning and the Making of the Administrative State," *Yale Law Journal* 127 (2018): 1538–1637; on rights and legalism, *see* Karen M. Tani, *States of Dependency: Welfare, Rights, and American Governance, 1935–1972* (New York: Cambridge University Press, 2016); Daniel R. Ernst, *Tocqueville's Nightmare: The Administrative State Emerges in America, 1900–1940* (New York: Oxford University Press, 2016).
31. For the sesquicentennial celebration of the Southwest Territory, *see* Russell Cherrington Driver, *Leslie Rowles Driver: The Fruitful Prince* (Maryville,

Tenn.: Script Press, 2002), 300 n.839. For accounts of the pageant and caravan by the organizers, *see* Northwest Territory Celebration Commission, *Final Report of the Northwest Territory Celebration Commission* (Marietta, Ohio: Federal Writers' Project, WPA in Ohio, 1938). An overview of the celebration appears in John Bodnar, *Remaking America: Public Memory, Commemoration, and Patriotism in the Twentieth Century* (Princeton, N.J.: Princeton University Press, 1993), 126–34.

32. On how Jackson's early experiences shaped his subsequent politics, *see* Opal, *Avenging the People*.
33. Bodnar, *Remaking America*, 126–34.
34. Joint Resolution of Aug. 2, 1935, ch. 429, 49 Stat. 511.

Index

For the benefit of digital users, indexed terms that span two pages (e.g., 52–53) may, on occasion, appear on only one of those pages.

Note: Figures are indicated by an italic *f* following the page number.